An Analyticial Guide to Television's
One Step Beyond, 1959–1961

ALSO BY JOHN KENNETH MUIR

Terror Television: American Series, 1970–1999
(McFarland, 2001)

The Films of John Carpenter
(McFarland, 2000)

A Critical History of Doctor Who *on Television*
(McFarland, 1999)

A History and Critical Analysis of Blake's 7,
the 1978–1981 British Television Space Adventure
(McFarland, 2000)

Wes Craven: The Art of Horror
(McFarland, 1998)

An Analytical Guide to Television's Battlestar Galactica
(McFarland, 1999)

Exploring Space: 1999:
*An Episode Guide and Complete History of
the Mid-1970s Science Fiction Television Series*
(McFarland, 1997)

An Analytical Guide to Television's *One Step Beyond*, 1959–1961

JOHN KENNETH MUIR

McFarland & Company, Inc., Publishers
Jefferson, North Carolina, and London

The present work is a reprint of the library bound edition of
An Analytical Guide to Television's *One Step Beyond*,
1959–1961, *first published in 2001 by McFarland.*

LIBRARY OF CONGRESS CATALOGUING-IN-PUBLICATION DATA

Muir, John Kenneth, 1969–
    An analytical guide to television's One step beyond, 1959–
1961 / John Kenneth Muir.
        p.   cm.
    Includes bibliographical references and index.

    ISBN-13: 978-0-7864-2849-6
    (softcover : 50# alkaline paper)∞

    1. Alcoa presents (Television program).   I. Title.
PN1992.77.A477 M85   2006
791.45'72 — dc21   2001018299

British Library cataloguing data are available

Cover photograph: Cloris Leachman from "The Dark Room"
episode of *One Step Beyond* in 1959 (ABC/Photofest)

Manufactured in the United States of America

McFarland & Company, Inc., Publishers
  Box 611, Jefferson, North Carolina 28640
  www.mcfarlandpub.com

For Amy, Frank,
Austin and Kiernan — a great family

and for John Newland,
our guide to the world of the unknown.

Acknowledgments

The author wishes to express his deepest appreciation to the late John Newland, an artist and gentleman, for speaking candidly about *One Step Beyond*, *The Next Step Beyond*, *Star Trek* and his long career in Hollywood on the afternoon of October 28, 1999. Special thanks also to Jerome Siegel, who arranged the interview at light speed efficiency. And last but not least, a warm word of gratitude to fellow writer Gregory Norris, who pointed the author in the right direction and told him to "go for it."

Table of Contents

Introduction

Have you ever stayed awake into the wee hours of the night and turned on your television set only to discover a smiling and good-natured (but sardonic) face staring back in stark shades of black-and-white photography? Have you ever listened, spellbound, as this mellifluous-voiced "guide to the world of the unknown" informed you, straight-faced, that the events you were about to watch unfold were a "matter of human record?" Have you ever felt your heart skip a beat as you then witnessed the "personal record" of a character who survived a terrifying and perplexing experience in the world of the paranormal or the inexplicable? If the answer to any of these questions is affirmative, then you have already taken a small step beyond. Now take a giant one...

For the uninitiated, the preceding paragraph revises and re-phrases the inaugural narration from one of television's true classics, the horror/paranormal anthology series known as *Alcoa Presents: One Step Beyond* (1959–61). Your guide to the "world of the unknown" was none other than Golden Age TV star John Newland, veteran actor of every notable TV program of that era, from *Tales of Tomorrow* (1951–53) to *The Loretta Young Show* (1953–61). And, for three remarkable seasons and 96 half-hour episodes on ABC television, this noted performer conducted prime-time audiences through a twisted, dark alley that most viewers had never envisioned: a voyage into the shadowy universe of paranormal and psychic phenomena.

Long before Chris Carter's *The X-Files* (1993–) made such sojourns a commonplace venture, *One Step Beyond* led viewers through gripping human ordeals concerning core parapsychological concepts, such as E.S.P. (Extra Sensory Perception), clairvoyance, reincarnation, precognition, poltergeists, apparitions, automatic writing, possession, out-of-body experiences, Bigfoot sightings and even alien abductions. Before this unique anthology series was finished unspooling, it had also dramatized for amazed audiences the mysterious psychic web that surrounded the sinking of the

1

Titanic ("Night of April 14"), examined premonitions about the assassination of President Abraham Lincoln ("The Day the World Wept: The Lincoln Story"), studied the world's foremost psychic investigator ("The Peter Hurkos Story"), recounted a peculiar true story about a phenomenon in Chico, California ("Where Are They?"), and even conducted a "hands on" study of the psychoactive properties of hallucinogenic mushrooms ("The Sacred Mushroom"). Today this TV series might accurately be described as a little off-kilter; in conservative 1959 it was positively "out there."

Each half-hour segment of this imaginative black-and-white anthology TV program was unique, not only for its highly unorthodox content but also for its distinctly eerie atmosphere. Effectively directed by John Newland, *One Step Beyond* remains a textbook example of low-budget, economical horror filmmaking at its very best. With intense performances from the likes of Cloris Leachman ("The Dark Room"), Warren Beatty ("The Visitor"), Jack Lord ("Father Image"), Christopher Lee ("The Sorcerer"), Elizabeth Montgomery ("The Death Waltz"), Donald Pleasence ("The Confession"), Ross Martin ("Echo"), William Shatner ("The Promise"), Robert Loggia ("The Hand"), Mike Connors ("The Aerialist"), Louise Fletcher ("The Open Window"), Joan Fontaine ("The Visitor"), Charles Bronson ("The Last Round"), Lois Maxwell ("The Room Upstairs"), Yvette Mimieux ("The Clown") and other future stars of TV and film, *One Step Beyond* was impeccably performed, as well as intelligently crafted. And, coupled with the timeless, chill-inducing music of composer Harry Lubin, the overall impact of *One Step Beyond*'s many paranormal excursions was a sense of pure terror, a case of the creeps so bad it would not go away.

There are many worthwhile reasons to acknowledge, study and remember *One Step Beyond* today, but perhaps the most significant of these involves television history. Today's audiences have seen psychic phenomena explored in a variety of TV programs, from Anthony Lawrence's *The Sixth Sense* (1972), starring Gary Collins, to the Shari Belafonte USA series *Beyond Reality* (1992–1993); from the popular *The X-Files* (1993–) and *Millennium* (1996–1999) to *Poltergeist the Legacy* (1996–1999), *Psi Factor* (1996–) and the new network program by Glen Morgan and James Wong, *The Others* (2000). Each of these popular genre adventures comes to the world of television with a distinct ancestry and a grounding in many of the paranormal concepts first explored successfully on *One Step Beyond*.

In addition to these notable dramatic productions, "reality" oriented paranormal programs such as *Sightings* (1994–1997), *In Search of* (1976–82) and even the Learning Channel cable series *Exploring the Unknown* (with

Mitch Pileggi of *The X-Files* as host) have adopted another piece of *One Step Beyond*'s mantle by depicting allegedly "real" accounts of psychic phenomena in elaborately staged "re-enactments." These programs flout the familiar dramatic components of anthology television (such as plot, character and story resolution), adopting instead a pseudodocumentary, almost journalistic approach to their fantastic material. This restraint, and the concerted effort to deal with the paranormal on accurate, research-based terms, was also a staple of *One Step Beyond*. "The Sacred Mushroom," a *One Step Beyond* classic, adopted the same format, being a travelogue and documentary rather than a fictitious account.

As the last days of the 20th century slipped away, these varied excursions into the terrain of the paranormal proliferated and proved extremely popular. The summer of 1999 even saw a hit film on the same topic, called *The Sixth Sense*.

On television at least, these marvelous and exciting new programs do share a common heritage, and that heritage consists largely of *One Step Beyond*: a well-spring of creativity from the late 1950s and early 1960s. It is time to celebrate this early example of the genre.

Before *One Step Beyond* captured the imagination of a prime-time audience back at the end of the 1950s and the commencement of the 1960s, no regular TV series had dealt exclusively with the subject of the paranormal (though, in fairness, horror series such as *Lights Out!* [1946; 1949–52] and *The Inner Sanctum* [1954] had occasionally touched on the subject, also with an accent on the terrifying). And, perhaps more significantly, a little-remembered or acknowledged historical fact in modern genre circles is that *One Step Beyond* bowed on the air well before *The Twilight Zone* was even created, let alone in regular broadcast. As *One Step Beyond* narrator and director John Newland revealed to this author during a telephone interview near Halloween of 1999, *Twilight Zone* creator Rod Serling actually met personally with Newland while *One Step Beyond* was shooting its first season roster to assure him that his upcoming anthology series would not be a "rip-off" of *One Step Beyond*. That fact alone demonstrates how worried Serling was that *The Twilight Zone* was similar to the established ABC anthology (then known as *Alcoa Presents*) in content and mood. Considering that encounter, as well as the timing, it is certainly appropriate to "revise" some official TV history books, as well as the words of several noted genre authorities who have stated widely that *The Twilight Zone* is the "father" of every fantasy-oriented show of the modern age. There is sufficient cause to believe *One Step Beyond* may be the true patriarch. For those who are inclined to look at things that way, this book can be considered a paternity test of sorts.

Another prime purpose in re-examining *One Step Beyond* concerns its oft-noted claim that its stories are based on documented and authentic cases of the paranormal and inexplicable. Indeed, much of *One Step Beyond*'s horrifying texture stems from this remarkable claim of accuracy and realism. The stories are frightening enough as mere drama, but buttressed by this claim of being "true," many episodes linger in the consciousness like unending nightmares.

This author has learned that many episodes of *One Step Beyond* do indeed report the "facts" of famous parapsychological incidents, if not the exact personal details (which were often rearranged for purposes of drama and pacing on the TV series). Additionally, *One Step Beyond* shepherded its core concepts (possession, reincarnation and the like) with a special care, accurately reflecting the literature on parapsychology of the day (and, for the most part, of today as well). Because *One Step Beyond* respected its audience and demonstrated this highly unusual dedication to accuracy, this reference book shall return that favor. It will honor *One Step Beyond* by, wherever relevant, noting the research (and the cases) supporting *One Step Beyond*'s claim that it is based on matters of "human record." It should be noted that this view into *One Step Beyond*'s nature in no way suggests that this author believes in or validates any so-called case studies in the world of the paranormal or psychic; only that *One Step Beyond* took remarkable pains (remarkable especially for television) to respect its subject matter and adhere closely to the "details" parapsychologists have ascribed to such phenomena as out-of-body experiences, psychometry, crisis apparitions, spirit rapping, and the rest. If *One Step Beyond*'s creators and writers could make the effort, week-in and week-out, to log so-called "paranormal" incidents with an eye towards history and reality, then any study of the TV series should surely assume the same responsibility of research, and this book does so.

In addition to researching and reporting on the accuracy of the concepts touted by *One Step Beyond* and making a case for the anthology's importance in genre television, this work also pauses to remember the short-lived 1978 syndicated sequel to *One Step Beyond* (called *The Next Step Beyond*), and to examine the genre contributions of director John Newland between the cancellation of *One Step Beyond* and production of *The Next Step Beyond* (including a truly terrifying episode of *Thriller* called "Pigeons from Hell" and an outstanding *Night Gallery* story entitled "There Aren't Any More MacBanes"). It also seeks to analyze several of the stories and themes that reappeared in both the *Beyond* series and later in modern genre TV.

Why were so many characters in *One Step Beyond* modern Cassandras, doomed to know the future but never be believed? Why were so many of the characters who faced psychic phenomena also battling to save their marriages? Why were many of the protagonists recovering alcoholics or mental cases on the mend? These and other questions will be addressed as *One Step Beyond*'s assumptions about people, psychic phenomena, drama, and television are investigated. John Newland's personal feelings and remembrances about *One Step Beyond* have also been included in the following text, thanks to Newland himself, who, shortly before his death, granted a rare first-person account of the creativity, hard work and fun that went into producing a television classic.

Some 41 years after its debut, *One Step Beyond* still speaks meaningfully to the world at large. Whether it does so in the language of television history and by the number of offspring it has generated (*The X-Files* and *The Twilight Zone* prime among them), as a legitimate example of parapsychological research, or simply as a fine example of craft and ingenuity from the Golden Age of TV is not necessarily important. All those facets work together to forge an indelible affection for the series in the hearts and minds of its viewers, and even a bit of a shiver too, as its most chilling moments are remembered.

So let us take that giant step...

Part I

History

The Times

It was truly a different world in 1959 when *One Step Beyond* (originally titled *Alcoa Presents*) was born. There were no DVD players, no VCRs and no cable networks like USA, TNT or TBS. There was no internet, no Fox Network, no UPN and no WB. Even the most commonplace of technologies, such as color TV, were barely out of development.

The black-and-white world of science-fiction and horror TV programming, the arena this anthology TV series often orbits if not totally inhabits, was also largely underdeveloped as 1959 began. *The Twilight Zone* (Fall 1959–65), *Star Trek* (1966–69), *Thriller* (1960–62), *The Outer Limits* (1963–65) *Lost in Space* (1964–1968) and nearly every popular icon of genre television did not yet exist as the year commenced. At the movie houses, even the great James Bond film series starring Sean Connery had not yet begun its forty year string of blockbusters (the first such film, *Dr. No*, premiered in 1962), and genre high-water marks such as *Planet of the Apes* (1968) and *2001: A Space Odyssey* (1968) were nearly a decade off in the future. These facts help to establish the historical context for this unusual and undervalued TV series, as well as secure the fact that *One Step Beyond* was a TV pioneer, predating the more popular and more renowned Rod Serling *Twilight Zone* anthology by several months (approximately ten months, or a full season).

On a wider scale, 1959 was the year that the Dalai Lama fled Tibet, John Foster Dulles resigned as the U.S. Secretary of State (under President Eisenhower) and seven men (Carpenter, Cooper, Glen, Grissom, Schirra, Shephard and Slayton) were chosen as having the "right stuff" to man the fledgling American space program. On the silver screen, up-and-coming stars had names like Shirley MacLaine, Hope Lange, Diane Baker, Lee Remick and Carolyn Jones, and the most popular director of feature films was a gentleman known as Alfred Hitchcock. One of his best-known and most exciting films, *North by Northwest*, opened that very year.

7

Recently, editor Ruth Reichl described these times (the 1950s) in ironic (if not wholly positive) terms in the introduction to her work *The Measure of Her Powers: An M.F.K Fisher Reader* (Counterpoint, 1999), a collection of writings from the noted food and wine critic and expert Mary Frances Kennedy Fisher:

> America was another country in the fifties. Spaghetti came in cans. Cheese mainly meant Velveeta. Nobody had ever heard of cappuccino. Most fancy restaurants were serving ... Continental Cuisine, and the only Chinese dish ... was chop suey.[1]

Such a colorful description may not paint a flattering picture of the era, but it underlines a critical point worth highlighting, even though the topic here is television, not food. Globalization and the age of information had not yet commenced, and Americans (as a whole) were far more naive about the world than one might remember. Without a 24-hour news cycle to bludgeon them with minutiae, it is fair to state that people in this country in the 1950s were almost a different breed from today's media savvy, web-connected U.S. citizens. To wit: At the beginning of the 1950s, few Americans owned television sets at all. However, by the end of the decade, a set was in virtually every home in the country (or at least 90 percent).[2] Thus the fifties encompassed a period of major change; and, as always, popular entertainment (i.e., television) reflected the growing pains of the country. Some may quibble with this description of the 1950s as a simpler, more naive time, but the facts are hard to ignore. Today "regular" people "e-trade" on the stock market (losing and gaining fortunes before lunchtime) and communicate instantaneously over vast distances through the use of personalized computers (an idea that would have been dismissed as downright frightening, if not immoral, by many Americans in the 1950s), and many homes are equipped with electronic security systems. Though the "chop suey" comment above may sound derogatory or mean-spirited, it simply reveals that the people of the 1950s were not connected and knowledgeable on the same scale as Americans are today. Whether that is a good or bad thing is a completely debatable argument.

Despite the fact that television was still a fairly young "institution" when *Alcoa Presents: One Step Beyond* began its network run, its world was not without controversy. The Quiz Show scandal, as it has since become known, was a major headline in 1959, thanks to a Congressional Committee investigating the incident. What happened was simple: The popular TV game show *Twenty-One* (1956–1958) was revealed to be a fraud when information came to light that the quiz show's fresh-faced 14 week champion, Charles Van Doren, had been coached to his victory over Herb

Stempel. As Ralph McGill, editor of *The Atlanta Constitution*, wrote at the time:

> television had robbed people of a kind of faith which it is dangerous to destroy in a democracy, and it is the more so because it is a reflection on all of us and our national character.[3]

Why is any of this prologue significant to the history of a paranormal anthology? Simply put, one must recall the very content of the series known as *One Step Beyond*. Host John Newland stood before the TV audience each week, in the very living rooms of the country, and made claims that the wild stories presented by his new show were "documented" and "based on real accounts." How could such a claim be accepted at face value when it seemed that so much of the programming of the epoch that appeared real, and that television producers claimed to be "real," was actually rigged from behind the scenes?

Perhaps understanding that a mood of cynicism had resulted from the *Twenty-One* fall-out, *One Step Beyond* was born a series obsessed with validating itself and its dramatized cases, week-in and week-out, during its three years on the air. Sometimes the proof offered on-screen was scanty, but in other cases it was startlingly specific and valid ("Night of April 14," "Tidal Wave," "Where Are They?"). Sometimes the proof offered by *One Step Beyond* was a clever form of misdirection, a kind of "if/then" equation that stated: "If A can happen, as it did here, then B can happen as well." Today, viewers are rarely tricked by such logic, but then modern audiences are blessed with forty years of "new" media exposure that those who watched *One Step Beyond* originally did not have any experience with, not to mention publications such as *The Skeptical Inquirer*, which investigate fraudulent claims of "truth."

Today's audiences are intimately familiar with so-called "reality" programming, such as *Sightings, Cops, Rescue: 911*, as well as genre items like *The Legend of Boggy Creek* (1973) and *The Blair Witch Project* (1999), both of which utilize documentary technique to make false horror stories appear as "true." In the case of *One Step Beyond*, it never made the claim that its dramatizations were "real" in-and-of-themselves or that it was a documentary. Instead, it argued that its dramatizations were based on fact and that the core concepts of those dramatizations (telepathy, precognition, alien abduction, Bigfoot) were valid and worthy of further study. On those grounds it is a resounding success. The Quiz Show scandal had undermined American faith in television as a purveyor of truth, and *Alcoa Presents: One Step Beyond* proffered a clever response that deflected, or at least deflated, some of that cynicism. Had *One Step Beyond* been born before this scandal, there need not have been any discussion of proof or evidence, but *One Step Beyond*'s timing assured that its format would be one in which "integrity" was on display regularly.

The year 1959 also fits into that era of TV that some historians refer to as the "sponsor identification" years. Though it apparently had "no provable relationship with sales effectiveness,"[4] major American companies such as Revlon, U.S. Steel, Philco and Alcoa, put up the considerable money for the production of television programming during much of the 1950s and very early '60s. Alcoa had *The Alcoa Hour* (1955–57), *Alcoa Theatre* (1957–60) and *Alcoa Premiere* (1961–63), in addition to *Alcoa Presents* (*One Step Beyond*). Philco had *Philco TV Playhouse* (1948–55), Revlon had *Revlon Mirror Theatre* (1953), U.S. Steel had *The U.S. Steel Hour* (1953–63), and so on and so forth. Because of this arrangement, the networks were not, as they are today, required to sell commercial time to various competing companies. Instead, *One Step Beyond* always featured aluminum (from Alcoa, of course) commercials during its run, and had no other sponsors whatsoever. Though this approach may sound distinctly undemocratic today, and even a tad monopolistic, it was the way things were done when *One Step Beyond* was created, and it explains why the series is often referred to in reference books as *Alcoa Presents*. Of course, that uninspiring title gives no indication of the series' fascinating content, but it does establish who, precisely, was putting up the money for the show. Thus the title itself is a form of advertising, and *One Step Beyond* boasts the distinction of being the only such "brand name" TV series of the sponsor identification era to achieve such long-lasting pop culture success that it actually outlived the business practices of its time. It survived long enough to see its very title changed to a more content-oriented one in syndication.

When establishing the time and place from which *One Step Beyond* sprang, it is also critical to enunciate the fact that the series was remarkably different from its contemporary competition. In 1959, seven of the ten top shows were westerns (*Gunsmoke, Wagon Train, Have Gun — Will Travel, The Rifleman, Maverick* and *Tales of Wells Fargo*). In fact, westerns totally dominated the airwaves in general. Although legal dramas (such as *Perry Mason*) and variety shows were also popular, TV really belonged to the Old West, a time of simple values and justice preserved. Seen in that light, *One Step Beyond* lived up to its title. It was very different, by at least a few degrees, from all its video brethren, and that fact alone makes it worthy of study.

Our Guide to the World of the Unknown

Although many artists contributed enormously to the success of *One Step Beyond*, from creator Merwin Gerard, musician Harry Lubin and editor Henry Berman to writers Larry Marcus and Collier Young, there remains one face who will be forever associated with this timeless anthology series. Of course, that gentleman is John Newland (1917–2000). Were Newland merely the host of *One Step Beyond*, his prominence here might seem a tad misplaced, but this talented actor was not just the on-screen presence who kept the series glued together, he was the artisan who endowed the program with so much of its look, style, feel, texture and pace. In an accomplishment truly rare in the annals of television, John Newland directed every episode (96 in all) of *One Step Beyond*. This rigorous and rewarding experience in television production should surely elevate the prolific Newland to the high level of respect afforded Rod Serling, who wrote 92 episodes of his own anthology, *The Twilight Zone*. But, strangely, Newland has never been idolized to the same degree as Rod Serling, or even *Star Trek*'s Gene Roddenberry, perhaps because his beginnings in the industry were not in the arena of writing, producing or even directing.

John Newland was not always the consummate director. A theatrical actor in the early 1950s, Newland quickly graduated to television and promptly became the Golden Age's foremost leading man. Yet, at the time, television did not have the same level of respect afforded it as film did. Many critics and industry insiders viewed television as but a "poor cousin" to film. Still, Newland understood the potential of TV as an art form and, looking ahead, chose that venue as his central career mode. Dedicated, he rose through the ranks of television production, all the while being a "star" of the medium:

> Any of the live shows you can name, I did ten of. Back then there were a handful of stars, Felicia Montealegre, Maria Riva, Margaret Hayes, John Baragrey, Richard Kiley ... and me."[5]

So John Newland was a genuine TV celebrity of the era, and for good reason. He headlined in some 13 episodes of *The Loretta Young Show* (1953–61), an uplifting, morally valuable dramatic anthology of the day. Featured alongside actors like Claude Akins, Ricardo Montalban and Jim Daly, Newland immediately created a humble but compelling screen persona that simultaneously suggested a degree of wit and sense of modesty. Along with Elizabeth Montgomery and Cliff Robertson, Newland was also a recurring player in the popular drama *Robert Montgomery Presents* (1950–57), a series on which he appeared some 40 times between 1952 and 1957.

During those incredibly busy days, Newland also logged in multiple appearances on *Kraft Television Theater* (1947–1958), *Philco Television Playhouse* (1948–55), *Armstrong Circle Theater* (1950–63), *Schlitz Playhouse of Stars* (1951–59), and even *Dr. Kildare* (1961–66).

Within the genre, Newland also made an impressive name for himself. In *Tales of Tomorrow* (1951–53) he played Victor Frankenstein to Lon Chaney, Jr.'s, Monster in an adaptation of Mary Shelley's classic novel *Frankenstein* that aired on January 18, 1952.[6] Newland also guest starred three times on the horror series *Lights Out* (1949–52), in the episodes "The Strange Case of John Kingman," "The Dark Corner" and "Grey Reminder." Appearing on *The Inner Sanctum* (1954), he starred in "The Sisters"; and on *Science Fiction Theater* (1955–57) he was in the futuristic tale "No Food for Thought."[7]

These experiences provided young Newland with three important ingredients for his future success in television. Firstly, he had seized a national and highly visible platform on which to prove his artistry. Secondly, he gained a familiarity with the science fiction and horror genres, territory he would return to (at least obliquely) for *One Step Beyond*. Third, and perhaps most importantly, Newland's hundred-or-so performances in 1950s television drama gave him the perfect opportunity to study, study, study. On the sets of those programs in which he starred, Newland watched carefully how programs were assembled and shot, and very quickly graduated to the director's chair. From 1957 to 1959 he directed several episodes of *The Loretta Young Show* and thereby honed his skill in the difficult and complex terrain of economical visual storytelling. Newland was therefore ready and experienced enough to mount *One Step Beyond* when the series started filming in 1958 (and began airing in 1959).

Newland's directorial work on *One Step Beyond* remains remarkably efficient, tight and even clever to this day. Indeed, it is Newland's many gifts as a behind-the-scenes player that grant the series so much of its creepy, dread-filled atmosphere. Once again, one is reminded of Rod Serling and his contributions to *The Twilight Zone*. The comparison between these two men and their shows is interesting and quite illuminating. Serling wrote so many installments of *The Twilight Zone* that his distinct writing voice often managed to come through loud and clear in the final product. In the final analysis, however, Serling the creative voice was at the mercy of the director of the week on *The Twilight Zone*, whose vision for his stories might differ by varying degrees from Serling's original idea and agenda. Though Serling was also executive producer of *The Twilight Zone*, what was actually shot — the film footage itself — did not bear his imprimatur.

By contrast, the buck stopped with John Newland on *One Step Beyond*. Every teleplay landed squarely at his feet, and ultimately it was he who was responsible for camera movement, performances, staging and the overall look of the series. In purest forms the argument is this: What creative contributions Rod Serling actually delivered to *The Twilight Zone* (in the form of teleplays) were filtered through the eyes of a troop of talented directors (such as Buzz Kulik, Don Medford, Alvin Ganzer, Robert Parrish, Douglas Heyes, John Brahm, Jack Smight, Boris Sagal, and Lamont Johnson).

Oppositely, John Newland served as the final filter through which all the written material (by a small but talented cadre of writers) on *One Step Beyond* traveled. This debate begs the important question: Who was more crucial in the creative process of film and television-making during the Golden Age, the writer or the director? The answer will probably not be resolved here, but it is important to note that John Newland's contributions to *One Step Beyond*, though different, are every bit as important as Rod Serling's efforts on *The Twilight Zone*. Ironically, one can answer this question about TV in the 1990s quite firmly. Directors are usually hired guns with little real authority; writers are constantly rewritten and often devalued; and the producer is the overseer of all things creative.

It should be noted that in diagramming this debate about the relative value of writer versus director, this author has no issue with the prolific, brilliant Serling, who created a classic TV series, but rather with the myth of *The Twilight Zone*, which has perpetuated some false statements over the years. For instance, on *The Treasures of The Twilight Zone* DVD, released in 1998, there was an impressive *Inside the Twilight Zone* history section written by *The Twilight Zone Companion* author Marc Scott Zicree. It stated that Serling's masterpiece was:

> the first great fantasy series of the television medium. *Twilight Zone* was there before *Star Trek*, *The Outer Limits*, *The X-Files* or any other such show. In a real sense it made them all possible.[8]

As *One Step Beyond* premiered a full season — ten whole months — before *The Twilight Zone* (January 20, 1959, for the former; October 2, 1959, for the latter), it seems not only inaccurate but actually unfair (from a historical perspective) to champion *The Twilight Zone* as the first great "fantasy" series of TV. As *One Step Beyond* dealt with the fantastic made utterly believable (in essence, the same effort as many later genre series), it clearly deserves at least a mention or nod in any such listing of genre heavyweights. Sadly, the mistaken belief that *The Twilight Zone* somehow inspired *One Step Beyond* is commonly held by even the most knowledgeable of television historians. Rick Marschall in *The History of Television* (1986), erroneously wrote of *One Step Beyond* that it came "hot on the trail of the successful *Twilight Zone*,"[9] rather than reflecting the truth of the situation: that it was *The Twilight Zone* which followed *One Step Beyond* ... almost a year later.

Also, an objective viewing of the details reveals that *The X-Files* (listed in Zicree's history) has far more in common with *One Step Beyond* than it does with *The Twilight Zone*, so again it seems fatuous to herald the Serling series as some kind of spiritual father to this particular, popular 1990s program. At least in its early seasons, *The X-Files* dealt exclusively with inexplicable happenings, most of them paranormal in nature. *The X-Files* format, which examined pyrokinesis ("Fire"), communication with the dead ("Beyond the Sea"), soul transference ("Lazarus"), reincarnation ("Born Again"), demonic powers ("Die Hand die Verletzt"), premonitions ("Clyde Bruckman's Final Repose"), astral projection ("The Walk") and precognition ("Oubliette"), has far more in common with *One Step Beyond*, which also dealt with those subjects in various episodes (pyrokinesis: "The Burning Girl"; soul transference: "Message from Clara"; communication with the dead: "Brainwave"; reincarnation: "The Riddle"; demonic powers: "The Voice"; premonitions: "Tonight at 12:17"; astral projection: "The Navigator"; precognition: "Tidal Wave").

While it is certainly true that the two series (Chris Carter's and John Newland's) take different approaches to their paranormal material, they each accomplish essentially the same thing. Both attempt to document or expose those things in life that remain inexplicable, either through science, religion or some combination thereof. Oppositely, *The Twilight Zone* tended to be a morality play set in fantasy, horror or sci-fi settings, and its didactic terrain was not really the paranormal (though there were significant exceptions, such as the episode "Nightmare as a Child").

In fact, every claim people assert for the breadth and scope of *The Twilight Zone*'s legacy can be made with equal validity about *One Step Beyond*. There are those who champion the Serling series because it offers the chance to see great early TV performances by future stars, such as Jack Klugman, Robert Duvall and Robert Redford. No doubt that is a terrific accomplishment, but *One Step Beyond* features early (and brilliant) performances by Warren Beatty, Donald Pleasence, Christopher Lee, Charles Bronson, William Shatner and Yvette Mimieux, to name but a few. Others will look at *The Twilight Zone*'s influence and state that it allowed for the birth of other anthologies, such as *Quinn Martin's Tales of the Unexpected* (1977), *Amazing Stories* (1985) and *The Outer Limits*. Again, that is quite true, but *One Step Beyond* laid the groundwork not only for *The X-Files* and its spin-off *Millennium* (1996–1999, in which protagonist Frank Black regularly experienced psychic visions), but *The Sixth Sense* (1972), *Beyond Reality* (1992–1993) and the "reality" TV shows *In Search of* (1976–82) and *Sightings* (1994–1997.) There are those who argue that *The Twilight Zone* must be a better series because it experienced its own revival in the mid–80s. Fine, but *One Step Beyond* was also revived in the mid–70s, as *The Next Step Beyond*. Interestingly, neither sequel came close to the quality of the original.

The point of this tit-for-tat battle is not that one series is necessarily better than the other, but that *One Step Beyond* and John Newland are certainly worthy of the respect that has been so graciously heaped upon *The Twilight Zone* and the work and career of Rod Serling. Newland's visual stamp is all over *One Step Beyond*, and a fine one it is, too. And, for the record, *One Step Beyond* did come along first.

The Series Unfolds

The TV series that became known as *Alcoa Presents* (and later, in syndication, as *One Step Beyond*) commenced in 1958 — not with a psychic cathexis of interconnected psychic mediums, but in the minds of a talented group of four friends from Hollywood, California, instead. Linked with actor-director John Newland, genuine star of the Golden Age of Television, was writer Larry Marcus, writer-producer Merwin Gerard and veteran producer Collier Young. This impressive brain trust was looking for a new TV series to develop and, furthermore, a way to break new ground in what was still a young art form at the time: television. This network of talent could have produced a western, a variety show, a dramatic anthology, a family situation comedy, a quiz show, or even a bonafide genre effort (such as *Lights Out!*, *Tales of Tomorrow* or *Science Fiction Theater*). However, each principal in this so-called "network of four" sought to break new ground rather than give birth to what was essentially a retread of someone else's idea.

Adroit radio scribe Merwin Gerard created *One Step Beyond*, and his initial concept for the series was a kind of omnibus genre anthology program. Titled first *Imagination* and then *Fantasy*, the proposed TV series would have highlighted fantasy one week, horror the next week, a paranormal excursion the third week, and a science fiction drama the fourth week, all in continuing rotation. Collier Young and creator Gerard would produce the new anthology, Larry Marcus and Gerard would write most of the stories, and Newland would serve in two important capacities. He would direct each half-hour episode, but he would also serve as the front man for the whole enterprise: appearing on-screen at the commencement and conclusion of each episode and thereby acting as a host of sorts.

Although Newland's presence as an accomplished director was no doubt more important overall to the tenor and feel of the new series than his on-screen duties as host, everyone involved in the effort understood that as an established star, Newland needed to be front and center for this particular venture to fly. The networks and the sponsors would surely have demanded the presence of a celebrity, especially on a TV show wherein the stories would be beyond the realm of most viewers' experience and familiarity. Therefore, Newland was to represent a friendly, welcoming face in a world of unfamiliar, even terrifying ideas. Although one goal of the new series was certainly to raise goosebumps, the terror generated always had to be manageable (or "tolerable," as the creators of *The Outer Limits* [1963–65] later coined the phrase), and Newland successfully put a grinning — but earnest — face atop that horror, thereby making it infinitely more digestible to viewers at home.

As *Fantasy* developed, the circle of four began to narrow the ideas that would serve as the playground for the proposed series. In short order, straight horror, straight fantasy and straight science fiction were eliminated from the format because, in one form or another, they had already been done before by the prominent genre programs of the 1950s. Thus it was decided instead that the new series would focus solely on psychic phenomena, a long-time subject of interest to creator Merwin Gerard, for two very important reasons. Firstly, no dramatic series had ever leant itself exclusively to the topic of parapsychology (except a short-lived audience participation program called *E.S.P.*, which was hosted by Vincent Price and aired for only a month in the summer of 1958); and secondly, there were a variety of available and legitimate sources to reference in writing numerous installments of the series. Histories, biographies, archives, even the American Psychical Association, could all be plundered for stories that might be dramatized on the new anthology. In other words, there would never be a shortage of material — a critical factor in a production intended to have a long run and to appear fresh, week in and week out.

The rub for Merwin Gerard, John Newland and the others was that their "paranormal anthology" could not simply be phantasmagoria. It had to be *real*, and some proof had to be offered for each scenario depicted. This was an important distinction, because it meant, essentially, that the men of *One Step Beyond* were going out on a very dangerous limb. They would present amazing stories each and every week, and then tell audiences that what had been seen was actually based on fact ... thereby generating a terrific scare.

As the blockbuster films *The Amityville Horror* (1979) and *The Blair Witch Project* (1999) later proved so dramatically, audiences react with genuine interest and heightened terror to productions that can make the claim of being "based on fact" or that seem like "true" stories. *Alcoa Presents: One Step Beyond* gained a kind of immediacy with viewers because Newland, as host, often made that all-important claim that these things had actually happened to real people. He would then buttress those claims with evidence. "It had to be real, and there had to be proof, either anecdotal or published," Newland established, and that rule became scripture on *One Step Beyond*. The series even enlisted a technical advisor in the person of Ivan Klapper, though Newland remembers his input as only moderately helpful.

Interestingly, *One Step Beyond*'s obsession with "proof" and "evidence" may be the very factor that has assured the series' longevity. Some of the best episodes of the series ("Night of April 14," "Moment of Hate," "Where Are They?" "Persons Unknown," "The Day the World Wept: The Lincoln Story" and "The Sacred Mushroom" remain chill-inducing even in the 21st century because the evidence presented at the end of these episodes remains difficult to dismiss out of hand. These stories resonate because, even forty years after *Alcoa Presents: One Step Beyond* ceased production, there are very few real answers in the field of parapsychology about why amazing things, such as astral projection, teleportation, precognition and the like, occur ... or appear to occur.

With their formula for a paranormal anthology cemented, and John Newland ensconced as "Our Guide to the World of the Unknown," Collier, Young, Newland and Gerard set about producing a pilot film to shop around to sponsors. The group raised $30,000 and subsequently shot a 30-minute drama entitled "The Bride Possessed." Starring Virginia Leith, Skip Homeier and Harry Townes, "The Bride Possessed" was lensed in a matter of days and Newland directed it efficiently. A taut drama, the debut story concerned the ill-fated honeymoon of two sympathetic newlyweds. The new wife (Leith) became unexpectedly "possessed" by the spirit of a dead woman who needed to prove to authorities that her hot-blooded husband had actually murdered her. In her possessed state of mind, the poor bride embodied behavior that was alien to her youthful, virginal character (including the ability to drive a car, explicit knowledge of love-making, and recognition of landmarks from places she had never visited before).

While putting together this pilot, other important figures joined the *One Step Beyond* production team. Perhaps the most important of these contributors was Harry Lubin, a musician who was responsible for writing the score of "The Bride Possessed" and all subsequent *One Step Beyond* episodes. In scoring the pilot, Lubin created the memorable "Fear," a creepy composition that came to be heard in every episode of *One Step Beyond* during its 96 episode run. Absolutely chill-inducing, the quality of this musical interlude is another reason why the series has remained fresh: It is genuinely creepy. In fact, John Newland still remembers the first time he heard this *One Step Beyond* signature piece, a kind of trademark for the series: "At that moment, I just knew that everything was coming together on the show. Harry was a very articulate man, and a great composer, and he really loved the idea of the show. I think the music reflected his genuine interest and feel for the material. When an album of his work on *One Step Beyond* was released many years later, it was quite successful." Indeed, to this day, Lubin's contributions to *One Step Beyond* can be ordered on the Internet in CD form. It may not be as well-known a piece as *The Twilight Zone* theme, but it is certainly an evocative work that captures the uncertainty and terror of *One Step Beyond*'s paranormal universe.

Also aboard for the pilot film was Bud Westmore, the legendary make-up artist who has toiled (over the years) on every major genre effort, from *The Twilight Zone* (1959–64) and *Star Trek* (1966–69) to *Rod Serling's Night Gallery* (1970–73). Another crucial figure in the series' genesis, Henry Berman, did not become involved with *One Step Beyond* until after the pilot was completed. However, Berman, a consummate editor, is another man whom Newland openly credits with making his series such a landmark production. "Cutters are incredibly important people," he told this author. "Henry Berman was a major reason for the success of *One Step Beyond*. After lunch on any given day of shooting, he would approach me and let me know what he thought he needed in order to deliver a satisfactory final cut. He would say: I need a two-shot here, John, et cetera ... and usually his recommendation was something that would never have entered my mind. Cutters are very helpful to directors, and I always listened to Henry and placed stock in his advice."

When completed, the pilot "The Bride Possessed" was shopped around, and Alcoa, the Aluminum Company of America, liked it enough to sponsor a full season of episodes. With a major backer such as Alcoa sponsoring the series, a network deal was rapidly arranged and ABC picked up the series, now called *Alcoa Presents*, for prime time. As Newland remembers, his presence in front of the camera was a "strong selling point" because he had very much been a star in the fledgling art form of television. As he recalls, "Having me as a front man helped get the series sold."

From there, *Alcoa Presents: One Step Beyond* was off and running. In January of 1959, a time of year usually considered the middle of a season, ABC dropped *Confession* (1958–59), an interview show filmed in Texas with host Jack Wyatt, which concerned the root causes of crime, and replaced it with the brand new *Alcoa Presents*. The paranormal anthology thus aired Tuesday nights at 10:00 P.M. against CBS's *The Gary Moore Show* (1958–67), a variety program, and NBC's *The Californians* (1957–59), a series about the Gold Rush in the 1850s. In the three seasons it aired (1959, 1959–60, 1960–61), *One Step Beyond* never moved from this time slot, a fact that would today probably seem a miracle in a world where networks demonstrate little faith or commitment to new programming. Just look at what happened to *Harsh Realm*.

The typical episode of *One Step Beyond* was shot in three days, with the crew shooting five days a week. The production team consisted of roughly 80 technicians, and the average budget per episode was $55,000. In its first two and a half-seasons the series was lensed at the Metro Goldwyn Mayer Studio in Hollywood, and one way to maintain the low cost of the installments was to utilize costumes left behind from various MGM film productions. Indeed, the *One Step Beyond* episode roster features many period pieces (including "The Death Waltz," "Night of Decision," "The Lovers," "The Day the World Wept: The Lincoln Story" and others), so that the production team could take advantage of these very expensive, very impressive MGM film costumes.

Script-wise, John Newland remembers very little improvisation or rewrites on the sets of the series, recalling that the show was erected on very solid foundations: "good actors, good movement, solid dialogue" and the "vast experience" of a well-trained writing team and director. Newland also praises the efforts of Collier Young and Merwin Gerard, who went far beyond their writing and producing duties to participate heavily in the casting of the show, for bringing such a high caliber of performer to *One Step Beyond*.

As far as the direction of the show was concerned, Newland says he had a totally "free hand," and that the network and Alcoa were not involved in the day-to-day, on-set decisions of filming the show. "Those were the great days," he reminisced with enthusiasm. Indeed, Newland worked in the TV industry long enough to see both the positive and the negative side of things: the good and creative early days when artists called the shots on their own TV series, and the contemporary, corporate days when business executives attempt to exercise a choke-hold of control over the dramatic and creative direction of a program.

Twenty-two episodes were produced in *One Step Beyond*'s first year, and they were an impressive bunch of stories by any standard, effectively dramatized and directed. Notable guest stars in the first sortie included Patrick Macnee (of *The Avengers* [1961–69] fame) in "Night of April 14," Cloris Leachman (of *Hold It Please* [1949], *Bob and Ray* [1951–53], *Lassie* [1954–57], *The Mary Tyler Moore Show* [1970–77], *Phyllis* [1975–77], *Backstairs at the White House* [1979] and the film *The Last Picture Show* [1971]) in "The Dark Room," Alfred Ryder (of *Star Trek*'s "The Man Trap") in "The Devil's Laughter," Patrick O'Neal (of *Diagnosis Unknown* [1960], *Kaz* [1978–779] and *Emerald Point N.A.S.* [1983–84]) in "The Return of Mitchell Campion," Mike Connors (later the titular character in *Mannix* [1967–75]) in "The Aerialist," and Werner Klemperer (later of *Hogan's Heroes* [1965–71]) playing a Nazi in "The Haunted U-Boat." The paranormal topics tackled in the freshman year included possession ("The Bride Possessed" and "The Captain's Guests"), premonitions ("Night of April 14," "Premonition" and "Emergency Only"), ghosts—or, more accurately, apparitions—("The Dark Room," "Front Runner," "Epilogue," "The Dead Part of the House," "The Secret" and "The Navigator"), OBEs—Out of Body Experiences—("Return of Mitchell Campion"), pyrokinesis ("The Burning Girl") and even "rapping"—tapping noises supposedly generated by the dead—("The Haunted U-Boat").

In each installment of *One Step Beyond* (or *Alcoa Presents*, as it was originally known), John Newland (sharp in a suit and tie) would greet viewers (in medium shot) with the reflection of a circular window on a bare wall behind him. Before the opening credits rolled, he would greet the viewers with a variation on the following narration:

> What you are about to see is a matter of human record. Explain it? We cannot. Disprove it? We cannot. We simply invite you to explore with us the amazing world of the unknown, to take that *One Step Beyond!*[10]

This explanation/disclaimer was a brilliant bit of writing, not to mention showmanship, because it elegantly, even artfully, established a few important things about the paranormal anthology. Firstly, it broadcast that the series would offer true stories that were a "matter of human record," a claim that gave the dramatizations an added weight of legitimacy. Secondly, the narration gave producers an out. They could back away from providing hard and fast scientific explanations ("Explain it? We cannot") yet keep a veneer of legitimacy by simultaneously claiming that the events portrayed within are both inexplicable *and* unable to be disproved. And finally, the narration lowered expectations for skeptics and cynics by "simply" inviting the viewer to "explore" the "amazing world of the unknown." A clever turn of phrase thus marked the parameters of the series' playground rather nicely.

Newland's pre-title narration was followed by a shot of the greatest mystery of all: outer space. A black screen, with stars moving inexorably across it, was seen. Finally, the title *Alcoa Presents* appeared, twisting and shimmering in the void as if caught in the current of a river. It was a simple presentation of the title, but an effective one. When the series became *One Step Beyond* (in syndication), the starscape remained intact but the words "One," "Step" and "Beyond" raced out of the nothingness towards the screen in pyramid formation.

Like *The Twilight Zone, One Step Beyond* did not limit itself to just one opening narration. As the series developed, other narrations came to the forefront. One of the most memorable — and eerie — is as follows:

> Have you ever been certain the telephone would ring within the next ten seconds? Or have you ever walked down a street and had the feeling you knew what lay beyond the unturned corner? Then you've had a brief encounter with the unknown, a small step beyond. Now take a giant one."[11]

Audiences found themselves inclined to accept these invitations from the smiling Newland, not merely out of curiosity but because *One Step Beyond* promised to be scary, chill-inducing and thought-provoking, all at the same time. By asking the viewer personal questions ("Have you ever been certain the telephone would ring...?"), Newland and the writers of *One Step Beyond* again made the paranormal hit close to home, and that, no doubt, helps to explain the series' perennial appeal and effectiveness.

Our Guide to the World of ... Aluminum?

At the same time that Newland was directing each episode of *One Step Beyond*, he was also showcased in various promotional clips that aired both directly before the episode of the week and right after the denouement. In many of these commercials, Newland's job was also to hawk Alcoa products. As Newland remembers, he very much enjoyed the task of playing aluminum promoter for the backers of his new series. "It was great," he said of the arrangement. "They were happy with my work, and I was happy with their money. It was a good relationship."

In contemporary America, TV programs no longer have only one sponsor, and some do not even have regular sponsors at all; but back in 1959, Alcoa's funding quite simply allowed *One Step Beyond* to exist. In return, the commercials seen on *One Step Beyond* were for items such as Alcoa Wrappers (a "super strength" aluminum foil) and Alcoa Downspouts (which resisted corrosion, wouldn't stain, remained attractive, and even came in three "attractive" finishes: natural, embossed and "special" alumalure).

In one commercial, which aired between segments of *One Step Beyond*, a pitchman (not Newland this time) held an ordinary black-and-white spotted house cat in his arms and made an announcement that seemed funny (if appropriate), considering the paranormal content of the Newland series:

> Meet an insulation expert. She's *psychic* about insulation in a wall. If a wall isn't insulated, she heads for the middle of a room … that's where the heat is.

In another spot for the show, John Newland was seen to be walking (almost gliding, actually) behind a shimmering curtain of aluminum. As he was viewed in close-up (superimposed over more swaying aluminum patterns), Newland delivered a narration that was one part series promo and one part sponsor commercial:

> *Alcoa Presents* … a journey into the world beyond reason. Alcoa … first in aluminum, its development and perfection for today's many uses, and in the world of tomorrow. *Alcoa Presents* … an adventure that may make you doubt your senses. Come. You'll witness things strange, unexpected, mysterious … but not to be denied. Join me now and take *One Step Beyond*.

And, although Newland recollects very little interference from Alcoa ("these were the days before Proctor and Gamble," he noted), at the end of each show Newland would return once more in the aluminum labyrinth to provide viewers with a tidy wrap-up that would leave them feeling secure enough to sleep peacefully and, again (nudge, nudge), remind them to patronize Alcoa products:

> A word of reassurance. Many things that seem mysterious can be explained. This maze is really of aluminum, that remarkable metal. Light and beautiful, yet strong and long-lasting, serving you better in new ways every day. Aluminum — developed and perfected by your host, Alcoa, The Aluminum Company of America.

Thankfully, commercials and series promos rarely blend so totally in one presentation today, but as John Newland reminds us, this approach was "just part of the business" back in the 1950s.

A *Detour into* The Twilight Zone

As John Newland directed one of the 22 first season episodes of *One Step Beyond*, he was called from the set to answer a very interesting phone call. When he picked up, Newland discovered that the party on the other end of the line was none other than Rod Serling, arguably the greatest writer of 1950s television. "I knew Rod, and he knew me as a director," Newland reported, "and he was a splendid person to work with and a real supporter." When Newland questioned Serling about the purpose behind the call, Rod proposed that Newland meet him for drinks at an L.A. restaurant, The Cock and Bull, to discuss something of mutual importance. Newland agreed to the date and met with Rod as planned. Once at the restaurant, Serling revealed flat out to Newland that he was going to be producing and writing his own genre anthology series, to be called *The Twilight Zone*. At first, Newland was taken a back by the revelation, as *One Step Beyond* had already been on the air for some time and was earning good ratings. But then, Newland remembers, Serling assured him that "his show was going to be pure fantasy, with no discussion of proof or psychic powers." As Newland recollects, Serling "just wanted to let me know in person that he wasn't going to rip us off." Rather than angering Newland with news of the competition, Serling's gracious behavior and personal notification only proved to Newland what he had already known for some time: that Serling was "a class act." Today, Newland remembers this meeting with good humor.

When *The Twilight Zone* finally aired, *One Step Beyond* consistently scored higher ratings, but forty years later it is the Serling show that remains better known.

The Second Season

Alcoa Presents was renewed for a second season without difficulty or fuss, and John Newland was back on board with Collier Young, Merwin Gerard, Larry Marcus, Henry Berman, Harry Lubin and much of the same behind-the-scenes personnel to present a whopping 39 new half-hour stories. Newland recalls that the response to the first season had been "enthusiastic" on the part of both the network and Alcoa, and audience response had also been strong. Although a few viewers (mostly from the Bible belt, apparently) had written angry letters to the show calling Newland "the Anti-Christ" and claiming that "only God" could do the amazing things that *One Step Beyond* regularly dramatized (i.e. mind reading, seeing the future, et al.), the overall response to the series was positive and a bit surprising. Specifically, people began to write in record numbers that they themselves had lived through circumstances similar to the ones *One Step Beyond* dramatized regularly. Creator-producer of *One Step Beyond* Merwin Gerard was bowled over by the content and source of these letters:

> I would say that approximately 30 percent of our mail is of the let-me-tell-you-what-happened-to-me variety and the other 70 percent is the usual fan mail except that most of it is highly literate. We hear from doctors, lawyers, engineers, students— that level. And I would say that perhaps only one letter of 1000 is uncomplimentary.[12]

Relishing its popularity with the high-brow crowd, the show's creators took the second season of *One Step Beyond* even further with its bizarre concepts. "Delusion" concerned a paranoid who believed that anyone who shared his blood would suffer a terrible death. "Ordeal on Locust Street" featured a boy who was a hideous mutation, part-fish and part-man. In "The Inheritance," a necklace took on a malevolent life of its own, becoming a murderous sentient creature. And there was even an opportunity to escape the limited world of psychic phenomena for a half-hour and study the case of a Bigfoot-like creature in "Night of the Kill." Despite the more colorful stories, there was still the commendable grounding in reality and the prominence of "proof," but many of the tales were better told and more daring in conception and execution. The guest stars were also an incredible bunch of performers. Norman Lloyd, a regular performer and director on *Alfred Hitchcock Presents*, starred with Suzanne Pleshette ("one of the best actresses I ever worked with," Newland told this author) in "Delusion"; Robert Loggia (*Jagged Edge* [1985], *Big* [1986], *Independence Day* [1996]) was tormented by blood that would not wash off his hands after a murder in "The Hand"; and the great Albert Salmi guest-starred in the series' only two part episode, "The Peter Hurkos Story," about a famous European psychometrist. Also highlighted in the second season of *One Step Beyond* was future Oscar winner Louise Fletcher (in "The Open Window"), and an impossibly young and handsome Warren Beatty guest starred in "The Visitor" with Joan Fontaine.

The bolder stories, the great casts, good word-of-mouth, and increased viewing base assured *One Step Beyond* a sophomore season that was even more successful in the ratings game than the season before had been. The series continued to be aired on ABC on Tuesday nights at 10:00 P.M. Its lead-ins were Chuck Connors' *The Rifleman* (1958–63) at 8:00 and Philip Carey's *Philip Marlowe* (1959–60) at 9:00; and *One Step Beyond* now competed against not one but two variety programs: CBS's *The Gary Moore Show* and NBC's *Startime*, the latter sponsored by the Ford Motor Company.

One Step Abroad — The Third Season

By the beginning of *One Step Beyond's* third season, some 61 episodes had aired in prime time, an amazing number when one considers that a full season of stories for a dramatic program in 2000 is usually 20 to 24 episodes. With so many stories in the can, creator Merwin Gerard, producer Collier Young and host/director John Newland began to suspect that their anthology might be running out of new ideas, if not steam. In fact, Gerard even made his now-famous remark about the limitation of *One Step Beyond's* playground, the paranormal:

> Actually, there are only about 15 basic psychic phenomenon stories. Every story we did was just a variation of one of those 15 basic themes.[13]

If that assessment were true, then the successful *One Step Beyond* had gone through each of those 15 stories some four times by the end of its second year. Despite a fear of repetition, the third year of the anthology proved to be a remarkable one, perhaps because its creators were cognizant of the fact that they really had to top themselves for the show to remain fresh. Thus the third year of *One Step Beyond* boasted a number of outstanding efforts to keep the show new. The season premiere, "Tidal Wave," was especially timely. It was based upon a bizarre incident in May of 1960 in which a deaf man "heard" the screams of a crippled woman as a deadly tidal wave approached Hawaii. Despite his hearing impediment, the man saved the woman because of what he supposedly heard. At the end of "Tidal Wave," the participants of the *real* event were brought on stage and interviewed by John Newland. They testified that — except for a bit of dramatic license — the show had correctly reported their paranormal experience. The same idea, bringing the actual "percipients" on the show, was also used for the third-season episodes "Persons Unknown" and "Signal Received."

Another incredible experiment became *One Step Beyond's* most popular — and most notorious — episode. It was called "The Sacred Mushroom," and it remains the only *One Step Beyond* episode to abandon the dramatic format altogether. Instead, it was a documentary about John Newland's journey to a remote Mexican village to discover (and sample) a special mushroom that was purported to enhance the psychic abilities of those who digested it. The episode featured authentic foreign locales, a local *brujo*, and a scene in which a team of scientists experience the "effects" of this mushroom before our very eyes. In the last portion of the episode, John Newland himself eats the mushrooms and describes its hallucinogenic effects to the audience. Nothing like that had *ever* been done on network TV, inside or outside the science fiction genre.

In *One Step Beyond*'s final season, the guest star performances were as powerful as any yet seen. A young William Shatner gave one of his best TV performances as an ex–Nazi bomb defuser in "The Promise," Joanne Linville was a portrait of paranoia in "Moment of Hate" (playing a woman with the power to kill with a thought), and Robert Lansing faced off against a demonic rodent(!) in the chilling "The Voice."

From verifiable current events ("Tidal Wave") to a stunning documentary and experiment in Mexico ("The Sacred Mushroom"), *One Step Beyond* felt as fresh as ever, even though it had long since exhausted its basic fifteen stories. Still, feeling that the series could be given an ever bigger face-lift, John Newland suggested a radical idea for the last half of the third season: moving the production of the series overseas to Great Britain for the last thirteen shows of the year. "I thought it would give a little boost to the show because Great Britain offered good actors, good situations, and good settings. We sought permission from Alcoa, and they okayed it." So, for the final 13 episodes of *One Step Beyond*, the setting was England, a land whose culture was "steeped in psychic phenomenon" and where "practically every house" had "a resident ghost."[14] The transplanted series was now shot (under the auspices of Lancer Films) at the MGM Studios in Borehamwood, England.

Behind the scenes, *One Step Beyond*'s established production crew melded with the best young film minds of England. Among these new talents was assistant director David Tomblin, an artist who would go on to become an important voice in British sci-fi TV. After his tenure on *One Step Beyond*, Tomblin would write and direct various episodes of the Patrick McGoohan series *The Prisoner* (1967–68), including "Living in Harmony" and "The Girl Who Was Death." Tomblin also scripted and directed "The Cat with Ten Lives" and penned "The Long Sleep" for Gerry and Sylvia Anderson's *U.F.O.* (1970). Later in the '70s, Tomblin directed American stars Martin Landau and Barbara Bain in some of the best episodes of *Space: 1999* (1975–77), including Johnny Byrne's "Force of Life," "Another Time, Another Place," Anthony Terpiloff's "The Infernal Machine," and the first season finale, "The Testament of Arkadia." Years after this work, Tomblin relocated to Hollywood and served as assistant director to Steven Spielberg on projects such as *Raiders of the Lost Ark* (1981).

The move to England turned out to be a good one on all counts because it gave *One Step Beyond* access to a new group of performers, such as horror icon Christopher Lee ("The Sorcerer"), Donald Pleasence ("The Confession"), Mark Eden ("Signal Received"), Lois Maxwell ("The Room Upstairs"), and Roger Delgado ("The Face"). The omnipresent, refined British accent even provided the psychic goings-on of *One Step Beyond* an additional air of legitimacy in some circles. And, despite what has been reported in various magazines, John Newland remembers that the series' ratings remained strong during the overseas experiment. By the end of the third season, nearly one hundred episodes of *One Step Beyond* had been produced.

Cancellation and Syndication

Despite an ever-more-courageous format and a bold approach to its paranormal material, *One Step Beyond* was not renewed for a fourth go-round, the 1961–62 season. During its third season and final slate, it aired after *Stagecoach West* (1960–61), a short-lived western that provided an inadequate lead, and once more found itself battling the variety program *The Garry Moore Show*. Sadly for Alcoa's series, *Garry Moore* had shown a steady rise in popularity since its premiere. In 1960 it finally broke into the top 25 shows, and then it catapulted up to number 12 in 1961. By contrast, *One Step Beyond* never vaulted into the coveted top 25 rated series in any of its years on the air. This is especially odd, because most television viewers or historians will not remember *The Garry Moore Show* today but they would certainly recall *One Step Beyond*.

Other things had changed since *One Step Beyond*'s premiere. *The Twilight Zone* had provided intense competition, and invidious comparisons were inevitably made. And, during *One Step Beyond*'s last year on the air, rival NBC spotlighted a suspense/paranormal block on Tuesday nights featuring *Alfred Hitchcock Presents* and the Boris Karloff anthology *Thriller*. It was possible, and highly likely, that viewers of genre programming were turning their attention to *The Twilight Zone*, the long-lived *Alfred Hitchcock Presents* (which began in 1955) or the spanking new *Thriller*. *Alcoa Presents* did not prosper amidst so much competition.

Still, John Newland recalls that *One Step Beyond* was not cancelled because of low ratings or because of more intense competition. Instead, it was simply a matter of familiarity and numbers. "You have to remember, we had done 96 episodes already, and there was the inescapable feeling that we were no longer the new kid on the block. The show was still drawing high ratings, but the decision was made to make room for a newer product." That newer product turned out to be *Alcoa Premiere*, a prestige drama with Fred Astaire acting as host and star. Featuring stars such as Charlton Heston, Lee Marvin and Shelley Winters, this new series took *One Step Beyond's* 10:00 P.M. slot from 1961 to 1963, before it too was cancelled. The last new episode of *Alcoa Presents* (*One Step Beyond*) aired on August 4, 1961, though reruns ran through October 3, 1961.

In any normal world, that would have been the end of things for *One Step Beyond*, but the world of television was changing rapidly in the early 1960s. Local stations all over the United States were cropping up in record numbers, and they needed to fill all the hours of the day (and particularly the early evening) with some manner of appealing programming. Network TV cast-offs seemed the best option, though networks had produced scores of variety shows and quiz shows, and both of those genres seemed instantly dated, hence unprofitable. Worse, many early TV shows had been filmed "live" and thus no longer existed as taped broadcasts to rerun at all. In this environment, shows such as *One Step Beyond* were as good as gold. Through the magic of syndication, local TV stations all over the United States were able to buy the series and "strip" it (i.e., run it five days a week). Since *One Step Beyond* ran for three years and 96 episodes, it was perfectly suited for this cause because it could be shown for approximately 20 weeks with no reruns. In fact, it was through the venue of syndication that *One Step Beyond* (its official syndicated title) really became a cult show. Run in the early evening (at 6:00 P.M. or so), it was soon seen by scores of children and young adults who had not been permitted to stay up until 10:00 P.M. during the show's original run. And the fantastic subject material at the heart of *One Step Beyond* promised that the comic book/science fiction crowd would greet the series with enthusiasm. They did.

Accordingly, it was not very long before John Newland realized that he had a cult sensation on his hands. His contract had stipulated that he be paid for the first six reruns of *One Step Beyond* only, and then nothing. When those six royalty payments arrived in fast succession, there was no doubt in anyone's mind that *One Step Beyond*, a cancelled network program, had a rerun resurrection beyond any expectations. By the mid–70s the series was actually entrenched as a cult classic, airing constantly on channels such as WPIX New York ... rounding out an hour that began with *The Twilight Zone*. As the seventies continued, the series was written about in glowing terms in such reference books as *Fantastic Television* (by Gary

Gerani and Paul Schulman) and in budding genre magazines like *Starlog*. So popular was the series that John Newland launched *The Next Step Beyond*, a syndicated follow-up to his classic series, in 1978. Hindered by a low budget and a cheap look, courtesy of the decision to shoot on video-tape, the series ran for only 25 episodes before cancellation. Still, *The Next Step Beyond* would never have been made had *One Step Beyond* not exceeded all expectations in the world of television reruns. It was quickly known as "one of television's most successful series ever to be syndicated" after original network (ABC) airings.[15]

It was a great and rewarding fact that *One Step Beyond* extended its video life well into the 1970s—more than a decade after its network cancellation; but the series just kept going and going ... even beyond the seventies. In 1988 *One Step Beyond* was still being broadcast regularly on stations such as WZTV-17 in Nashville, WGPR-TV62 in Detroit and KTZZ-22 in Seattle. As cable grew more popular in America, *One Step Beyond* went with it. In 1991 *One Step Beyond* aired on the cable network called "Nostalgia Television." It ran at 8:00 P.M. several nights a week as part of the "Nostalgia Anthology" viewing block, preceeding such classic movies as *White Zombie* (1932). Thirty years after its cancellation, *One Step Beyond* was still being aired in major markets.

The Sci-Fi Channel Rebirth

In 1992 a new network devoted to science fiction programming was born from the auspices of the USA Network. Not surprisingly, one of the Sci-Fi Channel's first major acquisitions was the 1959–61 anthology *One Step Beyond*. Of course, much time had passed since the program had originally aired, and *One Step Beyond's* distributor, World Vision Enterprises Inc., decided that it was time to update some facets of the aging series. Specifically, two new elements were added: a pre-title sequence which included one significant (and usually creepy) scene from the episode being broadcast (shaded in a deathly blue hue), and a new opening credits sequence. Instead of the simple starry backdrop and the title of the show in block-white lettering, it was decided to go ahead with new computer generated imagery in a revamped title sequence.

As of 1992, the retooled *One Step Beyond* credit montage began with a close-up of a glowing, full moon. After a pullback, in which it is revealed that viewers are seeing the moon framed between two bare tree branches, the camera pulls back even further and the audience finds itself inside an empty, modernistic house, looking out through a massive window. The camera suddenly zooms forward through a living room area with a spiral staircase. On a wall in the background, the round window reflection that Newland once stood before in his weekly introductions is visible (here as a skylight). The camera then rockets up the spiral staircase to a set of French doors at the end of a long hall. These doors swing outward suddenly, into deep space, and the words "*One Step Beyond*" pop up to windy sound effects.

In addition to this elaborate new imagery, Harry Lubin's title score has been re-synthesized. It now sounds electronic and far more pulse-pounding, accenting the scary aspects of the series. It is with this music and the new computer imagery that *One Step Beyond* has been introduced to a whole new generation. Interestingly, John Newland was never contacted about this decision to retool the series opening, and he reacted with surprise about it when informed of the revamp.

Despite the new credits, Worldvision's prints for the Sci-Fi Channel were the best that had been seen on TV in some time, and were far crisper than those rerun in the 1980s. In the years following 1992, *One Step Beyond* has been a continuing part of the Sci-Fi Channel, airing in prime time, evening, afternoon, and mid-morning. Most recently, it aired with *Tales of Tomorrow* and *The Invisible Man* as part of the late night/early morning Sci-Fi Channel bloc known as "Retro Television." One hopes it will soon return to a regular slot.

What a long strange journey it has been for the TV series *One Step Beyond*. It has lived so long (more than 40 years now) that its numerous children (*The X-Files*, *Millennium*, *Beyond Reality*, *The Sixth Sense*) are in reruns themselves and have even inspired generations of offspring of their own. Beyond *One Step Beyond*'s eternally provocative subject matter, it may have succeeded for so long simply because its crew loved making it. During the interview for this book, John Newland made a special point of thanking the fans for their undying interest and support in the series. He was also able to put the *One Step Beyond* experience into a special perspective: his long career in show business. "It was the best production I ever worked on, period. It was the best time I had working in this industry, and it was the most creative and satisfying atmosphere in my life, both personally and professionally."

And what of the persistent talk that *One Step Beyond* might be revived again, à la the Showtime version of *The Outer Limits* or the recent revivals of *The Twilight Zone*? Newland laughed about it, then confirmed that there had been some discussion on the topic. "We've talked about doing all kinds of revivals, even recently, but as *The Next Step Beyond* proved so dramatically, you just can't go home again. Recent talks have centered around the idea that there would be a new host — which is fine with me — but it would certainly be a whole different animal in today's television world. The fact remains, you can't go home again." Although Newland does not watch *The X-Files*, he is cognizant that it is a child of *One Step Beyond* and the work he pioneered from 1959 to 1961, and that fact makes him very proud.

A *One Step Beyond* without John Newland front and center is a thought no aficionado of television history would care to contemplate, especially considering how a colorized Alfred Hitchcock was "resurrected" by NBC for the short-lived 1985 version of *Alfred Hitchcock Presents*. Even if there is no revival of *One Step Beyond*, one can be grateful, as John Newland is, that the series has survived its historical context, outlived its network brethren, spawned countless imitations, and even become a legacy for its creators. One test of a great work is how well it stands up from one generation to the next. *One Step Beyond*, still going strong at 40 years plus, has passed that particular benchmark with flying colors.

A chapter of *One Step Beyond*'s history came to a close on January 10, 2000, when John Newland, 82, died of a stroke.[16] He was survived by two daughters, his wife of 32 years, and a legion of fans who still admire his work.

Part II

The Series

Critical Reception

Because horror and the paranormal are frequently scoffed at by mainstream critics (not to mention a slew of professional debunkers), *One Step Beyond* has often been met with a sense of what can only be described as grudging respect. Reviewers are quick to acknowledge that the series is well done from a technical standpoint — creepy and impressively directed by John Newland — but the same critics are just as likely to dismiss the program because of its "B movie" subject matter.

One Step Beyond's true critical success has blossomed from within the confines of the genre, where reviewers are more likely to appreciate *One Step Beyond*'s noble attempts to document the paranormal in believable and restrained (yet consistently frightening) fashion. As the paranormal becomes a more accepted branch of "science," *One Step Beyond* may even earn the title that has long eluded it: science fiction (or would it be science fact?).

Some of the more notable critical comments about *One Step Beyond* are sampled below:

The stories were all, apparently, based on real-life incidents, and were depicted as convincingly as possible. Effectively eerie segments and a determined authenticity place this show among the more notable examples of the genre. — Christopher Wicking and Tise Vahimagi, *The American Vein: Directors and Directions in Television*, E.P. Dutton, NY, 1979, page 252.

His [Newland's] direction was always intelligent and often brilliant. It was not a simple task to make half-hour episodes about E.S.P. or other supernatural phenomena appear believable. He usually succeeded.... Unlike *Twilight Zone*, *One Step Beyond* was based on fact, not fancy, and it took great pains to present psychic phenomena as realistically as possible.... Despite its integrity, reasonably favorable reviews and a devoted band of viewers, *One Step Beyond* received neither the critical acclaim nor the ratings that *Twilight Zone*... — Gary Gerani, with Paul H. Schulman, *Fantastic Television*, Harmony Books, 1977, page 26.

One Step Beyond can only be marginally termed science fiction.... Its baili-wick was the supernatural, psychic phenomena, ESP, reincarnation.... *One Step Beyond* was a genuinely scary look into the world below your mind.—John Javna, *The Best of Science Fiction TV*, Harmony Books, 1987, page 128.

Psychic phenomena of every sort were given a very restrained treatment which compared unfavorably with the melodramatics the audience had come to expect in presentations of this kind, while the documentation was usually too scanty to produce a deep sense of conviction. Nevertheless, there were a few interesting shows, especially one that abandoned the usual dramatic for-mat to present a study of hallucinogenic drugs.—Les Daniels, *Living in Fear: A History of Horror in the Mass Media*, Charles Scribner's Sons, New York, 1975.

One Step Beyond was most concerned with supernatural events that were explained by understandable psychic phenomena....The series was able to supply a weekly dose of barely believable, but nonetheless acceptable stories. The belief that what was being presented had actually happened was under-scored by Newland's desire for accuracy ... as in the case of a survey of hal-lucinogenic drugs ... when he tried a sample of peyote to test its effects. A decade ahead of the drug craze, Newland could have been television's orig-inal head.—James Delson, *Fantastic Films* Vol. 1, #6: "Science Fiction on Television," February 1979, page 58.

...studio-bound but seriously spooky ... the chilly series ... is virtually noth-ing but ghost stories, all of them supposedly based on true occurrences...—Jon Abbot, *TV Zone*, Special #7: "Spooky Anthology Series," November 1992, pages 48–51.

The men involved—Newland, creator-producer Merwin Gerard, and writers Larry Marcus and Collier Young—were intensely interested in the subject of the supernatural. Gerard contended that there were 15 basic psychic phe-nomena stories, and *One Step Beyond*'s makers labored to render each story as realistically as possible. The show elicited a great deal of fan mail ... much of it personal corroboration of the show's stories.—David Smith, *Starlog* #9: "Vintage Video: The Golden Age of SF Viewing," October 1977, page 54.

A sometimes silly show about highly unlikely "real life" occurrences ... despite its age, *One Step Beyond* remains far more tolerable than the spin-offs that followed.—Gloria Anchors, *Epilog Special* #5: "One Step Beyond," December 1992, page 40.

...Rod Serling's show was rarely scary or atmospheric and relied heavily on "surprise" or "twist" endings. *One Step Beyond* was genuinely scary and atmospheric throughout each episode. The moody black and white photog-raphy and the spine chilling background music only added to the atmosphere. This was a truly scary show.... Host John Newland was perfect ... and his monotone voice and unexpected appearances on the screen added to the sur-real feeling of the show.—edge-16, *Internet Movie Database* review: "Who Needs *The Twilight Zone*?" Posted March 23, 1999.

SEASON ONE (1959)

Cast and Credits

CAST: John Newland (Our Guide to the World of the Unknown).

CREW: *Producer:* Collier Young. *Series Created by the Associate Producer:* Merwin Gerard. *Special Consultant:* Ivan Klapper. *Executive Writer:* Larry Marcus. *Director of Photography:* William A. Horning. *Art Directors:* George W. Davis, William Ferrari, Alex Golitzen, Hans Peters. *Film Editors:* Henry Berman, Milton Carruth ("The Bride Possessed"); *Music:* Harry Lubin. *Assistant Directors (various episodes):* Stanley Goldsmith, Tom McCrory, Frank Shaw, Erich von Stroheim, Jr. *Set Decorators:* Henry Grace, Julia Heron, Keogh Gleason, Jack Miles. *Recording Supervisor:* Franklin Milton. *Sound:* Joe Lapis. *Make-up:* Bud Westmore. A Joseph M. Schenck Enterprises, ABC Films Presentation. Filmed at Metro-Goldwyn-Mayer Studios, Hollywood, U.S.A.

NOTE: The critical commentaries in the following section vary in length considerably, depending entirely on the content of the episode. As has been stated, an attempt has been made to note when and where *One Step Beyond* has been accurate in presenting the details of "recorded" accounts of psychic or paranormal phenomena. Since many later episodes do tend to repeat concepts already seen on the series, the discussion of accuracy and of documented antecedents most often appears during the review of the *first* episode that utilizes the concept. If there is an important variation in the concept (i.e. an apparition versus a crisis apparition), it is noted in the appropriate episode commentary.

The Episodes

1. "The Bride Possessed"

(Dramatized by Merwin Gerard and
Larry Marcus; Directed by John Newland;
Airdate: January 20, 1959)

SYNOPSIS: Matt and Sally Conroy's much-anticipated honeymoon is interrupted when Sally begins to manifest the uncharacteristic behavior of a woman she has never met, a woman who died at Eagle Point some weeks earlier. It seems that the restless spirit of Karen Warden is "possessing" the body of the new bride to prove that her untimely plunge from the hilltop was not suicide ... but murder.

GUEST CAST: Virginia Leith (Sally Conroy), Skip Homeier (Matt Conroy), Harry Townes (Dr. Alex Slawson), Ann Morrison, Janet Hughes, John Shay, Frank Richards, Duncan McLeod.

COMMENTARY: *One Step Beyond's* pilot episode immediately lands the fledgling series on solid ground, so far as its paranormal subject matter is concerned. The topic at the heart of "The Bride Possessed" is *possession*: the control of an unwilling individual by some external force or person, or as John Newland declares here, "the dead temporarily taking over the body of the living." In this tale, it is poor Sally Conroy whose body is manipulated by an outside agent, the dead Karen Warden, for the express purpose of righting the scales of justice and exposing her murderer. Though Newland states in the closing narration of "The Bride Possessed" that there are "thousands of cases" of possession that are "fully authenticated ... by respected scientists," possession is actually believed by psychical researchers to be a relatively rare phenomenon. That fact established, "The Bride Possessed" is remarkably faithful to the actualities of the most famous "true" cases of possession.

For instance, there is the strange evidence of a man named Pepe Veraldi and his vessel of possession, a girl named Maria Talarico, in 1936. In this seemingly genuine example of possession, young Maria passed under a bridge near a river (in the company of her grandmother) where Pepe Veraldi's corpse had been discovered some three years earlier. Pepe's death had been ruled a suicide by local authorities, but when Maria neared the site of his demise, she inexplicably began to speak in a male voice: Pepe's! Maria told her grandmother, in a voice not her own:

> My friends murdered me; they threw me into the river bed, then as I lay there, they beat me with a piece of iron and tried to make the whole thing look like suicide.[1]

Understandably concerned by this transformation, Maria's grandmother asked Pepe to leave her granddaughter alone, and he did so, ultimately returning Maria to normal. However, years later, a man *did* confess to Pepe's murder (with three friends as accomplices) and to the use of an iron pipe in the crime!

One Step Beyond's "The Bride Possessed" subscribes to the details of Maria's bizarre story with startling precision. An innocent (Maria/Sally) is possessed by a spirit of the deceased, who is seeking justice (Pepe/Helen). In both cases, the possessed person's voice alters cadence and sound (whether it be female to male, or from Southern accent to no accent), and important, highly specific details known only to the dead are revealed by the living and then verified through outside means. In both cases, a believed suicide is actually a cloak for murder, a fact which seems to suggest that the dead cannot rest without revealing the truth of their demise.

To be sure, "The Bride Possessed" retells the Veraldi/Talarico story with new locations, altered characters and variations on peripheral detail, but it nonetheless captures the essential jigsaw pieces of a real-life possession phenomenon. With such loyalty to real-life accounts, *One Step Beyond* immediately makes its case that these odd stories are a "matter of human record," even if viewers choose to "believe it or not."

"The Bride Possessed" is even more provocative as drama than it is as accurate depiction of the most common (and hard-to-dismiss) possession reports. In particular, the teleplay (co-authored by the writing giants of *One Step Beyond*: Merwin Gerard and Larry Marcus) boasts a surprisingly strong sexual subtext that succeeds in granting the episode a more immediate and interesting veneer than were it merely some clinical depiction of paranormal phenomena. Specifically, Sally Conroy is depicted in the early scenes of "The Bride Possessed" as a lovely, open-faced Southern belle. She is coy and sexy, and her charming Southern accent signifies her as being different and apart from new husband Matt and his friends at the bar where they raucously celebrate the marriage. Sally's white, sleeveless dress also sets Sally apart: as both an object of purity and innocence (again, she wears a *white* dress) and as an object of Matt's lust (she fills out the dress rather nicely). Because this is the first night of the Conroy marriage, Sally is implicitly a virgin (this *was* 1959), and this couple's desire to make love for the first time is almost tangible. Accordingly, the feelings of excitement and anticipation that accompany the typical newlywed dynamic is not far beneath the surface. When Sally fears aloud that Matt will be "too tired" from driving all day, she is musing worriedly not so much about her husband's well-being as she is about the fear that their wedding night, and his performance, may not measure up to her dreams for it.

Then the ultimate horror occurs when Sally suddenly and inexplicably changes. Ironically, the real terror in the situation is not that Sally has become possessed by the dead, but that Matt's sexual prize has suddenly become cold, distant and off limits to him. Sally no longer recognizes or cherishes her new husband, her charming accent vanishes suddenly, her very language coarsens, and worst of all, she reveals that, somehow, she is sexually experienced. It is a new husband's worst fear: Immediately after the wedding vows, the new wife is suddenly *not* the open, sexually innocent and interested woman he courted with such devotion. Matt's "prize" is no longer the prize at all, and Sally (as Karen) talks openly of the passion she shared with her former partner while he was "making love" to her, touching her, and coming on to her. Thus Sally, in this new form, is no longer the virgin that Matt has so much desired. The quest for Matt becomes how to get Sally back, not just as a person but as an innocent.

The sexual underpinnings in "The Bride Possessed" could represent many things: a metaphor about the manner in which men and women seem to change after marriage, or even a comment on the fact that some people marry under false pretenses and are more experienced than they have let on. But in "The Bride Possessed" the choice to make the possessed woman a new bride has a very specific and very technical purpose within the mechanism of the teleplay. Specifically, the "new marriage" set-up adds to the tension and urgency of the situation. The audience wants the "damage" of the possession repaired so that these two young, highly sympathetic, attractive and likable individuals can get on with their lives together. The wedding night is a vulnerable and special time, and "The Bride Possessed" exploits those feelings of vulnerability to lend the episode urgency. It works well, and "The Bride Possessed" is quite compelling. One really feels for this couple.

The husband-and-wife dynamic of "The Bride Possessed" is also important because it points in the direction the series would ultimately take. A multitude of *One Step Beyond* episodes depict the particulars of the spousal relationship. Sometimes it is a strong and loving relationship that is highlighted, sometimes it is a vulnerable one, and sometimes it is falling apart or in chaos. Into this situation of high personal stakes comes the unexpected, the psychic, and this force of the unknown inevitably resolves the personal dilemma of the piece. This is a distinction worth noting, because *One Step Beyond's* contemporary, *The Twilight Zone*, was afforded a much wider creative freedom. Because its stories were entirely fictitious rather than based on bizarre accounts of the paranormal, *The Twilight Zone* could depict astronauts on other worlds ("Elegy," "People Are Alike All Over"), aliens ("To Serve Man"), and societies in the distant future or alternate realities ("The Lonely," "Eye of the Beholder"). By contrast, *One Step Beyond* often chose to limit its dramatic range to the apparently mundane, the real, and the human: a normal husband (or wife's) sudden encounter with the inexplicable.

Seen in this light, *One Step Beyond* is very much the ongoing story of an "Everyman" or "Everywoman" butting up against inexplicable, great forces that are simply beyond his or her comprehension. On *The Twilight Zone* there was indeed a similar confrontation: Man versus a Place "whose boundaries are that of imagination." The difference is that Serling's zone of imagination was entirely fictitious (and therefore able to be manipulated without difficulty), and *One Step Beyond's* playground was the paranormal, a region of the bizarre that bordered on reality yet had a set of rules and precedents that had to be respected.

"The Bride Possessed" precipitates the trend of "common" people facing bizarre situations by spotlighting the journey of Matt Conroy, a regular Joe who loses his wife on his wedding night and is driven to near-hysteria by her (erotic) experience of possession. At the same time, however, the example of dead Karen Warden and her brutal murder is an especially valuable and potent one for the prototypical American couple, Sally and Matt, because it represents a path they need not take. Karen and her lover, her murderer, model an unsuccessful marriage. Matt and Sally learn about that tragedy (almost first-hand, in Sally's case) and are now equipped to go forward in their adult lives (starting from this night) with the knowledge not to make the same mistakes.

Another critical piece of *One Step Beyond*'s format puzzle is also locked into place in this remarkable pilot episode: the disbeliever. Inevitably, there must always be a disbeliever in these stories: someone who will invariably complain about "psychic hocus pocus" and rail against the (psychic) explanation that seems the most applicable to the situation. This character archetype frequently dismisses the paranormal to begin with (a surrogate, perhaps, for a skeptical audience), so that when he does finally have the experience with the unknown — that creepy moment of realization and truth — it seems all the more believable for his earlier reticence. In other words, the disbeliever dismissed the paranormal as hocus pocus primarily (from a dramatic standpoint, anyway) so that his ultimate belief seems legitimate. The audience is also left feeling satisfied and vindicated, since the disbeliever was not a crazy person to begin with or predisposed to believe in the patently unbelievable. Such disbelieving characters represent the audience's simultaneous need to believe and reluctance to believe.

"The Bride Possessed" is a tight little drama, well directed by John Newland. Impressively, Newland seems to know exactly when to hold his camera on a face and an expression, and for precisely just how long. The anguish evident on Matt's face when Sally (as Karen) discusses her "husband" making love to her truly captures the terror of this particular situation in a way that a reenactment of that event never could. The night shooting (outdoors) is also well handled. Sally stands out like a beacon in her white dress amidst all the blackness, and she performs as such by leading Dr. Slawson and husband Matt directly to the murder weapon.

In addition to Newland's fine direction, Harry Townes ("Anniversary of a Murder," *Star Trek*: "Return of the Archons"), Skip Homieier (*Star Trek*: "Patterns of Force" and "The Way to Eden") and Virginia Leith turn in intense, credible performances as the first ever guest stars on *One Step Beyond*.

Since "The Bride Possessed" aired in 1959, possession has cropped up repeatedly as a topic for genre TV series and films. Demonic possession, a variant on the subject, was a point of great interest in the 1970s with films such as *The Exorcist* (1973), *Abby* (1977) and *The Exorcist II: The Heretic* (1977). On television, possession has been featured on *The X-Files* (in "Lazarus") and on *Beyond Reality* (as "Asylum" and "The Dying of the Light"). Perhaps the most recent example of possession was seen in the film *Stigmata* (1999), which found atheist Patricia Arquette possessed by the spirit of a dead priest who had translated a new and controversial gospel of Jesus.

2. "Night of April 14"
(Dramatized by Collier Young; Directed by John Newland;
Airdate: January 27, 1959)

SYNOPSIS: In April of 1912 a young woman dreams of drowning in icy, dark water and then is shocked to discover that her future husband has booked their honeymoon trip on the maiden voyage of a supposedly unsinkable liner named *Titanic*. When the great vessel strikes an iceberg and goes down at sea, psychic repercussions are felt around the world: by a Methodist minister in Canada who changes the hymn of that evening to #446 ("Pray for Those in Peril on the Sea"); and by a magazine cartoonist who sketches the specifics of the disaster even as it occurs.

GUEST CAST: Patrick Macnee (Eric Farley), Barbara Lord (Grace), Isobel Elsom (Mrs. Montgomery), Gavin Gordon (Reverend Morgan), Jeanne Bates, Gavin Muir, Alan Caillou, John Hiestand, Marjorie Eaton, John Craven, Francis DeSales, Gil Stuart, Jack Lynn.

COMMENTARY: Movie and TV viewers seem to foster a never ending fascination for the tragic story of the *Titanic*. Various film versions, in 1915, 1943, 1953, 1958 (*A Night to Remember*) and 1997 (James Cameron's *Titanic*), have reminded the world of the details of the disaster in almost nauseating detail: the massive loss of life (more than a thousand people dead); the hubris involved in the (mistaken) belief that the ship was unsinkable; the bad planning that left *Titanic* terribly short on lifeboats; the panic that set in on deck once the disaster had come; the dictum that women and children should disembark first; and so on.

In genre TV the *Titanic* disaster has spurred dramatic stories on series as diverse as *The Time Tunnel* (1966: "Rendezvous with Yesterday"), *Rod Serling's Night Gallery* (1970: "Lone Survivor"), *Friday the 13th: The Series* (1988: "What a Mother Wouldn't Do"), *Freddy's Nightmares* (1989: "It's My Party and You'll Die If I Want You To") and *Forever Knight* (1995: "Black Buddha Part I"). Though *One Step Beyond*'s "Night of April 14" cost considerably less to produce than James Cameron's expensive block-buster, it certainly remains one of the best (and most unusual) tales of *Titanic* because it captures both the personal and epic side of the sea disaster, and then comes to a startling conclusion that aficionados of the paranormal have relished and debated ever since.

The psychic phenomenon which comes to light first in "Night of April 14," *One Step Beyond*'s second televised story, is *precognition*, the awareness through psychic means of a future event — one's untimely future death, in this case. In particular, young Grace experiences the recurring and highly disturbing nightmare that she will die by drowning in icy waters. In point of fact, Grace survives the *Titanic* disaster and it is her new husband's drowning death she witnesses in her terrifying dreams. Still, this precognition, this ability to peer, however obliquely, into the future, is, like possession, another well-documented psychic phenomenon.

On January 30, 1908, for instance, a young actress in a hypnotic state was questioned by her doctor about the specifics of her future. She replied that her career would be short and that she dare not repeat how it would end because her own death would be so terrible an event. After awakening, the actress remembered nothing of this fearful report, and the hypnotist did not reveal to her the subconscious prediction of doom. Approximately a year later, on February 22, 1909, however, the actress was at her hairdresser's when a flammable cosmetic suddenly caught fire on a nearby stove. The chemical fire spread quickly onto the actress's clothes and body, and in just a few hours she was dead from severe burns.[2]

In this case it is certainly possible to argue coincidence, as it is with Grace's case in "Night of April 14," but such an explanation does not seem the most natural answer. Whether such stories represent extreme coincidences, a sense of *synchronicity* or something more, *One Step Beyond* manages to accurately depict the situation of precognition reported by the above-listed case and thus lay claim to being a highly accurate dramatization of "documented" events.

About the second portion of the episode, *One Step Beyond* gains even greater points for legitimacy. The latter half of the drama concerns a kind of widening psychic web around the *Titanic*, as if the sinking of the great ship is an event so catastrophic that it sends telepathic ripples across a psychic ocean and affects people as far away as New York and Canada. This is difficult to prove, no doubt, yet it is representative of another recurrent theme of *One Step Beyond* as a speculative TV series: that great disasters, such as earthquakes ("Earthquake"), the death of a beloved president ("The Day the World Wept: The Lincoln Story"), a volcanic eruption ("Eye Witness"), and the sinking of a massive ocean liner, somehow trigger psychic responses across a psychically-connected human race, and even across time when necessary. One might rightly ask just how such a thing can ever possibly be established or proven, but then comes a surprise: the "proof." There is the matter of "the book."

At the very end of "Night of April 14," *One Step Beyond* host John Newland faces the camera and with deadpan earnestness plucks an innocuous-looking hardbound book from a shelf behind him. Clutched in his hands is a novel entitled *Futility*, written by a man named Morgan Robertson. The novel's plot concerns the maiden voyage of the largest ocean liner ever built. On an April night, this fictitious vessel struck an iceberg and, because there were not enough lifeboats aboard, more than one thousand passengers died in freezing waters. The name of the ship in the novel *Futility* was ... *Titan*. Amazingly, this novel by Robertson was written in the year 1898, some 14 years *before* the *Titanic* disaster occurred! This amazing bit of evidence points to the fact that perhaps, just perhaps, Robertson's inspiration for writing this tale of disaster at sea came from some strange knowledge of a future event ... a "precognition" he may not have been consciously aware that he experienced.

Even the most skeptical of investigators cannot deny that the similarities between the real life and fictional stories are quite eerie and quite numerous in this particular scenario. To wit: *Titan* was 70,000 tons in *Futility*, and the *Titanic* was (in reality) 66,000 tons. *Titan* was 800 feet long in *Futility*, the *Titanic* some 882 feet long in reality. The top sailing speed of both vessels was listed at 25 knots. And, even more bizarrely, both the fictitious vessel *Titan* and the real-life *Titanic* were described with the identical terminology: *unsinkable*. Both ships, real and fictional, unexpectedly struck icebergs (apparently a common fear of the time), and both sank in the month of April.

No matter how one tries to reason this so-called set of coincidences through, the similarities between *Futility* and the real *Titanic* tragedy point to a kind of extraordinary web of events that goes beyond what most would consider the normal progression of linear time. And, as has been established by experts in the field of parapsychology, "precognitive ESP, numerous observations indicate, involves, under certain circumstances, trespassing the barrier of time to obtain information about future events."[3] Is that what happened with author Robertson? Did he experience a glimpse of the future that compelled him to write his novel? One thing is for certain: It could not have been the other way around.

Assume, for instance, that Robertson's book was so popular a work in 1898 that the real ship *Titanic* was actually named after the *Titan* of the novel. Though that is difficult, if not impossible, to swallow (because no shipbuilder in his right mind would name his vessel after a fictional disaster), let us assume it happened that way for just a moment. How then can one still adequately explain that both ships sank in the month of April, and that the builders of the real *Titanic* did not learn from the mistakes of the fictional *Titan* and provide enough lifeboats for survivors? Unless some maniacal behind-the-scenes conspirator was plotting to sink the *Titanic* in identical fashion to the *Titan*, the explanation that *Futility* inspired the real-life events aboard *Titanic* simply does not hold water (excuse the pun).

Oppositely, from a purely logical standpoint, there is simply no way that Robertson could have "guessed" correctly about so many things in some half-assed, coincidental fashion. He simply could not have guessed correctly on so many fronts: that the *Titanic* would hit an iceberg, lack lifeboats, have the same number of stacks as the *Titan*, share the same name, and ultimately go down on an April night. One or even two of those happenstances *would* have pointed to a coincidence, but all of them together point to something far more mysterious ... and downright creepy.

If John Newland was really on the level about the content of *Futility* (subtitled *The Wreck of the Titan*), if that book really and truly existed and its substance was as he declared it to be on TV, then what *One Step Beyond* and "Night of April 14" were describing seemed a pretty amazing case. Early research indications were not good, however, that the book really existed at all. In fact, various authors have misreported and misdocumented the book's history and publication. In *The Best of Science Fiction Television*, writer Peter Pautz offered some inaccurate data. He said the book was written by an author named Richard Johnson, called *The Titan*, and written in 1901[4]—all facts which did not jibe at all with Newland's on-the-air narration. Another widely-read work on psychic phenomena pointed to an issue of *Colliers* from August of 1898 where *Futility: The Wreck of the Titan* was supposedly serialized. When going back to that issue of *Colliers*, however, this author found that the piece was actually called *The Liner and the Iceberg*, by one Hyn Cutliffe. It told not of the *Titan* or *Titanic* disaster, but of the last voyage of an old, slow vessel called *The Armenia*. Though the iceberg situation was present once more (again, a common nightmare of the time apparently), there were no other similarities to the *Titanic* disaster.

Just when all hope seemed lost that *Futility* existed at all, a hundredth anniversary edition was released in paperback (to cash in on the Cameron *Titanic* fever, no doubt), and all doubts vanished. The book does exist. It is titled *Futility*; it is written by Morgan Robertson, and it does tell the story of the *Titan* in the precise terms that *One Step Beyond* purports. The story of *Futility* and its predictions is true — case closed. De-bunkers are welcome to explain away the numerous similarities between the novel and the *Titanic* tragedy, but the important fact for this text is that *One Step Beyond* accurately reported the detailed case of *Futility*'s unwitting prediction and the *Titanic*'s demise.

One Step Beyond's claim that there were several psychic happenings surrounding the voyage of the *Titanic* has also been borne out by modern research. A professor at the University of Virginia, Ian Stevenson, apparently collected nineteen paranormal reports in regards to the Titanic tragedy. Of the nineteen stories documented, six were of the precognitive variety (like Grace Montgomery's) described in "Night of April 14."[5] One story even told of a *Titanic* crew member who fled the ship before it went to open sea, terrorized by dreams of drowning!

On a purely dramatic front, "Night of April 14" is not so unified or layered a story as the opening hour of the series, "The Bride Possessed." Though it is rewarding that the sweep of the story takes it from the personal to epic, it seems that too little time is devoted to stars Barbara Lord and Patrick Macnee (of *The Avengers* [1961–69], *The Howling* [1981], *A View to a Kill* [1985] and *Waxworks* [1988]). In the short time they share the screen and puzzle out Grace's nightmares, these performers manage to define another sympathetic newlywed couple in trouble, and one wishes to see more of them. Macnee, a performer whom Newland says was "charming then and is charming now," succeeds with the particularly thankless role that is repeated often on this paranormal anthology: the dismissive husband.

Even as Grace warns Macnee's Eric again and again about her bad dreams, he tells her not to "spoil the happiest time of our lives because of a bad dream." Later, when her terrifying dreams become reality, Macnee is appropriately ashen, promising that if his wife ever has another bad dream, he will listen to every word of it. Though Grace is ultimately vindicated, it is hardly a happy ending: Grace and Eric are forced to part. Though Grace survives the ordeal, Eric drowns with 1,500 others. Just another unhappy ending on a ship filled with unhappy endings, but the audience is made to feel this one rather intimately through the good performances.

Above all, "Night of April 14" successfully depicts how quickly a disaster can befall us, and the overwhelming personal fear that we will not be believed when we *just know* that something terrible is going to happen. Because it also deals accurately with the concept of precognition and tantalizes viewers with the strange and true case of *Futility* and *The Titan*,

"Night of April 14" stands proudly as one of *One Step Beyond*'s best and most provocative half hours. And, delightfully, with nearly a full season yet to go, "Night of April 14" was just the tip of the iceberg.

3. "Emergency Only"

(Dramatized by Collier Young; Directed by John Newland;
Airdate: February 3, 1959)

SYNOPSIS: At a ritzy Manhattan cocktail party, a psychic named Ellen Larabee, who is capable of reaching a hypnotic sleep, is goaded into predicting the future of a skeptic, Arthur Douglas. The fate she envisions for him is a frightening one: a terrifying encounter on a train, and a meeting with a mysterious dark-haired woman (armed with a knife!) who may just be Douglas's murderer.

GUEST CAST: Lin McCarthy (Arthur Douglas), Paula Raymond (Woman on Train), Jocelyn Brando (Ellen Larabee), Clark Howat, Nan Adams, Ann Staunton, Ross Elliott, John Maxwell.

COMMENTARY: A slowly dawning sense of horror permeates "Emergency Only," *One Step Beyond's* second story in a row about precognition. An unsettling atmosphere of doubt hangs heavily as cocky skeptic Arthur Douglas is driven to the point of hysteria because elements of a psychic's prophecy keep coming alarmingly true, one after the other. So dismayed by fate's hand is Arthur that he is reduced to repeating "What is this?!" time and again, as if permanently befuddled by the intrusion of the paranormal into his work-a-day, solidly grounded life.

Like many installments of *One Step Beyond*, "Emergency Only" is an episode that builds tension masterfully as it leads up to the climactic, fateful encounter on a train, and director Newland knows just how to achieve the effects he desires and reach the ultimate dramatic destination: terror. In explaining how "horror" works, it is sometimes useful to dissect the component parts and see what roles they play in the overall whole, and here the parts each serve their purpose.

As with all good episodes of *One Step Beyond*, "Emergency Only" commences with perhaps the most significant ingredient of effective horror: the routine, "normal" setting that will be shattered, in this case the fancy party at the apartment of Jim and Betty Hennessey. The apartment interior is seen first in a long, establishing shot brimming with mingling guests and laughing faces, but soon the focus narrows to the cynical Arthur as he plays skeptic to the female psychic. Importantly, Ellen is a character who gains some sympathy points with the audience because she is reluctant to use or trumpet her unusual powers of intuition. As she falls into a hypnotic trance ("you're sinking ... down, down, down ... to worlds faraway..."), Newland's camera appropriately adopts the perspective of a high angle, gazing down at Ellen with a sense of doom as she looks into the "dark" of her prediction. Then the camera comes in for a tight close-up as the visions become eerily more precise and detailed. Maximum suspense is wrung from this scenario when the psychic finally describes Arthur facing the knife of a strange woman, a mysterious *femme fatale.*

From that simple but elegant set-up (a routine setting turned fearful), "Emergency Only" need fly only on autopilot as events follow, step-by-step, the terse outline reported by the psychic at the party. Arthur ends up unexpectedly on a train; he meets a strange woman and is attracted to her; she is wearing the exact piece of jewelry (a ring with a serpent on it) that the psychic has described in her vision; and so on. The scenario is all the more delicious because Arthur is clearly receiving a comeuppance of sorts. He so cavalierly dismissed the psychic's abilities and the forces of the paranormal that there is a degree of satisfaction in watching him become totally overwhelmed by said forces. Nobody likes a know-it-all, and Arthur, while no villain, seemingly deserves to get a bit spooked. His terror is palpable as his "murderer" approaches him from the opposite end of a long train corridor. Tight framing (another ingredient for successful horror productions) accentuates the suspense, and then, in desperation, Arthur pulls the "for emergency only" brake on the train.

Following this climax, there is a double revelation and, finally, a sense of relief. First, the woman Ellen saw in her vision who was bearing the knife was actually a doctor with a scalpel tending to Arthur's injuries after he caused the train to stop short, *not* some frightening female murderer. Second, Arthur's decision to pull the brake at that precise moment was serendipitous and life-saving because it averted collision with a freight train on the same trajectory. Thus Ellen Larabee's prophecy was accurate in one sense (a woman did approach Arthur with a knife, and his life was threatened), and this paranormal foreknowledge ended up saving a skeptic's life. As Newland muses about the story at the end of the episode, the audience is left to wonder, is this precognition, clairvoyance or merely happy coincidence? And, as usual, Newland has no answer for us ... only a smile.

A simple tale of horror, the streamlined "Emergency Only" falters only when a voice-over from the psychic Ellen repeats the details of the prophecy, again and again. Such repetition of important plot points is unnecessary in a thirty minute production, and today it would probably not even be necessary at all. However, it is important to recall that in early 1959 audiences did not have four decades of experience with "psychic"-style TV stories (*The Sixth Sense* [1972], *The Next Step Beyond* [1978], *Beyond Reality* [1992–1993], *The X-Files* [1993–] and so on), and thus it was imperative that viewers be made to understand what precisely was happening each step of the way in "Emergency Only" as the prophecy progressed inexorably towards reality.

As for the validity of the concept of precognition, it had already been established rather potently by *One Step Beyond* with its report of the *Futility* incident in the previous "Night of April 14," and it is a bit surprising to see the same psychic concept reinforced so immediately after that episode. However, the distinguishing factor in "Emergency Only" may simply be the *hypnotic trance*, the state through which the psychic Ellen attains her insight into Arthur's future events. Forty years after *One Step Beyond* folded, hypnosis is generally viewed as a useful psychological tool that encourages a state of relaxation, rather than as a mysterious vehicle for psychic powers. However, one should remember that this is indeed a recent application and interpretation of hypnosis. The *trance* aspect, important to this story, is simply the state in which a person becomes easily suggestible to the influence of the hypnotist. The trance is not in any way mystical or magical either, as "Emergency Only" seems to suggest in its staging. If this particular aspect of "Emergency Only" seems exaggerated or incorrect, one can take solace in the fact that the setting and scenario of the finale (a train crash) figures prominently in psychic lore. For instance, in the 1950s W.E. Cox conducted a study that established that fewer people travel on trains that are destined to have an accident than on trains that do not.[6]

Another episode of *One Step Beyond*, "The Ordeal on Locust Street," would deal more directly with the breadth of hypnosis in the second season, and an early episode of *Rod Serling's Night Gallery* ("The Dead Man") followed up on some of the same "hypnotic" concepts in 1970.

4. "The Dark Room"

(Dramatized by Francis Cockrell; Directed by John Newland;
Airdate: February 10, 1959)

SYNOPSIS: A single American photographer named Rita Wallace moves into an old house in Paris and sets about documenting "The Face of France" for her fashion magazine. A mysterious male "model" shows up at her place to be photographed one day, starts to rave about an illicit affair, and then attacks Rita. She later learns that her mysterious and violent photo subject is a ghost who died in her home in 1926 after killing his adulterous wife.

GUEST CAST: Cloris Leachman (Rita Wallace), Marcel Dario (Jean Gabon), Paul Dubov (Inspector Marsac), Ann Cadee, Ivan Triesault.

COMMENTARY: "The Dark Room" is *One Step Beyond*'s first out-and-out ghost story, the frightening tale of a woman who encounters an angry ghost named Jean Gabon, but does not realize (at least at first) that her visitor is an *apparition*. The ending confirms this fact when a police inspector escorts photographer Rita Wallace to the grave of the man who once owned the house, and an old photograph on the tombstone identifies the man as the spirit who attacked her.

As is typical for *One Step Beyond*, the series finds itself adhering rigorously to the standards of the literature and research done in the field of ghosts. Specifically, "The Dark Room" fulfills several of the characteristics often applied to encounters with apparitions. Celia Green and Charles McCreery, two British Psychical researchers, noted a catalogue of eight commonly-held "sighting" characteristics in the mid–70s that work rather well for "The Dark Room," even though it was produced in 1959. "The Dark Room" successfully meets five of the Green-McCreery criteria for a typical apparition encounter. These are: that the background in any such appearance remains the same; that the percipient's actions while viewing the apparition may not tally with memory; that the percipient may not realize it is viewing an apparition at all; that the apparition seems— to all tangible senses— real (that is, it can walk, talk, stand and sit); and finally, that the apparition is viewed as a complete *solid* figure.[7]

Accordingly then, photographer Rita Wallace's encounter with the supernatural finds her running into a spirit who appears quite solid — as a short, stocky, average-looking man in her apartment. He is real and talkative; he stands, sits, moves around, and is at least moderately responsive to her directions. In other words, the spirit of Gabon could easily be mistaken for a real person, and, indeed, this is what occurs. Beyond getting these important details of real-life apparition encounters correct, "The Dark Room" establishes that ghosts do not show up in photographs, a long-held belief in horror movies that may not be exactly true. Often photographs of apparitions do reveal something odd, if not the same figure that people believe they saw in the so-called flesh. A speck of light, a glimmer of fog, a blurry dot ... ghosts have been allegedly photographed in all these mysterious forms. Still, it is important dramatically for Rita (Cloris Leachman) to find evidence that Jean Gabon was not really in her apartment, and the developed photographs, which reveal only chairs and corners where he *should be*, accomplish that end rather neatly.

As always, what *One Step Beyond* reveals to its audience about the social context of its time proves to be almost as interesting as the paranormal encounters it depicts. Here, an unmarried woman is a professional, living on her own, and in all senses the protagonist of the tale. Because this woman is alone, however, she is immediately disbelieved at first. It is easy to dismiss a single woman as being crazy, is it not? In fact, this was the somewhat sexist attitude of *One Step Beyond* on many, many occasions. Women were often the recipient of psychic knowledge (much more frequently than were men), and they had to fight societal perceptions of them as "silly" or inconsequential to be believed. Again, the idea was to engender audience sympathy, and making the percipient an underdog (a single woman) made it easier for other characters to dismiss her and for the audience to subsequently root for her (since they had "shared"/witnessed her experience with her).

Today, audiences watching "The Dark Room" will probably be well ahead of the narrative, by at least a step or two. Jean Gabon, the ghost, initially appears in Rita Wallace's apartment with no warning whatsoever. Since no door opened, there was no knocking, and Rita let nobody into her home, this is a suspicious entrance, to say the least. The trick employed by Newland was to make the entrance seem so regular, so commonplace, that it would not be suspicious at all (by having Gabon just sort of "be present"), but today it seems to have the opposite effect, immediately sending up a red flag. This guy just shows up from nowhere, deep inside the apartment, and his presence immediately arouses suspicions. However, it should be noted, again, that *One Step Beyond* got it right when adhering to details of the literature on the subject. Apparently, an apparition would *not* show up in a thunderclap and lightning storm, or a surge of special effects magic, but appear instead as a real, solid person. That "truth" plays as rather undramatic and restrained in "The Dark Room," but for *One Step Beyond* the goal was always accuracy and believability, not fireworks.

5. "Twelve Hours to Live"

(Dramatized by Merwin Gerard; Directed by John Newland;
Airdate: February 17, 1959)

SYNOPSIS: An angry, jealous husband scorns his wife's mind-reading abilities, but on one rainy night his car goes over a collapsing hill during a mud slide. Miles away, the man's wife, Carol, hears his screams for help, knows he is in danger, and sets out to save his life, even though authorities are skeptical.

GUEST CAST: Paul Richards (Will Janson), Jean Allison (Carol Janson), Douglas Kennedy (Police Sgt.), Larrain Gillespie (Debbie), Lillian Powell (Mrs. Ford).

COMMENTARY: "Twelve Hours to Live" commences with series host John Newland standing under an umbrella during a downpour as he poses the question that will inform the episode: "How many ways are there for humans to communicate?" Our Guide to the World of the Unknown then offers several possibilities, including a kiss, a glance and a stare ... before finally wandering purposefully into the realm of the paranormal, specifically *telepathy* or *E.S.P.*, "the acquisition of information without the use of any human sense organs."[8]

Along with its dramatization of telepathy, "Twelve Hours to Live" is a prime example of what this author terms "The Cassandra Complex," a recurring character arc in the world of *One Step Beyond*. In Homeric legend, Cassandra was the daughter of Troy's King Priam; but, more importantly, she was a seer (cursed by the God Apollo) who knew the course of the future yet was cursed never to be believed or heeded. Many, many characters (usually women) fulfill that same role in *One Step Beyond*. They are inevitably aware of approaching tragedy (such as the sinking of the *Titanic* in "Night of April 14" or a plane crash in "Tonight at 12:17"), important facts (that a distant husband has been injured), psychic communications (sometimes from the future, as in "Call from Tomorrow") and such, but are perpetually dismissed as drunk, silly, foolish, pregnant, neurotic, whathaveyou. Here, patronizing police officers ignore, question and even mock Carol Janson's belief that her husband is in danger and that she is hearing his desperate thoughts, despite the fact that she is armed with specific psychic information (such as the very markings on a restaurant sign near the site of her husband's accident). Earlier in the show, Allison's husband also refuses to belief that this Cassandra could have psychic powers (even though she has accurately predicted that a prospective client will call soon for her lawyer husband's services).

The Cassandra Complex accomplishes several important purposes on *One Step Beyond*. First, it stacks the odds against the protagonist with psychic powers, rallying viewers to the underdog's side even though they may not really believe in psychic phenomena themselves. By aligning viewer identification with the persecuted, unheeded person, the producers, writers and Newland are assuring that the final victory is one not just for the Cassandra (and audience) but for their ongoing argument about the validation of psychic powers. It all comes in one package — you feel for Carol and you align yourself with her sensibilities.

Secondly, the Cassandra Complex mirrors a sense of reality. Disbelief, skepticism and even ridicule are common characteristics of people, even family members, confronted with another human's claim of psychic insight. It is easier to dismiss (especially those whose faults are known to us in intimate detail) than believe in something that is not easily quantified or legitimized by science.

Thirdly, the Cassandra Complex fosters a feeling of fate, of inevitability, in the audience. Even though there is "psychic" knowledge of a future event, characters are frequently too skeptical to accept it and so go rushing towards their (usually) unpleasant fate. *One Step Beyond* thrives on the feeling of inevitability. That is often the primary conflict of an episode: A Cassandra must strain against the forces of time and fate itself if a happy outcome is to be accomplished. Audiences pick up on this feeling of inevitability and further tension is wrought. It's a clever set-up.

It is also worth mentioning that "psychic" phenomena help to repair yet another damaged marital relationship in "Twelve Hours to Live." Before the events which lead Carol to save her husband's life in a driving accident, their marriage is near the end of another dangerous road. He was jealous of her, she was trying to pay the bills, and together they were mired in domestic agony. Mostly, these two people are unable to communicate with each other about their feelings, fears and desires. After Carol saves Will's life with the ultimate form of communication, telepathy, there is time, opportunity and hope for a new start. Marriage saved, optimism restored.

Again, *One Step Beyond* finds special interest in the spousal relationship and comes to the same conclusion: When life's petty concerns nearly overwhelm a couple, a psychic experience can reconnect or refocus that couple on the things that really matter, like life and death!

Visually, "Twelve Hours to Live" continues the fluid storytelling that Newland has already established in the previous four stories. Echoing the best filmic tradition, this was an era when the camera's position and movement informed viewers about the drama at hand and conveyed mood as well as information. Dramatic television, such as *One Step Beyond* and *The Twilight Zone*, understood film grammar and was not merely a mish-mash of master shot/two shot/close-up, the visually illiterate format that dominates the airwaves today. Most memorable in "Twelve Hours to Live" is editor Berman's exquisite use of cross-cutting. The episode jumps from Will in his speeding car, in imminent danger, to his home where Carol is relaxing and easing down for bed. The cross-cutting, which suggests that the car ride and Carol's preparations for sleep are occurring simultaneously, forges a visual link between Carol and Will that is thematically reinforced when she becomes aware of his accident through the "linking" device of telepathy.

The marital relationship in distress, the Cassandra Complex, and a psychic phenomenon depicted as a therapeutic force for marital repair are all elements that would recur in the next *One Step Beyond* episode, "Epilogue."

6. "Epilogue"
(Dramatized by Don M. Mankiewicz;
Directed by John Newland;
Airdate: February 24, 1959)

SYNOPSIS: In Nevada, a recovering alcoholic named Carl Archer tries to patch things up with his wife, Helen, and his little boy, Stevie. When Stevie and Helen are suddenly trapped in a dangerous cave-in at a nearby silver mine, an apparition of Helen — who was actually killed in the mine — warns the alcoholic of the terrible danger his wounded son now faces. Later, a doctor tries to convince Archer that the apparition was a result of alcohol-induced hallucinations, but Carl is ultimately corroborated by a pair of eyewitnesses.

GUEST CAST: Julie Adams (Helen Archer), Charles Aidman (Carl Archer), William Schallert (Doctor), Charles Herbert (Stevie), Roy Glenn, Don Kennedy.

COMMENTARY: Another middle-class, American marriage is on the verge of imminent collapse in Don M. Mankiewicz's "Epilogue," a story that relies not on a "silly" female as the unheeded psychic Cassandra of the week, but a character almost as easy to dismiss: a recovering alcoholic! Carl Archer has been in a sanitorium for chronic alcoholism for some time at the commencement of this installment, and so he, like most Cassandras on *Alcoa Presents*, is in one sense or another a discredited man when he finally takes his "one step beyond" into the larger world of psychic phenomena. It is all the easier to dismiss Carl's "wild" claims of psychic intervention (in this case an *apparition*) because he is considered by society to be damaged goods, having had problems in the past with drinking; problems that have even caused him to hallucinate. And indeed, that judgment is the very answer of science here (voiced eloquently, if in infuriating and patronizing terms, by guest performer William Schallert).

Schallert plays Carl's psychiatrist, and he raises all the familiar "Scully-isms" of science and rationality that viewers have come to expect in this kind of drama. By Schallert's way of thinking, Carl has not really witnessed the specter of his dead wife at all. Instead, he is merely suffering from fatigue and emotional stress. To the doctor, Carl saw only what he wished to see, and the doctor even states that "out of thousands of wild hunches people get for one reason or another, some are bound to be accurate." This author calls such ludicrous thinking "The Law of Averages Excuse." It is a ridiculous assertion that Carl could *just happen* to dream or hallucinate a vision of his wife which, at the right moment in time, points him specifically to the exact geographical location in the world where his son is buried alive and in mortal danger. "The Law of Averages Excuse" is just that, an excuse for someone too literal-minded to accept that there are some things, perhaps, that remain inexplicable in this world. It is easier to write such things off as coincidence than accept parapsychology, it seems, and William Schallert makes for an exceptionally irritating *One Step Beyond* archetype: the disbeliever.

Much of "Epilogue" is a heated tête-à-tête between the skeptical doctor and the recovering alcoholic, the man who imagines that his wife's spirit somehow led him to save his son's life out there at the silver mine. The smarmy psychiatrist almost has Carl swayed to his way of thinking when two rescuers who were at the silver mine show up at Carl's hotel room and confide that they heard Helen's screams too. Now Carl the Cassandra is corroborated by objective sources, and John Newland declares that perhaps "love knows no boundaries, not even death!" Again, a psychic happenstance (an apparition) has led to a positive result. A boy's life is saved, and a man can hold his head high knowing that even with his own foibles (namely alcoholism), his bond to his family is so strong that it can transcend death. While this may sound hokey, *One Step Beyond* is again quite restrained in its dramatization of these themes.

In addition to telling its primary story, *One Step Beyond* also finds some social value in this story of alcoholism and redemption. Specifically, Carl shares with his doctor what remains today one of the most memorable and accurate motivations for drinking ever reported on TV: fear. It was fear of losing his wife, fear of not being good enough, that first led Carl to alcohol. And then, when he did drink, Carl really was not good enough anymore, and he became even more scared, which led him to drink more, and so on. This description of low self-esteem, of a self-fulfilling cycle of failure, is a remarkably progressive and insightful interpretation of alcoholism for 1959, and actor Charles Aidman handles his monologue on the subject beautifully.

In the world of the paranormal, "Epilogue" is not far off thematically from episode #4, "The Dark Room." Though Helen is not a malevolent ghost, like the murderous French home owner Jean Gabon who menaced

Cloris Leachman, she is nonetheless a spirit attempting to communicate something of vital importance (though not rage, fortunately). Remembering the Green-McCreery criteria for apparitions, Helen's appearance fits several of the categories. She is collectively perceived (the two rescuers hear her cries for help, *and* Carl sees her); the background around Helen remains the same; the percipient (Carl) does not realize she is an apparition (until he finds her dead hand under tons of rubble); she is quite close to the percipient (appearing in Carl's hotel room); she is seen as a complete figure; and she walks and talks, screaming that her little boy is trapped in the mine. So, as before, *One Step Beyond*'s interpretation of reported psychic phenomena is an accurate, if not innovative, one.

More than being just an apparition, however, Helen is a very special kind of ghost: a *crisis apparition*. The crisis apparition has been defined by researchers in the field as:

> a manifestation of someone at or near the time of death or other crisis … in both … research and in historical accounts, apparitions materialized to people who had absolutely no desire to imagine their loved one dead. In the most compelling, indisputable instances, the subjects do not yet know that the person they are seeing is indeed dead.[9]

"Epilogue" is a perfect example of this particular phenomenon. Helen (an apparition) bursts into Carl's hotel room screaming for help and Carl is totally unaware that she is a ghost, a crisis apparition, until he finds her body buried in the rubble of the silver mine some time later. The Society of Psychical Research has reported that most crisis apparitions are seen within 12 hours before or after the crisis at hand because they have so clear a purpose. "Epilogue" jells with that explanation as well: Helen clearly came back from the dead at this particular time so as to assure the survival of her son, Stevie, also buried in the mine.

For fans of horror and science fiction, "Epilogue" offers not one but two favorite performers. William Schallert has appeared in everything from *Star Trek* ("The Trouble with Tribbles," as Nilz Baris) to *Gremlins* (1984), and Julie Adams was the lovely screen siren abducted by the Gill Man after a memorable swimsuit scene in *Creature from the Black Lagoon* (1954). Both of these actors offer solid support to Charles Aidman in "Epilogue," but with his tortured face, scruffy countenance, and sad eyes, the episode remains his showcase.

7. "The Dream"

(Dramatized by John Dunkel; Directed by John Newland;
Airdate: March 3, 1959)

SYNOPSIS: In the dark time after Dunkirk in 1940, Britain stood alone against the overwhelming Nazi threat, and senior citizens and military rejects stood guard at remote outposts, expecting invasion at any moment. On one dangerous night, a gentleman named Herbert Blakeley has a dream in which he sees his beloved wife Ethel, far away in London, die during a Luftwaffe bombing. At the same time, Ethel dreams of Herbert's death at the hands of a Nazi advance party. This "double dream" spurs both parties to action, and ultimately saves two lives.

GUEST CAST: Reginald Owen (Herbert Blakeley), Molly Roden (Ethel Blakeley), Richard Lupino, Kendrick Huxham, Jack Lynn, Charles Horvath, Philip Tonge, Eric Snowden, Nelson Welsh, Peter Gordon, Jean Runsome.

COMMENTARY: Another married couple is saved from disaster by a psychic warning, a "double dream," in *One Step Beyond*'s first period piece. Of course, in 1959 the era of World War II may not have felt like a "period piece," since it was only fifteen years earlier! Perhaps because it was so recent an event in the memory of American TV viewers at the time it aired, *One Step Beyond* visited the era of the Second World War in a variety of stories, including "The Haunted U-Boat," "Brainwave," "The Promise" and "Signal Received." Of all those war-related stories, "The Dream" is probably the least interesting. The early portions of this John Dunkel story are largely ineffectual and meandering, a rare occurrence in the usually compact *One Step Beyond*, because so many characters and subplots are introduced, and for the most part they are unconnected with the climactic psychic payoff (the dream that saves two lives). The too-numerous characters are also interchangeable and fairly talky, and not nearly enough time is spent establishing the character of Ethel, who is one-half of the reciprocal "psychic" vibe that represents the finale of "The Dream."

The problem may be that this story wants to be too many things: a story of redemption (a soldier finds his courage after facing fears of being cowardly), a study about the home front (in which older men, priests and other unlikely "soldiers" are put in the position of fighting for their country), a gentle love story (with long passages in which Herbert talks about his sedate, happy life with the offscreen Ethel) and a tale of psychic phenomena. Unfortunately, "The Dream" manages no subplot very well, perhaps because of time limitations.

If large portions of "The Dream" seem dull, at least one sequence still stands out as excellent, even though it has little to do with paranormal phenomena. At one point, a Nazi infantry group sneaks onto the mainland and attacks Herbert and his cowardly friend in their small outpost. Though obviously restricted to the studio setting and the difficulty of an "interior" forest landscape, Newland stages the German attack with real flair. Nazi soldiers jump down from trees, scale rocks, pop up suddenly, duck and even open fire in a vicious assault that is well choreographed, while old Herbert defends himself ably with a pitchfork. *One Step Beyond* rarely featured such out-and-out action set-pieces, and it appears that Newland relished the opportunity to do something a bit different from the norm. In fact, *One Step Beyond* made it a habit to treat its material with respect, pacing its episodes slowly and methodically, and this rousing action sequence is all the more exciting because of its contrast to things as usual.

Even in its conclusion, "The Dream" feels like a story already visited by the young series. In his closing narration, Newland declares that people in love have sometimes been known to slip beyond the bounds of time and space. That worthwhile point is touching, but it is also highly reminiscent of his stance about love transcending even death in the superior previous installment, "Epilogue." And, unfortunately, "dreams" are extremely hard to pin down, since there are no eyewitnesses to "dream" beyond the percipient. Even if a dream is reported to a fellow person, it is still a report of a subjective, unverified event.

8. "Premonition"

(Dramatized by Paul David;
Directed by John Newland;
Airdate: March 10, 1959)

SYNOPSIS: In 1901 an 11-year-old aspiring ballerina is paralyzed by a frightening vision that a chandelier in her home will suddenly fall from its perch above and kill her. As a result of her terrible experience, young Lisa stays away from the chandelier room for ten long years, until the very day of her engagement. Amazingly, no calamity results on the special day, and the terror of Lisa's vision is forgotten until a dark moment in 1947 when Lisa's granddaughter's coming out party occurs below the chandelier...

GUEST CAST: Pamela Lincoln (Debbie), Paul Langton, Beverly Washburn, David Garcia, Julie Payne, Claire Corelli, Percy Helton, Skip Young, David Whorf, Maria Riachi, Jeanne Manet, Thomas B. Henry.

COMMENTARY: In "The Premonition," surely one of the best of *One Step Beyond's* first season episodes, a young girl dances rapidly in a circle below a chandelier and experiences a frightening *premonition* about a future calamity. Though the episode primarily concerns that heart-stopping vision of the future received in the present, it is unique because of the manner in which writer Paúl David has the ballerina receive her message of terror. Dancing or spinning quickly in a circle and suddenly receiving knowledge of the future is certainly a variation on *gyromancy,* an ancient form of divination (or auguring) in which people glean knowledge of the future, and sometimes even of the afterlife, by the position in which they fall following just such a rapid spin.

Director Newland understands that it is the spin, the dance frenzy, which precipitates the psychic phenomenon of "The Premonition," and so he makes some interesting choices in his staging of the event. The ballerina is seen in close-up as she dances and rotates, but to give the impression of incredible speed, the production team has also placed the young actress (an aspiring ballerina in real life, Newland remembers) atop a rotating platform. The spinning girl and the spinning platform in conjunction create a kind of double barrel spin, and the world consequently seems to spiral out of control. This method of dramatizing the gyromancy is effective because the audience is allowed to share visually in the dancer's experience: a kind of dizzying giddiness as her mind crosses from the realm of the real to the unreal.

Even more dramatic than the staging of the initial premonitory experience is Newland's decision to feature the offending chandelier as an important character in the drama. It is omnipresent, always threatening to come falling down, and thereby quite effective at generating suspense. To accomplish this feeling of anticipation and dread, Newland frequently shoots from a high angle (the chandelier's point of view almost!) looking down at the girl dancing. And, in another startlingly composed shot, the camera is actually looking down through the spires and lights of the hanging chandelier. Below, the ballerina is dancing round and round, but because of the composition she seems to be surrounded by the lighting fixture's decorative arms and flourishes. In other words, the chandelier visually dominates the girl in these shots, just as it does so psychologically. She fears it, and this shot shows us why — it literally surrounds her.

Of course, this selection by Newland is an appropriate shot because the chandelier plays so dramatic a role in the ballerina's life, just as another human character might, and its prominence makes us ask the questions the episode revolve around: Should we organize our lives around our fears? Should we heed that little voice that tells us to be careful, or do we need to live our lives our own way and say to hell with fate? "Premonition" comes down on the side of caution; and, as always, *One Step Beyond* suggests that one should always trust the instinct, the glimpse of the paranormal, because it is inevitably proven correct.

When asked about the staging of the dance and the dominant position of the chandelier in so many frames of "Premonition," Newland reported that he was aiming for a very theatrical, very big feeling that would foster suspense, and that the many high angles in evidence were his solution to that problem. In another artistically composed shot in "Premonition," Newland's camera stands back at a distance and, out of the blue, tilts up and back (starting from eye level) during a second dance sequence (this one at a party.) As the camera tilts up unexpectedly, the chandelier suddenly looms large in the foreground, reminding audiences of the danger in the scene. Then the camera, satisfied, tilts back down to those in jeopardy: the young people at the dance, blissfully unaware that there is disaster hanging right over their heads and that the sky is literally falling. By focusing so much on the chandelier, Newland is cleverly expressing the idea that it is a character in the drama with a heavy impact (in more ways than one!) on the other players.

Dramatically, "Premonition" relies once more on a "foolish" woman who plays the classic role of Cassandra. In this case, the ballerina is not heeded by either her fiancé or father, even though she *just knows* that somehow, some way, she is right to be fearful of the light hanging above. And, as in "Emergency Only," the dream of the future is misinterpreted. It is not the percipient who suffers and dies from the disaster, but rather the child of a future generation. By pulling this kind of trick, *One Step Beyond* was able to posit the idea that psychic phenomena may be reliable, but not always interpreted correctly by those who experience them. Frankly, it was also a way of throwing a surprise ending at an audience that may have been growing increasingly wise to the series' *modus operandi*. The psychic climax was becoming expected, but by throwing in a few surprising curves and turns, viewers at home still could not predict the outcome of the episode.

Because it examines the premonition in interesting terms, through gyromancy specifically, and because of John Newland's exquisite direction, "Premonition" is one of *One Step Beyond*'s greatest early victories. That damned chandelier takes on a presence of evil and menace throughout the half hour, giving the episode a kind of cohesion that segments such as "The Dream" lack. There are also some good special effects when, in Debbie's vision, the chandelier starts to pull and tug at the ceiling, ripping it apart. This sequence suggests that the chandelier is a malevolent entity trying desperately to break free from its restraints and go after its prey.

9. "The Dead Part of the House"
(Dramatized by Michael Plant; Directed by John Newland; Airdate: March 17, 1959)

SYNOPSIS: A widower with a young daughter moves into a home built in the 1880s with his divorced sister and the Asian manservant of the previous owners. The young girl, Anne, begins to hear voices upstairs in what has been called "the dead part of the house." The father feels distant from his daughter, a feeling made worse by Anne's insistence that her three dolls (Jennifer, Rose and Mary) are talking to her and teaching her things...

GUEST CAST: Philip Abbott (Paul Burton), Joanne Linville (Mina), Mimi Gibson (Anne), Phillip Ahn, Ken Drake.

COMMENTARY: Can the dead continue to inhabit, or haunt, the very places where they dwelled in life? That is the central question raised by "The Dead Part of the House," a tale in which three neglected girls who died from a gas leak in their bedroom during the 1920s somehow manage to "cross over" into our reality and time to communicate with the living. They do so, initially, by inhabiting three toy dolls (Jennifer, Rose and Mary), a scary notion popularized in horror productions immemorial, from *The Twilight Zone* ("Living Doll") to *Child's Play* (1988) and its three sequels. In *One Step Beyond*, the doll angle is decidedly subdued, and the audience never sees the toys talking or moving (such a thing couldn't be proven, could it?), but it is nonetheless vaguely aware that something is not quite right up there in that room...

One Step Beyond takes the premise that communication between the living and dead is indeed possible. In this case, as usual, the series is on solid ground with most established parapsychological research and speculation. In 1939 one Harry Price established the following about haunting episodes, such as those dramatized in this half hour:

> ...haunted rooms or houses become saturated with the personalties of those ... who once lived in them, to the point where psychic discharges occur in the form of paranormal manifestations.[10]

Again, it is important to note that this author is not validating the above-quoted research, or even the beliefs of parapsychologists as a whole, only indicating that *One Step Beyond* is a TV series that took special pains to be as authentic to research and reported "human records" as was possible for its time. No TV series could possibly authenticate the existence of ghosts or spirits, but *One Step Beyond* is commendable in that it always aimed to capture the details of such psychic-oriented phenomena in a correct, authentic and respectful fashion. One can contrast that considered, thoughtful approach with series such as *Poltergeist the Legacy* (1995–1999), wherein ghosts and apparitions shoot laser bolts out of their hands, shapeshift at will, manipulate objects and do virtually anything that the story of the week requires and expensive special effects can depict. *One Step Beyond* is notable for taking a high road and living up to its promise of accurately depicting the world of the paranormal. Debunkers and skeptics may feel that what *One Step Beyond* pledges a sense of loyalty to is bunk, but those inclined to look at parapsychology and its research objectively will see that it was trying to be evenhanded and fair. As in its pilot, "The Bride Possessed," this installment of *One Step Beyond* dramatizes a didactic story in which the example provided by the world of the psychic can easily be applied to "real life." In "The Bride Possessed," the spirit of a dead woman modeled a bad marriage for two innocent newlyweds, thereby providing an example for them to avoid. "The Dead Part of the House" uses the same outline, telling a story of neglect and pain in which three poor children die terrible deaths. That tragic story from the past is contrasted with the current situation, in which father Paul Burton feels isolated and alienated from his young daughter, Anne. Her mother (his wife) died recently, and the father can no longer relate to his child because of the sad memories their relationship naturally raises. The father is initially dismissive of the possibility of ghosts but is eventually receptive to the idea and then uses the ghost experience as a lesson: He will not abandon his child as those poor three girls were once abandoned. Today, this concept of dual, parallel storylines may sound a bit hokey or facile, but *One Step Beyond* rarely crosses the line into camp or cheesiness, and it maintains its dignity, even when so tidily resolving complex family issues.

As is natural for the times, an element of sexism creeps into *One Step Beyond* sometimes, and "The Dead Part of the House" is a good example of that fact. At one point it is stated that all girls should own dolls because "it's good for developing a maternal instinct." Boys, it goes without saying, should play with guns, apparently. And, throughout the episode, comments are also made about the fact that Joanne Linville's character is a divorcée and therefore unhappy and less desirable than are other women. Despite this sexism, "The Dead Part of the House" is buttressed by some creepiness, particularly in its orchestration of a haunting music box song.

In another oft-used cliché of *One Step Beyond*, it is the Asian manservant (along with an easily dismissed woman, a divorcée!) in "The Dead Part of the House" who perceives the supernatural or paranormal at work. Often in *One Step Beyond*, people of ethnic or foreign origin tend to believe in and accept the paranormal while the Western white man finds it harder to deal with (see "The Riddle" and "Forests of the Night" for additional details on this series pillar).

Star Trek fans will recognize Joanne Linville of "The Dead Part of the House" as the Romulan commander who seduced Mr. Spock in the third season episode "The Enterprise Incident." She provided an even more compelling performance in the *One Step Beyond* third season episode "Moment of Hate."

10. "The Vision"

(Dramatized by Larry Marcus;
Directed by John Newland;
Airdate: March 24, 1959)

SYNOPSIS: At 22:30 hours on November 14, 1915, four French soldiers witness something strange: a glowing light in the sky that compels them to abandon their posts and cease fighting. The men are arrested and tried by their superiors for cowardice in the face of the enemy, but each soldier remembers a feeling of peace and serenity at the moment they witnessed the heavenly light above the battlefield. Their strange testimony is corroborated when reports come in, from all sides in the war, verifying their unusual account of the heavenly rays.

GUEST CAST: Bruce Gordon (Tremaine), Pernell Roberts (Sergeant), H.M. Wynant (Private), Peter Miles, Jerry Oddo, Richard Devon, Jean Del Val, Rene Korper, Will J. White.

COMMENTARY: A strange, inexplicable light in the sky is the object of curiosity that precipitates the drama in "The Vision," a truly bizarre but nonetheless interesting episode of *One Step Beyond*. Not merely a meteorological light source, this object in the sky seems to cause men to embrace pacifism, a particularly troubling predilection for soldiers in the field who are required to fight the German enemy! What is this light in the sky? A flare? A UFO? A supreme being angry at mankind's unceasing warring? A bizarre cloud formation? *One Step Beyond* wisely chooses not to commit itself to any one of these specific answers, opting instead to dramatize a more personal story: the effect of the "peace light" on four French soldiers who respond to the phenomenon by laying down their arms and ceasing to fight altogether. Their decision comes back to haunt them when they are tried by their superiors for dereliction of duty, thereby providing viewers a full recitation of the bizarre encounter with the unknown.

The unusual light in the sky in "The Vision" is depicted as a glowing orb not unlike the sun, with rays of light emanating outward from its central point. One soldier claims he was blinded by the light initially and then was suddenly back home with his family, seeing the fields and hills of his homeland. Another man comments that after viewing the light, his rifle suddenly felt wrong — obscene even — in his hands. Yet another man looks into the light and sees the face of the first man he ever killed, up there in the sky. The face was forgiving him, but he felt bad because he was still killing, still carrying a gun. The fourth man recalls a feeling of being free, of being a "part of everything."

These incredible reports of instant and total pacifism in "The Vision" are examined by director John Newland in tight close-up, so the viewer identifies with the affected men who shared the experience. The episode relies primarily on the acting talent of the four central performers, because their persuasive feelings of euphoria as they recount the paranormal encounter are supposed to be the factor that sways the skeptic to their side.

John Newland's opening narration for "The Vision" is unusually precise, listing a day (November 14, 1915) and a time (22:30 hours) for the events portrayed in the story. He claims that something strange was seen all over Europe that involved thousands of soldiers, from the English Channel to Italy and Russia. By his reporting, Newland establishes that 1,000 men saw something in the sky and suddenly could no longer fight. This is a remarkably specific claim, but one that this author has not been able to corroborate through personal research. Although wartime psychic phenomena are apparently quite common, this particular event was not among the accounts this author studied, and this apparently revelatory incident does not show up in much parapsychological literature or in any histories of World War I. Though it must be based on an account that writer Larry Marcus unearthed in his research, that account has not been located, and this author was unable to secure an interview with Mr. Marcus for further information.

One possible explanation for the strange events depicted in "The Vision" comes not from the world of parapsychology, but from psychology. In his book *Emotional Intelligence*, author Daniel Goleman writes of a strange event that occurred during the Vietnam War. An American platoon was battling the Vietcong, exchanging heavy fire, when six monks walked through the battlefield:

"They didn't look right, they didn't look left. They walked straight through," recalls David Busch, one of the American soldiers. "It was really strange because nobody shot at 'em. And after they walked over the berm, suddenly all the fight was out of me. I just didn't feel like I wanted to do this anymore, at least not that day. It must have been that way for everybody, because everybody quit. We just stopped fighting."[11]

Although no bizarre light from above spurred this particular cease-fire, the reaction was very much the same as the one described in "The Vision": Soldiers (from both sides) ceased fighting because of an external stimulus, the very will for combat seemingly removed from their spirits. As author Goleman points out, even one man's desire to end the fight could have been communicated across the battlefield to others, including the Vietcong soldiers, because human beings send out emotional signals in every encounter, and those signals affect others. It stands to reason that those signals would be stronger in more stressful situations, such as combat, and so it is not beyond the pale to see how an "emotional" chain reaction could have begun in World War I (or, later, in the Vietnam War) that led to general dropping of arms across a wide area.

In addition, it is not difficult to believe that the light over the battlefield was an element of a mass hallucination, something *one* man thought he saw at the time but that other men later remembered seeing for themselves, picking up on the same imagery that seemed so vivid in the first man's description. Reginald Omez wrote of such possibilities:

> ...impressions made upon us by even the most accurate perception do not remain inert and immobile in the memory; they are frequently recalled, and every time this happens the subconscious modifies them a little, telescoping one series of incidents, linking others with associated imagery, tidying everything up in a way which, without our realizing it, may seriously distort the original picture.[12]

So, it would not be a leap of faith to consider the possibility that one man saw a light in the sky, perhaps an unusual cloud mass or ball lightning, that reminded him, for whatever reason, of his home and made him stop fighting. He sent that "emotional" signal in some way to his compatriots, and later, when trying to explain their combined actions, those men adopted the imagery and "light from above" story of the first soldier. Of course, that is just one possible explanation (and a Scully-like one at that!), and others are equally valid. The "real" answer as to the reason why some soldiers apparently lost the will to fight during battle is not really known and can only be guessed at. Some may prefer to believe that God sent the men a message to stop their warring, or that some powerful alien race intervened for a moment, but those answers smack of the superstition-reflex in the human animal. A light shines unexpectedly in the sky and man's instinctive reaction is to explain away this uncomfortable happenstance as divine intervention of external interest in man's affairs.

Whatever the cause (if the event truly happened at all), whatever the origin of the light in the sky in "The Vision," it makes for one hell of a provocative and controversial story. A mystery like this is a fascinating one to us because there are no answers to be found, only the belief that something unusual really happened. Akin to *Picnic at Hanging Rock* (1975), the great Peter Weir film wherein a group of school girls mysteriously vanish on a mountainous outcropping in the Australian outback (never to be heard from again), the idea that viewers are left to struggle with at the end of "The Vision" is that there remain some things in this world man is not capable of finding answers for. A world of riddles; that is what is suggested most notably.

If "The Vision" has any plot weakness, it is that the vindication of the soldiers at the climax of the tale is a bit hard to accept. The final twist is that a German soldier also reports, independently, being affected by the heavenly light. Though this corroboration is undoubtedly included by *One Step Beyond* so as to express the universality of the experience, it is highly unlikely that a single, second-hand account, from an enemy soldier no less, would save the French men from execution. More likely, the military would suspect that the condemned men were actually involved in some kind of conspiracy with the enemy!

There is, of course, one other simple explanation for the events of "The Vision." The light in the sky could be interpreted as a metaphor for man's better instincts. Most men do not desire to kill, and by putting down their arms, the four soldiers from France were literally "seeing the light." They realized that they were fighting and killing their fellow man over land, politics and other relatively insignificant things when compared with the joys and wonders of life and death.

11. "The Devil's Laughter"

(Dramatized by Alfred Brenner; Directed by John Newland;
Airdate: March 31, 1959)

SYNOPSIS: In 1895 a condemned man, John Marriott, is escorted to the gallows to be executed, but the noose snaps just as he is to be hanged.

The following day Marriott is to be hanged again, but this time the lever malfunctions and the gallows floor won't drop. Feeling invincible, John Marriott is released from prison only to meet with a most unusual, but preordained, fate...

GUEST CAST: Alfred Ryder (John Marriott), Patrick Westwood, Ben Wright, Leslie Denison, Lester Matthews, Gordon Richards, Keith McConnell, Alma Lawton, John Ainsworth.

COMMENTARY: It is quite a leap from "The Vision," a story that asks some big questions about the nature of the universe and man's role in it, to "The Devil's Laughter," a quirky little tale of (literally!) gallows humor. Considerably less ponderous than the typical *One Step Beyond* installment, "The Devil's Laughter" is also John Newland's personal favorite among the series canon. It is not difficult to understand why that is so, for this is a tightly focused drama, almost a one-room play, as characters come and go from Marriott's prison cell in pursuit of various purposes and agendas. In addition, it is an execution drama, with a doomed convict waiting anxiously to meet his maker and pleading to authorities for his life.

But "The Devil's Laughter" also has the strange sense of the oddball to it. There is no serious study of any particular paranormal phenomenon (except a remarkable streak of good fortune, perhaps), only a series of remarkable pratfalls as guest star Alfred Ryder (*Star Trek*: "The Man Trap," *Land of the Giants*: "The Night of the Thrombeldinbar") escapes unscathed after each attempt by the government to bring his sorry life to an end.

There is much bluster and fun in Ryder's performance as The Man Who Can't Be Hanged, a fellow who escapes the gallows twice (via a broken noose and a malfunctioning step/lever), and even the point-blank aim of a loaded pistol. All this luck leads him to consider himself invincible, until he meets his end just as it was promised him (at the foot of a lion). The devil is in the details, and the joy in "The Devil's Laughter" derives from Newland's attention to detail and protocol, and the manner in which his camera methodically follows each execution attempt. The final walk to the hangman's platform is labored upon, and all the while the viewer is wondering when Marriott's lucky streak is going to leave him up the creek.

The episode title, "The Devil's Laughter," is a clever one, because it might be interpreted in two manners. Firstly, if one accepts that some kind of diabolical force is involved, then the Devil is surely laughing because he is foiling all attempts by human law to kill the criminal Marriott (who is responsible for murdering his wife, as well as pushing a blind beggar into a gutter and robbing him of his tin cup). However, at the climax of the episode — as Ryder meets his maker after a long fall down a stone staircase — another meaning becomes plain. The Devil has been having his fun — not with the befuddled lawmen, but with Marriott himself, whose confidence and life he has toyed with so maliciously. All this plays out in a rather minor but enjoyable key, and "The Devil's Laughter" is an interesting episode, out-of-step with the remainder of the series. In some ways it is more like *The Twilight Zone*, as it concerns a flawed human being caught up in the cogs of a cosmic order or justice he tries to manipulate but clearly does not understand.

Despite the quasi-comedic tone, "The Devil's Laughter" does have an interesting historical precedent and therefore could be said to describe a "real" situation. In 1803 there was a fellow by the name of Josh Samuels who lived in Sydney, Australia. He was falsely accused of a capital crime and sentenced to be hanged. The first time Samuels went to the gallows, the hanging rope broke. The second time he went to the gallows, the noose unravelled. The third and final time he was to be hanged, the rope snapped just above Samuels' head ... sparing him once again. Samuels, who became known as "The Man Who Would Not Hang,"[13] was later set free, and the police soon found the real perpetrator. *One Step Beyond* toys with the details of this story for dramatic purposes, making the lucky fellow guilty instead of innocent (probably so he can receive his comeuppance at the climax), but "The Devil's Laughter" otherwise remains true to the bizarre Australia incident.

12. "The Return of Mitchell Campion"

(Dramatized by Merwin Gerard;
Directed by John Newland;
Airdate: April 7, 1959)

SYNOPSIS: After recovering from a car accident and coma, Mitchell Campion goes on vacation to a small island near Spain, only to discover that the natives there claim to have met him before ... even though he has never visited the island! Worse, Mr. Campion seems to be in some kind of trouble over his relationship with a local girl named Francesca. Can Mitchell Campion somehow have been in two places at the same time?

GUEST CAST: Patrick O'Neal (Mitchell Campion), Lilyan Chauvin (Francesca), Richard Angarola.

COMMENTARY: The subject of "The Return of Mitchell Campion" is what is commonly referred to as the OBE or the OOBE (the *Out Of Body Experience*), that strange event in which a slumbering or comatose human being manages to project an image of him or herself to another location, sometimes miles away. The OBE (not to be confused with the NDE — the Near Death Experience) might also be referred to as *teleportation, bilocation* or *astral projection*. In "The Return of Mitchell Campion," the protagonist is a man who was in a coma following a car accident, and who was dead for four minutes during a cardiac arrest. Despite the fact that his body was at rest in a coma state, Campion's image/astral projection somehow managed to "appear" on an island hundreds of miles away. Proof of Campion's psychic journey comes from two contradictory bits of evidence: one on paper and one established by eyewitness reports. First, official medical records for Campion confirm that he was not on the island but rather in a stateside hospital during the period in which he was supposedly seen by the islanders (and where he signed the hotel guest registry). Second, everybody on the island claims to remember him, from the maid and hotel clerk to a woman he supposedly carried on a romantic relationship with. The kicker, of course, is that a friend even took a photograph of Mitchell Campion with the woman Francesca during his "psychic" vacation on the island three weeks earlier. The medical records of a hospital stay in the U.S. and the eyewitness reports and photograph of Campion on the island, all from the same period of time, serve to "prove" that Campion was in two places at once. At least on *One Step Beyond.*

The OBE is a common concept in science fiction and horror circles. Jack Cassidy played a bitter, crippled man who "astrally projected" himself out of his ruined body to murder the man he suspected was having an affair with his wife in the final first season entry of *Rod Serling's Night Gallery,* entitled "The Last Laurel." On *The X-Files,* a second season episode called "The Walk" found a crippled Operation Desert Storm veteran also wreaking vengeance by psychically leaving his wounded body and committing acts of violence on those in the U.S. military he deemed responsible for his wounds. In *Beyond Reality,* the episode called "Justice" depicted how a prison inmate could depart from his body during periods of psychological trauma, such as beatings by a sadistic prison guard. *One Step Beyond's* "The Return of Mitchell Campion" pre-dates all of these adventures by a good twenty years and succeeds not only because Patrick O'Neal (*The Twilight Zone:* "A Short Drink from a Certain Fountain," *Rod Serling's Night Gallery:* "A Fear of Spiders") delivers an effective performance as the befuddled title character, but because the series again trades on a concept that has been studied at length by parapsychologists— thereby treating the material with respect and a sense of superficial, if not total, accuracy.

Witness the following case of OBEs, described by authors Lois Duncan and William Roll in their book *Psychic Connections: A Journey into the Mysterious World of Psi:*

> A doctor named Michael Sabom did a study … that compared the description of the resuscitation program given by thirty-two OBEers with the "educated guesses" of twenty-five medically savvy patients who had not had OBE. All were asked to describe what happened when a medical team tries to get the heart restarted. Twenty-three of the twenty-five non-OBEers made major mistakes, while none of the thirty-two OBE patients made any. They apparently had *seen* what happened while they were out of their bodies.[14]

There are two important details in that "real life" account that are transposed to "The Return of Mitchell Campion" on *One Step Beyond*. The first detail establishes that the OBE experience occurred to people who had been in the hospital and had suffered from heart-related problems. On this front, *One Step Beyond* manages to be quite accurate by providing Campion that very medical background. The second detail of importance in the above description is that the OBEers were able to awaken and recall in detail their amazing OBE experiences (looking down at the doctors perform surgery on their unconscious bodies). In "The Return of Mitchell Campion," Campion speaks of *déjà vu*, of a "door opening in a room" he somehow knew, but he does not remember the details of his out-of-body visit to the island. It comes as a shock to him, and it is a mystery he works to solve. This characterization does not mesh with most reported OBE experiences, so it is plain that *One Step Beyond* did take some liberties with the very concept of bilocation.

On the other hand, the storyline of "The Return of Mitchell Campion" works far better on a dramatic front because of its "mystery" nature. Campion visits an island he thinks he has never visited, only to find that everybody there recognizes him. That is a terrific *Twilight Zone*–like concept (before *The Twilight Zone* existed) that allows the protagonist to learn the answers as the episode progresses and the plot unfolds. The story would not have worked from a dramatic standpoint had Campion known immediately, at Moment One, that he had taken "one step beyond" the normal path of the vast majority of human beings. Instead, awareness comes to him slowly, and the audience is allowed to assemble the clues with him. For that reason, one can perhaps forgive *One Step Beyond*, or at least give it a pass, on this occasion for picking and choosing which aspects of a phenomenon it decided to incorporate in an episode. Accuracy and dramatic license had to fit together seamlessly — no easy task — and it is a credit to *One Step Beyond* that this synchronicity so often was achieved.

13. "The Navigator"
(Dramatized by Don M. Mankiewicz;
Directed by John Newland;
Airdate: April 14, 1959)

SYNOPSIS: Someone or some *thing* is inexplicably erasing and then rewriting the course of a sea vessel bound for Boston, and the suspects are many, including an elderly captain with growing memory problems and a young first mate who is secretly a company spy investigating the captain. The mystery is believed solved when a strange stowaway is found hidden in the ship's hold, clutching a piece of chalk. Events turn strange, however, when a ship in distress, *The Flying Eagle*, is rescued in an ice field ... and the stowaway found earlier on one ship is discovered to be among the dead of the other vessel!

GUEST CAST: Don Dubbins (Navigator/Mate Walter Blake), Robert Ellenstein (Captain), Don Womack, Joel Fluellen, Robert Osterloh, Olan Soule, Stephen Roberts.

COMMENTARY: There are two possible psychic explanations for the events that occur in "The Navigator." The first is that the mysterious stowaway died aboard his own ship, *The Flying Eagle*, but his crisis apparition traveled to the other vessel in time to rescue the remainder of his crew. This answer fits well with established research, since crisis apparitions are believed to appear within twelve hours of the motivating catastrophe, and that time scheme fits precisely with the timely rescue of the *Flying Eagle* in "The Navigator." The second psychic explanation harkens back to "The Return of Mitchell Campion": The stowaway, dying, had an OBE (out-of-body experience), with the same ultimate goal in mind — to save his dying shipmates.

More interesting than either of the aforementioned psychic possibilities, however, is "The Navigator's" real thesis: that the sea is a realm of mystery where strange things sometimes occur. In his opening narration, Newland appropriately reports that the sea and the unknown go "hand in hand," and later the old captain, an experienced sea dog, reiterates that stance by reporting that there are things that happen at sea that "just can't be explained." Those two comments form the foundations of this interesting tale, which relies not on a hard and fast paranormal concept (like OBEs, NDEs, crisis apparitions or the like), but on the viewer's almost instinctive feelings of unease with the sea.

To this day, the oceans of the world retain some of their mystery and wonder for mankind. After all, humans walk on land and are not equipped for life or survival in water. Importantly, the sea is one place that man, even with all his technology and know-how, has not tamed or conquered. He is not the master in the ocean, and, in point of fact, he does not understand everything that goes on beneath its waves and ripples. And those things that man does understand about the ocean and its inhabitants tend to make him even more nervous. Sharks and squids, barracudas and even jellyfish make the water their home, and these seagoing creatures are as alien to man as beings from a distant planet might be. Perhaps it is an irrational fear, but man has often felt threatened by the ocean because of its size, shape and the dragons that dwell beneath its surface. One only need look at the success of *Jaws* (1975) or *Deep Blue Sea* (1999) to understand the impact that sea monsters still have on man. And there are other dynamics to consider too. The ocean stretches to the horizon, and in man's early history, there was no guarantee that a brave traveller on the water would ever reach land (and safety) on the far side. Sailors once wrote on maps that "Here there be dragons," as if monsters indeed dwelled a certain distance from the security of home port. Throw in all the stories about ships gone missing in "The Bermuda Triangle" or other strange regions, knowledge of terrible sinkings like the *Titanic*, and it is easy to understand why *One Step Beyond* should choose to exploit this realm for a story about the unknown.

Other films that have successfully generated scares by highlighting the mysterious, otherworldly nature of our seas include John Carpenter's 1980 hit *The Fog*. In that picture, soggy corpses came up from the ocean's bottom to avenge a terrible wrong done to them. More importantly perhaps, the primary characters of *The Fog* (some of them fishermen) relayed chilly legends of the sea, including one about the discovery of a ghost ship, like *The Flying Dutchman*, wherein all evidence suggested the crew had just been aboard moments earlier — but in fact there was, strangely, no sign of them anywhere.

One Step Beyond's "The Navigator" also relies on yet another role that the sea unwittingly fulfills for frightened sailors journeying across it: isolation. On any lengthy sea voyage the sailors are limited to the cramped space aboard their ship, with no easy escape and forbidding water on all sides. As any true fan of the horror genre can attest, the best way to generate scares is to dump a few interesting characters (preferably with conflicts) into an isolated setting and then hammer them with the fear of the unknown. The student film crew exploring the vast forest in *The Blair Witch Project* (1999), the handful of scientists at an Antarctica research base in *The Thing* (1982), the troop of actors on a burial island in *Children Shouldn't Play with Dead Things* (1972), even the "space trucker" astronauts of *Alien*, swimming through a cosmic sea on the vessel Nostromo, faced continued isolation as well as a "real" fear in the form of something believed to be malevolent. Taking the same stance of isolated setting and character conflict, "The Navigator" takes its bickering crew to a region viewers share understandable apprehension about (the sea), then strands them there as something spooky occurs. It may not be a revolutionary set-up for a horror story, but it is an effective one.

"The Navigator" gains further frisson through writer Mankiewicz's decision to make the story one of a power struggle. "The Navigator" is really a generational battle between an old captain and a young officer who thinks he knows better than his elder. The captain is a hardass who gives unlawful orders (making his crew men empty their pockets for inspection at one point). The young man is secretly a company security agent from back home, sent to investigate the captain. Obviously, neither of these men trust each other one lick, so when the ship's course mysteriously changes time and time again, a sense of paranoia overwhelms the proceedings. Is the security agent, operating under orders, redirecting the ship? Or is the captain, perhaps senile, responsible for the changes in direction? This kind of character tension supports the general feeling of uneasiness Newland's camera generates in "The Navigator," and points to the future of many horror films as well. After all, a company "agent" hidden among a ship's crew has become *de rigueur* in the genre of late, featured in everything from the *Doctor Who* serial "The Robots of Death" in 1977 to *Alien* (1979) and *Aliens* (1986).

"The Navigator" is a unique addition to *One Step Beyond*'s catalog because it is more concerned with suspicions, fears and the "creeps" than it is about the documentation of a paranormal event. It is more drama than dramatization and seems all the stronger for its powerful characterizations, courtesy of Don Dubbins (as Walter Blake) and a heavily made-up Robert Ellenstein (*Star Trek IV: The Voyage Home* [1986]) as the ship's captain. The psychic angle (either a crisis apparition or an OBE experience) may be recycled from earlier entries, but the prominent role of the ocean as catalyzing factor finds the creepy "The Navigator" anything but lost at sea.

14. "The Secret"

(Dramatized by Michael Plant;
Directed by John Newland;
Airdate: April 21, 1959)

SYNOPSIS: The victim of a failing marriage, Sylvia Ackroyd spends her fortieth birthday alone and miserable, reminiscing about her exciting days in France during World War II. She finds a Ouija board in the basement of her home and summons an invisible spirit called Jeremy — the soul of a French soldier who was killed some 80 years earlier, in the 1870s — to help alleviate her lassitude. Her disbelieving husband scoffs at Sylvia's obsession and worries about a scandal, but soon Sylvia disappears with a man who just might be the spirit of a dead man.

GUEST CAST: Maria Palmer (Sylvia Ackroyd), Robert Douglas (Harrison Ackroyd), Albert Carrier, Molly Glessing, Robert Shafto, A.E. Gould-Porter.

COMMENTARY: "The Secret" is another none-too-subtle *One Step Beyond* warning to all the neglectful, cheating husbands of the world: Treat your wife respectfully or else she might disappear forever with the spirit of a dead man! In its depiction of a lonely forty-year-old woman who one day awakes to find (and abhor) an emotional distance from her husband, this episode is really about release from marital misery, and the ensuing discovery of a new soul mate who will not leave Sylvia feeling "dead" inside. Of course, this is an especially ironic conclusion because Jeremy, the very soul Sylvia connects with as her new long-time companion, is actually dead himself. He died during a war some eighty years earlier! Despite the fact that Jeremy is "dead" in a corporeal sense, he is very much alive in that he represents a rekindling of Sylvia's interests and psychological focus. She too lives in the world of the past, reminiscing about the French occupation during World War II and her exciting work with the Resistance during that conflict. Perhaps it is this connection of war, of heightened experience shared, that allows two souls from disparate times to find one another.

Sylvia's memories of an exciting time and a purposeful life, and her later general malaise with a more traditional postwar role as wife, would later be the central stuff of *Plenty* (1985), a film starring Meryl Streep as a woman undergoing the same crisis, but for *One Step Beyond* these memories help mainly to form a psychic link, not a portrait of despair. Sylvia sees hope and joy and meaning in the past, in the excitement of a time gone, and she thus forges a connection with a soldier from another past who shares her passions. Of course, such a thing is the stuff of miracles, but "The Secret" is first and foremost a comeuppance story in which a nasty husband, concerned only with scandal and appearances, loses his wife because of his gross mistreatment of her (he even forgets her birthday).

The paranormal device that robs Mr. Ackroyd of his long-suffering wife in "The Secret" is the *ouija board*, or witchboard. Employed to open communication with the dead, and usually made of wood, the ouija (pronounced WEE-JAH) board is a long-cherished tool of occult seances. The object that is moved across the ouija board to formulate answers from the spirit world is known as the *planchette*. During rapport with a spirit, the planchette seems to spell out answers to questions by landing on certain letters of the alphabet or brief responses such as "NO" or "YES." Popularized as a child's toy in the late 1960s and early 1970s by the Parker Brothers game company, the ouija board has also been an object of terror in films such as *The Exorcist* (1973), which found Linda Blair's Regan MacNeil communicating with a dead spirit called Captain Howdy — actually a demon — and the far less memorable *Witchboard* (1986), starring Tawny Kitaen.

Today, it seems that everybody who has ever utilized a ouija board can tell at least one scary story about it, and it is considered wise not to play with a ouija board when one is alone or in a vulnerable state of mind. Corroboration of these "spooky" ouija tales have, for the most part, not been forthcoming or overtly convincing. However, a long-held rule about ouija boards is that one should never ask specific questions about one's own death.

In a sense, "The Secret" is really a wish-fulfillment episode for lonely housewives. A neglected spouse spurns her philandering husband, finds a new, wonderful lover, and then leaves with him … disappearing from the world forever and confounding her disbelieving husband. When Jeremy finally arrives to take Sylvia, Mr. Ackroyd mistakes this apparition for the doctor he just sent for, and Jeremy knowingly tells Sylvia that she will be very happy where she "is going." Then the goosebumps are raised as, moments after Sylvia's departure with this man, the real doctor arrives and Mr. Ackroyd realizes he has been witness to an apparition. Worse than that, he realizes his wife has fled reality with one! In its depiction of an apparition as a solid being, *One Step Beyond* continues to adhere to paranormal research on the topic and follow in the tradition of "The Dark Room" and other early stories.

"The Secret" also represents a story type that *The Twilight Zone* would emulate during its five year run. A favorite "surprise ending" of that series found tormented souls finding final escape in other realms, much as Sylvia escapes her unhappiness in this *One Step Beyond* story. In *The Twilight Zone*'s "The Bewitchin' Pool," for instance, children neglected by their self-involved, bickering parents jumped into a swimming pool, disappeared from reality, and emerged at the swimming hole of a kindly old maternal woman named Aunt T. (who clearly fulfilled the same role as Jeremy in "The Secret"). It was clear that Aunt T. would love the sad children and treat them well for all of time. They had no need to return home, just as it is unlikely Sylvia Ackroyd would ever do the same.

15. "The Aerialist"

(Dramatized by Larry Marcus;
Directed by John Newland;
Airdate: April 28, 1959)

SYNOPSIS: The Flying Petrusscios, a family of trapeze artists, face off in a personal feud before an important circus show, and then the performance goes terribly wrong when Gino, the patriarch of the family and "Toast of Seven Continents," falls some 80 feet. Gino's eldest son, Mario, blames himself for the accident and later tries to commit suicide by performing the same dangerous stunt that left his father totally paralyzed. To Mario's total surprise, the two powerful hands of his father reach out to save his life at just the right moment, then vanish into thin air...

GUEST CAST: Michael Connors (Mario Petrusscio), Yvette Vickers (Carlotta Petrusscio), Robert Carricart, Ruggero Romor, Penny Santon, Charles Watts, Vernon Rich, Mary Patton, Ray Baker.

COMMENTARY: "The Aerialist" reminds viewers that man's academic explanations for the workings of the world are but grains of sand in "the Sahara of the unexplainable," a nice line of narrative explanation in a somewhat familiar story. In "The Aerialist," host John Newland refers to the process of allowing the body image to show itself and act at a great distance as *bilocation,* but the ability of old, paralyzed Gino to save his son by leaving his shattered body is really but a form of astral projection, or, more accurately, an out-of-body experience. Whatever one chooses to call it, it is clearly a paranormal "event" dramatized rather successfully in a previous *One Step Beyond* episode, "The Return of Mitchell Campion." There, a man recovering from injuries transmitted his body image halfway around the world, and here, another wounded man transmits his body image to a gymnasium miles away in order to save his son from death. Since "The Navigator" also handled a similar subject, "The Aerialist" feels a bit like a rehash of previous *One Step Beyond* stories.

The personal drama of "The Aerialist," which finds *Mannix* star Michael Connors feeling guilty because of his failure to perform a circus stunt correctly and in the process injuring his father, is interesting enough but hardly the stuff of a classic episode. And, in fact, "The Aerialist" is highly reminiscent, at least structurally, of "The Navigator" in one other important way. Instead of the inaccessible world of the sea, "The Aerialist" allows us to peer into the closed tents of the circus, another realm where many people find cause for fear. Freaks of nature, magicians with dark secrets, and clowns with unnaturally smiling faces all lend the venue of the circus an aura of horror. On the surface, it is a place of play and joy, but beneath that "happy" tent dwells a dark underworld. Tobe Hooper's nightmarish *The Funhouse* (1981), the frightening *Doctor Who* serial "The Greatest Show in the Galaxy" (1989), the surreal film *Killer Klowns from Outer Space* (1988), the *Star Trek: Voyager* episode "The Thaw" and even a later *One Step Beyond* episode called "The Clown" all manage to squeeze real scares out of the unsettling atmosphere of the Big Top. In fact, so many horror TV series and films have been set at circuses that it is a wonder parents still take their children to see Ringling Brothers at all! Nevertheless, it is easy to see how one realm of horror (the sea) in "The Navigator" has been replaced by another (the circus) in "The Aerialist."

"The Navigator" also highlighted a generational war, a battle between an old sea dog captain and a young upstart. The same war is carried on here, as young Mario Petrusscio and his father Gino duke it out over the questionable behavior of Mario's flirtatious wife. Gino is of the "Old Country" approach to love, family and loyalty, and Mario is an "assimilated American" who does not seem to take objection to the fact that his wife seems "promiscuous" and lacks a certain respect for the family. It is this battle of generations that breaks the family solidarity, allows for distraction, and paves the way for the terrible accident that injures Gino. Just as the lack of solidarity among the crew in "The Navigator" allowed for a heightened sense of paranoia, as well as the advent of wicked accusations and suspicions, so does the Petrusscio family's failure to stick together inform the psychic events of "The Aerialist." The difference is that the rift is healed in "The Aerialist." Though Gino is doomed to die, he is able, in a moment of forgiveness, to save his son via an OBE.

It is also fair to argue that by this episode of *One Step Beyond*, there is a high degree of expectation and anticipation associated with these stories. Any regular viewer understands that there will be a psychic twist at the end, and so, having experienced that fact several times, he or she begins to look for the "surprise" early on. This anticipation of the unknown "twist" actually tends to make one both impatient and uninterested in what seem to be "regular" dramatic developments (such as a battle between a husband and wife). For instance, in "The Aerialist" the family's fortunes fall drastically because of the father's terrible accident. The Brothers Petrusscio are now lacking a player in their act and are virtually unemployable. The family starts to run out of money and new problems erupt with Carlotta, Mario's wife. And, most of all, Mario fears climbing back on the horse: getting back up on that trapeze to perform again. These are all valid dramatic concerns for "The Aerialist," but they get swallowed up or ignored because viewers are looking past the "nuts and bolts" of the story structure for the big twist. They are looking to get ahead of the show's story and figure out where and how the tale is going to culminate. It is for this reason that *One Step Beyond* stories would soon feature twists, double-twists and some interesting format alterations. For it to stay relevant, the series had to keep ahead of an audience that was now expecting to be surprised, wowed and toyed with on a weekly basis! "The Aerialist" is a well-produced, skillfully acted and directed episode, but it lacks the feeling of surprise and innovation that would have placed it among the more memorable installments.

16. "The Burning Girl"
(Dramatized by Catherine Turney;
Directed by John Newland;
Airdate: May 5, 1959)

SYNOPSIS: A shy teenage girl named Alice has a history of starting fires when goaded by her cruel Aunt Mildred. These fires are not set intentionally, but by some strange power in her mind: through pyrokinesis. A doctor attempts to get to the truth of Alice's strange powers, but instead of answers he spawns only another deadly conflagration.

GUEST CAST: Olive Deering (Alice Denning), Luana Anders, Edward Platt (Will Denning), Sandra Knight, Geraldine Wall, Alfred Hopson, Hampton Fancher, Peter Waller, Phil Arnold.

COMMENTARY: Even the most cursory look at the classic *One Step Beyond* episode "The Burning Girl" reveals it to be a dead-on, early version of the popular 1974 Stephen King novel *Carrie*, later made into an exemplary film by Brian De Palma in 1976. Instead of social outcast Carrie White, "The Burning Girl" introduces audiences to social outcast Alice Denning, a girl who is ostracized by cruel-hearted high-schoolers and responds to the ongoing torment with psychic force (in this case, embodied by fire). Like Carrie, Alice lives under the thumb of an accusing, religious zealot and parental figure. In *Carrie*, Mrs. White considers her own daughter a creature of evil simply because she menstruates—a sign to dear old Mom that she is a harlot and a sinner. In "The Burning Girl," cruel Aunt Mildred fulfills the same negative role model, referring to Alice as a "jezebel" and a demon for "chasing after boys." In *Carrie*, Mrs. White decides she can no longer suffer the presence of a witch in her household and opts to kill her own daughter. Aunt Mildred also tries to destroy Alice by seeing that the poor girl is held responsible for the fires. She also makes claims that the girl is a devil and, specifically, a witch.

Though *Carrie* and "The Burning Girl" on *One Step Beyond* both concern psychic abilities, they really concern the sexual coming-of-age known as adolescence. In *Carrie*, the teenage protagonist is vilified for not understanding her period, and for being a virgin. In "The Burning Girl," a pack of boys attempt to rape the attractive but naive Alice, signifying her entrance into sexual adulthood. In their respective stories, Carrie and Alice are both girls who are blossoming into full womanhood and beauty ... as directly opposed to antagonists Mrs. White and Aunt Mildred, who are both well past their prime and resentful about it. Perhaps the last great similarity between *Carrie* and "The Burning Girl" is that the defense mechanism of both productions, the telekinesis or pyrokinesis, disappears when Carrie and Alice feel secure and loved. When things are good at the high school prom for Carrie, or when Alice is having a fun time with her school friends, there is no need to strike back or put up the defenses. But when life turns nasty and dangerous, these two teenage girls respond (unconsciously, one suspects) with a ferocious power that Newland suggests on *One Step Beyond* might be a leftover from ancient times and the dawn of man.

"The Burning Girl" is a great *One Step Beyond* episode because it effectively hits all the same notes as *Carrie* (and, to a degree, Stephen King's *Firestarter*), some twenty years earlier. Thus it can be said to be well ahead of its time. Secondly, the episode succeeds admirably as an examination of another dysfunctional family (a regular playground for *One Step Beyond*), *and* as a portrait of a lonely girl who desires only to be loved. Though there are some awkward moments in the episode (all of the supposed high-schoolers look to be well into their late twenties or early thirties), and Edward Platt (the Chief of CONTROL on *Get Smart* [1965–70]) seems miscast as a heartless father ("You won't spoil things *this time* will ya?" he asks at one point, sounding more beaten down than genuinely hostile), the story is filled with interesting touches and attention to detail. For instance, as Alice prepares to attend a Halloween party, she dresses up in costume as a gypsy. This is an appropriate choice of costume, since the teleplay reveals that Alice is always being forced to relocate, and that her family has, by necessity, moved three times in four years. Essentially, Alice lives the life of a gypsy, so it is rewarding that her Halloween costume reflects that truth.

In another powerful and vivid moment, Newland's camera finds Alice reclining on a bed as flames suddenly erupt behind her. As she stands up in a daze, the fire spreads rapidly over the area where Alice had been laying just previously, and the effect of the devouring fire is stunning and well timed. It looks very, very dangerous and it represents a well-orchestrated on-set effect that moves with real speed and vigor.

Pyrokinesis, the ability to generate fires through the power of the mind, is not a commonly studied or well-accepted paranormal phenomenon, though it has certainly captured the interest of genre filmmakers. In addition to *Carrie* (1976) and *Firestarter* (1984), this unique ability to bring about psychic flames has been seen in *The X-Files* episode "Fire" and the *Beyond Reality* episode "Enemy in Our Midst," among others. Of over 25 books researched by this author, not one made specific mention of pyrokinesis. However, it could be that the thing poor Alice is coping with in "The Burning Girl" is not pyrokinesis at all but actually a *poltergeist*, or a *recurrent-spontaneous-psychokinesis*. In some poltergeist-like situations, it is believed that a living person is the cause (or *agent*) of the seemingly unnatural physical disturbances. Importantly, these disturbances sometimes are thought to take the form of fire "spontaneously" igniting. Adhering to parapsychology studies, "The Burning Girl" suggests that it is the young or adolescent who are often the agents of poltergeist activity.

17. "The Haunted U-Boat"

(Dramatized by Larry Marcus;
Directed by John Newland;
Airdate: May 12, 1959)

SYNOPSIS: a German U-Boat #147 transports Bachman, a future leader of the Third Reich, to safety in 1945. When the submarine dives beneath the surface, a strange rhythmic pounding on the hull is heard. Though the U-Boat escapes Allied detection for a time, the inexplicable pounding leads a U.S. destroyer back to the fleeing sub and lands the entire crew in jeopardy. Even more strangely, the pounding always seems to occur in close proximity to Bachman's location on the sub. The cause of the unearthly tapping is soon unconvered: a wrench held in the hands of a skeleton ... the corpse of a laborer who died when the ship was under construction in a Nazi dock.

GUEST CAST: Werner Klemperer (Bachman), Eric Feldary (Captain), Kort Falkenberg, Wesley Lau, Siegried Speck, Paul Busch, Frank Obershall, Norbert Kerner, Sasha Hardin.

COMMENTARY: As it neared the end of its first season, *One Step Beyond* hit its stride again with a series of remarkable, compelling stories. With "The Burning Girl" and "The Haunted U-Boat," and then "Image of Death," the young series was stretching for more ambitious material and offering much more than a sedate, measured study of the paranormal. "The Haunted U-Boat" is a wonderfully creepy story about a bad man (Bachman), a Nazi, who finally gets his comeuppance via psychic means. The implication to this claustrophobic story is that there is a sense of justice in the universe, and that the Nazi butcher will not escape scot-free from the evil he has so mercilessly dealt to others. The mechanism through which the scales of justice choose to operate on this occasion are psychic in nature, as one might predict; but in this case, *rapping* is the phenomenon of the half hour.

Rapping is a repetitive pounding noise believed to be generated from a paranormal or spiritual source. There have been many documented cases of "rapping," and the most interesting one mirrors the details of "The Haunted U-Boat." In 1847 the Fox family moved into a cottage in New York and heard a series of strange rapping noises emanating from the walls of their newly purchased house. As they investigated the history of the house, the family learned that a gentleman named Charles Rosma, an itinerant salesman, was rumored to have been murdered there in the past by the previous tenant. Years later (on November 23, 1904) *The Rochester Democrat and Chronicle* reported that a possible source for the rapping noise had indeed been located. The paper wrote that "a disjointed skeleton had been found in the cellar of the house when an old wall collapsed."[15] Obviously then, the implication was that the corpse's spirit was generating the pounding noise to alert people to the fact that a crime had been committed. The climactic kicker in "The Haunted U-Boat" is reminiscent of this very story. In the end, it is discovered that the corpse of a laborer was trapped in the ship's hull during construction. As Newland explains in the aired episode, that dead man's hand still gripped a wrench. Was he someone whose hate for the Nazis did not die with his own death? Clearly this is all speculation, but again, it is important to note that *One Step Beyond* pays attention to details and manages to get things right. The location may have been changed (from a house to a submarine) for purposes of drama, but the paranormal concepts are investigated and reported on with an eye towards accuracy.

So memorable is "The Haunted U-Boat" that the story of a Nazi submarine besieged by vengeful ghosts has become something of an urban legend today, a story often-repeated as "fact" in ghost story circles. Years after "The Haunted U-Boat" aired on *One Step Beyond*, the story was revamped by Rod Serling on *The Twilight Zone* (January 10, 1963) as "The Thirty-Fathom Grave." In that adventure, starring Simon Oakland and Bill Bixby, a haunted submarine from World War II was also the focal point for a supernatural story of revenge from beyond the grave.

The element that makes "The Haunted U-Boat" so effective an entry for *One Step Beyond* is the sense of claustrophobia created by the production team. Larry Marcus's descriptive dialogue establishes that Bachman feels like he's "sealed up in a coffin, choking on the fumes of oil and dirty men," and this comment is buttressed by tight sets and a potpourri of annoying, nerve-fraying sounds. The unnerving psychic rapping is, at one point, coupled with the repetitive and irritating sound of a sonar "ping." This synchronization of sound is especially clever because both noises serve to do the same thing: pinpoint ships. One tool (the sonar) works to protect the Nazis, the other (the rapping) ultimately works against them, forcing them to surrender their ship to the Allies.

Fans of *Hogan's Heroes* (1965–71) will no doubt recognize guest star, the late Werner Klemperer. In "The Haunted U-Boat" he is the Third Reich Devil called Bachman, but on the CBS sitcom he was the hapless Colonel Wilhelm Klink, a much kinder and gentler brand of Nazi.

18. "Image of Death"
(Dramatized by Larry Marcus;
Directed by John Newland;
Airdate: May 15, 1959)

SYNOPSIS: In France in 1892, a common woman marries above her station after poisoning her new husband's former wife, the kindly, aristocratic Janette. Soon after Charlotte moves into the chateau of her new husband, a strange pattern emerges on a wall where the Janette's beautiful portrait once hung: the unmistakable outline of a human skull. As the screaming skull becomes more and more plain for all to see, the conspirators in Janette's murder are driven to despair, paranoia, and finally death...

GUEST CAST: Doris Dowling (Charlotte), Max Adrian (Jacques), John Wengraff (Ernest), Diedre Owens (Rose), Gregory Gay, Guy De Vestal.

COMMENTARY: "Image of Death" is a sterling example of what *Creature Features* author and horror movie expert John Stanley sometimes refers to in his reference books as a "slowly going bonkers" story. In this horror subgenre, *something* starts to drive guilty conspirators mad. Perhaps it is their guilty consciences; perhaps it is the scales of cosmic justice being righted; but for whatever reason, bad and guilty people are "exposed" as they slowly go mad and meet their just desserts. In the case of "Image of Death," two adulterers responsible for the death of a kind woman face punishment for their illicit crimes when an odd little stain appears on the wall and then starts to grow. At first the stain is just that, a blotch that happens to appear at the very spot where the dead woman's portrait hung. Then, however, the blotch starts to take on particular characteristics. Could that be an eye? A screaming mouth? In the end, the conspirators believe they are seeing a testament to their own evil staring back from the wall at them, and are consequently driven to terrible deaths.

On a purely literary level, "Image of Death" also recalls a facet of Shakespeare's bloody tragedy *MacBeth*. Just as poor Lady MacBeth could not seem to wash the blood from her hands after killing Duncan, the King, neither can Charlotte and Jacques manage to clean the terrible stain that mars their wall like an admission of their guilt. What is perhaps unusual for *One Step Beyond* is that there is no real psychic phenomenon at play in this story of "comeuppance" and of two conspirators "slowly going bonkers." On the contrary, to all indications, John Newland's explanation on the air fits best: The guilty conscience can sometimes do very strange things. In particular, the stain on the wall functions like a modern Rorschach or inkblot test. Charlotte and Jacques interpret it to be something it is not, and later the housekeeper reports that there was indeed a stain present there, but no, it did not seem to resemble anything (or anyone) in particular.

In his treatise about psychic phenomena, French researcher Reginald Omez wrote a relevant comment about the power of the human mind to confabulate:

> Even the most stable and critical persons are not always proof against the suggestive power inherent in a set of circumstances whose vividness is heightened by fear, by longing, or simply by tension, all of which form favorable soil for the growth of hallucination, individual or collective.[16]

Considered in context with the events of "Image of Death," it is not difficult to see how the mindset of the conspirators may have been one of what Omez calls "fear and tension." What they experienced together, what they saw on the wall in the chateau, was perhaps a *folie à deux*, a shared or joint hallucination. Since their crime was one they participated in together, it does not seem unreasonable to believe that their own individual fears played off one another until the duo became convinced that an innocuous stain on the wall came to signify something more meaningful than it really was.

On the other hand, "Image of Death" leaves viewers with a question. Is it possible that the screaming skull on the wall was real? That, like the corpse banging against the hull aboard the submarine in "The Haunted U-Boat," the spirit of the murdered woman in this story wanted to expose her murderers to the world? Is it possible that the skull somehow stopped Charlotte's heart? That she died not of some physical problem, but of pure and terrible fright? Appropriately, *One Step Beyond* understands that the key to atmospheric horror stories is to raise these very possibilities, offer few answers, hint at a warning (on the anniversary of her death, it is said that Janette's skull sometimes reappears on the wall...), and then amble off the stage before too much is said to ruin the mood of dread.

"Image of Death" is an effective story not so much because it studies *folie à deux*, mass hysteria, or the idea of shared hallucinations, but because it so clearly recognizes the core concerns of economical drama: a crime committed, a guilty conscience, and slow-boiling insanity. Many major motion pictures have been based on less than that formula, and "Image of Death" remains one of the most frightening half hours dramatic television has ever produced. The comeuppance story rarely gets better than this.

19. "The Captain's Guests"

(Dramatized by Charles Beaumont;
Directed by John Newland;
Airdate: May 26, 1959)

SYNOPSIS: A couple married for six years moves into a vacant old house on the New England coast that the realtor has termed "unfriendly." When the Courtneys move in, Andy becomes possessed by the house's former occupant, a bitter sea captain named Clausen. Now Andy is reliving a murderous love triangle from a previous life, and his wife, Ellen, must save him before the battle for Andy's soul ends in a murder.

GUEST CAST: Robert Webber (Andy Courtney), Nancy Hadley (Ellen Courtney), Thomas Coley, Felix Locher, Jon Lormer.

COMMENTARY: All old houses creak and groan, right? That is the question a character asks in "The Captain's Guests," even as it becomes abundantly clear that the old home on Cape Anne Road in scenic New England is really haunted. *Haunted houses* are a favorite trope of the horror genre and have been popular for several decades. *The Uninvited* (1944), *The House on Haunted Hill* (1959), *The Haunting* (1963), *The Legend of Hell House* (1974), *The Amityville Horror* (1979), *House* (1986), and the Jan De Bont remake of *The Haunting* (1999) are just a few of the numerous celluloid adventures that center on a domicile infested with an evil that will not die. In psychical research, some houses are indeed believed to be haunted by the spirits of past residents, though the famous Amityville house, importantly, is not believed to be one of them. Hauntings are sometimes associated with poltergeists, sometimes with possession, and sometimes with other phenomena (the rapping story in New York from 1847 would be a prime example of the latter).

But the crux of "The Captain's Guests" is not the house itself, but the impact that living in the haunted house ultimately has on Andy Courtney. Interestingly, he goes through both a physical and mental transformation, taking on the characteristics of the former owner, Captain Clausen. In particular, Andy develops a limp and has a change in appetite (preferring rum and biscuits to his wife's more traditional middle-class cooking). Most importantly, he starts reliving an adulterous love triangle from the past, casting his wife and best friend in the role of betrayers. The punctuation of all this metamorphosis is that handsome, urbane-looking Andy Courtney (actor Robert Webber, of *One Life to Live*) emerges as a white-haired, bearded sea captain at the close of the story. This kind of surprise physical change is a long-held horror cliché too. For example, in *Night of Dark Shadows* (1971) handsome Quentin Collins (David Selby) developed the limp (again!) and the facial scar of an ancestor, Charles Collins, when he took up residence in a house haunted by the ghost of Angelique, Charles' lover. In *The Amityville Horror* (1979) poor George Lutz (James Brolin) also underwent a dramatic physical transformation, becoming gaunt and disheveled enough to pass for the identical twin of the boy (Ronald DeFeo) who had killed his family in the Amityville house a year earlier. Though *One Step Beyond* also adheres to this convention, that a person can be physically changed into another when under the roof of a haunted house, there remains little objective evidence in paranormal circles that a person can physically "change" into the spirit who haunts him. It is more likely that people are inclined to see their loved ones as unfamiliar or different in such stressful, bizarre situations.

"The Captain's Guests" is significant in the *One Step Beyond* roster because it highlights another husband-wife team confronting the unknown, facing possible separation, and coming out of the traumatic events changed. It is not difficult to imagine that Andy in "The Captain's Guests" fulfills the same dramatic purpose as the young bride in "The Bride Possessed" or the psychic wife in "Twelve Hours to Live." Once again, the appearance of the paranormal proves important as a trial for a good marriage. The inference is clear: If the Courtney's can survive this, they can survive *anything*.

Importantly, the story of "The Captain's Guests" is also a "possession" rehash to some degree. Though the house is the primary stimulating factor for the paranormal happenings in "The Captain's Guest," it is the captain's spirit in Andy's body, attempting to right a wrong from his own life, that changes Andy for the worse.

20. "Echo"

(Dramatized by Merwin Gerard;
Directed by John Newland;
Airdate: June 2, 1959)

SYNOPSIS: Paul Marlin is legally exonerated for the murder of his wealthy wife, Julie, and he flees town to escape the violent past. While staying at a quaint hotel, Paul experiences a vision of a gunman opening fire and killing him where he sits ... but is the assassin (seen only in the mirror) real or imagined? And is this strange gunman aware of something Paul Marlin is keeping a safely guarded secret?

GUEST CAST: Ross Martin (Paul Marlin), Edward Kemmer (Roger), Leslie Barrett (Daniel), Rusty Lane, Edna M. Holland, Edmund Glover, Jim Reppert.

COMMENTARY: A guilty conscience is at work again in "Echo," a tense human drama about murder, betrayal, lies and guilt. The story is a reiteration of the "Image of Death" ethos; specifically, that those who commit moral wrongs receive their comeuppance (or just desserts), often from a psychic force of justice that seems to intervene at the appropriate time and place. The guilty man in this story is a wife murderer named Paul Marlin (Ross Martin, of *The Wild Wild West* [1965–69]), and he is one of those twitchy-looking characters who always seems to be looking over his shoulder, so much so that one suspects he has not even acknowledged to himself that he is guilty of the crime for which he was accused.

The "Echo" referred to in the title is Paul's vision in the hotel looking-glass: a murder committed in his very hotel room. Ironically, he is witnessing not his wife's death (which he committed himself), but his own. In a sense, this phenomenon qualifies as *clairvoyance* (literally seeing the future), though the term "clairvoyance" today often refers to information about the future garnered through means not necessarily limited to the visual spectrum.

More provocative in "Echo" than the message of death and revenge, however, is the medium from which it emerges: the mirror. In horror films and television, the mirror is often considered a portal to other dimensions (*Prince of Darkness* [1987], *Poltergeist III* [1988], *Beyond Reality*: "Mirror, Mirror" [1992]), but it is also frequently a symbol of identity found, lost, regained or manipulated. In "Dreamland," *The X-Files* sixth season story in which Agent Mulder trades bodies with bureaucrat Michael McKean, the mirror comes to symbolize Mulder's loss of identity. In one side of the mirror he is himself (David Duchovny), but on the other side he is McKean — a buffoon. Even though Mulder is still Mulder to himself, the world now views him in quite a different way, and the mirror makes that fact plainly visible. In *The Twilight Zone* episode called "The Mirror," the looking glass is used in another way. It reflects the paranoia of a fearful dictator (Peter Falk) who believes he is going to be assassinated. The looking glass shows the leader's trusted advisers sneaking up on him, threatening him. Eventually, the mirror's warped vision causes the dictator to kill all of his friends and become an isolated, insane figure.

The mirror is put to interesting, if similar use in "Echo." It reflects Paul's future — his very ending — symbolizing perhaps that Paul sees himself as a murderer worthy of punishment even though he has escaped man's justice. Another "bad" man would see his end come in the reflection of a mirror in the later *One Step Beyond* episode "The Clown."

21. "Front Runner"

(Dramatized by Larry Marcus; Directed by John Newland;
Airdate: June 9, 1959)

SYNOPSIS: A dying jockey, Ronnie Watson, recounts a strange story to a reporter from the *Chronicle*: He once cheated his beloved mentor, Sam Barry, out of an important victory on the racetrack because his girlfriend, Rita, had left him for the older man. Years later, Sam Barry exacted bizarre revenge of sorts when he cost Ronnie Watson a win on the track as well. Oddly, Sam Barry had died in Uruguay during a steeplechase the day before the race in which he successfully challenged Watson...

GUEST CAST: Ben Cooper (Ronnie Watson), Walter Burke (Sam Barry), Sandy Kenyon, Carmen Phillips, Rita Lupino, Jerry Hausner, Phil Chambers, J. Edward McKinley.

COMMENTARY: Those pesky scales of justice are righted once more in Larry Marcus' "Front Runner," a story of a friendship gone sour and of a revenge that stretches from beyond the grave. As with "The Dark Room," *One Step Beyond*'s "Front Runner" trades on the notion of an apparition, the spirit of a dead man who comes back from the dead, still obsessed with incidents that occurred during his life. This episode is different from "The Dark Room" and others not so much in its depiction of psychic phenomena, but in all the surrounding details. This story occurs in the cutthroat world of horse racing, features a deathbed confession, and involves a mentor-apprentice spat over the love of a woman. In this case, all the innovation has seemingly gone into the melodrama rather than the psychical research, so it is no surprise that "Front Runner" seems a bit dull and uninteresting when compared to some of *One Step Beyond*'s other entries. Remember that, according to series creator Merwin Gerard, there were only fifteen legitimate stories to tell involving psychic phenomena. Thus repetition can occasionally be seen creeping into *One Step Beyond* in various installments that fail to break new ground. After the high suspense and interesting stories of "The Burning Girl," "The Haunted U-Boat" and "Image of Death," the series was seemingly settling into a groove at the end of its first season. All shows near the end of the freshman outing, including excellent entries like "The Haunted U-Boat" and "Image of Death," and even more mediocre fare like "Echo" and "Front Runner," concerned the comeuppance: revenge from beyond the grave. And all feature a protagonist who is guilty of some crime, whether it be Nazism, adultery, murder or, as in "Front Runner," cheating. The idea of setting an episode on a claustrophobic submarine enlivens "The Haunted U-Boat," and the sheer hysteria of "Image of Death" makes that show endlessly interesting, but "Front Runner" feels humdrum in comparison.

Though this author found no direct evidence of the exact incident described in "Front Runner" (probably because names were changed and dates rearranged), the universe of horse racing has not been without psychic phenomena. British Professor of Experimental Physics John Hasted once recounted this story of the Melbourne Cup in Australia:

> The owner of one of the horses had a dream in which he saw his horse winning the Melbourne Cup two weeks later. But there was something curious in the dream: His jockey was wearing a black armband. He [the owner] repeated the dream to several people, so it was well-documented. Well, the dream did not, in a sense, come true because although the jockey did win the Melbourne Cup on his horse and was wearing a black armband, the owner did not see him — because he had died in the intervening two weeks. The armband was for *his* death.[17]

That sounds creepy enough to be a *One Step Beyond* episode, doesn't it?

The world of the jockey would later be the subject matter of *The Twilight Zone* in 1963's "The Last Night of a Jockey," starring Mickey Rooney.

22. "The Riddle"

(Dramatized by Larry Marcus;
Directed by John Newland;
Airdate: June 16, 1959)

SYNOPSIS: During a train ride in India, a married American man, Len Barrett, starts to behave strangely — seemingly terrified and angered by an old villager carrying a rooster in a cage. Len leaves the train to pursue the old man, Khumar, and Len's wife follows, terrified by her spouse's uncharacteristic behavior. When a dangerous confrontation ensues, a local lawman explains to Mrs. Barrett about a strange love triangle that ended violently on the very day that Len Barrett was born, July 17, 1925.

GUEST CAST: Warren Stevens (Len Barrett), Bethel Leslie (Mrs. Barrett), Barry Atwater, Patrick Westwood, Arthur Batanides, Leonard Strong.

COMMENTARY: For those who believe that the last breath of one human life becomes the first breath of another, as John Newland succinctly describes the concept in his narration for this episode, "The Riddle" is a story to cherish. The topic for debate is, of course, *reincarnation*, and it is one that has been handled with much controversy and intelligence in films, such as Robert Wise's *Audrey Rose* (1977), and TV episodes, such as "The Field Where I Died" on *The X-Files* and "Echoes of Evil" on *Beyond Reality*.

A major tenet of the religious movement known as Buddhism, reincarnation is believed by many in the world (more than an eighth of the planet's population) to be a simple fact of life. For instance, Buddhists believe in the *samsara*, a cycle of reincarnation that sees people die and then be reborn until they learn the lessons of the Buddha and attain a state of bliss known as Nirvana. The way to stop the cycle of life and death and reach this paradise of bliss is to follow "The Middle Way," or "The Eightfold Path of Living," a kind of Buddhist equivalent of the ten commandments. How to follow those rules? Well, one must keep the right company, understand what life is really all about, maintain right behavior, curb passions in "right effort" and so forth. Like all religions then, Buddhism offers what is apparently a guide by which people can choose to live, a code of morality wherein there is a reward at the end (Nirvana) for maintaining the principles of a good and righteous life.

Interestingly, reincarnation is a belief that has spread through the United States in recent years not only through Hollywood's fascination with Buddhism, but through a "new" facet of hypnosis known as *past-life regression*. In this manner, psychologists regress patients back to a time before their current lives and discover, apparently, previous existences wrought with psychological turmoil. There have been numerous reports of people who drowned in a previous life and therefore find bodies of water terrifying in their current existence, and so forth. Shirley MacLaine, author of *Out on a Limb*, is one celebrity proponent of reincarnation; but she is not alone, because a Gallup poll conducted in 1982 established that more than 30 percent of Americans believed in reincarnation.

Despite this belief, there is not yet an objective consensus on reincarnation or the belief that past-life regression is a valid scientific or psychological tool. And many scientists and professional skeptics suspect that less-than-honorable psychologists have actually planted these so-called past-life memories into their patients through a clever bit of trickery and pointed questioning.

Considering that Buddhism began in India, it is perhaps appropriate that *One Step Beyond*'s first study of reincarnation, "The Riddle," be set in that country. The drama of "The Riddle" finds an average American businessman, Len Barrett (Warren Stevens, of *Forbidden Planet* [1956] and *Star Trek*: "By Any Other Name"), suddenly consumed with hatred for an old villager in Calcutta who brings a chicken into his train compartment. The moment of revelation occurs late in the story when it is learned that the villager, Khumar, killed an artist named Ranjit on July 17, 1925 — the very day that Len Barrett was born. The inference, of course, is that the soul of Ranjit was reborn in Len, and that this wayward American soul would never have realized the truth of his past had he not taken the Bombay-Calcutta run and found himself at the home place of his previous identity.

In *One Step Beyond*, reincarnation plays very much like possession, as Len starts to act like the blind artist Ranjit and is consumed with murderous rage for Khumar. Len's poor wife is left to puzzle out the situation with the help of a friendly constable who understands the whole story, but ultimately there is nothing that can be done to save Mr. Barrett. Len has not learned the lessons of his past life and so is doomed to repeat the samsara, the wheel of rebirth, until he does. "The Riddle" very accurately depicts the tenets of reincarnation, although there are some controversies about just how long it takes for an identity to be reborn. Some people believe it is a simultaneous transfer (as depicted in "The Riddle" and the film *Audrey Rose*), and that a life passes between bodies one moment to the next, but others believe that reincarnation need not be so immediate a phenomenon, that generations may pass before a specific soul is reborn.

Is there any real evidence of reincarnation? It all depends on what one considers to be evidence, apparently. There are certainly documented stories that are difficult to dismiss out of hand. "The Riddle" tells of a happening in India, but in "real life" there was an interesting, documented case in Alaska:

> Victor Vincent was a Tlingit Indian living on one of the small islands off Alaska's southern coast. In 1946, when he knew he was dying, he told his beloved niece Mrs. Corliss Chotkin that he would be reborn as her next son and that she would know this by two scars the child would receive from him. Vincent had a livid, one-inch surgical scar on his back and a less distinct scar at the base of his nose. A year-and-a-half later, Mrs.

Chotkin gave birth to Corliss, Jr., who has two birthmarks that exactly match the scars on Vincent's body.[18]

The same story reviews other bizarre similarities that resemble those depicted in "The Riddle." Corliss Jr., the alleged reincarnation of Victor Vincent, was reportedly able to "spontaneously" recognize people on the street whom he had known in his past life (just as Len Barrett recognizes Khumar). Allegedly, he also spoke like Victor (with a stutter). As John Newland might say ... explain it, we cannot; disprove it, we cannot.

"The Riddle" is a fine climax to the first season of *One Step Beyond*, a mystery that involves the viewer from the first moment to the last. Efficiently directed with tight two-shots and close-ups, and also well cast, this episode artfully explores the possibility of hate at first sight, that a pain from a previous life could be so powerful that it would reach out and consume a new life. And because reincarnation had not yet been handled on the series, "The Riddle" feels much more fresh than "Front Runner" or "Echo," two recent "comeuppance" stories.

SEASON TWO (1959–60)

Cast and Credits

CAST: John Newland (Our Guide to the World of the Unknown).

CREW: *Producer:* Collier Young. *Series Created by the Associate Producer:* Merwin Gerard. *Special Consultant:* Ivan Klapper. *Executive Writer:* Larry Marcus. *Director of Photography:* William A. Horning. *Art Directors:* Phil Barber, George W. Davis, Feild Gray. *Film Editor:* Henry Berman. *Music:* Harry Lubin. *Assistant Directors (various episodes):* Donald C. Klune, Tom McCrory, Robert Saunders. *Set Decorators:* Henry Grace, Jack Miles. *Recording Supervisor:* Franklin Milton. *Script Supervisor:* Jane Ficker. *Make-up:* William Tuttle. A Joseph M. Schenck Enterprises, ABC Films Presentation. Filmed at Metro-Goldwyn-Mayer Studios, Hollywood, U.S.A.

The Episodes

23. "Delusion"

(Dramatized by Larry Marcus; Directed by John Newland;
Airdate: September 15, 1959)

SYNOPSIS: Tidy little accountant Harold Stern donated blood some 31 times and then mysteriously changed his name and dropped out of sight.

Now a girl named Marta is dying, requiring Stern's rare blood type, and the police demand that he donate his blood again. Stern refuses to cooperate with the authorities and then makes a startling admission: He believes he forms a psychic link with all those with whom he shares blood. When he saves Marta from a gas leak in her apartment, Harold invites the young girl to move in with him so he can keep a close eye on her and make certain that the same tragic fate does not befall her.

GUEST CAST: Norman Lloyd (Harold Stern), Suzanne Pleshette (Martha Wiczinski/Marta Lynn), David White (Lt. Barry), John Brennan, George Mitchell, Marjorie Bennett.

COMMENTARY: "Delusion" is a perfect example of the manner in which *One Step Beyond* truly came to mature and develop more intricate stories the longer it remained on the air. Though the plot involves a *psychic link* (the mental connection between blood donor Harold Stern and those with whom he shares hemoglobin), the tale reveals an unexpected wrinkle at the climax, becoming a meditation on obsessive love rather than a simple exploration of a paranormal phenomenon. Here, as in many second season *One Step Beyond* stories, the characterizations are of paramount importance.

Accordingly, "Delusion" commences as a portrait of Harold Stern (Norman Lloyd of *St. Elsewhere* and *Star Trek: The Next Generation*: "The Chase"), a man of rare blood-type who is terrified that the police will seek him out and ask him to give blood again. When this eventuality does occur, Stern reluctantly reveals his fear that something terrible will happen to the recipients of his blood, and that he will psychically see all of it in advance (making him another prominent *One Step Beyond* Cassandra). To buttress his point, Stern has even kept the newspaper clippings proving that those who shared his blood have died or suffered. This focus on the clippings, as well as Stern's miserly attitude (he is an accountant obsessed with numbers) seem to indicate that he suffers from a malady not unlike obsessive-compulsive disorder. Stern is a man trapped in his own paranoia and "delusion" of doom.

Not believing Stern's wild story, the police (led by *Bewitched*'s [1964–72] Larry Tate, actor David White) lay it on pretty thick about the plight of poor Marta, the girl who now requires Stern's blood. They play her up to be an innocent child, and Stern eventually acquiesces to the transfusion. As it turns out, Marta Lynn is a 19-year-old woman and not quite the sweet little darling portrayed by the police. She has worked at the Kitten Club, a strip joint, and after the transfusion she immediately starts smoking again. A sultry trumpet on the soundtrack indicates that the older Stern is soon in love with Marta, and he invites her to live with him. Ostensibly this arrangement is so the old man can keep an eye on the girl with whom he has shared blood, but there is much more going on, just beneath the surface. Marta agrees to move in, and before long the two have developed an unhealthy relationship. Though he is attracted to her, Marta calls Stern "Grandpa" and falls for a young stud instead. Stern claims he is being protective of Marta only because of his record (that every recipient of his blood dies), but it is clear his interest in Marta is (at least subconsciously) sexual. Eventually, Stern kills Marta in a rage, making his prophecy of her death a self-fulfilling one! He was so obsessed with her safety (and with possessing her himself) that his concern led him to murder.

Clearly then, Harold Stern precipitates the death of Marta, the very death he had foreseen in psychic fashion. So was his dream of death merely an obsessive delusion brought on by his own compulsions, or actually a vision of the future, a *premonition?* "Delusion" offers no clear-cut answer, but, as usual, a case can be made for the psychic. After all, Stern does present evidence of his gift of insight (the newspaper clippings), and he does manage to save Marta from a gas leak in her apartment, preventing her accidental death. On the other hand, Stern might simply have read the newspaper, found that those who received donations had died, and built up an egotistical confabulation around those facts. Saving Marta from the gas leak would then be seen as mere coincidence, and her death at his hands a logical, if tragic, outcome, considering his dementia and delusions of grandeur. In fact, Harold Stern's efforts to save Marta could be seen as a way to make himself important (and to put himself in a position of control). He believes his blood is unique (and it is a rare type!), and that with this special blood comes some great power for seeing the future. Whatever Stern's real problem, whether it be psychological or parapsychological, he is one of the most complex people yet seen on *One Step Beyond.* He could be read as simply an older man desperate to save a life, or as lonely obsessive-compulsive paranoid trying to control his relationships.

Like so many episodes of *One Step Beyond,* "Delusion" is directed with a minimum of flash. It is composed primarily of two-shots and tight close-ups, so as to foster audience identification with the characters. And much of the drama in "Delusion" leads up to the moment when Stern is forced to donate blood, despite his fear of seeing another person die. This is an interesting switcheroo for *One Step Beyond* because the revelation of the psychic component usually comes late in the half hour, as understanding of a situation finally dawns. In "Delusion" the story dictates otherwise: Stern must describe his fear (for the audience's sake) and then

watch as his own behavior makes that fear play out. The different structure, coupled with good acting, makes "Delusion" quite a good show.

When asked about the climax of "Delusion," in which Marta is killed
by Stern, John Newland recalled that he had ordered Lloyd to "strangle her
good." However, the print of "Delusion" this author viewed ended in very
abbreviated, abrupt fashion, with Lloyd just barely making contact with
actress Pleshette. Newland could not recall if this was a rare instance of
network interference (in which a cut was demanded), or simply an example of local stations tampering with the show because of time constraints.
Despite "strangling her good," Newland does recall that Pleshette really
gave her all in the role of Marta, and reported that she was one of the best
actresses he ever had the pleasure of working with.

Perhaps "Delusion" is really a meditation on *self-fulfilling prophecy*, a
term that describes an individual's ability to shape fate to a preordained
(usually negative) outcome. As the man caught in a web of his own making, Norman Lloyd is an extraordinary presence. A veteran of such motion
pictures as *The Unseen* (1945), *Beginning of the End* (1947), *Audrey Rose*
(1977) and the contemporary science fiction TV series *Seven Days* (1998–
), Norman Lloyd also has the distinction of directing some of the best and
most memorable episodes of *Alfred Hitchcock Presents*, including "Man
from the South" (with Steve McQueen and Peter Lorre) and "The Jar," a
Ray Bradbury story.

24. "Ordeal on Locust Street"
(Dramatized by Michael Plant; Directed by John Newland;
Airdate: September 22, 1959)

SYNOPSIS: Inside a dark house, the Parrish family hides a terrible
secret: Jason, their horribly deformed son, is responsible for the family's
collapse into petty squabbling. Hoping to preserve her family, Mrs. Parrish enlists the help of Dr. Brown, a famous hypnotist who believes in the
power of the "mind force," to help cure the monstrous son who sits silently
upstairs in the red velvet chair.

GUEST CAST: Augusta Dabney (Margaret Parrish), David Lewis (Dr.
Edward Brown), Suzanne Lloyd (Anna Parrish), Bart Burns (George Parrish), Jim Kirkwood, Jr. (Danny), Gary Campbell (Jason Parrish).

COMMENTARY: In the 1990s *The X-Files* gave the viewing world
many of the most memorable and horrifying genetic deformities ever seen
in genre television. There was Tooms in "Squeeze": the liver-eating, long-
lived man capable of elongating and stretching his body. There were the

Brothers Peacock in "Home": inbred siblings more animal than man. There was the Fluke Man in "The Host": a worm-human hybrid created from the radiation of Chernobyl. In the seventh season of *The X-Files* there was even a man-shark hybrid who worked (and preyed on victims) at a fast-food restaurant. Before this memorable gallery of monsters and mutants roared across TV screens nationwide, *One Step Beyond* offered its own take on genetic deformity in the dark tale called "Ordeal on Locust Street."

The tale begins simply enough with the tantalizing information that the Parrish family has lived in its dark house for a year ... but never invited any neighbors or visitors inside. The rich set design reveals a house crowded with details and objects; the feeling of a real home and a real family is forged instantly. Then the subject of Jason, a young sibling, is raised, along with a series of questions. Is he a human being? A monster? Does he belong in the house or in the sea, as one character suggests?

Much of "Ordeal on Locust Street" plays on the horror inherent in those questions and the suggestion of how horrid a mutant Jason really is. Wisely, the camera does not ever reveal Jason in his entirety, instead granting only teasing visual hints about his hideous appearance. When Dr. Brown arrives to hypnotize Jason, Newland's camera assume's Jason's point of view. Dr. Brown addresses the subjective camera, talking directly to Jason (and to the audience). He then asks to see Jason's hands and the camera tilts down just enough to reveal two scaly, misshapen things that could be fins. That glimpse of Jason's startling physical nature is all the viewer gets to see of "the creature upstairs," but it is quite horrifying in its implications. Though the special effects budget of the series at the time would not permit the creation of a convincing full-body suit, Newland was not deterred by the limitation. "It was more effective to leave it to the imagination," he affirmed. "We showed the fish man's hands and we thought that was enough."

So for the first time in the *One Step Beyond* episode roster there is a "monster" and a story revolving around a monster. As is typical, however, the monster turns out to be an accident of nature, a gentle creature who longs only to be loved. Jason may appear a monster on the outside, but inside he is "human," making "Ordeal on Locust Street" another example of that favorite genre TV fable: "Don't judge a book by its cover." On later shows, such as *The Twilight Zone* ("Eye of the Beholder"), *Lost in Space* ("The Golden Man"), *Star Trek* ("The Devil in the Dark") and even *The X-Files* ("The Post-Modern Prometheus"), so-called monsters would be viewed with empathy, and *One Step Beyond*'s "Ordeal on Locust Street" is an early example of that trend. And in keeping with *One Step Beyond*'s obsession for truth and at least a veneer of scientific accuracy, the nature of the Jason Parrish mutant — a hybrid of fish and man — was based on "the genetic fact that a fetus goes through levels of phylogenetic development."[19] This same theory of a throwback to a previous stage of genetic development (also known as *atavism*) was also the subject of a *Star Trek: The Next Generation* seventh season episode in 1994. In "Genesis," poor Counselor Troi (Marina Sirtis) was forced to find sanctuary in a bathtub as her DNA was rewritten to a phylogenetic stage of evolution. In *Prophecy* (1979), a monster movie directed by John Frankenheimer, methyl mercury poisoning caused fetuses to become horribly deformed, remaining at a primitive stage of evolution.

In addition to predating the genetic deformities of *The X-Files*, starting the trend on TV to view monsters as creatures worthy of empathy, and offering a semi-plausible explanation for Jason's bizarre nature, "Ordeal on Locust Street" also trades on another psychological concept, particularly *hypnosis*. Originally known as magnetism or *mesmerism* (after its most prominent early proponent, Franz Mesmer of Vienna), hypnosis was thought for a long time to be an altered state of consciousness that was somehow related to psychic powers. It is no longer held to be mystical at all, but rather a tool for relaxation. So its prominence in this *One Step Beyond* episode points to the fact that society's understanding of hypnosis has changed considerably since 1959. Though "Ordeal on Locust Street" rightly points out that while in a hypnotic state certain subjects can seem immune to pain, its final conclusion, that Jason can — through hypnosis and mind over matter — appear physically normal to other sighted individuals, is a real stretch of credibility. In this case, as in others, *One Step Beyond* builds an "if-then" style of argument. It hopes to persuade by stating, in this case, that if hypnotism can induce the mind to ignore pain, then it can also induce the mind to change one's very physical nature. This solution is an *extreme* exaggeration of the *somatic bridge*, a form of self-therapy that causes patients to see their physical pain as a message from the inner mind. When they understand the message, they heal the pain. Still, there is no "inner message" to a genetic deformity — only a fact of biology, so "The Ordeal on Locust Street" is certainly out on a limb of believability.

That stated, "Ordeal on Locust Street" is also one of *Alcoa Presents'* most effective segments and most oft-remembered shows. It boasts strong gothic overtones (a dark house, a family secret, a hideous thing hiding upstairs), a message beneath the characterization (that what is good is not necessarily beautiful), and not a little bit of the creeps, courtesy of Jason's secret nature. Though it features an antiquated and exaggerated view of both biology and the powers of hypnotism, it remains touching because, at heart, it is the story of a mother who fears losing her special-needs son and must weigh that fear against the possibility of destroying her whole family. And because it points to many *X-Files* stories, "Ordeal on Locust Street" can rightly be termed ahead of its time in the arena of televised science fiction and horror drama, if not scientific accuracy.

25. "Brainwave"
(Dramatized by Charles Beaumont and Larry Marcus; Directed by John Newland; Airdate: October 6, 1959)

SYNOPSIS: A navy pharmacist's mate serving in the Pacific in World War II is shattered when his pacifist physician brother is killed in action. When the commander of his ship is badly injured in combat, the mourning Harris must overcome his crisis of faith and perform surgery. At a critical moment in the procedure, Harris—a medical novice—is assisted by the voice of a dead man.

GUEST CAST: George Grizzard (Pharmacist's Mate Harris), Tod Andrews (Lt. Commander Stacy), Whit Bissell (Commander Will Feeley), Bob Osborne, Raymond Bailey, Harry Harrey, Jr., Bob Alabama Davis.

COMMENTARY: "Brainwave" lands on *One Step Beyond* courtesy of the collaboration between staff writer Larry Marcus and one of the most celebrated names in TV horror and science fiction: Charles Beaumont. "The Hunger," "The Vanishing American," and "Black Country" are just a few of the memorable short stories penned by this prolific author (and gathered in his 1957 Bantam Book *The Hunger and Other Stories: A Collection of Violent Entertainments*). On *The Twilight Zone* Beaumont was a prolific source of creativity, and he wrote some of the most memorable episodes, including "Perchance to Dream" (based on his short story of the same name), "Elegy," "Long Live Walter Jameson," "A Nice Place to Visit," "The Howling Man," "Static," "The Prime Mover," "Long Distance Call" (with Bill Idelson), "The Jungle," "Dead Man's Shoes," "The Fugitive," "Persons or Persons Unknown," "In His Image," "Valley of the Shadow," "Miniature," "Printer's Devil," "Passage on the Lady Ann," "Living Doll," "Number 12 Looks Just Like You," and "Queen of the Nile" (with Jerry Sohl). In all, Beaumont's output on *The Twilight Zone* was more than 20 shows, a staggering accomplishment. Somehow, between these many *Twilight Zone* assignments, Beaumont also managed to find time to team with Marcus for "Brainwave" on *One Step Beyond*, a tale concerning communication with the dead, as well as the first season's "Captain's Guests."

A story of redemption and faith, "Brainwave's" protagonist is a man named Harris who has resorted to alcoholism after the combat death of his brother, whom he once goaded into volunteering for the war effort. For Harris, there is nothing left in this life but his own death, and no belief that there is anything beyond that end. The story comes full circle, of course, when Harris communicates with Dr. Madison during a complicated surgery, despite the fact that Dr. Madison died early in the operation when his own vessel took a direct hit from enemy bombers. This "voice from beyond the grave" restores Harris's faith in an afterlife and a better world. For some viewers, such a set-up may smack of *Touched by an Angel*, but the schmaltz factor is low in "Brainwave," specifically because the episode has a gritty quality to it. Newland's cameras could not actually detail the specifics of a bloody emergency operation, so instead his camera lingers on close-ups of sweaty, desperate faces trying to save another human life. The military veneer of the story, with Whit Bissell (*I Was a Teenage Werewolf* [1957], *I Was a Teenage Frankenstein* [1957], *The Time Tunnel* [1966] and *Star Trek*: "The Trouble with Tribbles" [1967]) lending solid support as a hard-bitten commanding officer, also limits the episode's sentimentalist tendencies, even though the word "miracle" is brought up at least once.

"Brainwave" reflects two critical *One Step Beyond* story standards. The first involves the setting: World War II. As Newland states in this episode, there were many bizarre accounts from the war that were "not reported," and that "the sea was once filled with death." "Brainwave" was neither the first nor the last *One Step Beyond* episode to feature the sea and a wartime drama. Secondly, "Brainwave" remembers the lesson of "Epilogue," that an alcoholic is a promising protagonist for any drama involving belief and disbelief, since hallucinations, delusions, black-outs and the like are all part of the alcoholic symptomatology. The question here is this: Is Harris an alcoholic prone to hallucinations, or did he genuinely have a paranormal experience?

If "Brainwave" seems a little skimpy, it may be because so much stock footage of naval battles and swooping airplanes dominates the half hour. Also, it seems a bit odd (from a structural standpoint) that Harris should hear the voice of a relatively anonymous dead officer rather than the words of his own dead brother. One might have expected a sibling psychic connection instead of the one presented. But, again, *One Step Beyond* tried to avoid the predictable whenever possible.

26. "Doomsday"
(Dramatized by Larry Marcus; Directed by John Newland;
Airdate: October 13, 1959)

SYNOPSIS: In the 1600s the eldest son of the wealthy Earl of Donamoor lay dying from the Black Plague while the woman who loves him is accused of witchcraft in the matter. As the innocent woman is dragged to her public execution (by fire), she issues a curse damning the eldest son of every generation to die before his father, the Earl. Eight generations later the curse is still working its dark magic on William, the son of an Earl who is wasting away on his deathbed. Will the old Earl die first, ending the curse once and for all, or will the day end with the death of the eldest son first and then his father?

GUEST CAST: Torin Thatcher (Earl of Donamoor), Donald Harron (Jamie/William), Edward Atienza (Doctor), Fintan Meyler, Pat Michon (Catherine), Patrick O'Moore, Lumsden Hare, Beryl Machin.

COMMENTARY: Curse or coincidence? That is the choice one has to make in analyzing "Doomsday," a suspenseful *One Step Beyond* episode with a sense of icy precision and irony. Did the eldest boys in eight generations die young by mere happenstance (the odds of which are 3 billion to one, according to host Newland's narration) or by the design of a witch who expired hundreds of years ago when burned at the stake? It is certainly an interesting question to ponder because the episode itself makes it fairly plain that the young woman wrongly set aflame by the nasty Earl is not really a witch at all. She is completely innocent of that crime. And she only invokes "the curse" because her trial has been a sham, a miscarriage of justice. Knowing that her death will come no matter what the facts of the case, her final revenge is to put the fear of God into the Earl of Donamoor. Ironically, her words do become reality. Of this incident one might point to that old friend "cosmic justice," a benevolent overseer of the universe who assures that a wrong done is eventually punished. However, in the case of "Doomsday," it is not really the guilty who suffers, but his children, his grandchildren, and his progeny for generations to come. This does not seem like a situation where the punishment fits the crime. It would have been more appropriate, cosmically speaking, for the original Earl also to be accused of witchcraft and burned at the stake rathen than see his innocent offspring suffer untimely deaths. So, as a "comeuppance" story, "Doomsday" targets the wrong people.

And what of "the curse"? Certainly there is very little scientific evidence to support a belief that a human being can curse another one. Even the famous King Tut curse has recently been "outed" as a sham cooked up by an overeager journalist hoping to sell more copy. But if curses are superstitious bunk, then perhaps Catherine's dying utterance is actually an example of some mind-directed power: the ability to influence others through the power of suggestion. Still, for a suggestion to be so powerful that it goes on for eight generations is a bit remarkable.

Then again, ideas are like diseases, they spread and grow stronger over time. For instance, imagine that the first new Earl of Donamoor remembered the curse of death and shared the story with his eldest son. That boy probably believed the legend (in no small part because his father did) and became frightened by it, eventually dying of some natural or so-called "normal" tragedy. By the time the next Earl came into adulthood and power, the myth of the curse was cemented as true, because there was a previous example of death, and consequently an even more frightening story was passed on to the eldest offspring. Were the eldest sons and the earls of Donamoor merely poisoned by their fears and superstitions? That is one possible answer.

"Doomsday" has one of the most wickedly delightful trick endings of all *One Step Beyond* tales. Young William, the eldest son living in fear, is told by his wife that his father, the Earl, has finally passed away. Though sad at his father's demise, Will realizes that the multi-generational spell has broken. He has outlived his father, and the curse is over. So, relieved, William ventures into the Earl's room, unaware that his wife was actually lying to him. William is thus startled when the Earl, still hanging onto life, bolts up in his bed. Shocked and terrified, William trips backwards and falls off a ledge to his death far below. A chill-inducing ending to be certain, but an infinitely memorable one as well.

A multigenerational story that follows the curse from origination in the Middle Ages to contemporary reprise, "Doomsday" is notable too for a guest appearance by Torin Thatcher, an imposing actor with a booming voice and villainous screen presence. He has appeared in *The Seventh Voyage of Sinbad* (1958), *Star Trek*: "The Return of the Archons," *Voyage to the Bottom of the Sea* (1964–68): "The Secret of the Loch" and *Lost in Space* (1965–68): "The Space Trader." He makes a particularly nasty Earl, but one wishes that his children did not have to pay for his merciless attitude.

27. "Night of the Kill"

(Dramatized by Merwin Gerard; Directed by John Newland;
Airdate: October 20, 1959)

SYNOPSIS: Little Davey Morris has been lost in the woods for four days while 150 neighbors search desperately for him. When the boy is found safe and sound on a high, rocky outcropping, he claims that he was protected by a giant and hairy mysterious friend. This friend, a Bigfoot-type creature, soon returns to check on his ward, but is met only with hostility by Mr. Morris and the locals. They hunt the creature down and attempt to burn him in his cavernous lair.

GUEST CAST: Fred Beir, Ann McCrea, Dennis Holmes, John Marley, Tim Graham.

COMMENTARY: Just a few episodes after "Ordeal on Locust Street," *One Step Beyond* returns to the idea of a monster, this time that most famous of legendary creatures believed to live in North America, Big Foot (or Sasquatch). And, like "Ordeal on Locust Street," "Night of the Kill" adopts a stance of tolerance and compassion in dealing with a "monster" that some people believe is dangerous just because it is different. "Too often it is our way to fear what we don't understand," Newland comments near the close of the episode, after the audience has witnessed merciless hunters burn out the creature they believe is trapped, helpless, in a dark cave.

Unlike "Ordeal on Locust Street," however, there is not even a fleeting glimpse of the monster in "Night of the Kill." Instead, it is defined solely by its actions. It rescues Davey, a boy who has been lost for four days, and protects him in a rocky nest high above the earth (a place the boy could not possibly have reached himself). The creature has also taken food from the smokehouse and left giant footprints in the mud near the family homestead. And some people seem to recognize the creature's presence by a distinct odor, a musky animal smell that fills the air. The beast is also reported as walking upright, being tall as a man, and not being at all afraid of humans. Though the creature is never named "Bigfoot" in the episode itself, *One Step Beyond* attempts to stay true to the lore of the most believable Big Foot sightings.

For the most part, Bigfoot has been "seen" in the Pacific Northwest, and "Night of the Kill" is clearly set in that region of North America. The giant footprint in the mud, the only "tangible" evidence of most Bigfoot sightings, is also carried over into this drama, with the replete oohs and aahs over size and shape of the abnormally large print. Most Sasquatch (literally "Hairy Giant") sightings also seem to indicate that the creature is nearly seven feet tall and weighs somewhere in the neighborhood of 500 pounds. The creature of "Night of the Kill," though never seen, seems to match these dimensions, since it is capable of peering directly in second story windows and placing little Davey high out of danger on a mountainside.

Over the years there have been many Bigfoot sightings, including one near Chesterfield, Ohio, in 1902, which established a four-toed monster with a foot 22 inches long and seven inches wide.[20] In 1955 in the British Columbia town of Tete Jaune Cache, a witness named William Roe also reported an encounter with a Sasquatch creature in what could have been a scene straight from "Night of the Kill":

> ...it came across the clearing directly towards me. My first impression was of a huge man, maybe six feet tall, almost three feet wide, and probably weighing somewhere near 300 pounds. It was covered from head to foot with dark brown silvertipped hair.... Its arms were much thicker than a man's arms, and longer, reaching almost to its knees. Its feet were broader proportionately than a man's, about five inches wide at the front and tapering to much thinner heels.[21]

This eyewitness report tallies with others in the field of "Bigfoot" research, but it is rather disappointing that even today, in the new Millennium, there has been no "step beyond" these relatively undependable first-person sightings. No Sasquatch has ever been captured and no "spy" satellite has ever caught one on film (that we know of, anyway).

Interestingly, there is not even one word about psychic phenomena in "Night of the Kill," and instead this episode tackles the terrain *The X-Files* would later inhabit, opting to simply explore the unexplained. Even "Ordeal on Locust Street" had a psychic-oriented component (hypnotism), but "Night of the Kill" eschews that background and emerges as one of the most unique installments of *One Step Beyond*.

Like so many *One Step Beyond* stories, "Night of the Kill" begins with the normal, a little boy lost, and then escalates straight into weirdness like a rocket achieving escape velocity. The opening portions of the episode concern the search for little Davey as 150 neighbors fan out across the area, even though hope has faded that he will be found. In these early scenes there is no dialogue, only somber music over the gathering of searchers in the field, perhaps because the scene does not really require words. The actors' faces reveal that the search has failed and that things are getting desperate. From that almost documentary-style beginning, the episode cross-cuts from searcher to searcher, each coming up short, each on the verge of exhaustion. When the boy finally is found, in a place he could not possibly have climbed to, the "inexplicable" component of the story arrives front and center. How did Davey survive? Who put him up in that perch on the rocks? The boy claims that he has made a "friend" in the man-beast who took care of him, but the boy is not unlike that familiar *One Step Beyond* character type, the Cassandra. He is young and therefore (like alcoholics, former mental patients and silly women) easy to dismiss. When the boy is proven right about the existence of the beast, the adults can only think of killing the animal, and the didactic thread of the episode finally becomes clear. In going from documentary-like examination of a crisis to the revelation of a monster and finally to a moral standpoint, *One Step Beyond* again shows a flair for complicated story telling, equally as impressive as that seen on *The Twilight Zone*.

Bigfoot has still not been validated as a "real" creature, and society seems less concerned with him than it was in the past. The Sasquatch really had his heyday in the late 1960s and 1970s when a new film on the shaggy monster seemed to be released every day. *Big Foot* (1969) with John Carradine, *Sasquatch* (1977), and the pseudodocumentary *Legend of Boggy Creek* (1973) are just a few such examples. On TV, Bigfoot became a high paid guest star when he combatted *The Six Million Dollar Man* (1974–78) and *The Bionic Woman* (1976–78) on ABC TV. Strangely, these bionic shows purported that Bigfoot (played by actor Ted Cassidy) was actually a bionic robot from outer space! In the late 1980s a popular movie from Steven Spielberg called *Harry and the Hendersons* (1987) also recounted the story of a family befriended by a benevolent creature, much like the Bigfoot of legend. Once again, *One Step Beyond* might legitimately be called ahead of the curve in terms of content.

28. "The Inheritance"

(Dramatized by Larry Marcus; Directed by John Newland;
Airdate: October 27, 1959)

SYNOPSIS: An aging countess dies, strangled to death by her seemingly sentient diamond necklace. After her death the necklace passes to a new owner, an heir, and continues its murderous legacy. Through it all a gold-digging boyfriend plots to steal the jewels and get rich. He finally gets the necklace and offers it as a gift to his young mistress ... with terrifying results.

GUEST CAST: Sean McClory (Mario), Jan Miner (Grace), Estelita Rodriguez (Nina), Iphigenie Castiglioni (The Countess), Jose Gonzales, Robert Tafur, John Verros.

COMMENTARY: "The Inheritance" opens not with John Newland on the sidelines as simple narrator, but in the center of the action at hand. As the episode commences, we are told (by voice-over) that John Newland was recently on vacation in Mexico City when he heard a strange story at a local watering hole. Then the camera actually focuses on the tidy Newland in the dark restaurant as he meets a drunk who tells him the horrifying tale of the monster necklace. This is an odd way to begin an episode, and there is an uncomfortable artificiality about it. It is just plain hard to believe that this story really came to Newland in such fashion, and the opening moments of "The Inheritance" suffer for it. The decision to make Newland "part" of the actual story probably came from a few factors. The first fact was that the ratings of *One Step Beyond* skyrocketed whenever Newland played a larger part on-screen, so it is not surprising that in the second season of the show Newland had expanded roles in "The Inheritance," "Delia" and "Vanishing Point." Secondly, as *One Step Beyond* became more and more popular on TV, Newland was stopped wherever he went and met by people who did, indeed, have strange stories to tell him. So while it is doubtful that the tale of a malevolent necklace ever *really* came to Newland from an eyewitness in Mexico, "The Inheritance" nonetheless reflects the truth that people around the country (and world, in fact) were starting to regard the TV star as an expert on the paranormal and sharing their stories with him.

Since Newland is an on-screen player in the drama at the commencement of "The Inheritance," this episode offers the opportunity to comment on his unique screen presence. Newland is a tall, slim man with an unusually graceful carriage; he seems to glide when he walks. He is earnest in demeanor and precise in speech and diction. More importantly, Newland seems to take everything he hears very seriously, revealing an open, inquisitive mind. Most importantly, however, Newland boasts a tell tale sparkle in his eyes that suggests he loves a good scare as much as the next guy. Much of *One Step Beyond*'s enduring appeal is that Newland marshals these personal qualities (inquisitiveness, open-mindedness and sardonic delight) to his role as narrator (and to his sense of style as a director). Rather than the rat-a-tat-tat delivery of Rod Serling or the overblown pomposity of Alfred Hitchcock, Newland comes across in his monologues as quite laconic, and he is just as likely to punctuate his narration with a wicked smile, a shrug of the shoulders, or a sincere question as a simple explanation for what has come before. "Who knows?" he is often heard to ask at the end of an "inexplicable" tale on *One Step Beyond*. It is almost as if he has stated his case (the paranormal) but is open to any thoughtful interpretations. That casual attitude makes the whole psychic kit-and-caboodle wash down a bit smoother than on a TV series that tries to attack the viewer, head-on, with claims of "truth" and "reality" (like the quasi-newsroom approach of *Sightings*). So the opening of "The Inheritance" is a bit silly, with the pristine Newland entering a hole-in-the-wall bar in poor Mexico, but it does take advantage of Newland's "star qualities" at the same time that it genuflects to the fact that by the second season he had unwittingly become an expert in *One Step Beyond*'s subject matter to the general populace.

The central story of "The Inheritance" that follows Newland's sojourn to Mexico City is not one likely to be found in a legitimate parapsychology report. It concerns a diamond necklace with a malevolent life of its own (it moves of its own free will in two separate stop-motion shots!). At one point the necklace, of its own volition, curls up like a snake coiling. It is a frightening moment to be sure, but the idea of a cursed antique (apparently imprinted with the Countess' evil spirit) is one that seems more at home on a purely supernatural or horror oriented TV show. Indeed, the concept of cursed antiques passing from owner to owner, wreaking havoc, was later the central premise of the syndicated Paramount hit *Friday the 13th: The Series* (1987–1990). That stated, "The Inheritance" is a creepy little show and a change of pace for *One Step Beyond*. A case for legitimacy is made at the end of the episode when Newland reports that a woman in Brighton, England, was strangled by a string of pearls, but no further documentation about that case (or the case of the Countess) is provided.

It is not difficult to discern that the real subject of "The Inheritance" is not psychic phenomena, but materialism, or, simply, greed. An insincere Romeo romances an older woman just for her extravagant wealth. When she dies, her gold-digging boyfriend pursues the plain-jane servant who has inherited the fortune, inadvertently killing her with the necklace. The face has changed but his modus operandi remains the same. From there the 180-diamond inheritance goes to Mario's young mistress, Nina. In all cases, Marios' greed has been at issue. The necklace seems to have a hypnotizing effect on those who wear it, as money often does, and Mario sees it only as a thing that will take him where he wants to go. In the end the necklace causes Mario to lose Nina, the one woman he legitimately cares for. And, in a "comeuppance"-style finale, Mario ends up at an asylum for nine years, driven insane by his vision of the sentient necklace. All in all, a satisfying, if didactic, tale about the pursuit of things at the expense of real love.

An unusual show for its weird opening and its out-and-out supernatural premise, "The Inheritance" is a spine-tingling affair for *One Step Beyond*. Don't watch it alone at night, because you will never look at jewelry the same way again.

29. "The Open Window"
(Dramatized by Larry Marcus; Directed by John Newland;
Airdate: November 3, 1959)

SYNOPSIS: A struggling magazine artist in Greenwich village spies a woman gassing herself in the hotel room across from his own, but when he tries to prevent the suicide attempt he learns that the woman he "saw" has not checked into the hotel at all! The artist continues to witness the bizarre suicide attempt, again and again, until time finally catches up with his prescient psychic vision.

GUEST CAST: Michael Higgins (Tony March), Louise Fletcher (Jeannie), Charles F. Seel, Lori March, James Seay, Elizabeth York.

COMMENTARY: The window is a perfect object for *One Step Beyond* to construct an episode around. As a whole, this anthology TV series seeks to be a window or a portal to the unknown, and "The Open Window" literalizes that metaphor by landing a strange psychic vision just across an alley, through an open window. And just as one might also consider the television set to be a window into another world (both are square boxes; both are view ports into other places; and both feature a wealth of "stories" beyond their parameters), the window in Tony's apartment serves the identical function. It grants access to another time and place, in this case the galaxy of the paranormal. Accordingly, much of the episode is rendered in deep focus, with Tony's apartment in the foreground and the window and mysterious tenant of the other apartment in the background, behind the framed "box" of the window. In other words, the audience is given a view of Tony viewing the other apartment. Importantly, what occurs behind that window is very much like a TV show permanently set on rerun mode: a constant loop of a woman going about the preliminaries of her own death.

This comparison between the world of television and this psychic phenomenon is even extended to the dialogue of "The Open Window" when a hotel manager notes that running his establishment is "better" than watching TV. That is, he finds his hotel as interesting to "watch" as he does television. Tony could make the same argument.

By comparing Tony's startling "peek" into the world across the street and the viewer's "peek" into the TV world, *One Step Beyond* seems to tender a comment on man's voyeuristic impulses, and even his tendency to believe what his eyes tell him, whether it be on the tube in the living room or occurring as "real" across the street. At the time "The Open Window" was produced, TV was still relatively young, and the overall effect of transmitting stories into the family living room was still not fully known. Indeed, the effects are not fully understood now, which is why presidential candidates such as John McCain have suggested that the surgeon general of the United States needs to conduct an investigation on the very subject. "The Open Window" seems to demonstrate a fear that TV will make man less sympathetic to the lives of others. The impulse to watch, to be a voyeur, may become more important than the need to interact, to help. This fear is epitomized in the hotel manager's blasé attitude: He is more interested in the comings and goings of the hotel denizens than the possibility that someone may have died in one of his rooms.

Tony is also a "watcher" at first, at least before he bursts into action to save a life. He even declares that he "wants to see something exciting" to help him develop as an artist. And then, as the image is rerun, he comes to fear his sanity — a selfish reaction, perhaps, caused by the numbing effect of his witnessing the suicide attempt in rerun mode multiple times. "The Open Window" is quite interesting in this social subtext, though it is also reminiscent of Alfred Hitchcock's *Rear Window*.

All manner of excuses are made about the psychic phenomenon that occurs in "The Open Window." Has the Cassandra of the Week (Tony) had too much to drink (another example of alcoholism rendering a man's eyewitness account invalid)? Has he had a recurring nightmare? Has he witnessed a mirage due to "temperature inversion"? Or has time somehow skipped a groove, allowing the future to appear in the present? The latter appears the most likely, and that would be a solution also suggested in stories such as "Delia" and "I Saw You Tomorrow." However, rather than generalizing the concept (the universe altered time to save one woman), one could also make a case that Tony had a premonition: a view of the future that appeared in the present.

"The Open Window" is significant historically for an early appearance by Louise Fletcher, the 1975 Academy Award winner for best actress in *One Flew Over the Cuckoo's Nest*. Nubile and charming in "The Open Window," Fletcher spends most of the episode cavorting about Tony's apartment in a skimpy bathing suit! Fletcher has become a favorite in the genre for films such as *Brainstorm* (1980), the notorious *Exorcist II: The Heretic* (1977), and her many appearances on *Star Trek: Deep Space Nine* (1993–1999) as the evil Bajoran religious figure Kai Winn.

On top of its interesting comments on voyeurism, "The Open Window" also dramatizes the sexist attitude of the time it was produced, as happened from time to time on *One Step Beyond*. When Tony asks his doctor friend how his patients stand his arrogant attitude, the doctor replies with all seriousness, "Because I always deliver boys." One can't help but wonder what Gloria Steinem would make of that remark.

30. "Message from Clara"

(Dramatized by Larry Marcus; Directed by John Newland;
Airdate: November 10, 1959)

SYNOPSIS: A woman teaching English to a group of adult immigrants is given a cameo brooch by one of her students, a butcher from the

"Old Country," and suddenly she starts writing in a strange language she has no knowledge of. In fact, Miss Morrison is writing in the words of a woman, Clara, who has been dead for five years ... a murder victim. But why is Clara communicating, and what does she have to say?

GUEST CAST: Barbara Baxley (Miss Morrison), Robert Ellenstein (Mr. Tomachek), Celia Lovsky, Oscar Bergeri Jr., Renata Vanna.

COMMENTARY: How can a person write a passage in a language that he or she does not understand and has never studied? In the annals of the paranormal, the answer to that question would surely include a reference to the phenomenon known as *psychic* or *automatic writing:* the unique ability to write messages without conscious knowledge (or even control) of the content. In "Message from Clara" poor teacher Miss Morrison receives a gift, a piece of jewelry, that spurs within her the automatic messages of a dead girl, Clara. "Message from Clara" emerges as a clever episode not only because it accurately depicts *automatic writing,* a strange form of mediumship, but because it leads viewers on a merry path of misdirection.

At first the immigrant butcher Tomachek seems kind and loving. He admires Miss Morrison, and he gives her the gift of the brooch. There is no reason to suspect him. When Miss Morrison suddenly "seizes" and begins to write in the language and style of a girl from the "Old Country" who has been dead for five years, the viewer assumes the story is going to be another *One Step Beyond* romance. In particular, one assumes that Tomachek's lover, Clara, has returned from the grave to send a message of love to her man in mourning. The climax of "Message from Clara" tricks viewers, however, when the message is finally translated. "He is out there.... He will kill you!" are the very words from beyond the grave, and sure enough, Tomachek is revealed to be a freak who "loved" and murdered Clara and would like nothing more than to do the same thing to Miss Morrison. This is a genuine — and creepy revelation — and an unexpected culmination to the story.

"Message from Clara" includes a great performance by Robert Ellenstein (last seen as the Captain in "The Navigator") as the crazy Tomachek, and also a new arrangement of Harry Lubin's chilling "Fear" music. In this case the theme is rendered with human voices chanting, and the effect makes the skin crawl with trepidation.

Automatic writing was also the subject of the premiere episode of *The Sixth Sense* ("I Do Not Belong to the Human World") and an important plot element of the Stephen King novel *The Dark Half.* In that novel the cryptic warning "the sparrows are flying again" came unconsciously to a writer who suffered from a murderous alter ego.

31. "Forked Lightning"

(Dramatized by Merwin Gerard; Directed by John Newland;
Airdate: November 17, 1959)

SYNOPSIS: As a storm gathers high above the city, forked lightning spurs a double premonition in disparate individuals. One woman, Ellen Chambers, dreams of her husband's death at the bank where he works, and a widower caring for his wheelchair-bound daughter realizes his own death will occur on that very day.

GUEST CAST: Alex Peters (Ralph Nelson), Frank Maxwell (George Chambers), Roberta Haynes (Ellen Chambers), Candy Moore, Robert B. Williams, Logan Field, Frank Behrens, James Nolan, Peter Walker.

COMMENTARY: In a rare flirtation with nihilism, *One Step Beyond* presents the thoroughly depressing episode called "Forked Lightning." The story presents a variety of sympathetic characters (including a disabled child) and then confronts them with tragic fates as the mechanisms of destiny and a double premonition lead inexorably to disaster.

In an approach that seems almost to border on sadism, the day-to-day travails of a widower named Alex Peters are dramatized in "Forked Lightning." He has suffered a stroke and simultaneously experienced a vision of his own death that very day. This vision makes him desperate because he does not have the necessary amount of money in savings to take care of his crippled daughter in the event of his demise. He seeks to set up a trust fund, but cannot do it. He seeks to buy more life insurance, but has to wait for a physical examination in a few days before the money can be his. He faces uncaring bureaucracies in grim-faced fashion, the camera recording all of it dispassionately, and keeps coming up empty for his poor daughter. Finally, in desperation, he is reduced to robbing a bank. This is the act that precipitates his death and leaves his daughter *sans* a father and the resources to survive!

If that is not depressing enough, there is the parallel story of Ellen (another Cassandra character) who loves her husband very much and warns him not to go to work that day at the bank because of a vision of his death. He ignores her advice (partially because he has stolen money from the bank and needs to cover up his crime) and consequently ends up dead as well. Ellen, like the poor disabled child, is left in mourning at the conclusion of "Forked Lightning." Maybe a deal should have been brokered so Ellen could adopt the Peters girl!

Superbly directed by Newland and compelling throughout, "Forked Lightning" is worthwhile, despite its steadfast grimness. It looks again at the interesting concept of a self-fulfilling prophecy. Had Alex Peters not seen a vision of his own death, he would not have faced the bureaucracies on that day, felt frustrated, and ended up in an angry shoot-out at the bank. "Forked Lightning" also acknowledges that sometimes fate cannot be escaped.

In some *One Step Beyond* tales, understanding is forged and disaster is averted. Not so in "Forked Lightning," which has the courage to follow its depressing convictions all the way through to the finale. It may not be a fun show, but its tale of "psychic lightning" striking two individuals simultaneously, and the manner in which their fates cross, is well written by Merwin Gerard (whose teleplay captures a feeling of desperation so strong it is almost tactile) and well handled by the production team.

The tale of a bank robbery that ends in disaster for everyone involved was recently handled on *The X-Files* in an episode of its sixth season called "Monday." Its subject was not double premonitions, but a repeating time-loop that ended in the deaths of Mulder, Scully and a bank full of customers.

32. "Reunion"

(Dramatized by Larry Marcus;
Directed by John Newland;
Airdate: November 24, 1959)

SYNOPSIS: In September of 1939 a group of macho German glider pilots and their beautiful young groupie, Helga, promise to meet again and share a joyous reunion on the first Sunday after World War II has ended. One man, Peter, is jealous of Helga's friendship with pilot Hans, and he kills Hans just before the glider is swept away on a final flight. The glider with Hans' corpse aboard disappears for years behind a row of trees, only to return mysteriously for that post-war reunion...

GUEST CAST: Paul Carr (Peter), Betsy Von Furstenberg (Helga), Rory Harrity (Hans), Page Slattery (Theo).

COMMENTARY: Jealousy rears its ugly head in "Reunion," another "comeuppance"-style *One Step Beyond* account that witnesses a guilty man (Peter) apparently condemned by the universal "scales of justice" for his nefarious deed (murder) and eventually exposed for his crime (thereby eating his "just desserts"). The jealous man in "Reunion" is Peter (actor Paul Carr, of *Voyage to the Bottom of the Sea* and *Star Trek*: "Where No Man Has Gone Before"), a guy in love with Helga who worries incessantly that the more studly Hans will take that love away. In a moment of pure rage in 1939, Peter kills Hans before a flight, leaves his body in the glider cockpit, and hopes that the aircraft will crash into the nearby mountains, thus obscuring the murder. Instead, the glider modulates trajectory, as if controlled by some living source, and then disappears until that fateful Sunday some six years later, after the war.

When the dead Hans (or the mechanism of fate) finally lands the glider at the post-war reunion, it is a grinning skeleton who returns in the cockpit. Is Hans' ghoulish return merely a coincidence or fortuitous timing? Or does the glider's return on the precise date or the reunion signify the hand of another force? Is this merely an instance of *synchronicity* (the belief that there are no accidents or coincidences in life, only interconnected events) at work again? "Reunion" makes no real claim either way. And, regardless of the answer, there is a moral grounding in "Reunion" to leave TV audiences feeling secure: The bad Peter gets his comeuppance.

Some of the specific details make "Reunion" an interesting story. When Hans wants to go flying, initially just for an hour, Peter admonishes him that one of his hours "can go on for days." At the climax, Hans' "hour" has actually turned into years, but he (or *something*) lands his glider anyway. In another fun moment, the pilots are warned about the deadly nature of the winds, another possible explanation for Hans' extended orbit: The wind merely carried the glider away for six years, then "returned" it at the appropriate time. Finally, "Reunion" earns its "comeuppance" stripes by depicting Peter as a really nasty guy and one deserving of an unhappy end. By the climax of the show there is no doubt that Helga is with the wrong fellow. Not only has she selected a murderer as a boyfriend, but an abusive spouse as well. "Do you think you're still the little girl who used to fix us picnics?" Peter snaps at her in one nasty instance. In that moment the true nature of Peter's crime becomes plain: He killed Hans over a relationship he eventually loses interest in himself.

Perhaps the most effective moment in "Reunion" occurs just after Peter has killed Hans. Hans' corpse is tucked away silently in the glider cockpit, nobody knows about it, and then the car that is supposed to drag the glider into the air will not start. There is a pause, and eventually the vehicle does start after another attempt ... but for a moment the audience collectively holds its breath, wondering if Peter will be exposed. Why is it that audience members find themselves complicit with such a nasty character, even for a moment? This was some kind of psychological factor that Alfred Hitchcock was acutely aware of as a film director (as in the sequence in *Psycho* [1962] when, for an instant, Marion Crane's car stopped sinking — it's rear fender still visible — in Norman's favorite swamp; or when a brutish murderer had to retrieve incriminating evidence from the back of a potato truck in *Frenzy* [1972]). It is a side of human beings that isn't especially nice or pleasant, but apparently is part and parcel of our innate desire to see people get away with something. For whatever reason, this so-called moment of suspense works well in "Reunion," as does the rest of an episode about an ill wind that carries the accusing hand of fate back to a guilty man.

33. "Dead Ringer"
(Dramatized by Catherine Turney; Directed by John Newland; Airdate: December 1, 1959)

SYNOPSIS: Housewife Esther Quentin succumbs to a terrible fever and then experiences a vision in which she sees her twin sister commit arson by burning down an orphanage. Now Esther must prove to the doctors and police that the mental picture she witnessed is no delusion.

GUEST CAST: Norma Crane (Esther Quentin), Grant Williams (Bill Quentin), Ed Prentiss (Dr. Parks), Olive Blakeney.

COMMENTARY: Twins. The world seems to be fascinated with them, perhaps because it seems unfathomable to human beings, a race that prides themselves on individuality, that biology could create a "double," a carbon copy. Though twins obviously have their own minds and own personalities quite separate from one another, there is still something a tad creepy about the fact that nature would knowingly engineer "a set": two beings who resemble each other to such a degree that individual detection is sometimes impossible. The physical similarity among twins has led to much speculation among the scientific community about what other attributes two like-siblings might share. Would they share the same pain (as in the famous Corsican Brothers scenario, later dramatized in a third season *One Step Beyond* episode known as "The Trap")? The same thoughts? The same motivations? The same morals?

Speculation of that sort is the gas that propels "Dead Ringer," a tense yarn about unwitting psychic connection between separate twins. One commits a crime; the other becomes aware of it. As is usual, the percipient of the psychic experience is a woman (and thus easier to dismiss in the male-dominated 1950s), the doctors and authorities serve as naysayers, and there is even another mitigating factor (the psychic vision came during a fever and can thus be dismissed handily as hallucination, delusion or sickness). Grant Williams, who plays the concerned husband in "Dead Ringer," had already had a previous rendezvous with the bizarre prior to this episode of *One Step Beyond*: He was the star of *The Incredible Shrinking Man* (1957), one of the all-time great science fiction films.

In 1988 there was another story of twins entangled in a freaky situation in the similarly titled David Cronenberg feature *Dead Ringers.*

34. "The Stone Cutter"

(Dramatized by Gail Ingram; Directed by John Newland;
Airdate: December 8, 1959)

SYNOPSIS: A businessman, estranged from his father, returns home to Maine when a stone cutter named Menzies predicts his dad's impending death. The son, who has been running away from his family for years, must now contend with his father's terminal condition, as well as the stone cutter's gravestone (which lists the day of his father's death as ... today!). When Lockhart confronts the strange stone cutter, he discovers another alarming gravestone.

GUEST CAST: Joe Mantell (Stan Lockhart), Walter Burke (Menzies), Arthur Shields, Don Beddoe, Chet Stratton, Robert Lieb, Dick Reeves.

COMMENTARY: Everyone has a birth date. Everyone has a death date. Those are two inescapable facts of human nature: We live, we die and the span in-between is bracketed on tombstones by those two dates. "The Stone Cutter" recounts the tale of Menzies, a man who usurps nature by carving the tombstone, complete with death date, before the intended customer has even passed away! So accurate are his "predictions" of death that many people fear this strange man. They believe in his power. As for Menzies, it is a simple matter of using the information he gets: "I carve the truth when I know it," he says innocently.

Though he is a primary character, "The Stone Cutter" is not really Menzies' story at all. Viewers are not granted access to his life, his most private thoughts, or even the reasons why he has been granted this unique (and not altogether pleasant) ability. Instead, the effect of Menzies' psychic power (of clairvoyance) on another family is of paramount importance, as a businessman named Stan Lockhart faces the inevitable fact that his father is going to die and that Menzies has predicted it. Stan blames Menzies for that fact, but deep down one senses that he actually blames himself for a lot of things. He is depicted as a selfish man who feels a high degree of guilt because he has not visited with his father for years. He grew up, became consumed with the business world and, for all intents and purposes, left his father behind in a small town. Sure, he sends his Dad money every month, but his father does not want money, he wants his son's company. In fact, Mr. Lockhart has used his son's money not to support himself, but to purchase for Stan all the things young Lockhart desired while growing up; things that the family could not afford to buy back then (a fishing rod, a wristwatch, etc.).

These are the details that make the "The Stone Cutter" particularly worthwhile: the human drama of a short-sighted man who wants more time with his father and, in time-honored fashion, blames the messenger (Menzies). What is even sadder than the distance that separates Lockhart and his dying father is that he wastes the last hour of his father's life railing against Menzies, essentially railing against the inevitability of death. He loses what precious time remains with his father in a futile attempt to stop the hand of fate.

Because Stan Lockhart is not a terribly likable character, one is tempted to pigeonhole "The Stone Cutter" as yet another tale of comeuppance (following in the footsteps of "Echo," "Image of Death," "Front Runner" and the like). When Stan flies off the handle, he kills Menzies, only to see that Menzies accurately predicted his own death date. Afterwards, "justice" catches up with him as Stan is executed by the State for the murder of Menzies. Despite Stan's unpleasant fate, there is never really the overriding impression that he is a bad man, only a little man, a self-involved man who looks to blame others for his own failings. Because Stan is a human character, an everyman in a sense, the story plays as one of lost opportunities rather than one of cosmic justice being meted.

Menzies' gift of being able to predict the "death date" of people is an example of psychic insight or precognition, the ability to see the future. A common affliction in *One Step Beyond*, it had already been seen in "Night of April 14," "Emergency Only" and several others.

35. "Father Image"
(Dramatized by Merwin Gerard; Directed by John Newland; Airdate: December 15, 1959)

SYNOPSIS: A man inherits the estate of his dead father and learns that the bequeath includes a Burlesque Theater closed down some thirty years ago. Venturing into the boarded-up establishment, Dan Gardner has an accident and subsequently an encounter with the psychic that sheds new light on his father's character, reveals a tempestuous relationship with a show girl, and the reasons why the old theater was never sold.

GUEST CAST: Jack Lord (Dan Gardner), Cece Whitney (Valerie), Ian Wolfe (Timothy Welton), Frank Scannell (Barker), George Selk.

COMMENTARY: "Father Image" stands its lead character in the ill-fitting shoes of his dead father and then has him walk around in them for a while. Part travel story, part psychic experience, part murder-mystery solved, the story is a compelling one that proves there are secrets in every family, and sometimes dark ones at that. In its tale of a chorus girl who died and who longs for justice, "Father Image" reiterates the themes of several episodes already dramatized (especially "The Haunted U-Boat"), once more causing one to remember Merwin Gerard's theory that there are only 15 "types" of psychic phenomena stories. In this case, "Father Image" evokes the possession of "Bride Possessed," in that the psychic phenomenon exists to reveal a hidden truth. It also is reminiscent of "Image of Death," in that a murder wrongly committed precipitates the spiritual unrest. And the idea that time has somehow "skipped a track" is seen in stories such as "The Open Window." Despite these familiarities, "Father Image" is among *One Step Beyond*'s most popular episodes, perhaps because it features Jack Lord, the intrepid Steve McGarrett of *Hawaii Five-0* (1968–80) and the first in a long line of actors to portray Felix Leiter (in *Dr. No* [1962]) in the long-running James Bond film series. A talented painter as well as actor, Lord passed away on January 21, 1998, but his fans still populate many web sites on the internet in which they honor his many performances, including his notable turn as Dan Gardner on *One Step Beyond*.

36. "Make Me Not a Witch"

(Dramatized by Gail Ingram; Directed by John Newland;
Airdate: December 22, 1959)

SYNOPSIS: A farmer's daughter inexplicably develops the ability to read minds, and her family fears she now has the Devil inside of her. The telepathic girl proves she is no evil witch, however, when she uses her unusual gift to rescue two lost hispanic children.

GUEST CAST: Patty McCormack (Amy Horvath), Robert Emhardt (Priest), Eileen Ryan (Ma), Leo Penn (Pa), Deena Gerard, Jimmy Baird, William Greene, Pedro Regas, Preston Hanson, Charlotte Knight.

COMMENTARY: Ignorance is the issue that "Make Me Not a Witch" tackles. Young Amy Horvath suddenly develops telepathy, the ability to hear the thoughts of those around her. To a priest, this development is a miracle, a gift from God, but to her parents, raised in rural, Christian America, this telepathic gift is only a curse, a sign of evil. In some senses, this dynamic is reminiscent of the family politics that informed the first season entry "The Burning Girl." There a bitter old aunt and a nasty father blamed his telekinetic daughter for the fires her mind inadvertently caused at times of extreme insecurity. Here Amy's parents are conservative and ignorant, and the point is hammered home again by *One Step Beyond* that psychic powers are often feared by those who cannot understand them. The resolution, which finds that psychic powers can be utilized to help people (including two lost children), is a validation of the series' basic belief that those things that are at first feared can in fact become precious and valuable tools when ignorance is cast aside and understanding is forged. That is a valuable message, though "Make Me Not a Witch" suffers from a resolution that feels a bit too tidy. Amy loses her power ("it was a gift just given for a little while") after saving the children, and her parents welcome her back home with no reservations. This seems an unusually "sugar-coated" climax for *One Step Beyond*, and it is hard to swallow the notion that two such ignorant people would welcome a girl they consider a witch back into their house (especially since the parents were not present when Amy read the mind of the comatose man and telepathically garnered the information necessary to save the children).

Tidy conclusion aside, "Make Me Not A Witch," does feature an interesting aspect of telepathy not visited before in *One Step Beyond*. Amy's ability to hear the thoughts of the comatose man in his native language, and then repeat that language, could be considered a form of *xenoglassy*, the speaking of a real language unknown by a person in his or her regular state of mind.

Guest star Patty McCormack (Amy Horvath) gives a sympathetic performance in "Make Me Not a Witch" and avid TV watchers may remember her from her appearances on *The Chevy Mystery Show* (1960–61) and *Playhouse 90* (1956–61), and her recurring role on *Mama* (1949–1956). Horror fans, however, will always associate the talented McCormack with her memorable performance as the evil child in the 1956 film thriller *The Bad Seed*. Veteran TV director Leo Penn also appears in "Make Me Not a Witch." Years after "Make Me Not a Witch," Penn directed the popular *Star Trek* episode "The Enemy Within."

37. "The Hand"

(Dramatized by Larry Marcus; Directed by John Newland;
Airdate: December 29, 1959)

SYNOPSIS: A lovelorn pianist named Tommy Grant lashes out at his promiscuous former girlfriend, stabbing her to death in a back alley with a broken bottle. Afterwards, the murderous musician literally can't seem to get the blood off his hands. This strange stigmata, visual evidence of

Tommy's guilt, eventually contributes to the pianist's mental and legal undoing.

GUEST CAST: Robert Loggia (Tommy Grant), Miriam Colon (Alma), Joseph Sullivan, Warren Parker, Pete Candoli, Bob Hopkins, John Zaremba, Patric McCaffrie, Dick Winslow.

COMMENTARY: The story of a guilty conscience that drives a killer to go "slowly bonkers" is one that *One Step Beyond* visited with memorable results in the first season episode "Image of Death." Nonetheless, the similarly-themed second season story called "The Hand" emerges as one of the best episodes of the series. It's a stylish *film noir*, and the production team on "The Hand" uses black-and-white photography to its utmost potential, while a seedy but compelling performance by Robert Loggia wraps it all up together in one eerie little package.

Rarely in television has the psychological impact of a brutal crime (on its perpetrator, no less) been rendered so visible and tangible. But, in this rather graphic story, Tom's murderous hand just won't stop bleeding … even though there is no visible wound. Some viewers may associate this bizarre fact with the Midas story (everything Tommy touches turns to *blood*) or, again, with the plight of Lady MacBeth (that the blood of a slain king just won't wash away). Regardless of the literary allusion it makes, "The Hand" takes its premise of a "guilt stigmata" and lends it a visual punch through the consistent use of bright whites in its compositions. In shadowy black-and-white photography, red blood appears almost like oil — black and thick. To accent Tom's crisis then, the episode is suffused with examples of pure bright white, so that the pianist's bloody hand will totally mar that "clean" color. Indeed, to many in our society the color white signifies things good, clean and pure, and Tom's crime assures that he no longer merits any of those descriptions. Accordingly then, Tommy infects every white object he touches with a nasty dark ooze — the thick swath of blood from his hand.

The first such disturbing image of infection occurs immediately after Tom has murdered the promiscuous Alma. He returns to his piano and his bloody fingerprints immediately stain the ivory keys. Even in the gray, neutral hue of black-and-white television, this is a disturbing and memorable image. Next, Tom's bloody hand splatters messy "darkness" on clean, white towels— another significant example of a surface of purity marred. And when Tom handles a newspaper to read the details of his own crime, another white object is shaded with pigments of his guilt. Finally, Tom sees a doctor to have his hand — now a beacon of his guilt — bandaged up, and once more the blood seeps through another clean, white filter. In a 25 minute show, these four instances of purity destroyed represent a significant motif and effective visual dramatization of Tommy's guilt.

Delightfully, the "purity" symbolism so prominent in "The Hand" is even carried over in a clever manner to the climax of the tale, in which Tommy finally breaks. He is to stand trial for Alma's death, but when he takes the witness stand he is asked to put his right hand on a Bible: perhaps the ultimate symbol of good and purity in Western society. Unable to face his own infection and desecration of the Holy Bible, Tommy cracks up and confesses all. In conjunction with the white and "pure" objects, the appearance of a Bible at the resolution of "The Hand" is a reminder to Tommy of a state of perfect grace and innocence he has lost. His guilty conscience is forcing the truth out of him in a neverending fountain of blood! It is a good use of symbolism, an artistic idea rarely seen in series television.

Newland's eye for artistic composition is also in evidence in "The Hand." In particular, the episode boasts one terrific deep-focus composition. Outside the bar a drunken Alma stands in the foreground, waiting for her man of the hour. From behind her (in the background of the shot) appears Tommy — watching and waiting. She is unaware of him, though not for long. The shot nicely captures victim and perpetrator, hunted and hunter, in one frame, and hints at the stalking and violence to come. Another highpoint of "The Hand" is the sultry piano score that underlines the story, an appropriate choice of instrumentation by Harry Lubin, considering Tommy's career.

Actor Robert Loggia captures the essence of Tommy Grant, a drunk little nobody of a man who is driven first to a crime of passion and then to a slow-boiling insanity. The rough-hewed Loggia is familiar to modern audiences for his varied performances in hits like *Jagged Edge* (1995) and *Independence Day* (1996), but "The Hand" is an interesting link to another of Loggia's most popular performances. In "The Hand" on *One Step Beyond*, Loggia plays a pianist, and the song "Chopsticks" is heard three times in the episode. In the most memorable sequence of the hit film *Big* (1989), Tom Hanks and Robert Loggia share a "dance" on a giant electronic piano to the tune of ... "Chopsticks." One can only hope that Loggia did not leave bloody footprints behind in that instance...

38. "The Justice Tree"

(Dramatized by Merwin Gerard; Directed by John Newland;
Airdate: January 5, 1960)

SYNOPSIS: In the arid southwest in 1948 a dangerous criminal commits murder, escapes a deadly car accident and ends up at the homestead of a widowed mother and her young son, Joey. An oak tree that has been dead for 70 years mysteriously comes back to life, as if to warn the family of the new danger in its midst.

GUEST CAST: Frank Overton (Calvin Gannis), Charles Herbert (Joey), Sallie Brophy (Mom).

COMMENTARY: *One Step Beyond* officially entered the 1960s with "The Justice Tree," an early example of the common television story (now a cliché) that this author has termed "The Single Woman in Jeopardy" dilemma. In this subgenre (inexplicably popular with science fiction and horror TV series) a single woman and her son are menaced by some kind of villain, only to be saved by the series' star. Gil Gerard rescued a mother and her boy from a rampaging satyr in "The Satyr" on *Buck Rogers in the 25th Century* (1979–1981). Richard Hatch (as Captain Apollo) rescued another mother/boy combination from a renegade Cylon in "The Lost Warrior." On *V* (1985–86), Marc Singer (as Resistance fighter Mike Donavan) saved a mother and her daughter from the alien Visitors in "The Wildcats." Interestingly, one might also make the case that the real "star" of *One Step Beyond* (the inexplicable or paranormal) saves Joey and his Mom in this atypical second season entry. Of course, "The Justice Tree" arrived on television much earlier than the other series episodes listed above, so it might rightly be seen as a progenitor of the cliché rather than subscriber. Still, in another important way, "The Justice Tree" is familiar stuff. It is the same animal as "The Haunted U-Boat" and "Image of Death": "the comeuppance" or "scales of justice" story in which a bad person is punished by psychic means. Here a nasty criminal sentenced to the gas chamber chases an innocent boy up a tree, unaware that this old oak was once the local "hangin' tree" and that it is all too eager to carry out his death sentence.

Stories like "The Justice Tree" fail or succeed on the development of suspense. If the stories are tense and populated with believable characters the story usually works. And, in fairness, that is the situation here. The setting is one of total isolation: the Great Southwest in 1948, particularly a region or desert Newland describes as "137 miles of nothing." The boy and his mother are palpably "alone," and then little Joey starts to piece together Calvin's true nature, a little at a time, noticing the handcuff "burns" on the criminal's wrists. In addition to the setting and slow-building realization of danger, there is a certain level of sexual attraction between the lonely widow and the dangerous criminal. This is not prominent, vulgar or overdone (it never is on *One Step Beyond*), but it is there. Finally, the details about the tree (its branches are very brittle and very dangerous, but the boy claims that it is his friend) set up the climax. All these elements make for a compelling half hour, even if the story elements are mostly recycled from other episodes.

"The Justice Tree" ends with the hangin' tree picking up its old habits and executing a condemned man. However, this is one finale that could easily be viewed in terms of coincidence rather than the paranormal. To wit: Much is made of the fact that the tree branches are brittle and dead, yet it still supports the boy's weight when he climbs it. That may simply be a matter of weight. The little boy could weigh no more than 50 pounds, but Calvin is a big man, easily weighing 170 pounds. So it is not at all impossible to believe that the tree would hold up for Joey and then, seconds later, crack for Calvin. It is not a matter of a sentient, selective tree so much as it is one of mass, weight and gravity. And though it is ironic that the tree was once a hanging' tree, that fact could also be viewed as coincidence. On the face of the story, "The Justice Tree" is easy to explain: A big, nasty criminal too heavy to be supported is killed while climbing a tree in pursuit of a child. Case closed. Of course, that answer is not nearly as much fun as the *other* answer, that the tree somehow understood it should kill the criminal. And, again, there is the specter of *synchronicity*, the haunting idea that there are no coincidences in life.

Star Trek fans will recognize Frank Overton in "The Justice Tree" as the actor who portrayed Elias Sandoval, the leader of Omicron Ceti III in the classic first season episode "This Side of Paradise." Charles Herbert, who plays stubborn and determined little Joey, also appeared as the son of Charles Aidman and Julia Adams in the first season *One Step Beyond* installment "Epilogue."

39. "Earthquake"

(Dramatized by Larry Marcus; Directed by John Newland;
Airdate: January 12, 1960)

SYNOPSIS: On a hot day in San Francisco in mid–April of 1916, a lowly hotel bellhop and recovering alcoholic, Herbert Perkins, has a vision of a devastating earthquake. He knows the exact time the quake will hit (5:13 A.M.), but his warnings go unheeded by hotel management, the local newspaper and other authorities. Perkins grows increasingly desperate as the moments tick down to the moment when the quake will strike.

GUEST CAST: David Opatoshu (Herbert Perkins), Olan Soule, Elvira Curci, Herb Vigran, Gregg Stewart, Wayne Mallory, Harry Ellerbe, Martin Garralaga, Oliver McGowan, Steve Fenton, Nora Marlowe.

COMMENTARY: The Cassandra Complex, the plight of the visionary who sees the future but whose warnings are ignored, returns with full force in "Earthquake," a *One Step Beyond* episode that, like "Night of April 14," tells two stories simultaneously: a personal one (about the prophet ignored and disbelieved) and an epic one (in this case, the total destruction of an American city). On the latter front, *One Step Beyond* could hardly have selected a more deadly historical disaster. In April of 1916 an earthquake of massive proportions (later believed to have registered over 8.2 on the Richter Scale) struck San Francisco. With an epicenter along the San Andreas fault, the earthquake was—and still is—the worst disaster ever to occur in a United States metropolis. Over 500 city blocks were destroyed, and 450 deaths occurred as a direct result of the quake. Importantly, the quake was only a part of the overall disaster: Flames also consumed much of the city because the tremors and quakes had shattered subterranean gas pipes and started an unstoppable conflagration. In the end, 10 kilometers were destroyed and San Francisco stood in ruins.

"Earthquake" puts the audience into the head of the only man in the world (or "the most important man in San Francisco," as Newland calls him) who has a foreknowledge of the approaching quake. He is Herbert Perkins (actor David Opatashu, of the *Star Trek* episode "A Taste of Armageddon" and *The Twilight Zone* story "King Nine Will Not Return"). Perkins is a modest bellhop who works at a ritzy hotel. While taking a quick break in a supply room, he has a startling vision of the world seemingly falling down in rubble around him (a remarkable special effects sequence that also incorporates stock footage of the chandelier falling from the ceiling in the first season episode "Premonition").

When Herbert reports what he saw, he is dismissed by hotel authorities and eventually fired. In this case, Herbert is a Cassandra who is especially easy to dismiss for a variety of reasons. Firstly, he was experiencing fainting spells from the intense heat shortly before his premonition, and was thus seen as "sick" (i.e., undependable) in the eyes of his employers. Secondly, he is a former alcoholic, and thus easy to dismiss as crazy from drink. Thirdly, he was just a lowly bell-hop ... why should "God" or the "Forces That Be" endow this guy with such critical foreknowledge? Regardless of why it happened, Herbert's vision of destruction is dismissed and he remains powerless to stop the earthquake.

At this point in "Earthquake" (and in the *One Step Beyond* series as a whole), a few questions have to be asked. First, why is it that psychic visions always seem to come to those who are especially difficult to believe (mental patients, alcoholics, "silly" women)? And second, is it just a fact of human nature that prevents people from believing in such stories, regardless of the personality qualities of the messenger? Third, and most provocatively, why do so many terrible disasters (the earthquake in "Earthquake," the sinking of the Titanic in "Night of April 14") spur intense psychic phenomenon (*and* occur in mid–April!)? If not directly raised by "Earthquake," these questions all float to the surface on a more thorough examination of the episode. Not surprisingly, no real answers are forthcoming ... because there are no answers to give.

As "Earthquake" ends, Newland stands in front of a city aflame and reiterates the commonly held allegation that psychic phenomena seem to accelerate in frequency before great disasters occur. As corroboration, he tells the (verified) story of a strange telegraph message received in Ogden, Utah, a full four hours before the beginning of the earthquake. The message requested first aid supplies and assistance. Goosebumps anybody?

40. "Forests of the Night"
(Dramatized by Catherine Turney; Directed by John Newland;
Airdate: January 19, 1960)

SYNOPSIS: While rained in at a cabin on a weekend hunting trip, three friends carelessly play a Chinese occult game involving Confucius' "Book of Changes" and other strange spells. In this unusual Chinese game, Ted's icon is that of a tiger ... and he soon takes on the unmistakable characteristics of a wild feline.

GUEST CAST: Alfred Ryder (Ted Doliver), Mark Roberts (Pete), Douglas Dick (Alec), Stacy Graham (Mrs. Doliver), John Damler.

COMMENTARY: That all living things, from bats to birds, from humans to hippos, have their own distinct and recognizable spiritual essence is an element of a system of beliefs sometimes known as *animism*. "Forests of the Night" is an exploration of the idea that a tiger's feral essence could be transferred into a civilized man via the auspices of Chinese mysticism. In particular, a magic game brought back by China, a book of games, requires that Ted Doliver (Alfred Ryder of "The Devil's Laughter") renounce his humanity to play. "I will undergo change," he announces as part of the game, indicating that he will become "that which he is not," a tiger, specifically. From there, "Forests of the Night" depicts the strange changes in Ted's behavior as he goes on the prowl, infused with the spirit of a predatory cat.

More than adhering to any particular paranormal concept, "Forests of the Night" pays homage to the long-cherished Western belief that what is foreign is also strange; that what is foreign is also dangerous. Here a fear that Chinese mysticism may hold transformative powers dominates the episode. The real message is that arrogant Americans should not carelessly play around with the dangerous beliefs of a non–Western culture. That message plays out in semi-ridiculous fashion as Ryder grooms himself in imitation of a cat, hunts on all fours, comes to depend more on his sense of smell, and exhibits the other telltale attributes of a tiger.

The character touches interwoven through "Forests of the Night" demonstrate again that *One Step Beyond* was not afraid to feature less-than-likable protagonists. Ted Doliver is an interesting part for Ryder to essay because Doliver seems to enjoy his transformation into beast. Ted *likes* the idea that everything is afraid of him, that he is master of the jungle and king of the wild. Ryder's screen presence includes a healthy dose of arrogance when necessary, and he puts it to good use in this narrative.

"Forests of the Night" also boasts some unusually literate touches. Its very title quotes from poet William Blake ("Tiger, Tiger burning bright in the Forests of the Night") and at one point in the segment Rudyard Kipling is referenced as well ("For I am the cat who walks by himself and no one is a friend to me"). These meditations on catdom are appropriate in a story about the regal and individual nature of the feline, and they give the tale a veneer of the intellectual in a story obsessed with instinct and the call of the wild.

"Forests of the Night" takes the work of Chinese philosopher and spiritual leader Confucius as its starting point on a tale of transformation. Confucius did author *The Book of Changes*, a work on divination, but much of his writing on the supernatural was often misinterpreted or mistranslated (to be correct) by scholars in the early part of the 20th century. For though Confucius believed in the world of spirits, he also believed that to understand that world, one must first understand the world of man.

41. "Call from Tomorrow"

(Dramatized by Gabrielle Upton; Directed by John Newland;
Airdate: January 26, 1960)

SYNOPSIS: A famous stage actress, Helena Stacey, returns to her home in New York City full of fear and grief because of a terrible accident: Her daughter Didi died when struck by a car on a busy road. Cast in *Othello* as Desdemona by her director-husband, Helena begins to fear for her sanity when she hears the terrified cries of a child again and again. Is she losing her mind or is Helena experiencing a psychic call for help?

GUEST CAST: Margaret Phillips (Helena Stacey), Arthur Franz (Kevin), Mervyn Vye, Ben Hammer, Emily Lawrence, Daryn Hinton.

COMMENTARY: Familiar series elements dominate "Call from Tomorrow" as another fractured marriage hangs in the balance and an unstable woman with serious grief issues is perpetually disbelieved by her doubting spouse. For Helena Stacey the situation is serious. She has just recovered from a nervous breakdown, she has lost her dear child, and now she wants to "play act" at an "insane little game" that there is nothing wrong or bad in her life. This plan is damaged seriously when Helena starts to experience *clairaudio*, a close cousin of clairvoyance: the distinct hearing (rather than seeing) of things and events yet to come. In this case Helena is not hearing the cries of her dead daughter (who wandered into a busy street in pursuit of the family cat), but those of a lost little girl backstage who will meet the same unpleasant fate as Didi if Helen does not heed the voices in her head. The episode reaches a fever pitch as cries of "Mama!" are heard repetitively, and poor Helena is again driven to the brink of insanity.

This *One Step Beyond* episode also offers the usual science vs. paranormal debate, this time pitting the explanation of tinatus and abnormal hearing against the paranormal possibility of clairaudio. It also employs another allusion to Shakespeare: Just as Helena is at odds with her husband, she portrays Desdemona on stage, another woman at *serious* odds with her husband. Though the allusion is employed in only half-interesting fashion, it does add a layer of interest to events that seem somewhat familiar. In fact, "Call from Tomorrow" is reminiscent of several *One Step Beyond* episodes. Though it is interesting to center an episode around the concept of clairaudio, it is an unfortunate choice to drag out once again all the old standbys (the disbeliever, the scientific explanations, the damaged woman with history of insanity, et al).

42. "Who Are You?"
(Dramatized by Merwin Gerard; Directed by John Newland;
Airdate: February 2, 1960)

SYNOPSIS: Helen Mason is in mourning over the death of her child, Alice, and far across town another girl named Laurie is dying of scarlet fever. Laurie unexpectedly awakens from her feverish state, healed of the deadly disease, and travels across town to find Helen — whom she insists is her own mother! Can Alice, in the body of Laurie, revive a catatonic mother in grieving? And what of the real Laurie? Is she free to live again or will she be forever possessed by the spirit of Alice?

GUEST CAST: Philip Beurneuf (Carl Mason), Anna Lee (Helen

Mason), Reba Waters (Laurie), Phyllis Hill, Ross Ellicott, Mike Keene, King Calder, John Lormer, Jacqueline De Wit.

COMMENTARY: The explicit message of "The Bride Possessed" (that possession can serve a positive purpose) is given a more sentimental tweak in "Who Are You?" as a dead child's soul fills the spirit of a living child to save a mother in grief. A tear-jerker through and through, "Who Are You?" also displays *One Step Beyond*'s more spiritual side. In fact, "Who Are You?" proves with some validity (as does "Goodbye Grandpa") that, in addition to giving birth to *The X-Files*, *Sightings* and the like, it also fathered the *Highway to Heaven* (1984–1988) and *Touched by an Angel* (1994) school of television drama wherein "miracles" bring healing and love to people made despondent by the rigors of life. To that assertion, some genre experts may simply say "blecch!" Indeed, the syrupy charms of *Touched by an Angel* are not to everybody's tastes or liking. It is a series that plays on false sentimentality, a deep misunderstanding of Christian tenets (angels are not human beings doing good so as to earn their wings), and a propensity for schmaltz. Importantly, what differentiates *One Step Beyond* from these later shows is not subject matter but tenor and execution. *One Step Beyond* fosters a sense of real sentiment but does not push for maudlin melodrama at the expense of good storytelling. In other words, there is a degree of restraint in *One Step Beyond* stories such as "Who Are You?" that makes them tolerable rather than retch-worthy. The same efficient approach to directing that keeps *One Step Beyond* from veering into histrionic, over-the-top horror saves the show from overdosing on saccharine. Also, *One Step Beyond* has the dignity and unbiased approach to tell its upbeat and more inspirational tales outside the parameters of any particular religious faith. *Touched by an Angel* is tethered to, and therefore limited by, its Christian-based mission of "born again" storytelling.

Despite its inspirational tenor and heartfelt determination to save a family in distress, "Who Are You?" hits a sour note at its climax. The possession of Laurie (by Alice) ends when Helen becomes pregnant. The spirit of Alice is apparently no longer needed now that there is a bun in the oven. The inadvertent message of this timing seems to be that when it gets right down to it, a child *can* be replaced. Though a new life certainly gives Helen Mason something "positive" to live for, one assumes it will never take away the hurt caused by Alice's demise. The pregnancy angle of "Who Are You?" is a false lift, an attempt to provide an optimistic ending.

43. "The Day the World Wept: The Lincoln Story"
(Dramatized by Larry Marcus; Directed by John Newland;
Airdate: February 9, 1960)

SYNOPSIS: *One Step Beyond* offers an examination of the psychic phenomena surrounding the assassination of President Abraham Lincoln. Even as the beloved President has troubling dreams of his own death, people all around America become almost subconsciously aware that a tragedy is occurring. A printer in East Pennsylvania, for instance, hammers out a headline hours before the assassination: Lincoln murdered–NATIONAL TRAGEDY.

GUEST CAST: Barry Atwater (President Abraham Lincoln), Jeanne Bates (Mary Lincoln), Justice Watson, Amy Douglass, Tom Middleton, Jonathan Nole, Theodore Newton, Eric Sinclair, Riza Royce, Norman Leavitt, Robert S. Carson, Watson Downs.

COMMENTARY: When possessed of special confidence and considerable and compelling evidence of the paranormal, *One Step Beyond* occasionally forsakes the personal story of a single man or woman trapped in a psychic crisis to dramatize a story with a much larger scope and impact. In the first season entry "Night of April 14" the series examined the details surrounding the sinking of the *Titanic* and offered cogent evidence that the disaster was "detected" all over the world, even by an author writing a novel called *Futility* some 14 years before the disaster. "The Day the World Wept: The Lincoln Story" returns *One Step Beyond* to the same epic scale, spinning a story of psychic phenomena around the assassination of one of America's most adored historical and political figures. Although some may scoff at the notion of paranormal events buzzing about the doomed President Lincoln like a swarm of bees, there have, in fact, been many accounts of odd occurrences from those final days at the end of the Civil War, a time that John Newland refers to as a "time of portents."

First of all, "The Day the World Wept" turns out to be a remarkably apt title for any story surrounding the Lincoln assassination because there are indeed some validated reports that some six weeks prior to his untimely death, President Lincoln did hear the sound of sobs echoing through the White House, at least in his unconscious, dreaming mind. As has been described:

> Lincoln dreamed that he woke up in the White House to the sound of sobbing and was told by a guard that the President had been killed. ... Lincoln also had a recurring dream in which he was drifting away in a boat to an unknown shore.... He described this dream to members of his cabinet several hours before he was shot.[22]

Considering that the report of a dream could represent *precognition*, "The Day the World Wept" opens very faithfully to the established historical record, with President Lincoln awakening out of an afternoon nap in which he hears the weeping of a nation. From that accurate beginning, however, the dream changes form a bit for its TV dramatization. In the *One Step Beyond* story, Lincoln dreams not of being in a boat bound for an undiscovered country, but of glaring down at his dead body in an open coffin. This seems to relate, at least tangentially, to another dream of death that Lincoln has often been reported as having had:

> When Lincoln returned home after the 1860 presidential election, he saw two images of himself in a bureau mirror; in one, his face was normal, in the other it had a death-like pallor. His wife Mary's interpretation was that he would enjoy good health in his first term but die in his second.[23]

The specifics of this dream are reported correctly in "The Day the World Wept" as Lincoln confides to his wife that he has experienced a nightmares, in which he sees two faces in his mirror: one living and one dead. So *One Step Beyond* again is true to accounts of Lincoln's foreknowledge (in dreams) of his own demise, even if the coffin story is not completely corroborated.

Mary Lincoln's fear and foreknowledge that her husband was to die may be dismissed by some skeptics as mere anxiety and worry commensurate with Lincoln's position of importance and the raging conflicts of the period, but it is important to note that the spouses of important national figures often report being aware of just such things. For instance, former First Lady Nancy Reagan reported on C-SPAN in late 1999 from the Ronald Reagan Museum that she had felt a terrible sense that "something was wrong" while attending an art show on the very day President Reagan was shot by gunman John Hinckley. So strong was this feeling of unease that it caused Mrs. Reagan to excuse herself from her present company and the official gathering, leave the art gallery proper, and walk down a flight of stairs. There, at the bottom of the staircase, she was greeted by a subordinate who reported grimly to her that "there has been a shooting." What was the source of Nancy Reagan's strong feeling, a sense so powerful that it caused her to overcome protocol and duty, and flee her surroundings? One might never be sure, but there are persistent reports that people close to important figures sometimes register an "alertness" to danger just as Mary Lincoln reports so memorably in "The Day the World Wept."

The death of President Lincoln has also had other "psychic" phenomena attached to it over the years. Many Oval Office residents have reported the ghost of Lincoln — an apparition — wandering the halls of the White House. Another interesting theory called *retrosynchronicity* posits a unique link between two Chief Executives of the United States assassinated in their prime: Abrham Lincoln and John F. Kennedy. Consider the following similarities: Lincoln was elected to Congress in 1847, Kennedy in 1947; each man was killed by a bullet to the head in the presence of a spouse; both Lincoln's and Kennedy's secretary (the latter named Lincoln, ironically) warned the doomed Presidents not to go on the trips (to the theater and to Dallas, respectively) in which they were assassinated; both were succeeded by Southern men named Johnson; Kennedy and Lincoln have the identical number of letters in their last names; and assassins John Wilkes Booth was born in 1839 while assassin Lee Harvey Oswald was born in 1939. Though this theory of retrosynchronicity could easily be considered an accumulation of interesting coincidences, it is reported here merely to demonstrate what this *One Step Beyond* establishes so well: That Lincoln is indeed a central figure of much speculation in paranormal circles. "The Day the World Wept: The Lincoln Story" is essentially a story of omens ignored, as Mary experiences a "strange feeling all day" that she cannot explain (but which she confides to her husband is the very same feeling she experienced the day her son died). This strange feeling, this warning of horror to come, even makes Mary another *One Step Beyond* Cassandra. She begs her husband not to go to the theater but is not heeded. Meanwhile, President Lincoln grimly goes about making arrangements for a future he knows he will never see ("It must be *today!*" he emphasizes of a meeting with the Vice President, as if aware he will not live to see tomorrow).

Then, as in "Night of April 14," the episode's focus shifts to people all around the country who experience visions or foreknowledge of the Lincoln assassination before and as it occurs. Finally, "The Day the World Wept" ends in touching, poetic fashion as the camera slowly zooms in on a sculpture of Lincoln highlighted on a black stage, and Newland meaningfully reads from Shakespeare ("After life's fitful fever, he sleeps well...").

Like the best episodes of *One Step Beyond*, "The Day the World Wept: The Lincoln Story" induces chills not just through clever acting and camerawork but by accurately reporting a psychic-based event with a minimum of hysteria or fuss. The straight-faced approach to storytelling grants a sense of credibility to the admittedly amazing material, and suspension of disbelief is accomplished because, after all, it is almost as difficult to believe in a dozen bizarre coincidences as it is that somehow, some way, President Lincoln knew his end might be near.

44. "The Lovers"

(Dramatized by Joseph Petracca, Russell Beggs;
Directed by John Newland; Airdate: February 16, 1960)

SYNOPSIS: In Vienna during a "golden yesterday" of the late 1800s, a poltergeist strikes as a retired postman, Otto, courts the lovely young Elsa. Every time poor old Otto plants a kiss on Elsa, strange disturbances ensue: books fly, phonographs play of their own volition, and statues spontaneously shatter. Convinced he is to blame for these bizarre occurrences, Otto goes to see a psychologist.

GUEST CAST: John Beal (Otto Becker), Vanessa Brown (Elsa), Irene Tedrow, Rudolph Anders, Sig Ruman, Lili Valenti.

COMMENTARY: *One Step Beyond*'s increased level of confidence during its second season is demonstrated to good effect in "The Lovers," a funny little tale about a mismatched, May-December romance that must face more than just the disapproval of society, but also of some enigmatic psychic force as well! Though the story is thick with hard-to-understand accents (the tale is set in Vienna), the focus is on light-hearted romance and comedy, not terror, and the shift in tone is a welcome one after the somber explorations of "The Day the World Wept: The Lincoln Story."

Young Elsa and old Otto seem to have everything going against them. Her parents disapprove of her decision to marry an old postman; he is diffident, inexperienced and uncertain; and, worst of all, a *poltergeist* interferes every time the couple attempts to kiss! Of course, "poltergeist" is a German word for "noisy spirit," and it has come to be associated with "hauntings" by angry dead spirits ever since the popular 1982 film from Tobe Hooper, titled *Poltergeist*, premiered. However, many prominent researchers in the field of parapsychology actually believe that the poltergeist phenomenon may be caused not by a discarnate spirit at all, but rather a living person with unusual (subconscious) abilities. In its chapter on "Questionable PK [psychokinetic] Phenomenon," *Parapsychology: The Science of Psiology* discusses some common characteristics of poltergeist activity:

> Household objects move with a controlled type of flight that is often visible, sometimes navigating corners and seldom causing physical injury to the observers, although fragile objects such as crockery and windows may be broken.[24]

Those physical symptoms of a poltergeist "attack" mimic exactly the details of the unusual events Otto and Elsa witness when attempting to kiss in "The Lovers." Plates fly about, records start to play, and so forth. What "The Lovers" seems to suggest, then, is two-fold. The first theory is that old Otto is the one who subconsciously "causes" these events. He is so unsure of himself and insecure about young Elsa's commitment to him that his subconscious mind creates these disturbances, these bizarre distractions, when they become romantic. The second theory applied to "The Lovers" would posit that Elsa is really the cause of the poltergeist activity. Some research does seem to indicate that the young (and in love) have a special susceptibility to this unwitting psychokinetic behavior. The final answer, however, is a romantic and sweet one. Otto is indeed to blame (he is the so-called *agent* of the phenomenon) not because of his insecurities, but because he is simply "young at heart."

Regardless of which party is to blame for the paranormal seizures that shatter statues and crockery at inopportune moments, "The Lovers" is a fun episode, and its primary purpose is not a serious psychic examination but a humorous peek at the world of psychology. Specifically, the latter half of the story involves Otto's less-than-therapeutic experience with a Freudian psychoanalyst. On Otto's first visit the therapist promptly informs Otto that his hour consists of "fifty minutes." Later, Otto's problem with poltergeists is offhandedly dismissed as just another "sexual problem" by the professional, who quite obviously adheres to a Freudian interpretation of people and events. Since this story is set in an idyllic "golden yesterday," the contemporary skepticism about Freud and the jokes about a shortened hour are anachronistic stabs at humor meant to be enjoyed by *One Step Beyond*'s more psychologically aware 20th century audience.

In addition to its true-to-accounts poltergeist activity and humor, "The Lovers" offers an interesting thought about romance itself. One of the characters in the play states that love is a ghost "that inhabits a body for a while — then moves on." In a series rife with spirits, poltergeists, reincarnation, astral projection and possession, that unexpectedly poetic description for another truly inexplicable facet of human behavior — true love — seems particularly apt.

45. "Vanishing Point"
(Dramatized by Larry Marcus and J.G. Ezra;
Directed by John Newland; Airdate: February 23, 1960)

SYNOPSIS: A bickering husband and wife attempt to repair their crumbling marriage while summering at their lakeside cottage in Connecticut. After a particularly sobering coming to terms, Mrs. Graham gets the last laugh when she walks into her house and disappears without a trace. Consequently, her husband, at a loss for an explanation, is held for murder and forced to confront the bizarre history of his most unusual summer house.

GUEST CAST: Edward Binns (Fred Graham), Fredd Wayne (Lt. Barnes), June Vincent (Ruth Graham), William Allyn, Arthur Hanson, Amzie Strickland, Lindsay Workman, Byron Foulger.

COMMENTARY: To vanish, to literally pass out of existence, is the most frightening thing that can happen to a human being. To vanish is to silence all arguments forever. To vanish is to leave matters unfinished and people perpetually wondering. To vanish is to do much worse than die, because in death at least there is an ending. Accordingly, the horror genre is filled with stories of people who disappear, never to be heard from again. In the appropriately-named *The Vanishing* (1993) a man (Kiefer Sutherland) becomes obsessed by the inexplicable disappearance of his girlfriend (a pre-stardom Sandra Bullock). In *Picnic at Hanging Rock* (1975) a trio of school girls climb a rock in the Australian outback and somehow slip out of the mortal coil, never to be seen again. In *The Blair Witch Project* (1999) three film students disappear in the small town of Burkittsville, leaving behind only their ambiguous footage ... but no bodies and no explanation. Similarly, many *One Step Beyond* episodes deal with vanishings in rather tangential fashion. A tenet of the series seems to be that people who have vanished are usually murdered, and that their "spirits" so resent that their end is unresolved (a vanishing) that they make their presence known again by psychic means ("The Bride Possessed," "The Haunted U-Boat," "Father Image"). The disturbing and dramatic "Vanishing Point" goes beyond the realm of these previous stories and offers a negative spin on another *One Step Beyond* story, the first season entry "The Secret."

"The Secret," some may recall, concerned a lonely woman named Sylvia Ackroyd who was trapped in an unhappy marriage and who used a ouija board to conjure a ghost from a century past. At the climax of the tale, the ghost appeared in the flesh to take the woman to a "better place," and the duo vanished into thin air. In that story the vanishing had the overlay of release and freedom. Though "Vanishing Point" does suggest that Mrs. Graham is indeed free of her earthly bond, it does not seem a pleasant or happy release. Instead, it is a vanishing borne of her desperation, of her emptiness, of her feeling that she has no positive future. She feels worthless, and the universe seems to agree. Mrs. Graham simply walks into her house one day and the edifice seems to absorb her, as if she has willingly surrendered her identity to it and, like Jonah and the whale, it has swallowed her whole.

In "The Vanishing Point's" most disturbing and eerie moment, Mr. Graham re-enters his summer house (following closely on the heels of his wife), only to find it silent and vacant. As Harry Lubin's shiver-inducing music plays on the soundtrack, Mr. Graham searches one room after the other, and the audience fights a creeping awareness that his wife will never be found; that somehow, some terrible way, Mr. Graham is now irrevocably alone inside that house. The slow build to this realization is handled masterfully by Newland as his camera stalks Mr. Graham, and the concerned spouse urgently faces room after room of darkness, flipping on light switches, expecting the horrific moment to end. But he finds only thin air, and "Vanishing Point" captures the same mood of uneasiness and mystery that *Picnic at Hanging Rock* and *The Blair Witch Project* so expertly project. The world of reason has collapsed, and science, logic and the laws of physics as humans understand no longer apply.

Had "Vanishing Point" ended simply with Mrs. Graham's vanishing, it would have been an undisputed masterpiece of cerebral terror. However, this was 1960, and *One Step Beyond*, for all its artistic qualities, was still a product of its medium: television. The last half of the story undoes much of the preceding terror by going into elaborate detail and describing the history of the summer house. Specifically, Mr. Graham learns that a woman named Agatha Dunlop lived in it during the late 1800s. She feared she had nothing to live for, locked herself in a room, and disappeared without a trace. Before Agatha, back in 1821, Harrison Fraser built the house. He became morose after his wife died in childbirth and, again, the house seemed to swallow him up. Though this history adds to the overall feeling of horror, Mr. Graham sees an apparition of Ms. Dunlop at one signficant point, as she relives the moment in which she is fired from her job and elects to remain in her house permanently. Perhaps that is a little too much exposition, and one can only wish that the perplexing story of "Vanishing Point" had been allowed to remain a mystery.

Besides its fascinating central premise, "Vanishing Point" also harkens back to "The Inheritance" by featuring host John Newland in a more substantive part. The story proper begins when Newland arrives at the summer house and meets with the recalcitrant police officer who investigated the Graham case and fears for his own sanity. Newland implores the officer to tell him the story and interacts with the guest cast as if he is actually a character in the drama, a detective of the paranormal or some such thing. This breakdown of the "fourth wall," allowing Newland to play both host and participant, was a pattern that most anthology series never duplicated, perhaps fearing confusion on the part of the audience. In the 1990s, however, Wes Craven did revive the practice in his short-lived *Nightmare Cafe* (1992) series. His main character, Blackie (Robert Englund), would interact with the regular cast but often direct his sardonic comments to the audience as series narrator as well.

In 1972 a prime-time network horror series called *Ghost Story* offered an entry similar in tone and content to "Vanishing Point." In "The Summer House" a woman (Carolyn Jones) faced the strange fact that her husband may have disappeared in her house and that, outside the confines of linear time, she may have killed him there.

46. "The Mask"

(Dramatized by Joseph Petracca and Russell Beggs;
Directed by John Newland; Airdate: March 1, 1960)

SYNOPSIS: During World War II Lieutenant Wilenski escapes a terrible disaster when his plane goes down in Egypt. Though Wilenski survives the terrible ordeal and receives appropriate medical care, he comes to believe — with increasing fear — that he is possessed by the spirit of an ancient Egyptian prince.

GUEST CAST: Wesley Lau (Leonard Wilenski), Luis Van Rooten (Brimley), Stephen Bekassy (The Doctor); Joan Elan (Nurse).

COMMENTARY: There comes a time in every dramatic TV series when repetition replaces innovation, and *One Step Beyond* is far more suseptible to such "rerun" ideas than other programs, for a variety of reasons. Firstly, its "mission statement" to viewers promises that it will accurately depict the specifics of psychic phenomena. That mission statement limits the series' subject matter, while another series (like *The Twilight Zone*, for instance) could handle virtually any topic within the umbrella concept of a "twist" or bizarre conclusion. Secondly, the fallout of psychic phenomena tends to have the same effect on characters: either terror ("Image of Death," "The Haunted U-Boat," "Echo"), recovery ("The Bride Possessed," "Who Are You?"), plain astonishment ("Emergency Only") or a combination of all of the above. Thirdly, there is that familiar statement from Merwin Gerard that just cannot be ignored: only fifteen different stories of psychic phenomena can really be dramatized. So, frankly, there is an uncomfortably high degree of repetition on *One Step Beyond*. Some modern viewers may find this tendency to repeat story ideas, characters and concepts a tad annoying, but the joy in *One Step Beyond* is often in the creepy execution, and the series has an uncanny knack for improving on material the second time around or putting a different slant on the same paranormal concept. Sometimes, however, the weight of repetition is too great to bear, and the stories become overly familiar. In fairness to *One Step Beyond*, this trend may appear to occur because this author watched all of the ninety-six episodes over a span of weeks and months, not years, and was hence more cognizant of repetition. When run originally, *One Step Beyond* aired over a period of two-and-a-half years, and the tonal commonalities would have been diffused over that longer period.

Oppositely, a case could be made that consistency of theme, plot and characterization is actually an artistic trait that is worthy of praise. When viewing a painter's life work, a critic will look for commonalities, comparisons and contrasts, and make judgments based on those things. Much of the material in a painter's portfolio *is* similar because it is all created by one mind, one imagination, one vision. Though filmmaking (and hence TV production) is a collaborative art, it is to *One Step Beyond*'s credit that it appears so remarkably consistent, literally of one "hive" mind. John Newland directed all the stories, and most of the plots were written by two gifted gentlemen, Larry Marcus and Merwin Gerard. Therefore, the act of critiquing *One Step Beyond* becomes much more interesting than in a show where a different creative voice jumped in each week. Because there is a small group of talent calling the shots on *One Step Beyond*, the variations in common themes can be discussed in all their permutations. Reincarnation is a frightening experience in one story ("The Riddle"), only to re-emerge as a comforting idea in another episode ("The Nightmare"). Likewise, possession can be seen as terrifying ("The Bride Possessed") or as a surprise source for healing ("Who Are You?"). And the conflicts of marriage, and the debate about Eastern versus Western modes of belief, are all spread over a wide palette instead of a narrow, one-time half hour. Basically, a reviewer can have it either way, complaining that many episodes are derivative of others, or praising the series based on its dedication to consistency.

Regardless of the reasons why, "The Mask" is a somewhat familiar story. When viewed in light of the series as a whole, it seems to offer little thought that's new. War (an arena of heightened senses and perceptions) is the overall backdrop ("The Dream," "The Vision"), a non–Western ethic informs the terror/psychic encounter ("The Riddle", "Forests of the Night") and there are doubting authority figures ("Epilogue," "Vanishing Point"). Also, possession of the living by the dead is a key concept ("The Bride Possessed," "Who Are You?"). Thus, "The Mask" may register with the critic as a good story, well-acted and well-directed, but it is not in the same class as the *One Step Beyond* greats such as "Night of April 14," "Epilogue," "The Day the World Wept: The Lincoln Story" or "The Sacred Mushroom."

The lore and power of Egyptology dominates much of "The Mask." Though this may be yet another example of *One Step Beyond*'s continuing thesis about white man's misunderstanding of the world and his education at the hand of non–Western thinkers ("The Riddle," "Forest of the Night," "Night of Decision"), no doubt it is also a reference to what was, at the time of production, felt to be a legitimate curse: the opening of King Tutankhamen's tomb in Luxor. A reporter had written that an inscription reading "Death shall come on swift wings to he who disturbs the peace of the king" was engraved in hieroglyphs on the secret tomb of Tut. However, history now records that there was no such curse, only an overeager reporter hoping to make a story with legs. Still, the Western world thronged to this tale of an Egyptian curse, and soon facts occurred which allowed that fascination to reach a fever pitch. Particularly, one member of the archaeological expedition, Lord Carnavon, died in 1923 just months after Tut's tomb was opened and the so-called "Curse" was enacted. As has been reported:

> Carnavon died in the most excruciating pain. ... Three events make Carnavon's death all the more mysterious. Firstly ... a mysterious power cut reduced Cairo to total darkness. While on the other side of the world his faithful terrier, Susie, woke the staff of the house with terrible anguished baying. ... Finally, his pet canary was swallowed by a cobra shortly after his death.[25]

The same account goes on to reveal that the cobra is the protective deity of the Pharaohs and that its murdering presence may have been evidence of a 3,000-year-old curse still at work. Today, with the Curse of Tut acknowledged as a hoax, one can see that these three odd events are mere coincidences only believed to have some kind of synchronicity or connection. One wonders, will the same eventuality be proven in cases of psychic phenonema?

Unaware that King Tut's curse would one day be demonstrated a fraud, *One Step Beyond*'s "The Mask" works to elicit chills by putting its main character in a situation where Egyptology (believed legitimately responsible for a curse at the time) would terrorize another individual. That one soul could possess another is a concept common to *One Step Beyond*, and the Egyptian word for a spiritual presence or immortal soul is *Ba*.

47. "The Haunting"

(Dramatized by Gabrielle Upton;
Directed by John Newland; Airdate: May 8, 1960)

SYNOPSIS: Just days before his marriage to the beautiful Nancy, Collin kills his best man, Peter Duncan, in the Swiss Alps because he suspects an affair. Though no such relationship existed, Collin is a former mental patient with a paranoid bent. As the wedding ceremony nears, an unearthly chill sweeps through the house, encroaching on the murderer and all those who continue to associate with him.

GUEST CAST: Ronald Howard (Collin Chandler), Christine White (Nancy), Doris Lloyd, Anthony Eustrel, Keith McConnell, Cyril Delevant, Clive L. Halliday, Veronica Cartwright.

COMMENTARY: "The Haunting" is a frightfully good "revenge from beyond the grave" tale in which a man (and murderer) on the brink of sanity is driven out of his mind and straight from his wedding bed by the chill of a wrathful ghost. This tale of a murderer caught in his own web of deceit suggests a distinct dramatic connection between the murderer and his deed. With cold-blooded planning and execution, Collin murdered his best man, Peter, on no more than a suspicion of his guilt. And since Collin did the murderous deed while out skiing on a snowy mountain, the "cold-blooded" metaphor extends to setting as well as intent. It is thus quite appropriate that a man of cold heart who killed in a cold setting should himself become so cold that others cannot stand to be in his presence.

This revenge (a dish best served cold?) is also representative of a long held belief in parapsychology that the presence of a ghost nearby lowers the temperature of the surrounding area and results in an unnatural (or supernatural) chill. This particular effect has been utilized recently in major horror releases such as *The Sixth Sense* (1999) and *Stir of Echoes* (1999), wherein protagonists able to communicate with the dead recognize the arrival of ghosts when their icy breath becomes visible in ostensibly non-icy settings.

Likewise, a peculiar chill fills the air of Collin's home as the wedding arrangements are made. His clothes feel as if they have been in the snow all night, wedding flowers are frozen stiff, frost forms on the windows (though it is warm outside) and a gust of icy wind abbreviates Collin and Nancy's ceremonial kiss at the wedding altar. It finally gets so cold that Collin is unable to find comfort in anyone, as the dipping temperature around him drives everybody away. And, in a wicked joke, "The Haunting" culminates with a kind of visual double entendre. Collin and Nancy are to share their first night of intimacy together as husband and wife. However, Collin is so cold, so chilly, that his beautiful new wife will not let him touch her. There will be no intimacy because she is, literally and figuratively, frigid.

Though the "comeuppance" story had already been produced several times on *One Step Beyond*, "The Haunting" escapes its familiar plot outlining by an understanding that the devil is in the details. The detail of interest here, the cold, makes for a feeling of stark, icy terror, and a psychic wind that blows ill for all the protagonists.

Another familiar concept seen in "The Haunting" is Collin's history: He is a former mental patient, which automatically disqualified him from believability by his friends and neighbors. They understandably mistake his "haunting" for a mental relapse.

On a trivia note, the child actress in "The Haunting" would go on to make quite a name for herself in horror and science fiction circles. Veronica Cartwright, a mere girl here, would later appear in prominent roles in such classics as *Invasion of the Body Snatchers* (1978), *Alien* (1979) and *The Witches of Eastwick* (1986).

48. "The Explorer"

(Dramatized by Don M. Mankiewicz;
Directed by John Newland; Airdate: March 15, 1960)

SYNOPSIS: A famous explorer visits a geography teacher to tell him a bizarre story: On his last trip to the Sahara, the explorer's guide was killed and he became hopelessly lost in the desert until Eric, the geography teacher's son, led them to water and salvation. This account does not seem to mesh with the truth about Eric's condition, however. He died in bed the previous summer after a spinal disorder had rendered him paralyzed for the last ten years.

GUEST CAST: Jeremy Slate (Eric), Gregory Morton, Eddie Firestone.

COMMENTARY: Sounding as if he has come straight out of an atmospheric Jack Arnold film like *It Came from Outer Space* (1953), one of the characters in "The Explorer" declares that the desert can do "strange things" to a man's mind. And, indeed, that is one possible explanation for the bizarre events seen in this *One Step Beyond* episode. Is Eric merely a mirage to the three lost men who are dying of thirst and starvation out in the great desert? If he is only an hallucination of sorts, then why is the physical shape of this "fantasy" recognizably Eric, a person that none of the explorers has ever met in person? The answer, recalling "The Return of Mitchell Campion," concerns that favorite trope of *One Step Beyond*, the OBE (out of body experience).

Though Eric was cursed with a spinal disorder that left him paralyzed and bedridden for ten years, "The Explorer" would have viewers believe that only his body was confined. His spirit was free, and Eric called himself an explorer because his maps and his books could transport him anywhere in the world. In other words, Eric seems to have willed himself into having an out-of-body experience. Oddly, that strange idea jibes with much research on the OBE, as experienced OBEers have often concentrated on and even planned their journeys on the astral plane in incredible detail. Some OBEers claim they have seen the surface of Mars, the Moon, and even Mercury. Other OBEers have demonstrated remarkable success describing military and research installations at the South Pole that they claim to have visited while on the astral plane.

What is, perhaps, less in keeping with published OBE accounts in "The Explorer" is the fact that Eric's strength fails in the desert as a deep well is found to be dry, as if it is his physical body that is suffering rather than merely his projection. In most reported OBE occurrences, the wayward traveler is snapped back into his body (a feeling often described as like being connected to the body with an elastic band) when something "jars" the experience. Something as simple as flying through a STOP sign while traveling out-of-body has been known to bounce OBEers back into their bodies, frustrated. So how is it that Eric "astrally" visits the desert, but has no tether, no lifeline, with his body back in bed at home?

In "The Explorer" the final twist confirms both this oddity *and* the fact that the invalid Eric left his bed and somehow visited the desert he knew so much about. When Eric passed on, he died not of his spinal disease but of dehydration (although there was a pitcher of water beside his bed). In other words, Eric really did die of "thirst" in the desert. Though this ending denies the facts of most OBE experiences, it also serves to confirm the facts of Eric's bizarre journey, so perhaps one can again chalk up the inaccuracy to dramatic necessity. It is also fair to state that there has been quite a bit of new research on the OBE since 1960, so it is possible that "The Explorer" does reflect the most accurate research on the phenomenon available at the time of *One Step Beyond*'s production.

"The Explorer" makes for a good episode of *One Step Beyond*. It dramatizes another realm of the strange (the desert), adds another piece to its expanding puzzle about the power of mind over matter (with Eric overcoming illness to "psychically" travel the world), and it has a happy ending, with Eric's parents finally achieving a level of closure.

49. "The Clown"
(Dramatized by Gabrielle Upton; Directed by John Newland;
Airdate: March 22, 1960)

SYNOPSIS: A nasty, mean-spirited husband accuses his young, beautiful wife of being cheap and indecent when she befriends Pippo, a mute clown from the nearby S & S Carnival. In a fit of jealous rage, the husband stabs his wife with Pippo's scissors and kills her. Soon after the murder, which is pinned on the innocent clown, the guilty husband begins to see the vengeful Pippo's reflection everywhere: in a mirror, in windows, and even in the water.

GUEST CAST: Yvette Mimieux (Mrs. Nonnie Reagan), Mickey Shaughnessy (Pippo the Clown), Christopher Dark (Tom Reagan), Jack Daly, John Close, Karen Scott, Jim Nolan, Paul "Mouse" Garner.

COMMENTARY: "The Clown" is a scary little piece of work, a drama that selects a special icon of terror (Pippo the Clown) and then drops him into a marital dispute between two interesting and well-drawn characters, one kind and sweet, the other nasty and brutish.

In her first acting role, Yvette Mimieux (*The Black Hole* [1979]) convincingly portrays the sweet and innocent Mrs. Reagan. The saturnine-looking (and appropriately named) Christopher Dark essays the role of her nasty husband, and he sees a threat to his manhood every time his wife even speaks to another man. He calls her "cheap" and tells her he is tired of her "sweet act." He is a man obsessed with the idea that he could become a cuckold, and he is absolutely merciless to his wife, even chopping off her hair with a pair of scissors before plunging forward into a murderous rage.

Unlike the hard-hearted Mr. Reagan, Pippo the Clown understands implicitly that he and Nonnie have a different (*not* romantic) kind of connection: They are kindred spirits. A mute, Pippo is also very childlike and therefore drawn to Nonnie's fresh-faced innocence. Likewise, she is kind to him, allowing him to stroke her beautiful golden hair (as a curious child might), and she shows sympathy for his mutism. For Nonnie, Pippo is an interesting change because, unlike her husband, he can never say anything mean or nasty to her. The paranormal comes into play when Mr. Reagan steps into this bizarre relationship and shatters the friendship developed between Nonnie and Pippo. He accomplishes this by the murder of his wife, committed in a jealous rage. From that crime of passion the episode becomes a "comeuppance" story as the enraged Pippo is unleashed, becoming a specter of terror who materializes in mirrors, water and all other reflective surfaces. Terrified, Mr. Reagan soon sees Pippo moving in to strangle him in rear-view mirrors and such, unable to escape. Finally, Pippo does kill Mr. Reagan, though the Clown "never leaves" the trailer where he is held in custody after Mrs. Reagan is murdered.

"The Clown" is an engrossing story not only for its triangle dynamic but because of what it suggests about communication. Though Pippo is mute, he certainly can communicate. Perhaps because he has not developed the power of speech, his mind has given him another way to emote:

astral projection. The vengeful thing that attacks and murders Tom Reagan is not an apparition (nobody else detects it), is not merely a figment of Mr. Reagan's imagination (after the wrestling match in the water, the real Pippo is shown to be wet — though he never left his trailer), and certainly is not a dream (Mr. Reagan is conscious and all-too-aware the whole time he is stalked). It is possible then, that Pippo's murderous doppelganger is in fact an astral projection. Whatever his unique ability (bilocation?), he is a terrifying avenger, and John Newland reveals his usual delight in creeping out the viewer by suddenly planting the murderous Pippo in the background and foreground of many shots, his strangling hands reaching out to commit murder. The irony of this final psychic assault is that a clown represents joy, innocence, humor, fun, play and even childhood, but this one acts in a manner contrary to that character: committing murder! As has been mentioned before (in the review for "The Aerialist"), the world of the circus (and of the clown specifically) has been exploited many times for this very reason. People are afraid of clowns and see them as terrifying creatures who hide behind a mask of congeniality. "The Clown" certainly exploits that fear to its utmost degree.

In an elegant bit of camera movement, Tom's final doom is visually foretold as he enters a dark park and crosses a narrow bridge. The camera moves quickly and then rockets into a high angle, looking down on Tom in a stance that has traditionally represented doom in the cinema. From there, Tom gazes down off the bridge, looks into the watery reflection below, and spies Pippo preparing to make the kill. Before he can react, the frenzied Clown is upon him. It is a frightening moment told with exactly the right shot.

"The Clown" sets out to "disturb the secure curtain of reality," as John Newland states in the opening narration, and it accomplishes just that goal. Though it again features familiar series elements (a married couple threatened by the paranormal, as well as the oft-repeated comeuppance story template), it also finds intriguing method for revenge. "The Haunting" utilized the interesting motif of ice and cold, and "The Clown" offers the equally chilling sight of a clown bent on murder! "The Clown" is a better episode than "The Haunting", however, and one of *One Step Beyond*'s very best because Mimieux, Shaughnessy and Dark make for an instantly compelling triangle comprised of two corners innocence and one corner paranoia. Each character is trapped in a way, and that makes them interesting. Mr. Reagan is imprisoned by his own suspicions and hatred; Mrs. Reagan is trapped, in a marriage to a terrible man; and underneath the greasepaint smile and putty nose, Pippo is trapped by his inability to relate (i.e., to speak) to other human beings. When Mr. Reagan kills his wife and breaks Pippo's genuine connection to another human being, the clown bursts out of his cage with deadly psychic force. All of this plays out in solid, dramatic fashion and John Newland, as usual, makes the most of the situation with his effective (but not over-the-top) direction.

The killer who appears to a percipient only in reflections was resurrected in an *Amazing Stories* (1985–1987) episode directed by Martin Scorcese called "Mirror, Mirror." In that half-hour segment from the mid–80s Spielberg anthology, Sam Waterston played a horror novelist who perceived a murderous figure from his fiction in mirrors and even in the iris of a lover (Helen Shaver).

50. "I Saw You Tomorrow"
(Dramatized by Merwin Gerard;
Directed by John Newland; Airdate: April 5, 1960)

SYNOPSIS: An American visitor in a British bed-and-breakfast overhears a violent domestic squabble across the hall from his own accommodations. When he breaks in to intervene, he witnesses a murder. The only problem is that the murdered woman, Claire, and her angry husband, Carter, have not yet arrived at the hotel. Before long, the criminal and the victim *do* show up, and the perplexed Donald Stewart realizes he has been granted a preview of an unpleasant future.

GUEST CAST: John Hudson (Donald Stewart), Narda Onyx (Claire Seymour), Rosemary Murphy (Ellie Pelston), Francis Bethencourt (Carter Seymour), Barbara Morrison, Jack Raine, Rolfe Sedan, Christine Thomas.

COMMENTARY: In *One Step Beyond*, time seems to skip its tracks with a jarring frequency. "The Open Window" dramatized a situation much like the central scenario of "I Saw You Tomorrow": a vision of the future detected as real by the percipient, but which has not yet occurred in real time. In this case, American Donald Stewart is placed in the familiar role of Cassandra as he experiences a vision of murder yet to come and is not believed by others. The murder is not in the past, as one might rightly expect (indicating a haunting and a ghost seeking justice), but actually in the future. Is Stewart's experience a form of *déjà vu* (literally, "already seen"), or a half-forgotten memory of an event that has not yet occurred in linear time? Or is Donald Stewart simply facing the forward thrust of "inevitability," as a dinner conversation in "I Saw You Tomorrow" suggests? It is apparently inevitable that Claire will be murdered, and even Donald's intervention cannot stop fate's hand from acting. These are the questions which dominate "I Saw You Tomorrow," a competent, well-performed show with a nice air of urgency to it.

One Step Beyond's explanation for Donald's odd psychic experience is "mental radio," the belief that man's brain receives psychic signals (as if a radio) and then interprets those signals. Unlike most people, Donald Stewart's mental radio apparently is tuned not to the present but to the future, and thus he receives his vision. That answer may sound far fetched to some, but it is an interesting conclusion (and one that would also fit the events of "The Open Window"). Mental radio could easily be an alternate name for our old friend the premonition. Stated succinctly, Donald Stewart sees the future just as Grace Montgomery does in "Night of April 14" or Ellen Larabee does in "Emergency Only."

In addition to featuring a familiar theme (seeing the future), similar character dynamics (a Cassandra and a married couple in jeopardy), "I Saw You Tomorrow" concludes with a well-oiled *One Step Beyond* convention: accurate psychic visions misinterpreted. Donald experiences the vision of the murder and tries to protect Claire from her murderous husband. However, Claire and Carter leave the hotel, both alive and well, throwing a monkey wrench in Stewart's prediction of death. It is only in his closing narration that Newland reveals the stinger: Claire was murdered by her husband in the very same house, on the very same weekend ... but one year later. And, sadly, Donald Stewart was not there to intervene. The misread message was also seen in "Emergency Only" and "Premonition," among others.

51. "Encounter"

(Dramatized by De Witt Copp; Directed by John Newland;
Airdate: April 12, 1960)

SYNOPSIS: While in flight, a commercial pilot spots a U.F.O. and snaps a roll of film before both he and his plane vanish into thin air. An exhaustive search commences, but the pilot reappears mysteriously in a desert over a thousand miles away, claiming to have been "kidnapped" (i.e., "abducted").

GUEST CAST: Robert Douglas (McCord), Barbara Stuart (Ellen), Mike Forest (Jacques), John Carlyle, David De Haven, Ted Otis, Francis De Sales, Larry Berrill.

COMMENTARY: *One Step Beyond* blasts off into uncharted territory with "Encounter," an early example of one of modern science fiction television's most common (and most cherished) stories: the alien abduction.

From the crash of a "flying saucer" in Roswell, New Mexico, in 1947 and its ensuing alleged government cover-up, to the convincing testimony of Barney and Betty Hill about their own abduction by aliens on September 19, 1961, while returning home to Portsmouth, New Hampshire (a terrifying experience recounted in the book *Interrupted Journey*), audiences have found themselves fascinated with the topic of alien visitation. Even former President Jimmy Carter believes in U.F.O.s, alleging that he saw one on the night of January 6, 1969, in Leary, Georgia.

Accordingly, *One Step Beyond*'s "Encounter" displays a healthy curiosity about non-human life and the prospect that extraterrestrials have visited Earth. As one character in the drama lays out the argument so succinctly: Man is on the verge of space exploration, so why does he find it impossible to believe that somebody else out there beat him to it? After asking that question, "Encounter" hits all the notes that would later become *de rigueur* for the alien abduction story. An aircraft pilot spots the U.F.O. (an idea seen in the *UFO* episode "Exposed") and photographs it. His plane is subsequently abducted and the pilot ends up separated from his vehicle by hundreds of miles (*Close Encounters of the Third Kind* [1978]). True to many accounts, the UFO is reported as a giant cigar, but there is no physical evidence left of the unidentified flying object to merit a full-scale investigation (any "abduction" episode of *The X-Files*).

Dark Skies (1996–1997), *Beyond Reality* ("Return Visit," "Final Flight"), *The X-Files* ("Pilot," "Duane Barry/Ascension"), *Project U.F.O* (1978–80) and even *The Invaders* (1967–68) have all dealt with the same concepts that inhabit the core of "Encounter," and *One Step Beyond*'s willingness to peer into the world of the inexplicable as well as the psychic is no doubt indicative of its increased confidence after more than a year on the air. Already in the second season there had been a unique "Big Foot" story ("Night of the Kill") and a genetic mutant story ("Ordeal on Locust Street"), so "Encounter" does not feel at all like a stretch or betrayal of the series format. And, indeed, it is in the vernacular of the inexplicable and the bizarre that *One Step Beyond* explores this particular story. "The further man probes into outer space, the more riddles he encounters," Newland intones at the beginning of the tale, leading viewers through a story which, in the end, simply cannot provide objective, physical evidence of U.F.O.s, even if it does follow "abduction" lore quite accurately.

At the end of "Encounter" Newland plays a kind of nasty trick on the audience. In his narration he reports that in the matter of such bizarre cases, physical evidence is inclined to disappear without a trace. Then, suddenly ... POP! Without warning, Newland vanishes from sight, as if transported away. This optical trick is not only funny, but also sufficient evidence that film and television are manipulative arts. After all, Newland does not really disappear: The camera stops, Newland walks offstage, and the camera resumes shooting and obediently logs his "disappearance." This dramatic demonstration of the fact that TV can lie to viewers is one clearly at odds with *One Step Beyond*'s usual straight-faced approach to drama and mystery, even though it makes for a fun moment.

As far as evidence is concerned, in "Encounter" Newland reports of a strange incident in the San Fernando Valley in 1953 during which strange "Angel Hair" fell from the sky, dissolving in plain view of many eyewitnesses. That may not be actual proof of extraterrestrial visitation so much as it describes an *anomalous phenomenon* (see: "Where Are They?"), but it certainly helps to make "Encounter's" case that odd things can and do happen. Other incidents of falling angel hair "droppings" (a silky, gossamer substance that seems to melt away quickly) have also been reported in Port Hope, Ontario (September 26, 1948), and Iwae-Ken, Japan (October 4, 1957). Though some scientists speculate that this unusual material is created by spiders (i.e. webbing), there is no consensus as to how exactly the material ends up dropping high from the sky.

On the flip side of the coin, "Encounter" is filled with the same kind of bizarre logic that passes for skepticism and science on programs such as *The X-Files*. This author refers to these bizarre leaps of logic as "Scullyisms," since Agent Dana Scully (Gillian Anderson) is the prime exponent of them on modern television. For instance, the central mystery of "Encounter" involves Rand's plane and its disappearance. How could a small plane with only a two hour supply of gasoline and a top velocity of 120 miles an hour travel over 1000 miles in a day? The "Scullyism" excuse, espoused by skeptic McCord (Robert Douglas), is that the plane and its pilot were carried away on a freak wind. When Bob Rand is found, he dies of shock, but McCord thinks the death was exposure to heat (though Rand was only in the desert for a half hour). In cases like these it is appropriate to question, which seems to be the more rational and believable explanation? It requires fewer gymnastics of logic to believe in alien interference (especially since an unidentified object was reported by the pilot) than to propose all of these bizarre coincidences and happenings and then formulate a quasi-scientific excuse. Of course, even in 1960 the U.S. government might have been testing top secret warplanes that "appeared" to be U.F.O.s. That is another possible explanation, but one that *One Step Beyond* does not put forward.

A notable alumnus of "Encounter" would soon have other encounters with aliens in television drama. Mike Forest, who plays the pilot Jacques in "Encounter," played an alien himself in both *The Twilight Zone* ("Black Leather Jackets") and *Star Trek* ("Who Mourns for Adonais?").

52. "The Peter Hurkos Story" (Part I)
(Dramatized by Jerome Gruskin; Directed by John Newland;
Airdate: April 19, 1960)

SYNOPSIS: While being pursued by Nazi soldiers in Amsterdam, Dutch freedom fighter Peter Hurkos falls from the top of a high building (some fifty feet!) and is hospitalized for his injuries. When he awakens after a coma of six days, Hurkos finds he is now a "touch" psychic with the unique ability to see the life details and future of all those with whom he comes in contact. Tortured by voices he hears in his head, Peter Hurkos is driven to excessive drink, and he returns home to live with Aunt Elsa, a tarot card reader. There he becomes a house painter and contemplates a future in show business.

GUEST CAST: Albert Salmi (Peter Hurkos), Betty Garde (Aunt Elsa), Violet Rensing, Maurice Marsac, Robert Schiller, Leni Tana, Stephen Bakassy, Will J. White.

COMMENTARY: "The Peter Hurkos Story" is *One Step Beyond*'s two-part biography of a very controversial figure in psychic studies. Peter Hurkos (actually Pieter Van der Hurk) was born in Dordrecht, Holland, on May 21, 1911. He was the son of a house painter, and his advent into the world of psychic phenomena is not quite so heroic as "The Peter Hurkos Story" dramatizes. On TV, Hurkos is fleeing the Nazis as a member of the Dutch resistance when he falls from atop the roof of a high building. In reality, Hurkos had a simple accident in June of 1943: He fell off his ladder while painting a Nazi barracks. He slipped and plunged head-first from over 30 feet onto hard asphalt. Interestingly, it is true that Hurkos ran several secret missions for the Dutch resistance, but he was apparently not on such a mission when he was injured and developed his so-called psychic abilities. Clearly, *One Step Beyond* has adapted the story of Hurkos to make it a bit more "dramatic." It has mixed and matched the details of the accident so as to be more exciting to viewers. Still, this episode cannot claim to be completely 100 percent accurate, since the Hurkos power does not originate quite as the series claims.

John Newland, who consulted with Peter Hurkos several times, recalls that the Dutch psychic was a "curious man with the power to do curious things" and not a "little bit bizarre." But, as Newland recalls, Hurkos' story was considered perfect material for *One Step Beyond*. Therefore, the production company brought Hurkos, "The Psychic Model of the Century," over to the United States at its own expense and decided to film a two-part episode about his lifetime of paranormal experiences.

Eventually, "The Peter Hurkos Story" (both parts) was removed from the *One Step Beyond* syndication package because it was intended to run as a theatrical feature in Europe. Over the years there have been rumors and reports that Peter Hurkos initiated a lawsuit against *One Step Beyond* because he was unhappy with the final product. Newland states simply and emphatically that there was no lawsuit and has never been a lawsuit. Instead, it was apparently decided early on that "The Peter Hurkos Story" would be a feature film and that there would be an extra three days of shooting allotted to the production so as to procure the additional footage that would lengthen the episode to approximately 90 minutes. Eventually, however, it was decided not to release the *One Step Beyond* Hurkos material as a film, which is why, in the end, both episodes were returned to the syndication package sold to local stations.

The first part of "The Peter Hurkos story" follows Hurkos (a terrific Albert Salmi) as he recovers from his coma of six days (a symbolic number, no doubt, as God created the Earth in six days) and begins to have strange psychic experiences. He hears "voices" in his head and starts to develop the ability to hear thoughts when he touches certain objects or people. The story ends as Peter has become an "Instant Continental Success" but is unhappy that he is little more than a circus sideshow attraction.

53. "The Peter Hurkos Story" (Part II)
(Dramatized by Jerome Gruskin; Directed by John Newland;
Airdate: April 26, 1960)

SYNOPSIS: After a few years of performing as a novelty act, Dutch psychic Peter Hurkos' abilities are tested in the laboratory by a prominent scientist, Dr. Lindstrom. The scientist concludes that Hurkos' incredible power comes from electrical impulses, and then sets out to prove it. The pure research takes a back seat, however, when Hurkos is enlisted by the police to help solve a terrible murder.

GUEST CAST: Albert Salmi (Peter Hurkos), Andrew Prine (Byrd/Vogel), Alf Kjellin, Justice Watson.

COMMENTARY: The second portion of "The Peter Hurkos Story," *One Step Beyond*'s only two-part installment, focuses on two important aspects of Hurkos' life: his tenure as a guinea pig in the experiments of Dr. Lindstrom (really Dr. Andrija Puharich, of *The Sacred Mushroom* fame) and his frequent service to the police in the solving of certain heinous crimes.

Dr. Lindstrom's tests concerned the brainwave patterns of the famous psychic and how they were affected by various conditions setup by Lindstrom in the laboratory. In the episode, Lindstrom exposes Hurkos to a flashing strobe light that is supposed to "lessen the gulf between the conscious and unconscious mind," a 1950s variation, perhaps, on the current therapy known as EMDR (Eye Movement Desensitization Retraining). As his studies continue, Lindstrom finds that electricity is the key to Hurkos' psychometric power — a fact that reflects the reality of Puharich's research. As Edgar D. Mitchell wrote of the (real life) tests involving Hurkos and Puharich:

> Experiments with Hurkos conducted by Dr. Andrija Puharich in the 1950s indicated that under a special laboratory set-up in a double Farady cage, in which the outer cage was electrified with resonating current, Hurkos's abilities at telepathy became greatly enhanced.[26]

In this case, as in so many others, *One Step Beyond* reflects the truth of the "real life" situation even though a few minor details (such as the experimenter's name) have been changed for dramatic license.

Hurkos' tenure as a psychic detective dominates the last segment of "The Peter Hurkos Story," and it deals specifically in his particular brand of telepathy, which is known as *psychometry*. Psychometry, a term coined by the American neurologist Joseph Buchanan in 1849, is defined as:

> the faculty of obtaining paranormal knowledge of persons or events connected with a physical article by holding the object, which may be concealed by wrapper.[27]

In addition to categorizing psychometry (touch telepathy), Buchanan believed that all human bodies and objects produce an emanation or field which provides clues as to the nature of those bodies. Therefore, when Peter Hurkos touched a certain object or person, he received a psychic flash or insight into the characteristics of that object or person. In "The Peter Hurkos Story" he uses this power of psychometry to find and locate a vicious serial murderer named Byrd (Andrew Prine, of *The Town That Dreaded Sundown* [1976] and *V* [1984]). Hurkos' alliance with the police does reflect reality, because in the 1950s the real Hurkos was considered the best known and most accurate psychometrist in the world. Still, his results were not always as impressive as this *One Step Beyond* episode seems to indicate. For instance, among Hurkos' more notable misses were the following claims: that Hitler was still alive and living in Argentina, and that a certain suspect was in fact the Boston Strangler (but in reality was not). On one occasion Hurkos was even arrested by the F.B.I. and failed to see it coming (though, in his defense, he claimed his psychic power could not be used to acquire personally relevant information). Many police authorities who utilized Hurkos to help them solve crimes later claimed that he had exaggerated his own importance and accuracy in the various investigations. *One Step Beyond*'s "The Peter Hurkos Story" does not reflect those realities, choosing instead to view Hurkos as simply "the real thing."

At the close of "The Peter Hurkos Story" (Part II), the real Hurkos appears on stage and is briefly interviewed by host John Newland. Courageously, Hurkos offers himself up as a guinea pig for any experiments that science may impose on him to quantify his unique abilities. In the end, *One Step Beyond* chooses not to investigate the "negative evidence" of Hurkos' abilities. Still, it is rewarding that it should attempt to dramatize his story with at least one, if not both, eyes aimed towards verisimilitude. Overall, both parts of "The Peter Hurkos Story" tell an interesting tale that is based on fact. Yet if the devil is in the details, then the whole show would be a near miss for its decision to rearrange the events of Hurkos' accident and the choice to leave out vital information that counters Hurkos' claim to be an authentic psychic.

All that background established, "The Peter Hurkos Story" does accurately portray the psychic phenomenon known as psychometry, a facet of the psychic universe later explicitly examined in *The Dead Zone*, Stephen King's novel of another "touch psychic" whose unique powers develop (as Hurkos' did) after an accident and coma.

54. "Delia"

(Dramatized by Merwin Gerard;
Directed by John Newland;
Airdate: May 3, 1960)

SYNOPSIS: While on vacation at a beautiful and out-of-the-way tropical island, *One Step Beyond* host John Newland is approached by a retired islander named Bentley who has a strange story to share: A disillusioned, bitter man named Wilson once met and fell hopelessly in love with the beautiful Delia, a girl he felt he had been destined to meet (and love) all his life. Then Delia vanished from the island and Phil's desperate search began ... and lasted for eight long, agonizing years, until a tragic and unexpected resolution. Just days after Phillip died in an accident, the real Delia arrived on the island for the first time, nearly a decade after her first "phantom appearance."

GUEST CAST: Lee Philips (Phillip Wilson), Barbara Lord (Delia), Murray Matheson (Bentley), Maureen Leeds (Mrs. Garran), Peter Camlin, Salvador Vasquez.

COMMENTARY: After again transcending the role of TV host and narrator by interacting with the *dramatis personae* of the episode in question (in the fashion of "The Inheritance" and "Vanishing Point"), John Newland listens intently in "Delia" as an islander (why do these things always happen on islands?) describes a tale of tragic love. It is the story of Phillip Wilson, a disillusioned, bitter man with two ex-wives. Unexpectedly, Wilson has fallen for Delia, a beautiful young woman who disappeared after one fateful meeting, never to be seen by Wilson again. And as the years passed, Wilson grew ever more desperate to share even a moment with his beloved again.

If that set-up sounds like the stuff of a tear-jerker, it is. "Delia" is a sad story about lovers who have been crossed not by the stars but by time and the psychic mechanisms of an indifferent universe. In a virtual replay of the setting and concept driving "The Return of Mitchell Campion," a soul bi-locates or astrally projects to a distant island, only to find love there. In this case that loves proves devastating, and it destroys Phillip Wilson. And, like Campion in "The Return of Mitchell Campion," it is a devastation not shared by two. Some eight years after Wilson's crisis, Delia is still young and beautiful, and she is able to dismiss her love of Phillip as merely a dream she once had. He lost his life over a love that was unrequited and virtually unremembered. Depressing.

Despite "Delia's" obsession with tragic love, the story tends to play out as trite. Delia and Phillip meet and, in the tradition of all bad television, are *instantly* in love. They speak immediately of destiny and of love, and it all seems a little saccharine. Of course, they are pressed for time because the episode is only a half hour long, but still, the lock-step feel of the romance tends to take away from the feeling of a meaningful love shattered. Perhaps the most interesting thing about "Delia" is the sheer number of stock *One Step Beyond* ideas it recycles. The island setting (rerun #1), the out-of-body bilocation (rerun #2), the alcoholic protagonist (rerun #3), the insertion of Newland into the story by describing that he is "on a vacation" from the show (rerun #4), the time hiccup (rerun #5), and the protagonist's "Cassandra" status as disbelieved (rerun #6) all contribute to a feeling that this romance is really by-the-numbers rather than a truly meaningful love story.

In the remainder of the second season and in the third season, *One Step Beyond* would depict marvelous love stories of truly bizarre and original concepts in four superior episodes: "The Visitor," "The House of the Dead," "Legacy of Love" and "Nightmare." "Delia" is not in the same class as those stories, but in a way it is comforting in its steadfast reiteration of common series conventions. Like an old shoe, "Delia" fits well even if it doesn't look great.

55. "The Visitor"
(Dramatized by Larry Marcus; Directed by John Newland;
Airdate: May 10, 1960)

SYNOPSIS: After 17 years of marriage, Ellen Grayson is a recovering alcoholic who is unable to forgive her husband, Harry, for a heartless, off-handed comment he made a long, long time ago. When Harry's car unexpectedly goes off the road during a snowstorm, Ellen is visited in her mountain home by a handsome young man: Harry, 20 years younger, kind and gentle. The young Harry offers an important message of hope and love for his sad wife that the older Harry has not been able to express because of an increasing emotional distance from his heartsick wife.

GUEST CAST: Joan Fontaine (Ellen Grayson) Warren Beatty (Harry Grayson).

COMMENTARY: "The Visitor," which ranks among *One Step Beyond*'s most accomplished and touching episodes, has very little to do with "provable" psychic phenomena and a great deal to do with people, emotions, regrets and a shattered relationship. In this heartfelt story a married man in his fifties manages to escape his "cage of reality" and save his failing marriage by shedding the bounds of linear time. As a fresh-faced, optimistic youngster from the past, he is able to say some important things to his wife that he is incapable of telling her as an old man in the present, so filled with hurt and resentment. For his wife, this visitation is just the reminder she needed of her husband's love because they stopped communicating with each other a long long time ago.

Wisely, "The Visitor" does not dwell on technicalities. There is no valid explanation for how a man unconscious in his car manages to send a younger version of himself to make reparations with his wife. There is no discussion of OBEs, doppelgangers, astral projection, bilocation or teleportation. Instead, Newland observes only that as human beings we live our lives by the steady clicking of the clock while forgetting that time is merely a human invention. Somehow, Harry Grayson manages to escape the confines of that human creation and project exactly what his sick and emotionally-dying wife needs of him at that very moment. This "accident in time" is not an event that can be verified, buttressed or quantified through psychic research, it is merely the hook for a very engaging story about another marital couple at a crossroads in their relationship.

As is usual for *One Step Beyond*, it is a bizarre and inexplicable phenomenon that saves the collapsing marriage, that ultimately makes the couple's union a stronger one. And, in another common element of the series, Mrs. Ellen Grayson is depicted as a recovering alcoholic, so it is easier for her doctor to dismiss the claims that she was visited by her husband of twenty years in the past. Exhibiting the sexism of the time, he calls her a victim of "female emotionalism."

As a sentimental, resonant story of a second chance, of an old hurt finally healed, "The Visitor" succeeds so beautifully because its central performances hit exactly the right notes. Joan Fontaine conveys the hurt, cynicism and anger of a woman who never recovered from what she perceived to be her husband's snub: an off-handed suggestion early in their marriage that she have an abortion when she became pregnant and they were struggling to make ends meet. Warren Beatty, in heaps of old age makeup, plays the old Harry Grayson as a man who is simply tired of all the arguing and second guessing. Then, in his fresh-faced incarnation as the young Harry, Warren Beatty reveals the excitable, enthusiastic side of the same character. It too is an accomplished performance. John Newland remembers well what it was like to work with Beatty at the time. "He was just a nobody then, but Fontaine really wanted him for the episode, so we cast him. He was dating Natalie Wood, and together Beatty and Wood would come over and watch the dailies to see how he was holding up. He wasn't really in make-up that long, it wasn't *too* severe, and he became a good friend."

There is an overwhelming aura of redemption and miracles in "The Visitor." The omnipresent snowfall and the stopover by a ghost of days past imbue the narrative with a certain yuletide feel. And the fragile nature of this tender psychic experience is captured beautifully when the young Harry finally realizes whose house he has really stumbled upon. As recognition crosses the young man's features, he vanishes from the house and — miles away in the crashed car — the Harry of the present awakens. This "flashing out" of the young Harry at exactly the moment of recognition captures how gossamer-thin and delicate a miraculous moment like this might feel. You cannot touch it. You cannot hold onto it. When it is over, it is gone forever.

At the end of "The Visitor" Newland assures us that the path to healing has been forged and wonders about what really happened. Was all this an hallucination? A delusion? An accident in time? Did Grayson will himself back to become the man he once was to prove his love in the present? For once, those questions do not really matter, for this is a *One Step Beyond* episode that is all about humanity and the fragile bonds that can keep even the closest of people apart. It captures the melancholy of a love dimmed by time and an accumulation of perceived wrongs. "The Visitor" is a standout episode and perhaps the best of the series from a purely sentimental point of view.

56. "Gypsy"

(Dramatized by Gabrielle Upton; Directed by John Newland;
Airdate: May 17, 1960)

SYNOPSIS: A warden at a state prison contacts *One Step Beyond* host John Newland about an inexplicable happening that has him baffled. Four prisoners recently escaped from jail, and one of the fugitives, a gypsy, died in the attempt. Yet, after his own death, the gypsy apparently convinced a sensitive young kid on the path to a lifetime of criminal behavior to return to prison and salvage his future.

GUEST CAST: Robert Blake (Kid), John Kellog, Johnny Seven, Murvyn Vye, Addison Richards, Monte E. Burkhart, Kelly Thordsen.

COMMENTARY: Robert Blake, Emmy Award winner for *Baretta* (1975–78) and frequent guest on *The Richard Boone Show* (1963–64), gives a solid early performance in "Gypsy," a story of one convict's opportunity for redemption. As one might predict from *One Step Beyond*'s special nature, that redemption comes not from the spirit within but from a strange "outside" source: a psychic experience involving a gypsy.

In one sense, "Gypsy" is also a coming-of-age story. At first, Robert Blake's "Kid," an inmate, just wants to belong to something … anything. He wants to be part of a gang because his Mother is dead and his father is a drunk. When he becomes aware of an attempt to escape from State Prison, he insinuates his way into the group, trying to prove he is worthy of "membership." Blake is particularly good in this portion of the episode as his soulful eyes tellingly capture the sensitive nature of his character, a petty crook who could end up spending his life in prison if he does not change. Then, after the escape, the Gypsy tells the Kid to go back to prison and be a man, lest he be killed as an escapee. When the Gypsy dies in his arms, "Kid" makes the first truly adult decision of his life and returns to prison to take his medicine. The inference is clearly that he will be rewarded for his honesty and for surrendering himself. In returning to the prison, "the Kid" has redeemed himself and made room for a more positive future.

However, the psychic kicker in "Gypsy" is that the Gypsy died, unnoticed, during the escape attempt. He never even made it over the prison wall, so his heartfelt advice to the Kid came not as a living, thinking human being, but as a spirit. Clearly then, the Gypsy falls into that category that careful *One Step Beyond* viewers have seen before: the *crisis apparition*. In this case, the Gypsy appeared "alive" so as to save the Kid's future. And so he did, because the other fugitives all died after the escape!

Significant mainly for Blake's performance and the fact that John Newland is once again "in" on the action (this time visiting a warden who recounts the story), "Gypsy" is another relatively innocuous *One Step Beyond* episode, well-produced and directed without being particularly innovative or new. Another convention on display in "Gypsy" is the recurring *One Step Beyond* motif that the beliefs of a non–caucasian (i.e. a Gypsy) are in fact more powerful than Christian dogma. The foreign always represents a deeper "truth" on this anthology, an idea on hand in "The Riddle," "The Dead Part of the House," "House of the Dead" and even "Night of Decision."

Gypsy lore is a favorite element of genre TV, and *One Step Beyond* has not been the only series to exploit it. The Australian horror anthology *The Evil Touch* (1973) offered an entry entitled "Never Fool with a Gypsy Icon" in which two escaped convicts (again!) faced a Gypsy curse for their crimes. In *Buffy the Vampire Slayer* and its sequel *Angel*, the vampire Angelus (David Boreanaz) is also stricken with a gypsy curse that causes him to lose his soul if he ever has a moment of true happiness. In print and on film, Stephen King's *Thinner* also highlighed the negative impact of a gypsy curse.

57. "Contact"
(Dramatized by Paul David; Directed by John Newland;
Airdate: May 24, 1960)

SYNOPSIS: A man receives the gift of a pocket watch from his wife, and then has a psychic vision of someone planning to kill her.

GUEST CAST: Ron Randell (Bill Dermott), Catherine McLeod (Mary Dermott), Jason Johnson (Pawnbroker), Rodney Bell (Policeman), Jeanne Tatum, Alexander Lockwood.

COMMENTARY: Unfortunately, "Contact" was not available for review by this author at the time this text was written, and has not been rerun recently on the Sci-Fi Channel. Judging from descriptions in various sources, "Contact" appears, like "The Peter Hurkos Story" before it, to concern *psychometry*—the ability to discern information about people by touching their possessions (in this case, a pocket watch).

58. "The Lonely Room"
(Dramatized by Larry Marcus; Directed by John Newland;
Airdate: May 31, 1960)

SYNOPSIS: A diffident 23-year-old intellectual named Henri longs to romance his beautiful neighbor, the stunning Therese, but cannot seem to work up the courage to ask her out for a date. When he finally does manage to summon his manhood, Henri finds he has been beaten to the punch by his own doppelganger: an exact double with all the confidence and charm that poor Henri lacks.

GUEST CAST: Fabrizio Mioni (Henri), Lisa Montell (Therese), Carl Esmond, Maurice Marsac.

COMMENTARY: The doppelganger, literally the "double walker," is defined in literature as an apparitional duplicate or counterpart of a living person, and it is a concept that has been frequently explored in horror and science fiction circles. In *Beyond Reality*'s second episode ("The Doppelganger"), one man's nightmare comes to life as a vicious double. In *Poltergeist: The Legacy* (1996–1999), an imaginary friend of Katherine's goes on a spree of terror in "The Doppleganger" [sic]. The doppelganger or evil twin has also appeared numerous times on *Star Trek* ("What Are Little Girls Made Of," "The Enemy Within," "Whom Gods Destroy"), *Space: 1999* ("Seed of Destruction," "Another Time, Another Place"), *Doctor Who* ("The Androids of Tara," "Enemy of the People," "The Android Invasion"), *Star Trek: The Next Generation* ("Datalore," "Time Squared," "Second Chances"), *The X-Files* ("Small Potatoes," "Colony"), the new *Twilight Zone* ("Shatterday," with Bruce WIllis) and even *Knight Rider* (1982–85), making it one of genre television's all-time greatest clichés.

After explaining that Byron, Goethe and even Catherine the Great all had encounters with their doppelgangers(?), *One Step Beyond* host John Newland allows the mysterious events of "The Lonely Room" to unfold. In direct contrast to the above-listed stories, the doppelganger featured in this episode of *One Step Beyond* is not a villainous thing but rather a helper of sorts, a kind of romantic pinch-hitter. Henri's strange double nicely sets up things so that meek Henri can pick up with Therese where he leaves off. "The Lonely Room" also seems to suggest that psychic phenomena most often appear where intense emotions are in play (an idea also in evidence in the poltergeist attack dramatized in "The Lovers"). In this story, viewers are supposed to come away believing that Henri's love for Therese has somehow helped him to create a more romantic, more idealized version of himself, and that he has somehow willed this suave lookalike into being with his intense desire. What follows then is a meditation on the concept of identity, as "The Lonely Room" explores the notion that there is more than one side of our minds, so there must, by extension, be more than one side to our physicality as well.

The doppelganger in this story, a "spectral matchmaker," exists as an extension of Henri's desire, and its presence is not at all ambiguous or in doubt. It is seen interacting with Therese and by the employees of a restaurant in objective fashion, so it cannot be dismissed. This odd ability to see one's double is sometimes referred to in paranormal circles as *autoscopy*. Though the doppelganger is viewed by many people in "The Lonely Room," the episode does not provide evidence or documentation of such an encounter.

A fun story, "The Lonely Room" is a tale of romantic longing. Although in one sense Henri seems a terrible loser (he is literally outclassed by himself), in another sense he seems resourceful and even charming, following his doppelganger and would-be lover on a date, and finally, summoning the strength to fill in. Is the doppelganger an illusion? Who knows, but as John Newland suggests, imagination is a prime requisite for all those who take that "one step beyond…"

59. "House of the Dead"

(Dramatized by Don M. Mankiewicz; Directed by John Newland;
Airdate: June 7, 1960)

SYNOPSIS: In Hong Kong, Lt. Harry Fraser proposes to his beautiful Chinese girlfriend, Mai Ling, but she fears that her ethnicity will cause him turmoil in his military career if she marries him and returns to his home. When Mai Ling disappears without a trace, Fraser seeks the help of an Old Seer, a strange blind man with a stick. This street prophet draws a symbol that indicates that Fraser's beloved has gone to a place known as "The House of the Dead." But which "House of the Dead," and for what purpose?

GUEST CAST: Mario Alcalde (Lt. Harry Fraser), Laya Raki (Mai Ling), James Hong, Allen Jung, Gail Bonney, Barry Bernard, Beal Wong.

COMMENTARY: Many *One Step Beyond* episodes are constructed so tightly and move so swiftly that one emerges from a viewing with a sense of breathlessness. "House of the Dead" is just such an installment, filled with engaging characters and built on both a "time limit" and a "needle in a haystack search" that foster a true sense of urgency.

"House of the Dead" is erected with an eye towards generating suspense. John Newland's opening narration establishes that in "Hong Kong, all things are possible … and nothing is what it seems," hinting at that common *One Step Beyond* trope: that "ethnics" (Indians in "The Riddle," Gypsies in "Gypsy," Native Americans in "Night of Decision," et al). have a more well-rounded view of life and the universe; and that the white man is hampered by his traditional, Christian, Euclidian view of the world.

After setting up that thesis, the episode establishes a few important points. Firstly, Lt. Fraser is due to be shipped out of the country in a short amount of time. Secondly, he is in love with Mai Ling, a beautiful girl who gains the audience's sympathy instantly. She is so sweet and kind a character that one understands immediately why Fraser loves her. Then Mai Ling disappears and Fraser is forced (with only two hours left in the country before being shipped out) to undertake a search through the vast city that "only a man in love would ever attempt." The love relationship thus established (and threatened), the viewer is invested in Harry's mission, aware of his imminent departure, and therefore behind him all the way as he fights the odds to find Mai Ling.

Often it is illuminating to see how a writer stacks the deck in his favor, balancing one story element against the other to create a viewer's identification with the material. By making Mai Ling sympathetic (she is afraid that her ethnicity is a problem for Harry), by creating a "deadline" (Harry's departure from Hong Kong), by putting up an impossible obstacle (a search of all the Houses of the Dead in Hong Kong), Don Mankiewicz constructs a story so tight, so compelling, that viewers are completely engaged by the time that the paranormal enters the picture in the form of a "ghost cabbie" who leads Harry to Mai Ling.

And what is one to make of the fact that a man can be in two places in the same instant of time, as the cabbie directs Harry to his lover and simultaneously lays dying in a House of the Dead, tended to by the lovely Mai Ling? Though bilocation and the OBE are possibilities, one senses this episode may have been trying to grapple with a slightly different experience: the NDE (Near Death Experience). The screenplay establishes that the cabbie is at the final transition between existence and non-existence, hoping to conduct a last act of grace before he finds his destiny in the afterlife. This certainly sounds like a Near Death Experience, although most NDEs feature visions of the afterlife (and common elements like a tunnel of light; a feeling of peace and serenity; a meeting with friendly faces from life who have already "passed on"), not some attempt at redemption in this life. Perhaps the occurrence in "House of the Dead" is merely an OBE–like journey that occurs near the time of death. Whatever one calls it, it allows for a triumphant reunion and a happy ending, so one can be grateful for it.

The other "psychic" component of "House of the Dead" involves the blind street prophet who is able to (in a *very* general sense) determine Mai Ling's location. This seer draws sketchings with a stick and his grandson then traces over his drawings, which inevitably reveal something of great importance. How to explain the prophet's powers? Well, he could simply be a good guesser, since there are apparently dozens if not hundreds of Houses of the Dead in Hong Kong. This is rather reminiscent of a psychic who determines "telepathically" that a corpse has been buried near a "body of water." It is so general an answer that it will inevitably be interpreted as "correct." Bodies of water are frequent, and how does one "quantify" close? A mile, two miles? Thirty miles? On the other hand, one can assume that the Prophet's powers in "House of the Dead" are real if one accepts that old chestnut that one who has lost an important sense (such as sight) develops other radar (such as telepathy).

A great episode (and an involving love story), "House of the Dead" is notable also for an early performance by James Hong. This is the Asian actor who has appeared in films such as *Blade Runner* (1982) and *Big Trouble in Little China* (1986), and TV series such as *Forever Knight* ("Cherry Blossoms") and *The X-Files* ("Hell Money").

60. "Goodbye Grandpa"

(Dramatized by Gabrielle Upton; Directed by John Newland;
Airdate: June 14, 1960)

SYNOPSIS: At a dry, arid place where the railroad tracks rust and end, an old grandpa often imagines that he hears the whistle of that grand ole girl, the Silver Streak — a train on which he was once the engineer's brakeman. When Grandpa falls sick he promises that he will never die without saying goodbye to his young, sensitive grandson and his tough-nosed granddaughter. When Grandpa passes away, he keeps his promise, and his special signal — two long whistles and three short — echoes through the quiet desert, to the delight of the children.

GUEST CAST: Edgar Stehl (Grandpa), Candy Moore (Nan), Anna Karen (Cally), Donald Losby (Boy).

COMMENTARY: "Goodbye Grandpa" is a sentimental little show with enough intelligence to remember that the young and pure of heart do not stop to question that which is miraculous. "Goodbye Grandpa" is a simple, humble story about a teenage girl who, because of the poverty around her, has closed off her emotions. She misses her father (who abandoned the family) but will not admit to the pain. She wants her little brother to toughen up and learn the harsh facts of life, but in the end her grandpa teaches her a lesson about life ... and miracles. "There are amazing things around us if you have the patience to look and listen," Grandpa says wisely, and his comments become truth at the climax, as, after death, he travels by the old homestead in his beloved train (offscreen), and his distinctive whistle is heard all across the dead land.

If that episode description sounds schmaltzy ... well, "Goodbye Grandpa" *is* schmaltzy ... in a good way. It may be a simpleminded program that could be likened to *Touched by an Angel*, but its heart is certainly in the right place, and it has some interesting elements that elevate it above its corny premise. Since the program is set in the desert (a realm of mystery also established in "The Explorer"), the outlandishness of the premise is mitigated. After all, the desert produces mirages (like trains?) and strange sounds carry over vast distances in the dry air (like train whistles?). Anyway, the explanation of the miraculous is not as important as what it provides that poverty-stricken family living out there in the blistering desert: hope.

Perhaps the best testament to "Goodbye Grandpa's" enduring value is the fact that in 1985 Steven Spielberg opened his heralded anthology *Amazing Stories* with "Ghost Train," a story very similar in tone and substance, if not mood or effect. In "Ghost Train" a curmudgeonly old grandfather (Roberts Blossom) tells his grandson (Lukas Haas) that a train he should have boarded once will come back for him and carry him away at the time of his death. The family disbelieves this story, but in the million dollar climax the ghost train literally races through the family's living room, destroying their house. Then, in a "tender" finale, Grandpa boards the ghost train for destination unknown, while his beloved grandson waves him off, buoyed by the proof of life after death.

It is actually rather interesting to contrast these two stories. In "Goodbye, Grandpa" there is a real sense of place and time (of rusted railroads, crumbling homes, poverty and desert life), but in "Ghost Train" there is the typical Spielberg suburban family living in a fancy new house (the same family could have appeared in *E.T.* or *Poltergeist* without much difficulty). In "Goodbye Grandpa" the miracle is an understated one: The Silver Streak returns, with Grandpa aboard, and he sends the children his special whistle. If one felt so inclined, it could be argued that the light of the train was a mirage (or an anomalous phenomenon) and that the whistle was just a sound carried from some great distance away. There is room for debate, and that fact gives "Goodbye Grandpa" a degree of subtlety.

In "Ghost Train," fiery spectacle is the order of the day as all hell breaks loose and a family's home is destroyed in an action-packed special effects setpiece. Of course, *One Step Beyond* could not have afforded (on $55,000 per half hour) to destroy its sets with a real-life train, and every fan, critic and casual audience member can be glad for that. It is rather difficult to get all sentimental and worked up about a personal story when the final twist in the plot is not a sentimental "whistle blowing" heard out there in the desert, but rather a razzmatazz, blow-out special effects show-case whose primary purpose is not to send the old grandpa off but to feature massive destruction.

Despite the different approaches in storytelling, *Amazing Stories* certainly owes "Goodbye Grandpa" a serious debt, as it apes all the same plot elements: a train, a grandpa-grandson relationship, a miraculous affirmation of life after death and a vehicle bound for nether regions.

61. "The Storm"

(Dramatized by Jerome Gruskin;
Directed by John Newland; Airdate: June 21, 1960)

SYNOPSIS: "La Tormenta" (i.e. "The Storm") is a beautiful oil painting with a bizarre pedigree: It was painted just recently, but its artist died more than three years ago—during the Korean War! La Tormenta's claim of authenticity haunts Adelle, a married woman who once had feelings for Pedro, the dead painter. Adelle and her doubting husband, Joe, visit Pedro's mother in Mexico ... and are surprised when she talks about the deceased artist in the present tense.

GUEST CAST: Lee Bergere (Joe), Rebecca Welles (Adelle), Danny Zardivan, Ernest Sarracino, Argentino Brunetti, Joe Dominguez, Raoul De Leon, Abel Frances, Donald Foster.

COMMENTARY: A painting of dubious or perhaps psychic origin is the fulcrum of "The Storm," the final episode of *One Step Beyond*'s sophomore season. This "hotly disputed" canvass is a point of obsession for Adelle, and that obsession provides the episode its most interesting subtext. Though Adelle denies to her husband Joe that she ever harbored romantic feelings for Pedro the painter, Adelle's overriding interest in his work seems to suggest otherwise. Though Adelle is pregnant with Joe's child (which makes her, like alcoholics and recovering mental patients, easier to dismiss on *One Step Beyond*), she really seems to carry a torch for the dead Pedro. Is it possible Adelle did love him, and that this search for authenticity is her way of somehow keeping him alive? If so, that plot point makes for an interesting parallel to the psychic story, which finds Pedro alive indeed, inside the body of the blind Tomas, who now paints with the same vision as the dead man.

The *One Step Beyond* convention that non-white, non–Americans share a wider world view (last seen in "House of the Dead") also haunts "The Storm." Joe and Adelle get kicked out of their hotel room and are expelled from Pedro's village for asking questions. The natives do not want them there, and the American Adelle and Joe are really strangers in a strange land. The Mexicans of "The Storm" seem to understand and accept the idea that a dead man could come to a living man in his dreams and tell him to paint in a certain way, whereas the grounded Americans refuse to believe in such things. This episode also plays on a fear which is certainly a corollary to this cliché: that Americans in a foreign land should be a little afraid. They do not understand the laws or the rules of the land, let alone the guiding philosophies. They are alone, without the resources of America, and are way out of their element. This feeling of isolation, of ignorance even, creates a subtle anxiety in *One Step Beyond* stories such as "The Riddle" (which was set in India), as well as "The Storm."

Ironically, the questing protagonists of "The Storm" are satisfied that a "miracle" (i.e. the supernatural) has occurred with regards to Tomas and Pedro only when it is confirmed in their own lexicon. A Catholic priest, a trusted authority in America, confirms the strange story of this union of souls, and only then, couched in terms of Christianity, do Adelle and Joe accept what was previously unacceptable. Perhaps this is a sign of the times, or merely an unconscious reflection of *One Step Beyond*'s origination in a Judeo-Christian culture.

Surely another sign of the times is that, in the tradition of *The Dick Van Dyke Show* and *I Love Lucy*, Adelle and Joe in "The Storm" sleep in separate twin beds. Here that fact makes one wonder how Adelle managed to become pregnant in the first place.

"The Storm" also reflects another soon-to-be cliché of the horror genre. Paintings are often the center of odd stories—invested with an almost supernatural power in many genre stories. *Night Gallery* featured paintings as portals to worlds of horror in stories such as "The Cemetery," *Friday the 13th: The Series* explored the same concept in its final episode, "The Charnel Pit," and the psychic-based programs *Beyond Reality* ("The Color of Mad") and *Poltergeist the Legacy* ("The Painting") have followed suit.

And just how believable is "The Storm," a tale of "automatic art" (the dead painting and drawing through a living medium)? Well, in support of "The Storm's" thesis, there is the case of Luiz Antonio Gasparetto, a Brazilian psychologist who has been reported to go into a trance and channel a master of the art of painting:

> Not only is his range impressive (he has successfully executed the styles of Leonardo, Rembrandt, Van Gogh, Renoir, Lautrec, Matisse, Modigliani, and Picasso ... but he uses no brushes. He paints with his feet as well as his hands and occasionally channels an artist through his left arm, another through his right

arm ... Gasparetto is convinced that the discarnate masters paint through him for the sole purpose of revealing that life continues after death.[28]

Whether this is an elaborate hoax or a true example of "automatic art" is uncertain, but Gasparetto's alleged ability lends "The Storm" an all-important veneer of believability. *One Step Beyond* again shows that its mind is on getting the details right, even if at the same time it is shaking its head with wonder.

SEASON THREE (1960–61)

Cast and Credits

CAST: John Newland (Our Guide to the World of the Unknown).

CREW: *Producer:* Collier Young. *Series Created by the Associate Producer:* Merwin Gerard. *Special Consultant:* Ivan Klapper. *Executive Writer:* Larry Marcus. *Directors of Photography:* William A. Horning, Brendan Stafford. *Film Editors:* Henry Berman, Derek Hyde-Chambers. *Music:* Harry Lubin. *Production Coordinator:* Peter Marriott. *Director of Photography:* Brendan Stafford. *Camera Operator:* Frank Lown. *Art Director:* Frank White. *Assistant Directors:* Donald C. Klune, David Tomblin. *Casting:* Barry Gray. *Sound Supervisor:* A.W. Watkins. *Sound Mixer:* John Bramall. *Continuity:* Davis Martin. *Make-up:* Jim Hyde. *Hairdresser:* Alice Holmes.

Filmed in Hollywood California, and then at Metro-Goldwyn-Mayer British Studios, Boreham Wood, Hertfordshire.

The Episodes

62. "Tidal Wave"

(Dramatized by Charles Larson; Directed by John Newland; Airdate: August 30, 1960)

SYNOPSIS: After a series of devastating earthquakes in 1960, dangerous tidal waves encroach on the peaceful Hawaiian islands. A polio victim, the wheelchair-bound Mrs. North, misses the island-wide alert to evacuate because of a malfunctioning radio. Separated from her husband on the other side of the island, Mrs. North is unexpectedly rescued by a stranger who heard her cries for help ... despite the fact that he is deaf!

GUEST CAST: Jean Allison (Margaret North), William Schallert (Dick), Dennis Patrick, Cliff Hall, Ted Knight, William Quinn, Larry Burrell.

COMMENTARY: *One Step Beyond*'s third season opened with a powerful bang in August of 1960 by dramatizing a "true life" story of recent vintage — one that had, in fact, occurred only three months before the airing of the show. Specifically, "Tidal Wave" involves a series of earthquakes which struck Chile on May 21, 1960, and then generated "seismic sea waves." These tidal waves moved at an amazing 425 miles an hour and were reported as high as 16 feet as they surged towards Hawaii on Wednesday, May 25, 1960. The specific story of "Tidal Wave" concerns the tsunami's touchdown in Hawaii and the experience of one Margaret North, a woman handicapped by polio, whose cries for help were inexplicably heard by a "deaf" military man. In a bold move, *One Step Beyond* ends this dramatization by ushering the real participants on-screen to confirm their odd psychic experience. Though this final interview is brief and a bit stilted, and the two interviewees seem terribly nervous in front of the camera, it is still a powerful testimonial that lends credence to *One Step Beyond*'s ongoing attempt to document the personal record of those who have survived so-called paranormal experiences. Unless one assumes flat out that these real witnesses are liars, their presence makes the tale of telepathic communication a difficult one to dismiss out of hand.

Sometimes truth is stranger than fiction, and the experience of Mrs. North in May of 1960 proves that adage. The details of the story could not be more compelling had they been invented. Specifically, Mrs. North makes for a perfect protagonist. Left alone in her home, she is physically confined to a wheelchair and terribly lonesome because she and her husband have just moved to Hawaii. She does not know any of the neighbors yet, and they are unaware of her handicap. So, when Margaret becomes trapped, aware that a tidal wave is approaching, there is no hope of escape. The episode becomes almost unbearably suspenseful as North pulls herself to the door, falls from her wheelchair, tries to crawl out to the street, and then shouts for help. Her anguished, desperate pleas are heard by Thomas Powers, a hearing-impaired military officer who finds himself inexplicably lost in the North's neighborhood. Hearing her cries for help, Powers stops his car, looks around, and saves Mrs. North.

How did he hear her? Was it thought transference? Telepathic communication? Fortunate happenstance? In this case, one cannot establish how or why it happened, only confirm that it did happen, since the actual participants made themselves available to tell their personal story. In a court of law (or even a court of skeptics), personal accounts such as these would not hold up, no doubt; but this is television, after all, and *One Step Beyond* gains some "accuracy" points for bringing the witnesses on the air. Again, one should remember that *One Step Beyond*'s mission was not to authenticate all its stories, only to dramatize real accounts in a way commensurate with the research and literature of the time. In that regard, "Tidal Wave" succeeds admirably. It shares a tale of recent interest (May 1960) around a confirmed event (earthquakes, tidal waves) and lets the participants air their side of the story.

An interesting footnote to "Tidal Wave" involves the performers. Jean Allison and William Schallert had both appeared on the series before (in "Twelve Hours to Live" and "Epilogue," respectively), but there is a noteworthy newcomer in a supporting role. Playing a seismologist in "Tidal Wave" is none other than Ted Knight, Ted Baxter of *The Mary Tyler Moore Show* (1970–77) and Henry Rush of *Too Close for Comfort* (1980–83).

63. "Anniversary of a Murder"

(Dramatized by Larry Marcus and Jane Anna Pritchard;
Directed by John Newland; Airdate: September 27, 1960)

SYNOPSIS: Two lovers involved in an illicit affair are haunted by the voice of a bicyclist they inadvertently struck down on a dark road one year earlier. Despite their attempts to cover up the crime, their guilty consciences—and the voice of a dead boy crying out from beyond the grave—lead them to a justice of sorts.

GUEST CAST: Harry Townes (Jerry Sims), Randy Stuart (Frances Hiller), Amzie Strickland, Alexander Lockwood, James Maloney.

COMMENTARY: *One Step Beyond*'s first comeuppance episode of the third season may also be the series' very best. "Anniversary of a Murder" is one of those classic episodes that nearly qualifies as an urban legend in the 21st century. Viewers may incorrectly remember it as a *Twilight Zone* episode, or as an installment of *Alfred Hitchcock Presents*, but "Anniversary of a Murder" is nonetheless remembered as a particularly frightening story about two selfish lovers who become involved in a hit-and-run accident and choose not to do the right thing. So common a story has this tale become that the hit-and-run accident and the vengeful victim has also become something of a genre standard.

In *Creepshow 2* (1987) driver Lois Chiles strikes down a hitchhiker on the way home from an illicit rendezvous with a lover, only to be attacked by the dead man (who keeps repeating the line "Thanks for the ride, lady..." to horrific and hilarious effect). In the popular *I Know What You*

Did Last Summer (1997) it is a group of teens who have something to lose (scholarships, college, their futures) and who consequently cover up a hit-and-run accident to deleterious effect. "Anniversary of a Murder" pre-dates those stories by many years (decades actually); but in fairness, the "hit and run" comeuppance has a distinct E.C. Comics (*Tales from the Crypt*) feel to it as well.

"Anniversary of a Murder" differs from these other productions in its focus, despite sharing a common theme. Where a *Tales from the Crypt* comic from William Gaines (or *I Know What You Did Last Summer*) might obsess on the mechanisms of revenge (i.e., killings), "Anniversary of a Murder" instead looks close-up at what Newland terms the "faces of guilt." Simms and Fran are not bad people, but they do make a bad decision. Instead of doing the right thing and reporting the death of the bicyclist to the police (which would require they explain their affair), they do nothing. The guilt of inaction and the knowledge that a little boy died alone on the roadside in the dark, eats at this couple over a long year. It is not surprising then that the relationship between Simms and Fran fades after the accident — it leaves both parties feeling bad about themselves and their co-conspirator. "Just erase me," Fran begs at one point in "Anniversary of a Murder," but the point is that a crime cannot not be erased — not from reality and not even from Simms' accusatory dictaphone, which plays the voice of the dead boy again and again. Petty selfishness has turned an illicit act into a more serious crime. Simms pays for this crime with his life, killed while avoiding another bicyclist on the road, and Fran finally confesses.

Harry Towne (who appeared in "The Bride Possessed") and Randy Stuart give focused, solid performances in "Anniversary of a Murder." When Hiller hears the dictaphone, with its deathly "voice of conscience," Stuart's reaction is one of jaw-dropping astonishment, and it plays as very natural. For his part, Towne registers a more somber sort of distress as the camera zooms in on an extreme close-up of Simms recalling the fateful incident. Perhaps one of the main reasons this story is so enduringly popular with audiences is the fact that one of the earliest couples to go through the stress, represented here by Townes and Stuart, are so well-drawn and believable.

As far as psychic concepts go, "Anniversary of a Murder" is pretty muddy business. No one besides Simms and Hiller actually hear the incriminating dictaphone recording (except the audience), so it is easy to accept that their experience was a delusion, an auditory manifestation of their guilt. Or, on the other hand, it really could have happened the way they claim, with the voice of the dead boy proving to be an apparitional event. Whatever the truth of this dramatization, it is interesting to report that, again, *One Step Beyond* does not attempt to provide evidence of a comeuppance tale. The series has offered some interesting documentation about premonitions ("Night of April 14," "The Day the World Wept"), mind-over-matter powers ("Moment of Hate"), psychometry ("The Peter Hurkos Story"), telepathy (the preceding "Tidal Wave") and the like, but comeuppance stories, for whatever reason, rarely seem to merit a serious discussion on the lofty plateau of proof and truth. Perhaps this results from the fact that it would be downright odd, if not self-destructive, for "the guilty" to go running to a parapsychologist with the exciting news that he or she is being haunted by a ghost.

64. "The Death Waltz"

(Dramatized by Charles Larson; Based on Material from Amanda Ellis;
Directed by John Newland; Airdate: October 4, 1960)

SYNOPSIS: At Fort Union in New Mexico, America's soldiers wage war against the savage Apaches. Two such soldiers are in love with the beautiful but highly manipulative Lilly, a general's daughter, and both men ask her to a fancy ball that weekend. When Lilly arranges for Lt. Fairchild, one of her suitors, to be away on a dangerous mission, he is killed in action and she is free to pursue the handsome Lt. Buchanan, her man of choice. Then, at the ball, the deceased Lt. Fairchild claims Lilly's last waltz of the evening for himself.

GUEST CAST: Elizabeth Montgomery (Lilly), Joe Gromin (Buchanan), Robert Sampson, K.T. Stevens, Ed Prentiss, James Parnell, Mark Houston.

COMMENTARY: "The Death Waltz" is another comeuppance (or "scales of justice righted") segment for *One Step Beyond*, but unlike the duo just depicted in "Anniversary of a Murder," who were short-sighted and accident-prone but not villainous in any meaningful sense, this episode depicts a truly nasty, mean-spirited human being in the person of Lilly Clark (*Bewitched*'s star Elizabeth Montgomery). It is rare for *One Step Beyond* to offer a glimpse of a truly evil human being ("The Haunted U-Boat" would be an exception), but this episode goes the distance in depicting a selfish young woman with a cold and calculating side. So cruel is Lilly that she actually sends one of her suitors, apparently the lesser of the two in her eyes, out to be killed simply so she can go to the dance with another man. It is surprising to see so negative a view of somebody, and even more shocking that she is a young woman — seemingly not old enough to be so manipulative and deceitful.

In retrospect, Lilly should have made her decision about suitors more carefully. "I'd come back from Hell to be with you," Fairchild warns her at one point in the episode. That is not only a point of foreboding for the audience to register, but it should have served as a warning of sorts to Lilly. And Fairchild makes good on his promise. He shows up in plain sight of everyone at the ball and dances with his beloved ... even though he is dead! This strange happenstance (for which Newland provides an exact date: March 30, 1869 — unconfirmed) seems to fit the lore of the *apparition*, that *One Step Beyond* concept that had been seen as far back as "The Dark Room" in the first season. Specifically, the apparition in "The Death Waltz" seems real to those who perceive it; its background remains the same; it is seen quite close to the percipient; and it is "collectively perceived"[29] (i.e. people other than Lilly see Fairchild). What is even more interesting, however, is that this apparition commits a murder in front of several witnesses. He dances with Lilly, and their rhythm rapidly becomes a frenzy. Newland's camera adopts a high angle as the duo circle together again and again, and (like the moment of gyromancy in "The Premonition") the very act of spinning proves to be dangerous. Lilly finally collapses on the dance floor, dead of fright, and the witnesses to the event report three distinct stories. Some perceived Fairchild; others claim Lilly Clark danced alone; and another group states that she danced with a man that they "did not recognize." In other words, there are conflicting accounts that make an exact determination of what really occurred effectively impossible over a hundred years later.

Though, like "The Vision," "The Death Waltz" provides an exact date and time for its psychic happening, this author was unable to locate the exact "incident" from which this episode was drawn.

65. "The Return"

(Dramatized by Larry Marcus; Directed by John Newland;
Airdate: October 11, 1960)

SYNOPSIS: In combat during the Korean War, an American corporal is rendered blind by an accident. Miraculously, Cpl. Fred Cossage finds the insight and vision to find his way back to camp — despite his visual handicap.

GUEST CAST: Dick Davalos (Corporal Fred Cossage), Jack Mullaney (Captain Young Blood), Charles Gray (Sergeant Kersh), Chris Winter (Lieutenant), Rex Holman (Private Atley).

COMMENTARY: "The Return," by Larry Marcus, could be seen as a confirmation of another *One Step Beyond* trope: That those who are sightless in fact have greater insight/knowledge/wisdom than those with 20/20 vision. In this case, a soldier during the Korean War is able to find his way home via psychic means, just as a blind man named Tomas "paints" in "The Storm" or a blind prophet on the streets of Hong Kong miraculously "sees" the location of a missing person in "House of the Dead."

"The Return" also continues another commonly expressed *One Step Beyond* thematic strand: the wartime psychic event. Seen as far back as "The Dream" and "The Vision" in the first season, this tale seems proof positive that *One Step Beyond*'s writing staff attributed a high frequency of inexplicable events to the already-traumatic environment of combat.

A young Rex Holman appears in "The Return," and he would later make a splash in various *Star Trek* productions. He played a "ghostly" Earp brother in the third season episode "Spectre of the Gun," and the farmer J'onn of Nimbus III in the fifth motion picture in the series, *The Final Frontier.*

66. "If You See Sally"
(Dramatized by Howard Rodman and Roberta Martin;
Directed by John Newland; Airdate: October 18, 1960)

SYNOPSIS: Young Sally Ellis reluctantly leaves her grieving family after her hard-hearted father blames her for the accidental drowning of her brother, Paul. Sally lives in the big city for a time, barely eking out a life as a waitress in a greasy spoon, until her Pa realizes he has been unfair and summons her to return. Jubilant and happy to be returning to her loved ones, Sally is killed en route in a terrible road accident. Nonetheless, Sally's spirit keeps trying ... and failing ... to make it all the way home ... year after year after year ... as lonely drivers encounter her spirit in the dark chill of the night.

GUEST CAST: Anne Whitfield (Sally Ellis), George Mitchell (Pa), Mary Lou Taylor (Ma), Rusty Lane, Harry Jackson, Bernard Kates, Pat McCaffrie.

COMMENTARY: John Newland remembers a funny story about the lensing of "If You See Sally," one of the very best episodes of *One Step Beyond.* "It was shot late at night, and we had an 80 man crew shooting on this hill. On the other side of the same hill, Frank Sinatra and Peter Lawford were filming some war movie. Anyway, we were going along fine when Frank Sinatra sent a messenger over to our side of the hill to tell us to keep it down," Newland recalls with a laugh. "Well, I gave the guy a message of my own: I said he should tell Sinatra to go fuck himself. The messenger returned to his side of the hill, we resumed shooting on our side, and everybody thought everything was fine. Then, suddenly, it got *really* quiet on our side of the hill. I was behind the camera so I didn't know what was going on, but when I turned around, Frank Sinatra was right there, standing just a few feet from me. 'Johnny,' Sinatra said deadpan, 'I got your message.' There was a silence for a second, then everybody laughed ... and it was over. But it was a wonderful moment." As Newland remembers, Sinatra enjoyed the encounter as much as he did, and the experience was a powerful testimonial to Sinatra's "star" power and good humor.

Behind-the-scenes encounters with Frank Sinatra aside, "If You See Sally" remains one of the most remarkable and (like "Anniversary of a Murder") best-remembered episodes of *One Step Beyond*. It is a sad story and one that, like "The Secret," offers a succinct warning to short-sighted people who do not cherish their loved ones: Take care of those you love; guard their feelings; be fair and forgiving. For if you don't, they may never find their way home again, just like poor Sally Ellis.

That moral is certainly the lesson that Pa Ellis learns here, to heartrending effect. Early on he blames his daughter for the death of his son (and even wishes her dead), and he lets his anger destroy his family. Pa Ellis' punishment for this behavior is a cruel one, but perhaps fitting, considering Ellis' crime.

Like the mythological Tantalus, doomed to dwell in Hell, forever out of reach of all his desires, Pa Ellis is cursed always to *just* miss Sally again. Other people (traveling salesmen) see her and experience her radiant, determined life force again, but she never quite makes it home to him. To Pa Ellis, Sally is a child forever lost — and that is the albatross he wears around his sad neck. Sally's spirit has tried seven times in seven years to find her way home, but she is always gone — vanished again to that strange limbo — when Pa Ellis goes out to the salesman's car to reunite with her. What is distinctly unfair about this perpetual tantalizing disappointment is that Ma Ellis shares the punishment, despite her innocence in the events that led up to Sally's departure. Still, this sad result, and the fact that viewers can so easily identify with the Ellises, makes the episode a heartfelt one.

"If You See Sally" succeeds not only because its final twist is absolutely haunting (Sally was never in the salesman's car at all; she died on the road seven years earlier and her spirit is still questing to get home, like some modern-day Odysseus), but because the episode is written and shot with such poetry. In the writing category, Howard Rodman and Roberta Martin have created a classic. Early in the story they establish Sally's desperation and pain, and then the tale takes on a feeling of longing and hope as she optimistically begins the long journey home. When she never completes that mission, audiences are devastated because Sally seems so sweet, so innocent, so undeserving of this pain.

In one especially moving sequence, Sally (a remarkable Anne Whitfield) delivers a soliloquy in a truck cab about her brother's death. She muses on blame, guilt and conscience in a meaningful manner, explaining the paradox that her brother's accident both *was* and *was not* her fault. At another time she sees, with an eerie sense of foreboding, that nothing in the world seems real except the road ahead and "the black night passing you by." As she eventually becomes a very special sort of Flying Dutchman, a human vessel doomed to wander the roads and highways of the dark, this view of the road (and her future) seems apt. It is a tribute to the authors' writing skills that they were able to capture these sentiments without sounding hokey.

John Newland's direction of "If You See Sally" never fails to be informative and stylish. The episode begins with an over-the-shoulder view (from inside the salesman's car), and the most prominent sight in the frame is the road ahead. That road, always rolling forward, represents the unknown, the future, and the inexplicable. It is a perfect first shot, and it fits well with Newland's voice-over, which states that the traveling salesman is about to encounter something beyond the realm of human experience. Thus the road is a concrete player in "If You See Sally," both the physical location of a tragedy and a metaphor for the going forward into the great unknown.

In other sequences Newland sticks close to Anne Whitfield, catching every meaningful look on her face and every shift in her expressive eyes with a kind of unblinking clarity. Sally is depicted in close-up so frequently that the tight framing heightens audience identification and actually makes her travails and eventual death feel like a tangible pain.

A devastating story of a ghost in the road, "If You See Sally" actually does seem to have some "real" precedent in concept, if not plot and character detail. The imagining of a traveler that he/she sees some kind of character on his/her road journey (usually at night) has been described as:

> a rare hallucinatory event brought about by folklore that lingers in our collective imagination from a time when man first drove horses and chariots. Late at night, exhausted and alone on a dark road, the vulnerable driver may summon the ancient hitchhiker from his unconscious; in his weakened state, he becomes convinced that the eerie fellow is truly sitting beside him.[30]

The same source goes on to describe a series of events in the mid–1970s in Southern England, near the village of Nunney, wherein there were frequent reports of a so-called "phantom" hitchhiker on the road. The above-listed explanation blames the subconscious (or some kind of genetic memory) for the strange appearance — a factor explored in the *One Step Beyond* story "Legacy of Love" — but that does not seem totally satisfactory. Often in encounters such as those dramatized in "If You See Sally," the driver actually converses with the "ghost" or keeps an article of clothing from the phantom sojourner. These permutations cannot be explained away as an unconscious reflection of genetic memory.

An ultra-creepy version of the events of "If You See Sally" was reported in *Fantastic Television* in 1977 in a chapter on *One Step Beyond*:

> This broadcast ["If You See Sally"] elicited a spate of letters — forty-five in all — in which viewers described their own similar experiences. In one variation, the man lends the child a sweater. When he is told that the child is dead, he ... immediately asks what happened to his sweater. The garment is retrieved on the headstone of the child's grave"[31]

Like that story, "If You See Sally" can give one a terminal case of the creeps, in no small part due to the fact that this kind of thing seems to have happened to real people.

In the more comfortable world of dramatic television, the hitchhiker or traveler on the road who may be a ghost has been seen frequently. "The Hitchhiker" on *The Twilight Zone* is one such repetition, as is "Ghost in the Road" on *Poltergeist the Legacy*. Rarely, if ever, has the story been done with as much emotion and utter conviction as on *One Step Beyond*'s "If You See Sally."

67. "Moment of Hate"

(Dramatized by Charles Larson; Based on material from David Peltz; Directed by John Newland; Airdate: October 25, 1960)

SYNOPSIS: In a raw tête-à-tête with her doctor, a tortured dress designer cursed with a terrible temper confesses her darkest secret: She can wish people dead — and they promptly die. Recently, both Karen's up-and-coming assistant and her boss have died from spontaneous cerebral aneurysms after she desired them dead. But the power to kill with a thought can also be turned inward...

GUEST CAST: Joanne Linville (Karen Wadsworth), John Kellogg.

COMMENTARY: "How complex is the human mind?" John Newland

wonders in "Moment of Hate," a *One Step Beyond* installment with real dramatic punch. Much like in the early first season story "Epilogue," that central question of psychic abilities is confronted in a grueling face-to-face confrontation and verbal ballet between one viewpoint, representing the irrational believer (Karen), and another, representing skeptical science (the doctor). And, as in "Epilogue," it is the scientific perspective that is found wanting in the end. When Karen turns her destructive power inward on herself at the climax, she dies instantly and punctuates the argument once and for all.

The power to "wish someone dead" is one that human beings have long imagined, hence the saying "if looks could kill..." Appropriately, the horror genre is filled with examples of stories in which people employ potent mental forces to destroy other living creatures. David Cronenberg's *Scanners* (1981), in which concentrated mental assaults not only kill people, but blow apart human heads, is one egregious example. The psychokinesis of the titular teenager in *Carrie* (1976), and of the psychic teenagers (Andrew Stevens and Amy Irving) in Brian De Palma's *The Fury* (1978), represent others. But what "Moment of Hate" really concerns is the power of suggestion. In a fit of rage, Karen says "I hope you die," and behind her an assistant tumbles off the roof. Was Karen somehow able to plant that suggestion in the mind of her intended victim? Or, as the doctor explains, has Karen simply created a "guilt bridge" between two unconnected events: her own thoughts and an unrelated (though concurrent) death? In this case, it is pretty clear that *One Step Beyond* comes down on the side of the paranormal, arguing that Karen has an involuntary, amazing and horrifying mental power. This fact is also verified when the doctor hypnotizes Karen and she relates an incident from her youth (age 7) when she wished a friend dead for stealing her favorite hat. Importantly, the child died immediately after transmission of the murderous thought.

To buttress this story of mental murder, John Newland closes "Moment of Hate" by offering specific documentation on the subject. In this case, he references an article that appeared in *Time Magazine* on April 13, 1959. As Newland recounts the story, two rows of seeds were planted for a special experiment. One group was prayed over, the other was cursed. The plants over which prayers were lavished all flourished, and the cursed plants withered. This is an interesting story about man's ability to "send out" positive or negative thoughts, but there are some other interesting facts to report on the subject. Though that article does indeed appear in *Time Magazine* in the April 13, 1959, issue (on pages 95 and 96), it is reported not in the SCIENCE section of the weekly periodical, but in the RELIGION department instead.

The report, by Reverend Franklin Loehr at the Religious Research Foundation in Los Angeles (and author of *The Power of Prayer on Plants*), concluded rather prematurely from this experiment that "prayer is fact." On the contrary, what was established by his experiment was that man's *belief* in prayer (both positive and negative) was fact. There is no evidence that the prayers were heard by some supreme being and then answered by same.

Regardless of Reverend Loehr's conclusions, it was also reported that a woman involved in the experiment had incredible success with wielding "negative prayer," hurling epithets of "disdain, scorn and active dislike" at one sample of seeds. The result was that the "positive prayer" group saw 16 seedlings flourish and the "negative prayer" group saw only one seedling survive ... while the remainder of the cursed plants seemed to "twist and writhe under the negative power showered on them."

Though one must question the source here, as it seems to have a religious motivation and agenda (to prove that prayer is fact), it is interesting again to note the power of suggestion. Apparently, as suggested by author David Goleman in *Emotional Intelligence*, human beings do send out an array of emotional signals to other life forms, including plants and animals. "Moment of Hate" takes a belief in that ability and then expands it to suggest that human beings cannot only affect others with mental forces, they can actually kill! Though that is a difficult claim to substantiate, even considering the plant experiment of Reverend Loehr as documentation, it does lend a surface credibility to this particular story.

This is not the first time *One Step Beyond* used an interesting kind of evidence that seems to suggest that if A is true, then B is true as well. Here it is suggested that if people can affect the life and death of plants, they can also affect the life processes of other human beings. Not exactly an airtight or logical argument, but an interesting one that provides the story enough frisson to give an observer pause. Importantly, however, *One Step Beyond* provides no evidence whatsoever that a human being has ever successfully "wished" another human being dead.

68. "To Know the End"

(Dramatized by Larry Marcus; Directed by John Newland;
Airdate: November 1, 1960)

SYNOPSIS: In 1939 a woman named Emily is haunted by a strange vision: Soldiers break into her beach house and a dying gallant calls out her name, as if she is his dearest beloved. Although this odd occurrence is at first dismissed as an hallucination, Emily soon realizes that she has witnessed the death of a husband she has not even married, let alone met, as of yet. In 1943 the war catches up with Emily's terrifying premonition, and she must face a terrifying reality.

GUEST CAST: Elen Willard (Emily McDougall), Alex Davison (Harry McDougall), Sally Fraser, Noel Drayton, James Forrest, Jean Fenwick, Anthony Eustrel.

COMMENTARY: "To Know the End" defines an hallucination as the projection of objects that can't possibly be present, usually arising from a "fault" in the nervous system. However, an hallucination cannot even come close to explaining the experience of Emily McDougall, whose *premonition* of future events is so specific that she not only sees her future husband in precise detail for the first time, but sees his death to boot!

At first glance, "To Know the End" seems a reiteration of the premonition prototype seen in other *One Step Beyond* episodes such as "Night of April 14" or "The Day the World Wept: The Lincoln Story." There is a Cassandra (Emily), a disbelieving authority figure (this time in the military rather than the medical profession) and the specter of war (another common facet on the series, last seen in "The Return"), but these factors are played for a different purpose here. "To Know the End" is actually a meditation on choice, on free will. Newland's final remark makes the distinction clear. "Would they have chosen differently even if they could have?" he asks. In other words, being the person that she is, could Emily McDougall *not* have fallen in love with Harry? Could Harry, being the person he is, have chosen not to fight in the war? Probably not, in either case, and so destiny was not only unavoidable, it was a *choice* that the couple willingly made.

At first, Emily tries to scuttle the premonition by taking action against it. Knowing that Harry is due to die soon in the war effort, she arranges a car accident that will leave him injured. It does not work, and he goes off to fight and die anyway. Thus fate is depicted as immutable, and with a purpose. Specifically, we learn that the characteristics of the people involved assure a certain fate, whether it be Emily's heart or Harry's patriotism.

"To Know the End" also raises some interesting questions about the nature of human relationships. How would anybody like to know the outcome of a relationship (either marriage or death) before he or she has even met his prospective mate? And if "the end" is known, should it be revealed? Or, conversely, is it better not to reveal the end because any such knowledge of the future will inevitably pollute the relationship and, in fact, precipitate the feared "end" of the relationship? These are interesting issues well worth examining, and in "To Know the End" one feels for Emily and Harry. They are a charming, loving couple, but they are caught in the cogs of a fate that will destroy their romance. As Emily's dream comes true a piece at a time, the viewer starts to become aware that this is indeed a doomed love and that no intervention will allow for a happy ending. It is a troubling realization, but one that makes for interesting drama, especially if one is to contrast this couple with the husband-wife team in an upcoming episode, "Tonight at 12:17." In that story there is another couple troubled by a premonition, but the couple is able to escape death.

69. "The Trap"
(Dramatized by Larry Marcus; Directed by John Newland;
Airdate: November 15, 1960)

SYNOPSIS: In windy Chicago, turmoil ensues when Dominic, an average, happily married man, starts to behave strangely by referring lovingly to some mysterious woman named Edna. Then Dominic becomes sick: dehydrated and starved for air. Dom's wife, Florence, seeks medical help for her husband, unaware that Dom's heretofore unknown identical twin is dying of thirst in a collapsed mine shaft in Arizona, and that Dom is feeling the sympathetic pains of his identical brother.

GUEST CAST: Mike Kellin (Dominic), Ruth Storey (Florence), Alex Gerry, Jeanne Bates, Bert Remsen, Francis de Sales, Joan Dupuis.

COMMENTARY: Just about everyone has heard of *The Corsican Brother* scenario: Poke one twin brother in the gut with a sword, and the other twin feels the twitch of pain in his stomach too. For whatever reason, many people assume that the connection between identical twins is among the strongest in biology. In the world of the psychic, however, that truism does not always hold true. For instance, Remy Chauvin wrote of twin studies in the field of E.S.P. and other psychic phenomena that:

> Identical twins who did not get along well together gave poorer results than non-identical twins who had a friendly relationship.... Also, it was evident that a romantic relationship between two members of opposite sex strongly favored transmission.[32]

That quotation establishes two things: First, that identical twins are not necessarily the most connected of souls when the two siblings are totally unaware of each other (as is the case in "The Trap"), and second, that the male-female romantic relationship is actually among the strongest in E.S.P. circles (a fact reflected accurately in *One Step Beyond* because so many stories involve the marital relationship and psychic connections among romantic mates).

More interesting than its depiction of twins unknowingly sending telepathic vibes to each other back and forth across the continent in "The Trap" is the way that Dominic and wife Florence are portrayed. The teleplay states that they have been married "just about forever"; accordingly, they seem a more "real" couple than many on *One Step Beyond* (who are often either newlyweds or on the verge of divorce). Instead, the teleplay by Marcus is successful in its attempt to portray a "routine" but happy marriage in just about "the middle" of a long relationship. The jokes, the teasing, the easy rapport and the understanding of a spouse's idiosyncrasies all come through loud and clear, and there is a genuine sense of affection between these two souls. They are not young and attractive ("The Bride Possessed") and they are not dealing with alcoholism ("Epilogue," "The Visitor") or infidelity ("The Secret"), they are just "regular folks" who end up in a very strange situation. In some senses, that dynamic of normalcy makes Dominic's transformation all the more frightening. Florence starts to wonder if she is smothering her husband, but in fact he is in the grip of a very real physical pain brought on by a heretofore unknown connection with his brother.

"The Trap" is neither the most exciting nor the most accurate *One Step Beyond* installment on record, but its unique view of an "average" Chicago couple struggling against the inexplicable is strangely optimistic and even a little bit refreshing.

70. "The Voice"
(Dramatized by Charles Larson; Directed by John Newland;
Airdate: November 22, 1960)

SYNOPSIS: In a small New England community in 1902 a group of fearful villagers burn down a barn where they believe a demon called Roger dwells. A reporter named Corning covers the trial of the arsonists and is surprised to discover that the demonic Roger is actually a talking raccoon fluent in German, French, Latin and four other languages. Is this poor animal possessed by the Devil, or is there another answer?

GUEST CAST: Robert Lansing (Mr. Corning), Luana Anders (Joan Goss); Carl Benton Reid (Brian Christopher), David Lewis (Stang), Paul Genge, James Anderson, William Keene, Clark Howat, Harry Strang.

COMMENTARY: "The Voice" is really out there; a bizarre episode that is scary for long stretches of time because it *really* does seem that a demon called "Roger" has taken possession of a raccoon, endowing it with the human power of speech. Before the raccoon is even revealed as the source of the speech, the episode is effective because the little voice ("Je suis fatigue!" it declares with an odd world-weariness) seems to be originating from inside a small potato sack in the barn. This is an occasion when *One Step Beyond* is way ahead of its audience, and a viewer cannot possibly imagine what tiny, monstrous *thing* is speaking French inside that bag. Even the admittedly humorous revelation that a raccoon is the talker cannot take away the audience's level of discomfort. When it is revealed that some local children have died for laughing at "Roger," the fearsome nature of what should be a cute animal is established quite well. As in "The Clown," *One Step Beyond* fosters fear and unease by creating a valley between what is expected (a cute raccoon or a funny circus performer) and what actually occurs (an excursion into terror).

Beyond its depiction of a loquacious critter (who quotes Byron), "The Voice" has a great deal on its mind. It studies witch hunts to some extent, as one concerned character notes that there is not much difference between 1690 and 1902 in the remote mountains, a place where superstition runs rampant. This comment is borne out when, sure enough, fearful villagers come a-callin' for Roger, hoping to kill the demon once and for all.

"The Voice" also concerns *ventriloquism*, because the final twist (a bit of a cop-out after so compelling an opening) attempts to suggest that it was Joan Goss, possessed by the soul of a witch named Betty Randall, who threw her voice to make it seem that Roger the Raccoon was really doing all the talking. Another possible explanation for the odd happenngs of "The Voice" is that Roger was indeed a possessed raccoon until threatened by the townsfolk. At that point he jumped into Joan Goss, the nearest available body (a resolution that is also seen in *The Exorcist* [1973] and *The Possession of Joel Delaney* [1972]).

In his closing narration, however, John Newland does something unusual for *One Step Beyond*. Instead of promoting the mysterious aspects of the demonic possession, the host pins the whole incident on Joan, a demented individual. And, as punishment for her misdeeds, Joan Goss dies, the audience is told, of scarlet fever soon after the incidents depicted in this episode. The message is clear: Don't fool with the Devil!

Robert Lansing, the star of "The Voice," later starred in *The Man Who Never Was* (1966–67), a short-lived tale of international intrigue that featured John Newland as director of several episodes. Lansing is well remembered not only for his appearance as an alien called Gary Seven on an episode of *Star Trek* ("Assignment Earth"), but his turn as a stalker of the undead in an entry of the Laurel series *Monsters* (1988–1992) entitled "The Vampire Hunter."

"The Voice" seems to tread on a more symbolic plane than many *One Step Beyond* stories. The number of the superstitious, 13, crops up once (in an important address), Joan *Goss* proves to be an interesting name, as *gossamer* is defined as something delicate, light or insubstantial (much like Joan's mental state), and the good reporter who combats evil (Lansing) is appropriately named *Christ*opher.

71. "The Promise"

(Dramatized by Larry Marcus; Directed by John Newland;
Airdate: November 29, 1960)

SYNOPSIS: In London, after World War II, an ex-German soldier with a knowledge of munitions has promised his pregnant wife, Lois, that he will never handle another bomb. However, a British officer and friend, Lt. Davis, asks Carl for help one more time when a 500 pound undetonated bomb is discovered intact at a London construction site. As Carl attempts to defuse the deadly and irregular device, he makes a promise that no matter what happens to him during the operation, he will carry on the tradition of his beloved German village and breathe life into the body of his soon-to-be-born son.

GUEST CAST: William Shatner (Carl Bremmer), Ben Wright (Lt. Davis), Leslie Denison (Lois), Peter Gordon, Guy Kingsford, Lester Matthews, Queenie Leonard, Ollie O'Toole, Kort Falkenberg, Mollie Roden.

COMMENTARY: William Shatner is at his best in "The Promise," a tense segment about one German's search for redemption after World War II and the lengths to which his quest drives him. This episode features a softer, more vulnerable Shatner, and his performance is not at all in the "in command" mode one has become accustomed to while watching *Star Trek*.

In "The Promise" there is no sign of Shatner's later-in-life tendency to go over the top or beyond the bounds of the role at hand (even though he must contend with a wobbly German accent). For that reason "The Promise" really flies. It is a remarkably tense and involving installment, highlighted by an exceptional performance. When asked about Shatner, Newland (who later directed the actor on *Star Trek*) reminisced about the time they spent together on *One Step Beyond*. "At the time, he was really a working actor," Newland recalls. "He was easy to work with and quite charming. I thought he gave a great performance in that episode ['The Promise']." Indeed, Shatner's acting skill in "The Promise" rivals his best television appearance (in *The Twilight Zone* episode "Nick of Time") as a career high.

Shatner is aided in "The Promise" in no small part by writer Larry Marcus, who provides the actor a character he can really sink his teeth into. Shatner's Bremmer is a former German officer (a Nazi) who was captured by the Allies after his plane crashes. Since the war he has tried to pay for his "sins" by defusing bombs and saving countless lives. Now his wife is pregnant and Bremmer is tired of living in the past. He has paid his dues to Western society, and his goal is simply to be a good father and a good husband. He wants only what we all want: a happy family life, a successful career and a chance to live to a ripe old age. That all goes out the window, however, when Bremmer is called for one more defusing job.

As he steps into the hole with an undetonated bomb, Shatner nails the reluctant heroism of this remarkable character. He is clearly unhappy he is there, once more facing down death, but he looks to the task at hand with a grim efficiency.

The direction in "The Promise" is impressive too. Newland's camera gazes down on Shatner in the pit from up high as Bremmer does his precision work. The revelation that the bomb has an irregular configuration brings sweat to Shatner's face and eyes, and (in tight shot) he is left to defuse the bomb by feel (since he cannot see the bomb's internal mechanisms). Face to face with the bomb, Bremmer meets his unpleasant fate in a moment that might best be described as highly disturbing. Young Shatner is such a likable screen presence here — fresh-faced, handsome and sympathetic — that the audience has truly become invested in his life and dilemma. The mildly sappy ending, which allows a ghostly Bremmer (mercifully offscreen) to "pass on the breath of life" to the next generation, is tastefully done, but it hardly eases the pain of his death.

In the "psychic" finale of "The Promise," Carl Bremmer returns from the dead to slap his baby boy's behind, and the apparition (seen by a nurse) gives hope to his devastated wife. Because Lois has given up hope and no longer believes in Heaven until this strange experience, this is one more example of *One Step Beyond*'s sometimes inspirational nature. The creators of the series seemed to share a belief that encounters with the psychic or paranormal could actually be therapeutic at times: repairing relationships or giving a kind of hope to the hopeless (as in "Who Are You?").

This "Promise" is not the only one that Shatner has become involved with during his long career in TV and film. In the seventies the actor was the spokesman for "Promise" margarine as well. Coincidence or synchronicity? And he found himself wearing Nazi regalia once more in the *Star Trek* episode "Patterns of Force."

72. "Tonight at 12:17"

(Dramatized by Larry Marcus and Jane Anna Pritchard;
Directed by John Newland; Airdate: November 29, 1960)

SYNOPSIS: An expectant wife hears an airplane in distress high above her house every night at 12:17 A.M. Although her doctor believes she is being a "goofy" pregnant woman, Laura Perkins' experience gets more detailed each time she relives the vision, and finally she can even read the plane's registration number as it crashes through the roof. Mr. Perkins refuses to believe this vision of disaster, though his wife insists that *tonight* the plane will finally, in reality, crash down upon them.

GUEST CAST: Peggy Ann Garner (Laura Perkins), John Lasell (John Perkins), Gene Lyons (Sam Black), Jack Lester (Doctor), Barbara Bell Wright, David De Haven.

COMMENTARY: Another *premonition* of impending death informs "Tonight at 12:17." Unlike the recent "To Know the End," this startling vision of the future involves a plane crash, not the specific death of a loved one. Adhering to *One Step Beyond* tradition, the percipient in the case is a woman, she is disbelieved (the Cassandra Complex), she is dismissed because of her condition (not alcoholism or a nervous breakdown this time, but pregnancy), and her vision is ultimately proven correct, if misinterpreted. On this last front, the kicker is that by evacuating the house where Laura feels the plane will crash, she is transferred to a motel where the plane actually does crash. Fortunately, the Perkins escape the disaster and survive intact. As John Newland succinctly describes the climax in his final narration, "You can't change fate. But if you know what's coming, you can duck!"

Like so many *One Step Beyond* stories, "Tonight at 12:17" is basically a character piece with a psychic twist. Laura Perkins has been trying to get pregnant for six years, but she has miscarried before and has been told that she is not suited for childbirth. After she becomes pregnant, she starts to have the vision of the plane crash. This psychically-gained information is ignored by her husband, who, with the doctor's support, brushes off her experience with the simple explanation that she is pregnant and therefore "silly." Laura, the girl who cried wolf, cannot convince anyone that what she witnessed feels real to her. This creates an interesting dilemma. Laura is constantly told by her husband and doctor to relax and sleep so as to save the baby, who is in danger of a miscarriage if she does not calm down. But, in truth, if Laura ignores her reflexes and does sleep, she will be dooming the baby to death in the plane crash! Laura is damned if she does, damned if she doesn't, so the tale turns desperate as she tries to get someone, anyone, to validate her concern.

As interesting as Laura's catch–22 situation is the knowledge that her vision of precognition is precise enough to scare her (and to reveal the registration number of the plane), but imprecise enough to be wrong about the details (i.e. the plane crashes into a motel, not her house). This bit of psychic knowledge misinterpreted actually fits in with the theory of "psychic" J.W. Dunne, who wrote that:

> we all have precognitive elements in our dreams, but we do not know how to recognize them. They can be very unexpected, and often an adventitious detail turns out to be the precognitive element.[33]

In other words, though Laura Perkins may have a premonition that she understands in incredible detail at some points (the plane registration), she may very well misinterpret another detail, such as the location of the crash. *One Step Beyond* has acknowledged this kind of misinterpretation in stories such as "Emergency Only," and it does seem to fit with research on the topic. As for the cause of Laura's unusual (and obviously atypical) vision, there is only one answer: the pregnancy itself. Some research (and some old wives tales) seem to indicate that a mother-to-be will often have a heightened sense of "survival," both for herself and her unborn child. This psychic message of doom may be a corollary of that effect.

As for the incident of "Tonight at 12:17" (a plane crash predicted), there have been many instances in which people have reportedly had premonitory dreams of upcoming disasters. One of the most famous occurred in 1979 (after this story had been re-made by *The Next Step Beyond* as "Dream of Disaster") and involved a man named David Booth. For ten nights in a row he dreamed that a plane was going to crash. On May 22, 1979, David warned the FAA and American Airlines that a DC-10 jetliner was going to crash somewhere, and in the process, flip over on its back. Three days later, on May 25, 1979, 273 people were killed when an American Airlines DC-10 went down at O'Hare International airport. Booth had correctly guessed the plane type, the airline carrier and even the nature of the accident (the plane was inverted — upside down — upon crashing).[34]

Despite the fact that dreams of death and destruction have been the bread and butter of *One Step Beyond*, "Tonight at 12:17" is memorable and exciting, perhaps because one is made to sympathize so deeply with Laura's plight. With a baby at stake, the jeopardy of the episode is very intense. The plane crash scenario is also an interesting one, and it would be repeated in an *Amazing Stories* episode, starring Charles Durning, called "You Gotta Believe Me." In this case, the protagonist had a vision of a terrible plane crash in a dream, and he walked through the disaster area (his living room) in his bare feet and pajamas. As the title of this *Amazing Stories* indicates, one might appropriately term Durning's character a Cassandra as well.

73. "Where Are They?"

(Dramatized by Larry Marcus and Merwin Gerard;
Directed by John Newland; Airdate: December 13, 1960)

SYNOPSIS: John Newland presents two stories about strange appearances and disappearances. The first occurs in the small town of Chico, California, in March of 1922 when a man calling himself "the Ghost" claims credit for a rock storm that falls inexplicably from the sky every day at precisely 3:00 P.M. Then one day "The Ghost" disappears, never to be heard from again. In the second story a man named Charles Elton flaunts his miraculous invention: a pellet that can cheaply transform water into gasoline. Just when Elton is to be rewarded for his invention by the United States government, he disappears from the face of the Earth, never to be seen or heard from again.

GUEST CAST: Philip Pine (Harry Call), Joan Tompkins (Jenny Call), Alan Dexter (Towers), John Alvin (Bradley), Robert Williams (Joe Tomlinson), Herb Patterson (Garner), Richard Devon.

COMMENTARY: Briefly adopting a different style of format (two stories per half hour), "Where Are They?" asks some interesting questions about two inexplicable appearances and disappearances. In the first tale the town of Chico, California, is besieged by a daily rock storm. Stones literally rain out of the sky every day at 3:00 P.M. Strangely, the rocks come down *warm*. In the second story a man named Charles Elton offers the United States government a miraculous formula that turns water into a fuel. Before the government can make use of this incredible new power source, Elton disappears, and not even the F.B.I. can locate him or prove that he ever existed.

Both stories in "Where Are They?" manage to be pretty creepy. The falling rock story involves a letter from a crank who calls himself "The Ghost." Supposedly, he can manipulate the strange rock fall (much like another character controls the weather in *The X-Files* sixth season episode called "Rain King"). Oddly, the idea of strange things raining down from the heavens actually jibes with a number of paranormal reports. In addition to the story that Newland reports about fish falling from the sky in Chico in 1878, there have been many reports of stones raining down on villages in Europe—apparently a common poltergeist manifestation.

In an even more bizarre story, *The Anomalist* recounted two incidents in the 1800s wherein blood and human organs rained down from the sky in North Carolina. Since this was the era before air flight, the blood rain reported in Sampson County (February 15, 1850) and Chatham County (February 25, 1884) is doubly mysterious. Author John Hairr's "High Strangeness Report," entitled *When Flesh and Blood Fell from the Sky*, published a newspaper (*The North Carolinian*) account of the first blood fall:

> On the 15th Feb'y, 1850, there fell within 100 yards of the residence of Thos. M. Clarkson in Sampson County a shower of Flesh and Blood, about 250 or 300 yards in the length. The pieces appeared to be flesh, liver, lights, brains and blood. Some of the blood ran on the leaves, apparently very fresh.... During the time it was falling, there was a cloud overhead having a red appearance like a wind cloud. There was no rain.[35]

Like the rock fall, this "blood" rain was never adequately explained.

One Step Beyond's answer for Chico's anomalous phenomenon is that "The Ghost" somehow manipulated the rocks with an anti-gravity device. Since such technology remains unknown even to this day (nearly a century later), this seems highly unlikely, or at least improbable. The fact that the rocks fell at the same time every single day, however, does seem to indicate a man-made or at least *designed* phenomenon. Would nature be so orderly as to drop rocks every afternoon at 3:00 P.M.? Taken as a whole, the falling rock story, the falling flesh and blood story, and the falling fish story add up to more than just a crazy fish story. It does seem that, for whatever reasons, strange objects sometimes do fall from the sky. Tornadoes, tidal waves and other meteorological disturbances are known to sometimes carry objects in the air for miles, so this could be one possible explanation. Whatever the true cause, the story of Chico makes for a provocative segment, and the "High Strangeness Report" can be seen as one possible validation of the general concept, if not the specifics.

As far as the specifics are concerned, "Where Are They" is right on the money. History records that from July to November of 1921 rocks fell from the sky in Chico, California, for no explainable reason. A lawman, J.A. Peck, investigated the strange case, and *The San Francisco Examiner* reported on the situation in March of 1922. Peck came to believe that someone with "a machine" was responsible for the rock fall. Professor C.K. Studley reported his own findings in the *San Francisco Examiner* as well:

> Some of the rocks are so large that they could not be thrown by any ordinary means. One of the rocks weighs 16 ounces. They are not of meteoric origin as seems to have been hinted, because

two of them show signs of cementation, either natural or artificial, and no meteoric factor was ever connected to a cement factory.[36]

So, like "Night of April 14," "Where Are They" finds *One Step Beyond* on solid terrain. Right down to the dates and locations, it accurately portrays the details of a documented encounter with the inexplicable.

A similar incident occurred in Charleston, South Carolina, on September 4, 1886, and like the events of "Where Are They," this rock fall centered outside the offices of a newspaper, *The Charleston News and Courier.*[37]

The second story depicted in "Where Are They?" set in 1917, involves the disappearance of a genius who has developed a chemical catalyst to turn water into fuel. This segment goes to great lengths to prove the validity of Charles Elton's formula, as he leads a secretary from Congress and other officials through a test run of his amazing discovery. Then, just as it seems that Elton will be paid his one million dollars for the formula (though his catalyst costs less than two cents to produce), he disappears without a trace forever. The FBI searches for him. They never found him, and worse, never found any evidence he existed!

Did Elton have second thoughts about sharing his formula? Or was he a visitor from the distant future who traveled back to a "primitive" past hoping to exploit the populace with a future age technology? Was he snapped back to his own time when the authorities realized he was attempting to corrupt the timeline? That may sound like a premise from the film *Time Cop*, but "Where Are They" leaves itself open to that very interpretation.

Both short stories in "Where Are They" prove tantalizing, perhaps because they are so direct, so terse. Sometimes in *One Step Beyond* the psychic element only crops up near the end of a story, or well into the plot. Linked by strange occurrences, the twin tales of "Where Are They" grab the audience from frame one and hold on until the climax of Part II. It is both an interesting experiment in format and a chilling but fascinating exploration of the truly inexplicable.

74. "Legacy of Love"

(Dramatized by Howard Rodman; Directed by John Newland; Airdate: December 20, 1960)

SYNOPSIS: Despite all attempts to visit the town of Woodmere, fate conspires to send a female traveler to the out-of-the-way town of Seaside. There she finds herself mysteriously drawn to a married man she has never met before. As they are compelled to be together, the couple starts to experience strange memories which are not their own, memories that only someone of a previous generation could adequately explain.

GUEST CAST: Norma Crane (Mari Anne), Charles Aidman (John Brownley), Barbara Biler, Louise Lorimer, Olan Soule, Al Hopson, Charles Calvert, Joe McGuinn.

COMMENTARY: What does science really understand about memory? The mental storage system of the human being has been described as essential for the process of learning, and it is known that memories are formed by chemical changes between nerve cells. There are different types of memory (motor-skill memory and factual memory) and different levels of memory as well (immediate, short-term and long-term). Memory can be lost (amnesia), impaired (Alzheimers) or erroneous (paramnesia — i.e. *déjà vu*). *One Step Beyond*'s episode "Legacy of Love" asks the viewer to believe that there is yet another type of human memory: a *genetic* or *hereditary memory* that is passed from one generation to the next.

As a parallel to this perceived development, John Newland's narration offers the example of the starfish. If the parent body of a starfish loses a limb, the lost limb will, by itself, regenerate a new body. Is this limb a "child" of the original body, thus "remembering" the whole of which it was once an important component?

By extension, is Mari Anne in "Legacy of Love" remembering a relationship that her mother once experienced? Is she, in essence, a genetic regeneration of her mother, somehow encoded with the same memories? Does she, as a part of her mother's genetic material, remember the whole? Do we only inherit the color of our eyes, or is there a deeper memory locked in our minds too? Are flashes of *déjà vu* actually inherited memories of a different lifetime? These are the issues of "Legacy of Love," and new ones to the *One Step Beyond* ouevre.

The concept of a genetic memory that goes as far back as the caveman is often used to explain man's baser, seemingly instinctual responses in situations of extreme fear or danger. When somebody acts violently in these situations it is often said that he has "regressed" to an earlier stage of human development. The implicit suggestion is that somehow he remembers his ancestors' battles with the giant mammoths or the sabretoothed tigers and is thus calling on that long-suppressed experience today to fight a very different set of dangers. Though many experts do espouse the idea of a genetic memory, established science does not generally accept it as a valid concept, perhaps because the very mechanisms of memory are not yet fully understood. Like other "psychic" experiences described on the show, the genetic memory facets of "Legacy of Love" would best be described as speculative. Carl Jung termed this concept *the collective unconscious*, a universality of human experiences and fears that are the result of predispositions inherited from distant ancestors. On a more personal scale, *racial memory* is the inheritance of personal memories of ancestors, and that would seem to be the case in "Legacy of Love."

In content, "Legacy of Love" focuses on another couple whose love is doomed not to be. Like the time-crossed lovers in "Delia" or the couple shadowed by a premonition of death in "To Know the End," Mari Anne and John are trapped in a love which cannot live or thrive. After all, their love is but an echo of their parents' affair, and their duty here is to resolve that original relationship (which ended sadly) and not destroy the lives of John's family (he has a wife and children) in the process. So, again, *One Step Beyond* seems to suggest that a psychic experience can be healthy, even cathartic, when handled correctly. Mari and John "act out" the roles of the forbearers in harmless fashion, and in some sense they close the issues that left the romantics of a past life feeling incomplete. Of course, on an absolutely skeptical level, Mari and John also have a great excuse they can use to legitimize their weekend affair. "I'm sorry dear, I wasn't responsible. It was this hereditary memory thing that made me unfaithful…"

The climax of "Legacy of Love" reveals that Mari Anne's mother had a relationship with John's father, and that she had been thinking of this special relationship of late, dreaming about it. Was that "dreaming" the impetus that spurred John and Mari Ann to go to the same place at the same time and finish what their parents had started long ago? Perhaps, but regardless of the answer, "Legacy of Love" makes for an involving and mysterious episode.

75. "Rendezvous"
(Dramatized by Merwin Gerard; Based on material from Josefina Seiler; Directed by John Newland; Airdate: December 27, 1960)

SYNOPSIS: Bachelor Fred Sommers has proposed marriage to widow Kate Maxwell a million times, but she has always refused the offer out of loyalty to Jim, the husband she loved who is now presumed dead after an accident in the Pacific. Alone in the park one night, Kate is stalked by a creepy, murderous suitor, and protected from his amorous advances by the spirit of her dead husband.

GUEST CAST: Georgann Johnson (Kate Maxwell), H.M. Wynant (Cooper), Donald Murphy (Fred Sommers), Warren Kemmerling, K.L. Smith, Fred Coby.

COMMENTARY:. A protective apparition materializes at just the right moment to save his wife from harm in the interesting "Rendezvous," a *One Step Beyond* installment about "letting go."

The ghost of Mr. Maxwell not only saves wife Kate from a creepy, pushy stalker in a park, his sudden appearance as a ghost proves to Kate that it is time for her to move on with her life. She has put romance and love and a new relationship on hold because she was not certain her husband was really dead. The apparition provides her the freedom to go on, as well as the physical protection she needs in a dangerous situation. As one character states of the experience, "the important thing is this ... what does this mean to you?" As is usual for *One Step Beyond*, it proves to be more interested in the human answer to a dilemma than in flashy action scenes or special effects. The intervention of the psychic only serves to highlight and resolve a personal problem of human proportions.

A case could probably be made that Mr. Maxwell's apparitional appearance at the right moment to prevent his wife's death would qualify him as a *crisis apparition*, but according to research, most such appearances occur within twelve hours of a person's death. "Rendezvous" establishes that Mr. Maxwell has been presumed missing since the war in the Pacific, so it is more likely that he has been dead for some time. Still, there is no doubt he intervenes at the right moment, and one can be thankful for that.

The most interesting twist in "Rendezvous" occurs near the climax when Kate does not see the ghost of her husband for herself. Instead, it is the killer who sees a burly marine and later describes him to the police. Kate recognizes her husband from this description, but she is, in fact, denied the chance to see her husband "in the flesh."

As Newland intones at the ending, sight is not really understood by science. Is it possible that there was no ghost at all, only Kate's mental projection of an image that gave her comfort and security at a moment of intense stress? As if to prove his point about sight, host Newland then appears to walk directly through a door. This flashy moment recalls "Encounter" (when Newland popped out of existence while sitting in a chair), and reminds viewers again that what we see on TV cannot always be trusted.

76. "The Executioner"

(Dramatized by Bob and Wanda Duncan; Directed by John Newland;
Airdate: January 3, 1961)

SYNOPSIS: A lost Confederate soldier and his dog are captured while trying to steal food from a Union supply depot. A hard-drinking and malicious Union colonel frames the boy for espionage and plans to execute him at dawn. During the night the same colonel heartlessy shoots the boy's howling dog. At daylight, however, a loyal dog nonetheless arrives at the gallows to protect his master's life.

GUEST CAST: Graham Denton (Colonel Martin), Buzz Martin (Jess Bradley), Jeremy Slate (Captain Adams), Tom Middleton (Sergeant Evans), Will J. White (Corporal).

COMMENTARY: "The Executioner" is a testament to the unique bond that sometimes develops between man and animal. Here even death cannot stop a loyal dog from protecting his master. A pet's psychic "connection" with a master is an interesting topic for *One Step Beyond* to tackle, and one that has precedent in paranormal circles. For instance, in many OBE experiments, cats were reportedly able to "visually" detect their masters on the astral plane when they came to visit them, suggesting that animal sight/senses differ significantly from man's. In other instances cats and dogs have found their way back to distant homes and families after being lost. Bucking the odds, these "lost" animals sometimes return home from as far as hundreds of miles away. Also, it is a long-held belief (a wives' tale, no doubt) that dogs and cats can detect ghosts, a belief repeated on film in movies such as *Poltergeist* (1982) and *Stir of Echoes* (1999). Whether all of this information is but a notable example of anthropomorphizing (as debunkers would no doubt claim), or a genuine trait exhibited in the animal kingdom is still unresolved. Still, ask any cat or dog owner if their animals seem to perceive things in a different but oddly insightful manner, and you will have your answer.

Aside from featuring the "ghost" or apparition of a dog, *One Step Beyond* returns to three of its most common templates: the war setting (the Civil War this time), the comeuppance (or "scales of justice righted" tale) and the depiction of the main character (the villain colonel here) as an alcoholic (so as to make his wild claims easier to dismiss). In this case, the Colonel is a brute of a man who is so rotten a character that he shoots a dog. On TV, killing an animal is just about the worst thing a person can do, and accordingly the audience enjoys it when the malicious colonel gets his "just desserts" and is mauled by the apparitional canine.

An unusual story because it portrays the Union in an unsympathetic light (and makes a Confederate soldier a major protagonist), "The Executioner" also takes time to remember that old wives' tale that a howling dog signifies that someone is going to die. In a bit of irony worthy of *The Twilight Zone*, the Colonel soon learns that the bothersome dog is howling not for his master or himself, but for the Colonel, who will have his throat ripped apart by a creature that others insist was never there!

77. "The Last Round"

(Dramatized by Don M. Mankiewicz;
Directed by John Newland; Airdate: January 10, 1961)

SYNOPSIS: A slightly past-his-prime boxer living in England during World War II encounters the ghost of another boxer — a famous former middleweight champion named Paddy who now appears only to fighters about to die in the ring. Although Paddy's appearance is thought to be a hoax, fate takes a strange twist when four people distinctly see Paddy sitting in the back row of the arena.

GUEST CAST: Charles Bronson (Yank Dawson), Felix Deebank (Chipper), Ronald Long (Alfie), Wally Cassell (Collins), Stewart Taylor, John Indrisano, Gordon Richards, Peter Fontaine.

COMMENTARY: Charles Bronson (*Master of the World* [1961], *Death Wish* [1975]) dropped in on *One Step Beyond* in the episode "The Last Round" before achieving superstardom in the 1970s. As fighter Yank Dawson, Bronson does a creditable job by demonstrating the right mix of aggressive physicality and psychological reluctance to continue in a sport that has not always been good to him. The episode Bronson stars in, however, is a shaggy dog story that tries to lead viewers one way but then veers in another direction. The final twist demonstrates that, perhaps, the series has (temporarily) misplaced its moral compass.

"The Last Round's" teleplay reveals to viewers early on that the ghost of a boxer, Paddy Calhoun, haunts the auditorium called the East End Arena where Yank Dawson is to fight his next bout. Frighteningly, Paddy Calhoun only appears to those boxers who are about to die. Because the fight is expected to be hotly contested, an unscrupulous promoter for Dawson's competitor plants a Paddy Calhoun lookalike in the audience to startle Dawson, who is already a tad nervous because of a recent skull fracture. This hoax is perpetrated, but then the story's twist comes in: The "fake" Paddy leaves the ring early in the match, yet both boxers and both managers claim to have seen Paddy during the last round anyway. Before this inconsistency can be explained, German bombs drop suddenly on the auditorium, killing all the characters inside (all of whom really *did* see Paddy after all...).

It is a good final twist, if laboriously setup, but the problem with "The Last Round" is that Yank and the others do not really deserve their grim fate. This is not a comeuppance episode, and the boxers have no real crimes for which to atone. They are just workaday joes trying to make a living, and it seems a little cruel that they should all come up short at the finale.

Buttressed by Bronson's performance and by Newland's bravura staging of the fight sequence (a rousing combination of high and low angles, tight shots, and perspectives of cheering audiences), "The Last Round" comes off as enjoyable. Still, one ends up feeling sorry for Yank Dawson. Though it mirrors the arbitrary reality of life and death — that things are sometimes cut off in the middle —"The Last Round's" climax is not an especially satisfying way to end a drama in which the audience has come to care for the protagonist. After all, Yank cannot avert his fate, is not even aware of his options, and the German bombing feels more coincidental than ironic.

That said, "The Last Round" puts some more notches in the continuing catalog of *One Step Beyond* dramatic conventions. The episode takes place during wartime (like "The Vision," "The Return," "Brainwave" and others) and features an apparition ("The Dark Room," "Epilogue," "The Executioner" and others).

78. "Dead Man's Tale"

(Dramatized by Merwin Gerard; Based on material
by C.V. Tench; Directed by John Newland; Airdate: January 17, 1961)

SYNOPSIS: A married couple teeters on the brink of desperation, having lost their farm and gone broke. When they stay in Port Williams, a frontier town, however, the Werris couple finds a goldminer's handbook in their hotel room. From that odd discovery the Werrises uncover a tale of greed, as two brothers see their trust and love shattered by the destructive power of human avarice. This bizarre story of human foibles literally types itself out on a typewriter, using Mr. Werris as a vessel in a sort of "psychic seizure." After his wife reports the story to the newspaper, Mr. Werris feels compelled to learn the accuracy of what his typewriter has reported.

GUEST CAST: Lonny Chapman (Phillip Werris), Jean Engstrom (Jan Werris); Lucy Prentis (Mrs. Barton), Charles Tannen, Walter Reed, Charles Seel.

COMMENTARY: Automatic writing was the concept of "Message from Clara," and a variation of that phenomenon, *automatic typing*, seems to be the psychic phenomenon of the day in "Dead Man's Tale," as another couple in distress (this time suffering from a financial meltdown) faces the world of the unknown. What makes "Dead Man's Tale" feel unique is its interesting observations about writers and the act of writing.

Mr. Werris, a former newspaperman, types out a story that he claims to have no first-hand knowledge about. He pounds it out on a typewriter as if in a trance. This is an interesting metaphor for the writing process, since even writers themselves do not always consciously understand or realize the source of their inspiration. In this case, is it possible that Mr. Werris' inspiration is psychic? Did the goldminer's handbook leave a kind of psychic residue that Werris was able to subconsciously understand and translate into words? That is certainly one possible explanation, and it works well for this episode

In generic terms, Phillip's experience also qualifies as ESP, the acquisition of data without the use of any human sense organs. Another possibility is that this is actually a simple case of precognition: Paul's sudden insight into information he will eventually learn first-hand when he goes out to the field to research his story.

"Dead Man's Tale" also follows the same terse outline as the pilot episode of *One Step Beyond*, "The Bride Possessed." In that story two newlyweds had a disastrous marriage modelled for them so they knew what pitfalls to avoid. In "Dead Man's Tale" two very unhappy people who are tired of "eating spaghetti and hamburgers" and who do not have even enough money for a train ticket out of town are given the opportunity to see the end result of rampant materialism. They hunger for money and are willing to do anything to get it, even publish what they believe to be a false story. Yet when the story of the Bartons is revealed, it is a story of greed and avarice: Two brothers in search of gold lost their futures over the possibility of wealth. That is an experience that Phillip and Jan can learn from, since money and wealth is a core issue for them as well. There is clearly a didactic purpose here: One should not jettison human values for materialistic ones. This moral underpinning may not be as artfully integrated as it has been in other stories (particularly "The Bride Possessed"), but it does say something interesting about human nature.

79. "The Sacred Mushroom"
(Material assembled by Larry Marcus and Collier Young;
Directed by John Newland; Technical Consultant:
Andrija Puharich; Airdate: January 24, 1961)

SYNOPSIS: Series host John Newland, Dr. Barbara Brown (a brilliant neuropharmacologist), David Grey (a spiritual leader in Hawaii), Dr. Jeffrey Smith (a professor of philosophy at Stanford) and Dr. Andrija Puharich (author of *The Sacred Mushroom*) fly to a remote village in Mexico to determine if a special mushroom with hallucinogenic properties (called "X") is capable of enhancing extra sensory perception and telepathy in humans. The group meets with a spiritual leader (called a *brujo*), who allows them to sample peyote. Upon returning to America, *One Step Beyond* host Newland also consumes a special mushroom in Dr. Puharich's Palo Alto lab and is tested for an increase in psychic power and perception.

GUEST CAST: Andrija Puharich (himself), Dr. Barbara Brown (herself), David Grey (himself), Dr. Jeffrey Smith (himself).

COMMENTARY: In its strangest and most notorious half hour, *One Step Beyond* sheds its dramatic shell and offers a stirring travelogue/documentary about host John Newland's journey to Mexico with a group of scientists and philosophers who are hoping to learn the truth about mushrooms rumored to enhance human telepathic ability. As Newland reports before the camera, there are "no actors, no script ... for this psychic report can only be recorded at the moment it happens." What follows is an interesting document of culture clash, of advanced 20th century civilization arriving in a world of the primitive. Or as Newland says, an effort to bring a TV crew to a place that has never even heard of radio!

A genuine sense of location is immediately forged as the camera captures John Newland standing in front of the ruins of a massive Mexican temple. Later, the camera watches through a window as the crew's plane is forced to set down on a narrow runway deep between giant mountains. From there the camera walks the narrow streets of an isolated village. In all, it is an impressive visual journey, and one very different from the stage interiors usually employed by *One Step Beyond*.

In both voice-over and on-camera narration, Newland reports the progression of the mission as the American searchers open up a free medical clinic for villagers in exchange for information about the secret mushroom ritual that they have come so far to observe. Then the camera watches intently as Dr. Brown (an early proponent of bio-feedback), Andrija Puharich and the others literally "get high" before our very eyes, exposed to the fumes of the hallucinogenic mushrooms. Amazingly, a medicine man (or *brujo*) is then able to report significant facts about each of his visitors. He tells Dr. Brown that she is "sick in the chest," an accurate description of a heart problem that she has kept secret from her fellow sojourners.

All of this material lensed in the previously unseen village called Juquilla (south of Wahaca) would have completed "The Sacred Mushroom" escapade as originally intended, and John Newland was quite proud of the footage his crew garnered down in Mexico. "It was a spooky trip," he remembers. "We landed at a tiny airstrip near a mission. From there it was a donkey trip of four days to reach the village. It was a dangerous journey, but we got phenomenal footage." The only problem was that Alcoa and ABC would not air the program as it had been shot! "Alcoa told us that the show was so bizarre that 'we don't dare put it on the air,'" Newland told this author. Of course, this was a terrible problem for the production team because considerable money had been invested in the voyage and filming of "The Sacred Mushroom."

Just when all seemed lost, Merwin Gerard, Collier Young, John Newland and Andrija Puharich came up with an idea that they hoped would salvage the unusual documentary segment of the series. Upon return to the States, Puharich asked Newland: "Why don't you take the mushroom?" Newland was game, so he packed up his camera crew and drove to Palo Alto and Puharich's laboratory in hopes that this desperate gambit would save the show.

Once at the laboratory, Newland sampled the distilled mushroom material, which he recalls had a very powerful effect on him. That was all right, however, as he had prepped his film crew to be ready for *anything*. "I had three cameras rolling the whole time, and I told the cameramen to just keep shooting until we had run out of film. We decided to shoot and shoot and shoot and see what happened." To Newland's surprise, he did start to feel light-headed and a "sense of well-being." Later, as he was exposed to a strobe light, he saw magnificent colors and dizzying shapes and images. And, as the final episode ultimately reports, Newland's exposure to the mushrooms improved his ESP ability!

In a card test Newland scored 12 hits out of 50 (a remarkable score after his first, pre-mushroom score: 5 out of 50). In a picture detection test (for which he wore a blindfold), Newland managed 6 adequate descriptions of 8 pictures after consuming the mushroom, versus no adequate descriptions the first time around.

When Alcoa saw the new footage from Palo Alto, they backed off from their earlier position of protest and said that John's testimony about the effects of the mushroom was "proof enough" to air the episode. This was a good decision for *One Step Beyond*, Alcoa and ABC because "The Sacred Mushroom" soon proved to be the most popular episode of the series in terms of ratings. Although Alcoa attributed this success to the fact that John Newland was on the air in more of the show (and the ratings always went up the more he was involved on-camera), Newland was humble about the reasons for "The Sacred Mushroom's" success.

Ironically, what John Newland did not report on the air in the finished episode was that the mushrooms left him with a lingering mental effect. "I had flashbacks and hallucinatory moments for about a month," he told this author with a laugh. Still, there have been no long term deleterious effects, and Newland still does not feel that he had a genuine "psychic" experience. On the contrary, when asked if he has ever had a flash of psychic insight or any first-hand experience with the paranormal, Newland replied with disappointment: "None. Not a grain. I've always believed, but I've not had one single experience. I'd like to have one, and if I was offered one, I would jump at it instantly." Today Newland is not a hundred percent sure that he would sample "X," the so-called "sacred mushroom," again, even to save a TV episode. "I'm an adventurous guy, all right, but I'm not exactly 22 anymore," he said.

So what is one to make of "The Sacred Mushroom?" The first portion of the story is surely authentic in its location details and its study of the mushroom. The last portion of the story, set in the lab, is a little more difficult to establish as real because there is a tremendous amount of cutting. With the medium of film, anything is possible via the editing process, so the bottom line is that the footage *could* have been manipulated to make Newland appear more successful on his second round of tests than he was on his first. Though Newland, a reliable and honest man, claims that everything that happened in that lab is "100 percent true," the bottom line is that viewers have only the word of the filmmakers that the truth is exactly as it appears on screen. Of course, this is not terribly difficult to believe, since the cutting and editing in the laboratory sequence was necessary to bring the footage down to a reasonable length for airing in a half hour slot, especially since, as Newland reported, he had *three cameras* running for hours in hopes of catching something remarkable.

Today the hallucinogenic properties of mushrooms are very well documented, so it is rather shocking to see an authority figure like John Newland sitting down before the camera and literally "getting high"; but if nothing else, one must respect the director's determination that "the show must go on"!

Interestingly, the final moments of "The Sacred Mushroom" do not necessarily back-peddle, but nor do they make the excessive claim that psychedelic mushrooms absolutely positively enhance psychic ability. Although Newland did feel something "profound" in the lab, it was an altered state of consciousness, not necessarily a doorway to telepathy. In a round-table discussion at the climax of "The Sacred Mushroom," each expert reveals his or her findings about the mushroom, and those findings are modest. Barbara Brown notes simply that the mushrooms are a tool to explore the capabilities of the mind; the Kahuna suggests that the mushrooms took him into worlds "beyond perception"; and Puharich, ever the optimist, declared that the chemicals within the mushroom were "most promising" for E.S.P. efficacy. What that all comes down to, in essence, is that the "sacred mushroom" was a mind-altering chemical, and no more. The journey to Wahaca was the "ultimate trip" in more than one way.

A great travelogue with beautiful and dangerous locations, "The Sacred Mushroom" may just be the strangest half hour in anthology television history. Series hosts Boris Karloff, Rod Serling, Truman Bradley and Alfred Hitchcock certainly never made the same "one step beyond" that John Newland so boldly took in this bizarre episode. Today it seems downright disconcerting to see a TV host getting stoned before our eyes, but it is yet another example of how *One Step Beyond* is a TV series that puts its money where its mouth is and earnestly attempts to explore new, even dangerous, ideas in accurate fashion.

In 1980 the film *Altered States* followed *One Step Beyond*'s lead by involving its protagonist, William Hurt, on a quest for mushrooms with hallucinogenic psychic properties. Like "The Sacred Mushroom," *Altered States* took its team of investigators to Mexico for the study and found some interesting results. Of course, *Altered States* was wholly fictional, and its final twist was one that fortunately did *not* mirror John Newland's experience: Investigator Hurt was transformed into a prehistoric man by his consumption of the mushrooms.

80. "The Gift"

(Dramatized by Charles Larson; Directed by John Newland;
Airdate: January 31, 1961)

SYNOPSIS: A charlatan palm reader gets the surprise of her life when she has a genuine psychic experience. While conducting one of her frauds, she has a vision that shows her son choking a wealthy client to death. Can she stop this brutal crime before it is too late?

GUEST CAST: Betty Garde (Lola), Scott Marlowe (Mario), Mary Sinclair (Maude).

COMMENTARY: Most anthology programs feature episodes of but a half hour in length. *One Step Beyond, The Twilight Zone, Night Gallery, Tales from the Darkside* (1984–1988) *Tales from the Crypt* (1989–1996) and *Alfred Hitchcock Presents* all adhere to this general rule. Because time is short, these programs will occasionally rely on the most facile of character types to propel a drama. "The Gift" dramatizes one such occasion when it depicts a favorite cliché of genre TV: the charlatan fortune teller who suddenly develops "real" psychic powers, surprising him or herself in the process. On *Night Gallery* the story was called "The Dear Departed"; on *Tales from the Crypt,* "Seance" was a variation on the idea. The notion has even cropped up in longer, non-anthology TV shows, such as a *Poltergeist the Legacy* twosome starring a recurring character called Jeffrey Star

("Mind's Eye," "Out of Sight"). In film, the concept has been used in *Amityville 3-D* (1983) and even *Ghost* (1990). *One Step Beyond*'s "The Gift" is part and parcel of this general tradition, but it also plays on the specific conventions of this paranormal anthology, including the Cassandra Complex, the comeuppance and the premonition.

It is also interesting to note at this point just how many *One Step Beyond* episodes associate murder with a psychic phenomenon. "Image of Death," "Echo," "The Riddle," "Delusion," "Reunion," "The Stone Cutter," "The Hand," "The Haunting," "The Clown," "I Saw You Tomorrow," "Anniversary of a Murder," "Moment of Hate" and "The Executioner" all feature psychic events precipitated by a murder. There are two possibilities as to why this concept has been most often repeated. The first is that the act of killing is so egregious a deed that it sends out "mental shock waves" that are picked up by percipients (and, indeed, most of the above-listed stories are of the comeuppance variety). The second option is that *One Step Beyond* was exploiting the easiest and most dramatic concept available — a murder and its fallout. Again, it is fair to note that television thrives on similarities, not differences. *Alfred Hitchcock Presents* was a series that traded in strange murders with regularity, so it is possible that *One Step Beyond* was attempting to carve itself a piece of the same pie.

81. "Persons Unknown"

(Dramatized by Larry Marcus; Based on material from James Crenshaw; Directed by John Newland; Airdate: February 7, 1961)

SYNOPSIS: In Mexico a physician for a deposed president named Dr. Atl hides out in a supposedly abandoned convent. The haunted building, constructed on the site of an ancient Aztec shrine, also houses the angry spirit of a deceased warrior: a giant who was sacrificed by his king. When the deadly ghost murders a sadistic soldier, the physician is accused of a crime he is at a loss to explain in rational terms. His only salvation is a plaster of paris mold of the dead man's face that reveals the handiwork of this most strange of assailants.

GUEST CAST: David J. Stewart (Dr. Atl), Rudolph Acosta (Colonel Ferraro), Jay Novello (Gonzalez), Robert Carricart (Captain Alvarez), Argentina Brunetti, Rodolfo Hoyos, Martin Garralaga Danny Bravo, David Renard.

COMMENTARY: Following the tradition established at the start of the third season, with "Tidal Wave," *One Step Beyond* brings the actual percipient of a psychic or paranormal event on the air for an interview with

John Newland in "Persons Unknown." The man with the experience in this case is Dr. Atl, a fellow of some renown in Mexico as an artist and critic. An old man by this time, Atl sits down with John Newland and affirms on the dark, vast stage that the episode "Persons Unknown" accurately reflects his strange encounter of 20 years past.

Delightfully, that encounter is an original, spooky and compelling one that feels not unlike your typical *X-Files* episode. In this case, a malevolent invisible spirit strikes out at those who have invaded a monastery. At first, an innocent man is accused of murder even though his hand prints do not match those found around the victim's throat. More investigation is done and a plaster of paris sculpture reveals a murderous hand the size of a giant's! When that strange fact is coupled with the fact that an Aztec warrior is believed to have died at this very location, an Aztec shrine, the show comes together nicely. How could it be possible that a seven-foot-tall Aztec ghost haunts the convent? Could the spirit of this monster have lingered here for years after his death? These inexplicable happenings are verified as "true" by Dr. Atl even if there is no satisfying or rational explanation. (One wonders what Scully would make of the situation.)

The story of "Persons Unknown" is representative of much literature about hauntings. However, many sources differ about the capabilities of ghosts. Some researchers believes that ghosts have no ability to induce harm on living human beings, while stories such as "Persons Unknown," *The Amityville Horror* and every episode of *Poltergeist the Legacy* ever produced obviously indicate otherwise. Invisible or not, one would not want to spend a night in the monastery with that Aztec thing!

82. "Night of Decision"

(Dramatized by Merwin Gerard; Directed by John Newland;
Airdate: February 21, 1961)

SYNOPSIS: In the "winter of despair" of 1777, George Washington experiences a crisis of faith at his headquarters in Valley Forge. Should he continue his fight for independence in the face of so much death, the blistering cold, and the paucity of supplies, or should he settle with the British for a lesser peace? An Indian chief who once tried — and failed- to kill George Washington informs the contemplative general that "the Great Spirit" is protecting him for a greater purpose. That night George Washington dreams that he will be the father of a great civilization, one which stretches from Canada to Mexico and which connects the Atlantic and Pacific Oceans.

GUEST CAST: Robert Douglas (General George Washington), Richard Carlyle (Lafayette), Donald Buka, Richard Hale, Arthur Hanson, Stephen Franken, John Cliff, Ken Drake, Dehl Berti, Richard Tyler, Robert Curtis.

COMMENTARY: Arriving right around Presidents' Day 1961, "Night of Decision" is *One Step Beyond*'s effort to resurrect the magic of "The Day the World Wept: The Lincoln Story," a popular and well-researched installment, by casting another great American president in a mysterious web of psychic phenomena. In this case, the story is not so believable, because there is little evidence (and little corroboration in history books) that George Washington (1732–1799) ever really experienced a vision of the United States at its fullest potential (stretching from coast to coast, from Mexico to Canada).

Though that final dream is surely a stretch of reality, the other historical details of "Night of Decision" are quite correct. Washington was at Valley Forge (some 20 miles northwest of Phillie) after the battles of Brandywine and Germantown in the fierce winter of 1777. He was billeted with some 11,000 men of the Continental Army, and the situation was quite severe, as many men either abandoned their posts are died from the icy grip of the elements. Furthermore, "Night of Decision" is also quite correct when it points out that Washington survived the Battle of Mononga- hela in the French-Indian War over incredible odds, and that he emerged from the bloody day without wounds (despite the fact that there were three bullet holes in his hat and three bullet holes in his uniform jacket). Chief Otumka's assertion in this matter is that God was somehow favoring the Colonial general for a greater destiny, a fact that seems to indicate God likes America better than he does other countries, since he so obviously "intervened" to assure its future.

"Night of Decision" represents another one of those classic "if-then" logic equations that sometimes appeared on this paranormal anthology. If a viewer can believe that Washington was spared injury at the Battle of Monongahela by some greater force, then it is also possible that he had a prophetic dream about the future of the United States. And, conceptually, "Night of the Decision" has precedent. It is true, for instance, that over the ages some people have had extremely precise dreams about the future. Though this author found absolutely no corroboration that Washington ever had such a dream (one that was so wide-ranging that it even pre- dicted the Civil War!), it is interesting to note that wars (whether the American Revolution or World War I) tend to foster such predictions. To wit: In World War I, two letters by a man named Andreas Rill reported that a French civilian had been captured by his regiment. This Frenchman accurately predicted Germany's defeat in the war, the ascension of a man of "low birth" who would bring on the Second World War, the *exact* date the War would start, and the economic problems that preceded Hitler's rise to power.[38] Considering that odd story (set in wartime too), it is not completely impossible to believe that Washington might be blessed with a prophetic dream.

However, one must remember that the world was seen on a different scale in 1777–78. Is it at all realistic to assume that Washington could have imagined a unified state that stretched from ocean to ocean, from Mexico to Canada, when there was no nation of that size or coherence existing anywhere else in the world? How could he have conceived of a thing that, at the time, would have been pure fantasy? It is highly unlikely that someone of Washington's "vintage" could have thought in such vast, progressive terms. That fact alone tends to diminish the possibility that Washington had such a dream, even if the concept of the premonition is valid (see "Night of April 14" or "Tonight at 12:17" for compelling evidence).

Ask this question: Even if Washington did have such a dream, would he have understood it well enough to know what he was truly seeing? And such an important, nationalistic dream would certainly appear in the history texts, right? One fears that, like the story of the cherry tree, this is one Washington tale that is more fiction than fact.

Heaping on the improbabilities, "Night of Decision" also asks viewers to believe that Washington met with an *apparition*, the spirit of the deceased Otumka (who had died two years earlier). Perhaps that is a little too much to believe without a scintilla of corroboration. For whatever the reason, this episode does not carry the psychic weight of the Lincoln story in "The Day the World Wept." There are multiple accounts of psychic phenomena in that particular circumstance (the President's assassination). Here this author cannot tell a lie: "Night of Decision" is wholly entertaining and fun, but woefully lacking in corroboration.

83. "The Stranger"

(Dramatized by Larry Marcus; Directed by John Newland;
Airdate: February 28, 1961)

SYNOPSIS: While scouring debris after a devastating earthquake, two workers rescue a family in the rubble and discover the corpse of a stranger who supported and buttressed the trapped people during the crisis. Fingerprints of the dead stranger match those of a convict who, riddled with a guilty conscience, died some twenty years earlier and who has since been reported in Mexico saving a village from cholera as well as in other cities, where he saved families from fires.

GUEST CAST: William Nacy (Jerome Cole), Peter Dyneley (Hadley), Patrick McAlliney (Warden), Graham Stark (Peter), Ken Wayne, Larry Cross (Guard), Mark Baker (Doctor), Harold Kasket.

COMMENTARY: A mysterious stranger who miraculously appears in the right place at the right time to save the lives of innocent people may sound like the premise from some long-forgotten 1970s superhero TV show, but *One Step Beyond* invests the concept with some gravitas in "The Stranger," thanks to Larry Marcus' meaningful teleplay and Newland's restrained direction. The story of Cole is actually a touching one that suggests even the most "guilty" of souls can seek forgiveness and try to be better people.

A prisoner on death row, Cole was once scheduled to donate his eyes to a 17-year-old blind girl, but because he received clemency for a time, the donation of the sight-giving organs was never made. The blind tyke later writes Cole a letter stating that she is glad he has not been executed. This child's complete goodness in the face of her own pain reveals to Cole his own terrible badness. Her words that "the meaning of life" is found only when one "reaches out" to another human being comes to haunt him. It becomes his mantra, and even after the letter has been forcibly taken from him, the words of purity and goodness ring in his ears. At first Cole cannot handle the pressure, the guilt of those words, but then he is lead to seek forgiveness and redemption.

Thus, in his own death (and after-life, apparently) Cole becomes a figure for good. Having learned his lessons in life, Cole apparently spends his eternity helping those in need. He was sighted at a fire, then at a cholera epidemic, and now at an earthquake. This is not an *out-of-body experience*, since Cole is already dead, but his appearance could qualify as some manner of apparition. What muddies the water a bit concerning the psychic concept of "The Stranger" is that Cole's body is depicted as substantive, real. His corpse is found at the earthquake and its fingerprints match those of Cole, who is known to be buried in a cemetery some 6,000 miles from the disaster. There is no doubt, then, that Cole is *physically* (rather than spectrally) in two places at once: at the sight of a calamity and resting eternally in his own bed of dirt.

Since science tells us that no two set of fingerprints are identical, "The Stranger" leaves behind a chilling riddle. If you're ever in need of help and an American man appears out of nowhere to keep you alive … look at him closely and see if he is wearing a prison jumpsuit.

84. "Justice"

(Dramatized by Guy Morgan; Directed by John Newland;
Airdate: March 7, 1961)

SYNOPSIS: In England a banker falls asleep at church during a sermon and yet, at the very same instant, appears half-a-mile away to confess to a policeman that he has committed murder. The policeman falls under suspicion as the murderer himself because Mr. Roberts has an airtight alibi: All those witnesses saw him sleeping at chapel at the time of the confession. But, driven by guilt, a second teleportation soon occurs which rights the scales of justice.

GUEST CAST: Clifford Evans (Constable), Meredith Edwards (Roberts), Barbara Mullen, Pauline Jameson, Edward Evans, Ewen Roberts, Helen Sessions, Jack Melford, Martin Benson.

COMMENTARY: Though it reads like a catalog of common *One Step Beyond* elements (the bilocation or OBE, the guilty conscience, the comeuppance, the murder), "Justice" is nonetheless a solid, well-dramatized episode that concerns the failings of human law as much as it does a bizarre psychic happenstance. What is justice, after all, but the meting out of a fair and impartial verdict that goes straight to the truth of any matter in question? *One Step Beyond* discusses the essence of justice by arranging an interesting fight. In one corner is the solid, sturdy, practical tenets of English law. In the other corner is the paranormal. These two forces—common sense jurisprudence versus a "force" that does not conform to any known laws of science—go head-to-head to suggest an interesting point. By *One Step Beyond*'s thinking, there can be no real justice when laws are unable to account for the unexpected.

In this case, human law cannot adequately support the truth (as personified by the police officer, Jones) because another set of laws (those of physics) have proclaimed that a person cannot appear in two different places at the same time. Furthermore, the laws of man actually support the murderer's assertion of innocence, despite his guilt, because many witnesses (churchgoers, no less) can place Roberts in the chapel all Sunday morning, when Jones supposedly heard his confession. Yet the police have both the corpse and the knowledge of a murder: two bits of evidence they could not possibly have ascertained unless Roberts confessed to Jones. Thus the law is revealed to be limited in that it seeks not "truth" but only those facts that can be empirically supported and proven through the confines of science and Western thinking. In a trial it is the case with more tangible, concrete proof that wins, regardless of objective truth or justice.

One Step Beyond's conclusion about this matter is that God, not the laws of Man, will assure justice in the end. In the case of Mr. Roberts, his guilty conscience again allows him to bi-locate — this time in full view of the authorities. For once, there can be no argument about his guilt. "For God shall bring each thing into judgment," Newland declares at the end of "Justice", a recitation suggesting there is a cosmic scale of justice overseen by some supreme being. That conclusion may sound like a cop-out ending, but it is clear that "Justice" finds faith not in man's legal mechanisms (which are concerned with winning and burdens of proof), but the Eye of God, who sees and judges all. It is an uplifting finale; but in fairness, how exactly could the paranormal be fairly incorporated into law? Until OBEs, NDEs, possession and the like are quantified and proven by science, human law simply has no business trudging through bizarre psychic explanations for events. *One Step Beyond*, though indicting man's law, does not seem to have any answers about how the paranormal might fit into the system.

Still, *One Step Beyond* tends to put psychic phenomena to legal tests throughout its run. "The Vision" involved a trial of four so-called "cowards" who fled the battlefields of World War I because they witnessed an anomalous phenomenon. "The Voice" offered a trial over the murder of a raccoon who was thought to be possessed by a demon. "The Confession," which would soon follow "Justice," also involves a trial and its psychic repercussions (this time in the form of an *apport*). In these instances, as in "Justice," human law is found to be wanting until the judge or some other legal authority experiences the paranormal for himself.

Like so many *One Step Beyond* tales, "Justice" is a human story of consequences and characters. There are no flashy special effects and no dramatic action scenes, merely a kind of kitchen-sink drama that happens to concern an element which can only be described as "beyond" normal. In that sense, *One Step Beyond* is really the perfect title for this anthology. The encounters it depicts are inevitably "one step beyond" normalcy. *Poltergeist the Legacy* or *Beyond Reality*, with their focus on shimmering apparitions and such, are three, even four steps beyond.

85. "The Face"

(Dramatized by Derry Quinn; Directed by John Newland;
Airdate: March 21, 1961)

SYNOPSIS: In Liverpool in 1873, young Stephen Bolt has a terrifying nightmare in which he sees a stranger stab him to death with a knife.

As the boy grows up, withdrawn from family and friends, he continues to have the terrifying dream and becomes convinced he has glimpsed his own fate. Determined to avoid a frightening death, Stephen decides to find and kill his attacker before his dream comes true.

GUEST CAST: Sean Kelly (Stephen Bolt), John Bown (Mark), Penelope Horner (Rosemary), Roger Delgado (The Face), Victor Platt, Robert Cawdron, John Scott, Erik Chitty, Andrew Faulds, Derek Sydney, Michael Peake, Leon Cortez, Paula Byrne.

COMMENTARY: Little Steven Bolt has a nightmare in which he is attacked and murdered by a bearded stranger with flinty eyes. His harsh father, who has a striking inability to understand sensitive Steven, is rough with the boy and heartlessly tells him not to be afraid.

That is the set-up for "The Face," another superb (and suspenseful) episode of *One Step Beyond*'s third season. In this case, a *nightmare* precipitates the action, and the series takes special care to adhere to the literature on the subject of bad dreams. Specifically, the episode is clever (and accurate) enough to begin its tale in Bolt's youth, with a highlight on the disapproval of his father (and Steven's understandable fear of his remote Dad). Why? Simply put, that is the terrain of many recurring nightmares:

> The most frightening nightmares in adults seem to relate to the same basic childhood fears. Even when adult nightmares appear to express the hostile impulses of adults and frightened reactions to them, there is a link to childhood fears: the absolutely helplessness experienced to one extent or another in childhood is an essential background to the nightmare.[39]

"The Face" shows the viewer that Steven's fears stem from his childhood relationship with a cold paternal figure. It may be that very fact of familial life that opens his mind to the precognitive elements of his vivid "death dream." And Steven, like most frequent nightmare sufferers, grows up to be "alienated, distrustful, or quick to withdraw emotionally."[40] In "The Face" these personality factors are seen primarily in his relationship with his brother and with women. He never marries and spends most of his life feeling isolated and alone. Steven is dramatized as a sensitive fellow who does not feel comfortable in the company of anyone. He seems a bit "off," a bit too sensitive, perhaps because the recurring nightmare has made him an outsider to society (thus alienated) who is afraid to forge bonds with others (thus distrustful).

In addition to presenting a textbook example of a nightmare sufferer, "The Face" is a fun show because it raises interrogatives about a bugaboo of human existence: free will and fate. At the climax of "The Face" Steven dies at the hands of his nightmare assailant because, in the end, he sought out that very encounter. Not content to be killed suddenly by the glowering, steely-eyed assassin, Steven wastes his adult life seeking out a phantom, an example of the hunted becoming the hunter. Had he not hired a sketch artist to draw a picture of his nightmare man, and had he subsequently not gone to the docks to show that picture to the men there, he would not have been kidnapped and been forcibly made a crewman aboard a ship. Had he not been on that ship, Steven would never have met his nightmare man. And, had he not been driven to kill his own assassin and thus make a terrible mistake (the murder of the wrong man), he would not have died at the nightmare man's hands for the crime he committed. So Steven's aggressive, obsessive desire to change his unpleasant fate actually cements it.

At the end of "The Face" Newland wonders if we make our own fate or if somehow it is written for us. His answer, that it is probably "a little bit of both," does not quite fit the fact that every action Steven takes in "The Face" (seemingly of his own free will) hammers another nail into his coffin.

Like the *One Step Beyond* episodes "Emergency Only," "The Premonition" and "Tonight at 12:17," "The Face" is also the drama of a psychic experience misinterpreted. Bolt's *veridical dream* (a premonitory dream in which some details provide information about events unknown) culminates with two images: the seaman's cold face and the appearance of a knife. Bolt comes to believe that these images connect or equate to a single act of violence — the seaman stabbing him to death.

In reality, the final moment of his life is quite different than he had interpreted it in his dream. Bolt is to be hanged, and though the seaman's icy face is the last visage he sees, he is not stabbed to death. Instead, the seaman's knife cuts the noose, dropping Bolt's (now) dead body into the sea. "In the end, it wasn't a bit like the dream," Bolt asks a fellow shipmate to report to his brother back on shore. By that, Bolt means, perhaps, that he has played a different role than he expected. A young boy when he had the dream for the first time, he was an innocent. In reality, Bolt's behavior (the murder of a shipmate he assumed to be his assassin) was the event that led to his untimely demise. His dream gave no indication of that fact either.

That Steven Bolt's recurring precognitive nightmare told him only a piece of the puzzle is another accurate reflection of the documentation in these matters. In the review for the episode "Tonight at 12:17," J.W. Dunne was quoted on this very subject, and his discussion of the precognitive elements of dreams fits well here as well. Sometimes the details are unsuspected or unnoticed, and sometimes a detail the dreamer fails to dwell on is, in fact, the most important aspect of the dream.

Much of "The Face's" terror stems from the dramatization of Steven Bolt's nightmare of death. Superimposed over the sleeping boy's troubled head is the image of a man walking in the mist. His eyes grow large, and the coldness in them is evident. Then there are grasping hands, the flash of a knife, and finally the realization that the poor boy is experiencing a bad case of the night terrors. The dream is doubly effective because the face of Steven Bolt's assassin is the face of evil itself: the late Roger Delgado! Delgado gained fame in the early seventies by playing the black-garbed scourge of the universe called "The Master," clashing with Jon Pertwee's third incarnation of the time lord on the BBC series *Doctor Who* (1963–1989). Delgado's striking features make for an explicit menace in "The Face," and even though he remains a silent figure of doom and death, his screen presence is a powerful one.

86. "The Room Upstairs"
(Dramatized by Merwin Gerard and Larry Marcus;
Directed by John Newland; Airdate: March 21, 1961)

SYNOPSIS: Pregnant Esther Hollis is terrified that both she and her unborn child will suffer from the insanity that plagued her mother and great aunt. Her fears seem confirmed when Esther hears the plaintive cries of a sick child coming from the unused sewing room upstairs. Soon both Ester and her husband Will learn that their house is haunted by the echo of a terrible crime. They seek out the former tenants and discover a sin of omission.

GUEST CAST: Lois Maxwell (Esther Hollis), David Knight (Will Hollis), Anthony Oliver, Gilda Emmanueli, David Markham, Jane Hylton, Carl Bernard.

COMMENTARY: In "The Room Upstairs," Lois Maxwell (Miss Moneypenny of every James Bond film from *Dr. No* [1962] to *A View to a Kill* [1985], and a recurring performer on the Gerry and Sylvia Anderson series *UFO*) plays Esther Hollis, a protagonist who fears for her sanity. Her mother and her great aunt both had nervous breakdowns, and now Esther believes that she and her baby are somehow tainted by a genetic predisposition to madness. In this environment of fear and worry, Esther soon experiences a frightening vision: A sick child appears in her sewing room, crying out for help. Fortunately, Mr. Hollis, Esther's husband, breaks with long-established *One Step Beyond* tradition and proves to be a supportive spouse! He not only supports Esther, he actually shares in her vision late in the story, proving conclusively that Esther is not deranged.

Besides that twist, "The Room Upstairs" echoes some of the plot elements of "The Dead Part of the House." In that early episode, three children who died from neglect inhabit a house long after their deaths, much as poor Judy inhabits the Hollis house in "The Room Upstairs." That the primary percipient of the psychic phenomena should be pregnant (and therefore easier to dismiss) recalls the character dynamic of the premonition story "Tonight at 12:17".

The psychic happening in "The Room Upstairs" comes from two guilty consciences, though this is definitely not a comeuppance or just desserts episode. Instead, the Morrisons are treated with understanding. Apparently, their daughter Judy was dying a slow death from disease and rather than see her suffer, they "forgot" to give her medicine one night and thus hastened her demise. The aura of that emotional crisis now inhabits the house, perhaps because the Morrisons themselves have not resolved the issue of what they did. They have told no one of their "sin of omission," and so their guilty conscience projects the last hours of their daughter's life into their old home, again and again. That may sound farfetched, but such is the inference to be drawn from "The Room Upstairs." The episode then ends in uplifting fashion as the Morrison's decide to admit their "crime" to authorities, and Esther Hollis, determined that she is not crazy, can have a baby in good health and the comfort that she is not insane. This plot outline is similar to the structure of "The Bride Possessed" and "Dead Man's Tale" in that a couple undergoing an important life experience (marriage; financial breakdown; pregnancy) experience a psychic phenomenon that models just such an experience (usually negative) for the couple to avoid. The Conroys saw a negative marriage modeled in "The Bride Possessed"; the bankrupt Werrises saw the end result of materialism and greed in "Dead Man's Tale"; and the Hollises are given an example of parental neglect in "The Room Upstairs."

For those noting commonalities in *One Step Beyond*, "The Room Upstairs" also makes a comparison between psychiatry and witchcraft, and uses hypnotism as a tool for healing and data-gathering ("Ordeal on Locust Street," "Moment of Hate").

87. "Signal Received"

(Dramatized by Derry Quinn; Directed by John Newland;
Airdate: April 4, 1961)

SYNOPSIS: Three British sailors during wartime have psychic experiences about their future aboard the H.M.S. *Hood*. One man hears a radio broadcast from the future revealing the *Hood*'s destruction; the second man's mother has a recurring dream that her son is reported killed in action; and the third sailor plays a ouija game which, strangely, indicates safety and a long life. The three friends rejoin shortly before their duty resumes and discover that the third man, who is foretold to live a long life, has been transferred off the *Hood*.

GUEST CAST: Mark Eden (Watson), Terry Palmer (Breed), Richard Gale (Hughes), Viola Keats (Mother), Patrick McLoughlin, Patrick Jordan, Anne Ridler, Sally Layng, Gerrard Green, Jennifer Daniel, Susan Richards, Mark Burns, Charles Lamb.

COMMENTARY: *One Step Beyond* experiments with structure again in "Signal Received," offering three interwoven "psychic" stories about a wartime disaster: the sinking of the H.M.S. *Hood*. The concepts of clairvoyant dreams, divination via a ouija board and clairaudio are the psychic concepts that round out the half hour and predict a specific future for three friends. Adding a degree of authenticity to the proceedings, actor Robin Hughes appears at the denouement of "Signal Received" to reveal that he was the sailor transferred off the *Hood*, and that these experiences, as depicted by *One Step Beyond*, are accurate.

"Signal Received" offers one of the best moments of realization yet portrayed on the long-lived series. All three sailors have had psychic warnings about the fate of their ship. Two sailors are told that all hands aboard the Hood will die, but the third sailor is told he will live to a ripe old age. That last message of survival and hope buoys the two men fated to death. After all, if all hands are to die, how come one man will live? This contradiction in psychic warnings proves to the men that such predictions are bunk, and they merrily prepare to board the Hood. Then a transfer order comes suddenly for the third man as he is boarding the ship, and the triumvirate experiences a cumulative moment of realization. The two men fated to die *will* die on the Hood, and the transferred officer, serving elsewhere, *will* survive. There is a long, dramatic pause and then the two men fated to die march grimly aboard their ship. They are fully cognizant that death is around the corner, but they go ahead nonetheless, totally shattered by the revelation. It is an icy moment that leaves one with shivers.

Fans of British television will recognize one of the three sailors in "Signal Received" as actor Mark Eden, a man who has appeared on series such as *Doctor Who* (in a "lost" serial, "Marco Polo"), *The Prisoner* and *Coronation Street*. In an interview with the magazine *TV Zone*, Eden remembered his experience working on "Signal Received" and a fate he chose not to pursue:

The director was American, and he told me to tone down the Cockney accent, as they wouldn't understand me in America. I remember he said to me, 'Mark, you must come out to Hollywood; you will clean up.' In those days, I was very young and I was in love with a lady and I asked her to come out with me to America but she said no. So I didn't go.[41]

Though Eden may have eventually come to regret that career decision, it is certain that the actor's regret was small compared to that of the characters portrayed in the drama of "Signal Received" who did not heed their psychic warnings. Two of the three friends depicted in this episode died on May 24, 1941, when the Hood was sunk in combat with the Bismarck and 1500 sons of England died.

88. "The Confession"
(Dramatized by Larry Marcus; Directed by John Newland;
Airdate: April 11, 1961)

SYNOPSIS: A brilliant but unappreciated British barrister makes a choice of conscience: He prosecutes a man for murder even though he knows that the believed victim, Frank Malone's wife, is actually alive and well and in hiding. The man is hanged and the lawyer soon becomes a judge, but his past returns to haunt him in the form of a handwritten confession note that just won't go away.

GUEST CAST: Donald Pleasence (Harvey Lawrence), Adrienne Corri (Sarah Malone), Robert Raglan, Eileen Way, Jack Newmark, Douglas Ives, Gerald James, Julian Orchard, Brenda Dunrich.

COMMENTARY: The great Donald Pleasence, a horror and science fiction icon, delivers a remarkable performance in "The Confession," another memorable *One Step Beyond* story of "conscience" and "comeuppance." Pleasence, veteran of films such as *Fantastic Voyage* (1966), *You Only Live Twice* (1967), *Halloween* (1978), *Dracula* (1979) and *Escape from New York* (1981), grapples with an interesting moral dilemma in this tale of a man who makes a bad decision. His character, Harvey Lawrence, has written the most beautiful summation of his legal career in a highly-publicized case involving murder. It is so brilliant an example of legal thinking that it could assure Harvey a judgeship. Lawrence has longed for just such an opportunity for years, and now he has the ammunition with which to escape the lower rung of the prosecutor's office. Then, suddenly, evidence comes to light that the man convicted of murder, the man Lawrence's brilliant work condemns, is not actually guilty of the crime at all. In fact, there was no crime, and the victim, Malone's wife, is alive and well! Suddenly, Lawrence sees his entire future, including the judgeship, go down in flames. He has become attached to his own work of genius and he wants his summation to see the light of day, not only out of ego but out of that desire to move up in his career. So, ignoring the evidence, Lawrence destroys the note which proves conclusively that the alleged murderer is innocent. He gives his brilliant summation, Frank Malone dies, and Harvey Lawrence gets his long-desired judgeship.

What Lawrence discovers upon his ascension to the bench, however, is that he cannot forget his own crime. The destroyed note keeps reappearing in jacket pockets to remind him of his crime, to torment him. In the end, Lawrence is a man devastated not so much by the miraculously reappearing evidence (a tool of the paranormal to right the scales of justice, called an *apport*), but by the fact that he is so completely capable of doing the wrong thing. He has an awareness that he is no better than the criminals he condemns.

Pleasence is remarkable in this role. As his character slowly goes crazy, Pleasence stands in an empty courtroom and retries the case of Frank Malone as it should have gone. Fighting the ghosts of the past, Lawrence relives the trial that cost him his morality, and one realizes, both through the intelligent teleplay (by Larry Marcus) and through Pleasence's insightful performance, that the trial is not really a re-staging for Frank Malone at all; it is the trial of Harvey Lawrence. In the end, Lawrence goes just a bit batty, his hair turning stark white, and he loses everything he gained in that moment of corruptibility. He is removed from the bench and doomed to "confess" his crime to the masses in a park.

Charting the rise and fall of this unique character, "The Confession" is beautifully done, from its location shooting in London to its artful one-man re-staging of a trial. Though it certainly falls into the category of "comeuppance," and the reappearing note is no different from the blood on the hands of the pianist in "The Hand," or the voice of the dead boy on the dictaphone in "Anniversary of a Murder," the narrative still works. The viewer becomes involved with Harvey Lawrence's ethical problem and, as in the best of TV drama, is left to wonder what he or she might do in the same situation. How easy would it be to watch a golden opportunity, a once-in-a-lifetime chance, slip away? Lawrence's decision, which pits self-interest versus justice, makes for exciting and didactic drama.

89. "The Avengers"

(Dramatized by Martin Benson; Based on material from Rosamund Harcourt-Smith; Directed by John Newland; Airdate: April 25, 1961)

SYNOPSIS: In 1943 an arrogant Nazi general and his treacherous French girlfriend plan an extravagant party in a captured French chateau — which happens to be the home of some very old ghosts. The Nazi general plots evil against 50 French workers whom he hopes to send to a forced labor camp, but the spirits of the dead have other plans. As the general's party begins, a 150-year-old legacy comes to life.

GUEST CAST: Andre Morell (General Gunter Haukman), Lisa Gastoni (Mari Anne), Stanley Van Beers, Walter Gotell, Richard Leech, Steve Plytas, Carl Jaffe, Carl Duering, Jan Conrad, Charles Russell, Robert Crewdson.

COMMENTARY: Nazis make the best villains. Put an actor in an S.S. uniform and the audience assumes his evil nature almost *a priori*. Like the charlatan fortune teller who is stunned by his/her sudden real experience with the paranormal, the villainous Nazi deserving of a cruel fate is a facile character for TV dramas. His allegiance to Hitler and participation in the fascist movement establishes evil instantly, and no further comment on his character is necessary.

That stated, "The Avengers" is a "just desserts" story in which two evil characters get their comeuppance. The Nazi and his girlfriend are plagued by a ghostly voice, windows that open of their own volition, a fountain that comes unexpectedly to life and other evidence of a haunting. Though this is an interesting story, "The Haunted U-Boat" was a better view of Nazi evil and punishment, and the chateau setting employed here is reminiscent of a similar location in "Image of Death" (another comeuppance story). The thrust of this story is that history repeats itself. One hundred and fifty years earlier, peasants stormed the chateau to protest tyranny. Now they have returned to protest a newer version of the same old tyranny, with murderous results for Gunter Haukman. All this is fine and dandy, but relatively uninspired.

"The Room Upstairs" featured Lois Maxwell, a future James Bond film star, and "The Avengers" features another: Walter Gotell. Gotell later played General Gogol in *The Spy Who Loved Me* (1976), *Moonraker* (1979), *For Your Eyes Only* (1981), *Octopussy* (1983), *A View to a Kill* (1985) and *The Living Daylights* (1987).

90. "The Prisoner"

(Dramatized by Larry Marcus; Directed by
John Newland; Airdate: May 2, 1961)

SYNOPSIS: In Warsaw in 1943, a refugee who survived the Nazi death camps explains her triumph: Every day of her imprisonment she fantasized that she ruled the world and could punish those who had witnessed the atrocities of war without intervening. Later, in the refugee house, Ruth encounters a Nazi soldier who begs her for sanctuary and who ultimately puts her in the very position she has so long desired: control of another human life. But, strangely, this particular German soldier has already been dead for six years.

GUEST CAST: Anton Diffring (Wilhelm), Faith Brook (Ruth), Catherine Feller, Sandor Eles, Gerard Heinz, Annette Carell.

COMMENTARY: "The Prisoner" is both a testament to humanity's indomitable spirit and a probing look at the inefficacy of revenge. On the former front, Ruth kept her sanity in the Nazi concentration camp through the powers of her imagination. She dreamed of winning a lottery that would allow her to be ruler of the world for 24 hours, and that vision kept her going. Her mind pushed her to live, and she dwelled in a world of imagination.

However, beneath Ruth's vision was a slowly blossoming undercurrent of something less pleasant: very natural and very human anger at her situation. Ruth desperately wanted those who did nothing during the war to suffer as she did in the camps. Interestingly, the psychic situation of "The Prisoner" helps Ruth to exorcise these powerful feelings. Suddenly, she has a Nazi soldier at her mercy and the opportunity to toy with him as she was once toyed with. So Ruth plays with the desperate man, giving him false hope the way she once had false hope. Of course, this extended interlude of revenge does not make Ruth feel any better, and the hard-hearted woman starts to identify with the soldier, even though she hates the Nazi menace.

The notion that Ruth is an emotional, psychological cripple and unable to cope with her anger is expressed visually in "The Prisoner." When Ruth shoots at the soldier, he suddenly disappears, and it is revealed that she shot a mirror instead. The cracked mirror, with a bullet hole in it, shows a fragmented reflection of Ruth. This shot reveals that Ruth has only shot herself emotionally, that somehow she is "cracked" because of her need and desire for revenge.

Later it is learned that no Nazi soldier was there with Ruth at all. Instead, his corpse is found in the basement of the building. That means, of course, that he was an apparition of some kind. And one has to wonder why he appeared at all. Was it to repair some damage his soul felt responsible for (though he never knew Ruth in life)? Was his spirit giving Ruth what she desired so as to prove that revenge solves nothing? Did the apparition appear simply so that Ruth's suffering would end and she would have some closure in her life? The episode does not explain the situation in any significant way, but one is left with the feeling that the apparition is actually exorcising the deep hatred from Ruth, who is aged physically and emotionally beyond her years, courtesy of the Nazi mistreatment.

Set in wartime and featuring an apparition, this is a *One Step Beyond* story that looks beyond the obvious answer. The Nazi soldier (Anton Diffring, who played a Nazi in the *Doctor Who* serial "Silver Nemesis" as well) is not depicted as pure evil (as the Nazis were in the previous episode, "The Avengers") but as a human being. He longs to make contact with his wife. He is sick, wounded and weak, and he needs Ruth's mercy. Ruth is also depicted in strikingly ambivalent terms. Impatient, lonely, a little testy, this refugee has both good and bad inside her too. As much as she is a survivor and her courageous story is one of mind over matter, she is equally bent on revenge and finding outlet for her hatred. Her experience with the supernatural allows Ruth to vent these demons in a most satisfying manner, even if many of the so-called psychic details in this episode have been seen before.

91. "Blood Flower"

(Dramatized by Merwin Gerard; Directed by John Newland;
Airdate: May 16, 1961)

SYNOPSIS: In South America a visiting political science professor from the United States is unexpectedly possessed by a "blood flower," a psychic parasite. Soon the professor's pacifist nature is undercut by the flower, which leads him to become a fiery revolutionary and, ultimately, an assassin.

GUEST CAST: Larry Gates (Professor Gavin Carroll), Eugene Iglesias, Peggy Santon, Raoul de Leon, Marya Stevens, Renatta Vanni, Robert Tafur, David Garcia, Dick Crockett.

COMMENTARY: Every TV series has featured at least one episode that its creators probably wish would just vanish from the face of the Earth. For *The Twilight Zone* that episode might be the failed comedy "Cavender is Coming," for *Star Trek* it might be the absurd "Spock's Brain." For *One Step Beyond* host and director John Newland the episode which he dreads any mention of is "Blood Flower." This is the story of a sedate American professor who visits a South American country and becomes possessed by the spirit of a dead revolutionary following his unwitting exposure to a plant that was nourished on the revolutionary's spilled blood. And, as John Newland reports, he thought the concept of "Blood Flower" was "silly, dumb and just the pits."

It is not often that a *One Step Beyond* episode is less than successful, but "Blood Flower" is the rare exception to that rule. The story takes on an unintended sense of the ridiculous as Professor Carroll, a slightly overweight, balding "everyman," suddenly becomes a fire-spitting revolutionary who barks orders at swarthy-looking Latin types with names like Emilio and Alfredo. Amazingly, he is obeyed by these men, even though they do not know who he is or why he should suddenly be invested in their cause. Even more humorous is the scene in which the staid academician (Carroll) becomes an assassin (while still wearing his suit and tie), crawling through the grass to murder El Presidente. Perhaps the ultimate sign of desperation in "Blood Flower" is that the episode is jam-packed with voice-over narration that explains the story *ad nauseum*, an awkward device that brings to mind one of this author's ironclad rules of TV drama: Any story with a surplus of on-screen explanation did not work in the first place, and the voice-over exposition is simply a last-minute move of desperation to pull things together. That seems very much the case with "Blood Flower," a story that attempts to suggest that a plant nourished on a man's blood not only reflects that man's personality but transmit that personality to another human being.

Part of the problem with "Blood Flower" is certainly the main character. Professor Carroll is portrayed as a coddled American "authority" who supports the local dictatorship because it pays his bills; he knows nothing of local custom and is therefore naive at best and a fool at worst. When this pragmatic man of academia then starts to feel drawn to an "odd-looking vine" and becomes an unwitting revolutionary, the story loses all semblance of reality.

Despite the problems inherent in this odd tale, John Newland still directs the show with aplomb. A shaky, hand-held camera tracks Carroll tensely as he strides towards the bedroom of El Presidente to murder him, and there is, for at least a moment, a feeling of pace and suspense.

At the end of "Blood Flower," a dying Professor Carroll, shot down after assassinating El Presidente, mutters "I don't understand." The same might be said for the viewers who sat down to watch "Blood Flower."

92. "The Sorcerer"

(Dramatized by Derry Quinn; Directed by John Newland;
Airdate: May 23, 1961)

SYNOPSIS: In February of 1915 a German officer goes before a military tribunal and demands a trial, claiming that he is "guilty" of a crime for which he was not even present to commit. It seems a clairvoyant farmer, a "sorcerer," helped the man to project or teleport himself back to Berlin to kill his unfaithful, promiscuous lover.

GUEST CAST: Christopher Lee (Willem), Gabrielle Licudi (Elsa Brook), Martin Benson (Klaus Koenig), Alfred Burke, Joseph Furst, George Pravda, Frederick Jaeger, Peter Swanwick, Edwin Richfield, Richard Shaw.

COMMENTARY: Recounted in flashback structure, "The Sorcerer" is the dramatic tale of a man who is instantly teleported across country (some eight hundred kilometers away!) to commit a crime of passion. In this story the percipient is Willem, and the actor portraying him is Christopher Lee, who shortly before the filming of this episode gained stardom by playing Bram Stoker's Transylvanian Count in the Hammer film *Horror of Dracula* (1958). Like Donald Pleasence, Christopher Lee has become an icon of the horror genre and appeared in films such as *Count Dracula* (1970), *The Wicker Man* (1971), *Dracula A.D. 1972* (1972), *Horror Express* (1973), *The Man with the Golden Gun* (1974) and *Gremlins 2: The New Batch* (1990).

The teleportation of Willem is accomplished via the auspices of a strange farmer, "a sorcerer" who seems to have clairvoyant abilities. He informs Willem that Germany will lose the war effort (World War I), and hints that Willem's lover has not been faithful to him. This information leads Willem to commit murder, but the military tribunal is incapable of believing that Willem traveled to so distant a location so quickly, despite the fact that his gun has been fired. Since justice cannot accommodate the paranormal and Willem feels guilty for his crime, he solves his dilemma by murdering the sorcerer. This time he has committed a crime for which he can be punished, and so he is punished. In theme and concept, "The Sorcerer" is similar to "Justice." It demonstrates how man's laws cannot accommodate the inexplicable.

Teleportation is usually thought to be the process of instantaneously moving objects, not people; but there is no other explanation for Willem's strange journey in "The Sorcerer." He did not have an out-of-body experience because he is not seen in two places at once (bilocation). His body physically disappears from one locale and reappears at another, which makes the phenomenon different from the one explored in "The Return of Mitchell Campion" (wherein the protagonist was perceived on an island and in the United States, in a hospital, at the same time). In "The Sorcerer" Willem is instantly transported over miles and then returned through some miraculous means.

Christopher Lee makes for a stony but powerful central presence in "The Sorcerer," but this episode is not the sterling character piece for him that "The Confession" was for Donald Pleasence. Too much of "The Sorcerer" feels like a leftover from "Justice," though it is interesting that this episode features a psychic "agent" of sorts, rather than some mere force. The farmer is a sorcerer, warlock, witch, whathaveyou, and is not only clairvoyant but capable of seemingly magical acts. And he definitely has an agenda. One senses that he is all too happy to rid the world of Willem, an enemy in time of war.

93. "The Villa"
(Dramatized by Derry Quinn; Directed by John Newland;
Airdate: June 6, 1961)

SYNOPSIS: At a party Mrs. Mary Lowe sits before a flashing strobe light and experiences a frightening vision of someone trapped and dying in a lift in a dark villa. When she visits Milan with her estranged husband, Mary learns that the Villa Orlando is real, and thus she fears that her vision of doom might be true as well. When Mary disappears, her husband goes to the villa alone to find her, and a dark prophecy comes true.

GUEST CAST: Elizabeth Sellers (Mary Lowe), Michael Crawford, Ronald Lewis, Geoffrey Toone, Marla Landi (Stella).

COMMENTARY: The strobe light that pscyhometrist Peter Hurkos faced under the direction of Dr. Lindstrom (in "The Peter Hurkos Story") and series host John Newland faced under the direction of Dr. Andrija Puharich (in "The Sacred Mushroom") returns as the central prop of "The Villa," a dark and terrifying chapter in the *One Step Beyond* canon.

The protagonist of this segment is Mary Lowe, a woman trapped in a "dead end" marriage, a woman who knows that her husband is involved in an adulterous affair and that divorce is imminent. Then Mary goes to a business party with her husband, and a strobe light, a kind of party trick, causes a barrage of "foreign" images to explode inside her mind. Though quick strobing or flashing has been known to cause seizures in certain people (just ask the Japanese children who seized while watching the dazzling images of a *Pokemon* episode in 1998), it has quite another effect on Mary: She has a psychic vision of a dark place and a premonition of someone's death inside an ornate-looking elevator.

One Step Beyond episodes rarely trade in absolutely terrifying, relentlessly hopeless scenarios, but "The Villa" is a rare and powerful exception to the rule. Besides dramatizing the specifics of yet another failed marriage, Mary's premonition of death is one of stark horror. As we see into her mind's eye, a darting camera casts the viewer into a world of pitch blackness. Then, in a subjective P.O.V. shot, the camera stalks the blackness of the isolated villa: a grim, lonely world where someone is trapped, waiting to die. It is a nightmarish look into an unfamiliar place, and thus its no wonder poor Mary is terrorized by what she sees.

Bouncing forward after this scary vision, "The Villa" tracks an obsessed Mary as she determines to find the strange, dark villa for herself. Eventually she locates the Villa Orlando in Milan, and as she enters she feels a strong sense of *déjà vu*. Shortly she comes face to face with the episode's instrument of horror: the lattice-work lift that will cage someone until death.

"The Villa" is especially masterful at building suspense here. Against her better judgment, Mary enters the rickety but beautifully decorative lift (and the camera assumes a high angle, suggesting doom and entrapment). At this point the audience is convinced that it has anticipated the outcome: Mary will become trapped in the lift, and what she actually witnessed in the vision was her own imminent death. Then relief follows this tense scene, as Mary escapes the lift and the villa. The kicker comes, of course, when her husband goes to the villa to find Mary and ... the lift jams. Then a chill of fear and inevitability lands on the audience as realization dawns— Mary was actually seeing her husband's death! Horribly, Mr. Lowe screams to be freed, and the story ends with these shrieks and then Newland's ghoulish revelation that Mr. Lowe's body was not found for six months. A terrifying resolution, this ending is one of stark horror.

Besides trading on the very common *One Step Beyond* story elements of the *premonition* or *precognition* (see "Night of April 14" or "Tonight at 12:17"), "The Villa" does revisit several other "standards" of the series as well. There is the disbelieving spouse (Mr. Lowe) who suggests medical help; the Cassandra Complex (Mary, who just knows someone is going to die, sees her warnings dismissed); the comeuppance (Mr. Lowe pays for both his infidelity and his disbelief with his life); and the obsession with the psychic vision. In the latter situation, Mr. Lowe makes a telling, interesting comment about Mary. He says that her obsession has trapped her. "It is you who is in the lift," he spits, "trapped between floors!" This is a nice analogy, as Mary is indeed trapped by a future she fears and a present that does not seem to connect to that future—two distinct floors of reality, if you will. And, of course, there is the literal meaning too: Her vision *is* of an elevator stuck between levels. Not a bad metaphor.

"The Villa" ends with a man dead, a marriage destroyed, and a psychic warning not heeded — possibly the grimmest of all conclusions on *One Step Beyond*. This chilling climax works just fine, and the episode is a remarkably taut, suspenseful one, though regular viewers can take solace that *One Step Beyond* did not often reach a plateau of such inevitable, unstoppable terror.

94. "The Tiger"

(Dramatized by Ian Stuart Black; Directed by John Newland;
Airdate: June 20, 1961)

SYNOPSIS: A cruel governess becomes the caretaker of sweet young Pamela and promptly uses harsh methods to assure the child's proper behavior, such as locking the poor girl in a dark "punishment room" in the basement. Little Pamela, alone in the darkness with no company, tries to make her wishes come true by bringing life to a stuffed animal tiger. Despite Pamela's good behavior, she is still met with hostility by her governess. Pamela finally retaliates by unleashing her pet tiger, now very much alive, and wreaking vengeance on her abuser.

GUEST CAST: Pamela Brown, Elspeth March, Pauline Challenor, Edward Unbderdown, Patsy Smart, Brion Parker, Michael Collins.

COMMENTARY: The familiar conceit of "the comeuppance" is mated to a story of "mind over matter" in "The Tiger," another one of those delicious *One Step Beyond* episodes that finds a truly despicable woman meeting her just desserts at the hands of a psychic or paranormal event. Though the format is a familiar one, the joy of this particular story is in watching a nasty, arrogant governess become undone by a little girl's fantasy that her pet tiger (an imaginary friend) has come to life. Before long, fantasy is reality and the furniture is being mysteriously ripped apart by the claws of some invisible monster. Soon the cruel governess realizes she has picked the wrong child to pick on, and meets her unpleasant (but oh-so-deserved) destiny.

It so easy to hate Mrs. Cartwright in this episode. To little Pamela, this tyrannical woman has "Scaredy Eyes" (a wonderful, child-like description of the adult woman, and one worthy of Stephen King). Worse, Mrs. Cartwright's behavior is absolutely atrocious. She locks Pamela in a closet at one point and then casts her into a dark basement while she goes out to see a movie. This wicked caregiver, a reference to fairy tale stepmothers like those in *Cinderella* perhaps, finally gets torn apart by a marmalade yellow tiger and a little girl whose wish has come true; and despite the violence, the audience has found itself wishing for just such a conclusion.

"The Tiger" may not be progressive or original material (this was at least the tenth instance of the comeuppance on *One Step Beyond!*), but it is wicked, enjoyable fun and a memorable show. Fitting in with themes from the past, a child is seen to be the possessor of vast psychic powers ("Make Me Not a Witch," "The Burning Girl"), and the scales of justice are righted when the tiger makes lunch out of the governess.

95. "Nightmare"
(Dramatized by Martin Benson; Directed by John Newland; Airdate: June 27, 1961)

SYNOPSIS: A prominent painter upsets his talkative rich client when he paints a portrait not of her, but of some mysterious beauty named Claire. This also upsets Jill, the woman that Paul Rollins is to be married to in six days, who fears that he is having an affair. Paul soon finds that he can paint nobody but the mysterious Claire — as if her face is possessing his art and his mind. Driven mad by these visions of a woman he has never met, Paul instinctively drives to a rural town that overlooks the ocean, called Cadgwith, where an old woman has been in mourning for 40 years over the death of her groom-to-be.

GUEST CAST: Peter Wyngarde (Paul Rollins), Mary Peach (Jill), Ambrosine Philpotts, Jean Cadell, Ferdy Mayne, Patrick Holt, Richard Caldicott.

COMMENTARY: Is the human soul but a single flame, passed from torch to torch, life to life, as advocates of reincarnation might ask us to believe? *One Step Beyond* certainly thinks so, as it returns to the fascinating topic that also informed the ultimate episode of the first season, "The Riddle." In that story it was a legacy of hate and vengeance that was carried on from one life to another, but in "Nightmare" it is, instead, a legacy of love and remembrance.

At first, "Nightmare" moves rather slowly as it belabors the point that Paul has become obsessed with the painting of some unknown woman named Claire. As these seemingly alien images come to his head, audiences are left to muse on an interesting topic. Where do artists "find" the images that they create? From inside their own heads? Their subconscious? Their fantasies? Or does the muse that guides painters come from some other place, some psychic point of origin instead? That very question would make for an interesting episode of *One Step Beyond* all by itself, but before too many thoughts on the subject can be raised, "Nightmare" moves to its central thesis on the topic of reincarnation.

The story culminates in scenic Cadgwith, over the ocean, and the answer to Paul's obsessive behavior becomes clear: He is the living reincarnation of Jean, an old woman's dead fiancé. In this final revelation the episode reaches its emotional apex. The old lady, the elusive Claire, has lived alone in her house for some forty years, living for a love that was not meant to be. In 1916, the second year of the First World War, her fiancé died, and she has kept their house ever since as a shrine to the love they shared ever so briefly. Now Jean's soul has returned to life in Paul and is still consumed with the love he felt for Claire when he went to the grave. It is a beautiful premise, and, in fairness, it is more representative of the idea of reincarnation than the more harsh-minded (but compelling) "The Riddle."

If "Nightmare" fails anywhere, it is simply in its final resolution. Realizing he is indeed Jean, Paul leaves the old lady's home after a simple hug with Claire, approaches the camera, and smiles enigmatically. There is no follow-up and no real exploration of how this revelation has changed the artist's life or work. For instance, why would it be so impossible to believe that Paul would still seek to live with Claire, even though she is elderly? If their love was so powerful that it pulled Paul back to Cadgwith in a different lifetime, then certainly it was strong enough to weather the admittedly vast age difference between the lovers, right? Regardless of the answer to that question, the wrap-up of "Nightmare" seems contrived, as Newland conveniently reports that Claire soon passed away and Paul went on to great fame as an artist. One is left to wonder about the wheel of life: Would Claire soon return as another reincarnation, still looking for Paul/Jean? Are these two lovers always doomed to *just* miss each other, never at the right age at the right time to find the companionship they seek? That's a grim fate, and one certainly undeserved by two such sympathetic characters. Still, "Nightmare" is memorable for a sweet and tragic story about love crossing from one life to the next.

Fans of genre films may recognize Paul Rollins as actor Peter Wyngarde, the actor who played Ming's right hand man, Klytus, in the 1980 production of *Flash Gordon*.

96. "Eye Witness"
(Dramatized by Derry Quinn; Directed by John Newland;
Airdate: July 4, 1961)

SYNOPSIS: A night editor for the *Boston Star*, Henry Soames, has a seizure one August night in 1883 and then writes an alarmingly accurate story about a massive volcanic eruption on the distant island of Krakatoa that kills 36,000 people. At first Soames is met with skepticism for his bizarre article (which no other newspaper or magazine in the United States can corroborate), but then reality supports his assertion about the catastrophe. Years later, after a life of undesired celebrity as a "psychic," Soames returns to the *Star* to make another disturbing prediction.

GUEST CAST: John Meillon (Henry Soames), Rose Alba, Anton Rodgers, Robin Hughes, John Phillips, Robert Ayres, Gordon Stern, J.G. Devlin, Howard Knight, Janet Brandes, Patricia English.

COMMENTARY: "Eye Witness," *One Step Beyond*'s final episode, is a straightforward reiteration of the themes of "Earthquake," a well-done second season episode and an example of the Cassandra Complex. Though there is a different cataclysm to explore in "Eye Witness," the story of a man who experiences a precognitive moment (he receives psychic knowledge of a disaster) is one that is familiar. The disaster *du jour* in "Eye Witness" is the eruption of the volcano Krakatoa on August 26, 1883. Considered one of the most catastrophic events witnessed in modern history, the eruption caused earthquakes, tidal waves and other nightmares for the surrounding environment. Flying ash even obscured the sun for some two days in the immediate of the eruption. More than 36,000 people died in Java and Sumatra as a result of eruption-generated tidal waves, and plant and animal life did not re-establish itself in the region of Rakata for some time following the earth-shattering blast.

As far as disasters go, they do not come much more dramatic than the eruption of Krakatoa, and "Eye Witness" effectively utilizes that cataclysm to propel this psychic adventure. Interestingly, Mr. Soames (the man with the psychic experience) may be a thinly-disguised version of a real man rumored to have lived through a similar ordeal. There is the case of J.W. Dunne, a man now famous in psychic circles. Apparently, Mr. Dunne dreamed that he was in Martinique in the West Indies when Mount Pelee erupted and caused thousands of deaths.[42] The eruption may be from a different volcano, but the precognitive experience shared by the fictitious Soames and the real Dunne is the same.

Beyond establishing Soames' incredible experience of clairvoyance, "Eye Witness" concerns itself with the fallout of becoming known as a successful psychic. Henry Soames comes to feel like a "carnival freak," and soon everybody wants something from him. Should they buy or sell stocks? Can he find a missing boy? These questions overwhelm Soames until he is forced to give up his job as a newspaper man and seek respite from his newfound but most unwelcome celebrity. *One Step Beyond* thus suggests that mankind actively looks for seers, for easy answers to hard questions, when there really are none. Hounded into social retreat by his fellow man, the climactic twist of "Eye Witness" finds Soames returning only once to the *Boston Star*, years after his accurate vision of destruciton on Krakatoa. This time he pounds out another clairvoyant story on his typewriter: the shooting of President McKinley! After revealing this information, Soames quietly leaves the office and disappears into history, a one-time wonder who wishes to remain anonymous.

Not particularly original or fresh in concept, "Eye Witness" nonetheless makes some worthwhile observations about celebrity and the kinds of people who are attracted to it. It may not be the best episode for the series to go out on (especially considering the gut-punch power of "The Face" and "The Villa," or the uplifting finale of "Nightmare"), but it does epitomize the unchanging *One Step Beyond* approach to storytelling. It combines several common elements (such as the Cassandra Complex), treats its subject material with respect, and is shot with a subdued, understated grace.

Rod Serling once stated of *The Twilight Zone* that the show "had some real turkeys, some fair ones, and some shows I'm really proud to have been a part of."[43] A similar comment might be made about *One Step Beyond*. Though there were few outright turkeys ("Blood Flower" is the only one that immediately comes to mind), the series had many repetitive moments that flatten out the quality of some otherwise impressive series installments. Yet it also had some real, undisputed high points. Today, "If You See Sally," "Night of April 14," "Epilogue," "The Premonition," "The Haunted U-Boat," "Anniversary of a Murder," "The Day the World Wept," "The Sacred Mushroom," "Moment of Hate," "The Villa," "The Face" and many other *One Step Beyond* half hours still capture a cerebral feeling of horror and carry a real "psychic" weight. Every show has its own highs and lows, but *One Step Beyond*, even with its repetition of stock story elements, certainly has more of the former than the latter.

One Step Beyond Credits for 1992 Version on the Sci Fi Channel

For completists, the credits for the computer-generated revamp of *The One Step Beyond* that aired in 1992 (on the Sci Fi Channel) are included below:

A World Vision Enterprises, Inc., Presentation. *Executive in Charge of Production:* Mitchell Black. *Production Supervisor:* Howard Lester. *Additional Music:* Peter Wetzler. *Sound Re-Recording:* Richard Fairbanks. *Computer Animation:* Christopher Laskey. *Special Effects Photography:* Steve Decker. *On-line Editor:* Mark Nieves-Topal. *Electronic Graphics:* Melissa Snyder. Copyright 1992 World Television Programming Inc.

Part III

Newland Between Steps

TV Series

After *One Step Beyond* was canceled, John Newland found his talents as director in demand all over the television landscape. In fact, before the dust had even settled on *Alcoa Presents*, an example of Newland's most chilling and memorable work within the genre was on display in *Thriller*, the short-lived Boris Karloff–hosted horror/crime anthology.

"Pigeons from Hell," a ghoulish story by Robert E. Howard, was adapted for *Thriller* by writer John Kneubuhl, and director John Newland led actors Brandon DeWilde and David Walton through a terrifying and violent tale of indestructible zombies (or, more accurately, zuvembies) who dwelled in an old plantation house. Widely regarded as one of *Thriller*'s finest entries, "Pigeons from Hell" aired June 6, 1961, and met with rave reviews. It has been called "one of the most truly frightening journeys into small-screen fantasy,"[1] and Stephen King singled it out in his nonfiction book *Danse Macabre* as the "favorite of many who remember *Thriller* with fondness."[2] A chilling (and gory) tale, "Pigeons from Hell" demonstrates an attentive Newland at his stylish best. So successful was this *Thriller* installment that Newland returned as a recurring director in the series' second (and final) season. He starred in and directed both "The Return of Andrew Bentley" (based on a story by August Derleth) and "Portrait Without a Face," a tale of a painting with psychic overtones (shades of "Nightmare and "The Storm" on *One Step Beyond*!). Newland's last directing job on the excellent *Thriller* was "Man of Mystery," a tale written by Robert Bloch. It starred Mary Tyler Moore and William Windom and aired in April of 1962.

Also in 1962, John Newland lent his talents to the long-lived *Alfred Hitchcock Presents* (1955–65), which by that point in its broadcast history was well into its seventh season. By directing an episode of this anthology, John Newland joined the prestigious ranks of Don Medford, Normal Lloyd, Francis Cockrell, Herschel Daughtery, Robert Altman, Arthur Hiller, Don

Taylor, Stuart Rosenberg, Boris Sagal, Lewis Teague, William Friedkin and Hitchcock himself.

"Bad Actor" (remade in the 1985 version of the *Hitchcock* series as "Method Actor," with Martin Sheen) starred Robert Duvall and was a tongue-in-cheek tale of murder (and the cutthroat world of acting) from the pen of Robert Bloch. Newland directed "Bad Actor," "Burglar Proof" (with Robert Webber, of "The Captain's Guests") and "The Twelve Hour Caper" (with *Bewitched*'s Dick York) for *Alfred Hitchcock Presents* between other assignments on popular (but non-genre) programming, such as *Route 66* (1960–64; "There I Am — There I Always Am"), *The Man from U.N.C.L.E.* (1964–68; "The Double Affair"), *Dr. Kildare* (1961–66), *The Defenders* (1961–65), *Alcoa Premiere* (1961–63; "Mr. Easy"), *Naked City* (1958–63; "Strike a Statue") and the Robert Lansing ("The Voice") series *The Man Who Never Was* (1966–67).

In 1967 John Newland landed one of his most famous and well-known directing assignments when he was hired by series creator Gene Roddenberry to direct a first season episode of *Star Trek* entitled "Errand of Mercy" (by Gene Coon). This episode was an extremely important historically because it introduced a "new villain" that would go on to become *Star Trek*'s most enduring and most popular: the Klingons. The adventure concerned Captain Kirk and Mr. Spock's attempt to rescue the planet Organia from Klingon occupation. The climactic turn of events revealed that the Organians needed no protection at all since they were incredibly powerful, non-corporeal balls of energy.

Newland was instrumental in the casting of the first Klingon captain ever seen on *Star Trek*, Kor (Jon Colicos, of *Battlestar Galactica* [1978-79]); and Newland began a long friendship with Gene Roddenberry and his wife, Majel Barrett (who later appeared in *The Next Step Beyond* episode "Drums at Midnight"). Newland was quite pleased to work on *Star Trek*'s "Errand of Mercy," and he found it a delightful experience to work with William Shatner again after four years. Though Newland also enjoyed working with Leonard Nimoy, he remembers that at times Nimoy became so entrenched in the character of the dour Mr. Spock that he would resist direction and even refuse to carry out the imperatives of the script.

"Leonard is a *very* serious guy," Newland stressed to this author, with sincerity and a sense of admiration. "I remember that I asked him to do something relatively minor, and there came this long pause. He looked at me and said, 'John, I don't think a Vulcan would do this.' There was another long pause, so I looked to Bill [Shatner] and said, 'Bill, would a Vulcan do this?' Bill shrugged with indifference, but Leonard still would not take the direction. I finally had to say to Leonard: 'I really don't give a shit about Vulcan behavior, Leonard, because the script says you need to move now and do this thing.' Well, he didn't like that, but he finally did what I directed him to do ... after some difficulty."

After *Star Trek* Newland joined forces with longtime friend Rod Serling on his new horror anthology, *Rod Serling's Night Gallery*. During the show's second season (1971-72), Newland was asked to direct a teleplay by Alvin Sapinsley (based on a short story by Stephen Hall) called "There Aren't Any More MacBanes." This entry of the supernatural horror show (produced by Jack Laird) concerned a dabbler in the occult named Andrew MacBane (Joel Grey) who hoped to kill his uncle (Howard Duff) before the old man could disinherit him. Andrew utilized the magic spells of a warlock ancestor, one Jedidiah MacBane, to conjure up a demonic servant that would do his bidding. Though the spell was successful, MacBane found that he had brought a loyal, unswerving and *jealous* creature out of the blackness of the void. Once called, there was no way to vanquish the bloody thing, and now the creature was intent on killing every friend, lover or acquaintance for whom MacBane showed any affection.

Also starring a young Mark Hamill (*Star Wars* [1977]), "There Aren't Any More MacBanes" was an intense *Night Gallery* segment, a Lovecraftian story that featured a horrible, dog-like thing "scratching" malevolently behind doors for the affections of its horrified master. Personified at first as a thing with beady red eyes, the mystery of the "MacBane" monster was undercut only in the finale when the make-up and special effects revealed the dog-like creature to be a blue, hook-nosed witch of barely menacing proportions. Despite the underwhelming production values at the climax, "There Aren't Any More MacBanes," like "Pigeons from Hell," has been acknowledged as a classic of its genre and one of *Night Gallery's* best segments. Of Newland's direction it has been written that the artist:

> guides and visualizes the story with a sure hand at achieving his desired effects. Director also of the classic *Thriller* episode "Pigeons from Hell," Newland here seals the impression that his best work lies in the creation of shadowy worlds and gothic suspense. He successfully evokes the Lovecraftian sense of something lurking on the threshold, and the segment's shadowed photography and musty sets produce a brooding, archaic atmosphere.[3]

That atmosphere works wonders in "There Aren't Any More MacBanes," and Newland, as ever, makes use of film grammar to heighten tension and fear. In one especially impressive moment, Howard Duff is seen walking (by night) alone in the foreground of the frame when two devil eyes materialize behind him (in the background). Duff's murder is then inter-cut with a ghoulish close-up of MacBane (Grey) as he stands just beyond the confines of his fireplace. The crackling fire below MacBane lights Grey's expressive face and casts evil-looking shadows across his cruel visage. The cause-and-effect nature of this moment is consequently captured in effective visual shorthand. On familiar but fascinating thematic ground ("the comeuppance"), Newland again flourished as a director.

From *Rod Serling's Night Gallery* Newland moved on to a sister Uni-versal series, the hour-long psychic drama *The Sixth Sense* (1972). This series, developed by Stan Shpetner and created by Anthony Lawrence (based on the telefilm *Sweet, Sweet Rachel* [1971]) followed the adventures of Dr. Michael Rhodes (actor Gary Collins), a professor of parapsychol-ogy. In some ways the series was an attempt to go beyond *One Step Beyond*'s example and inject a continuing character into stories of automatic writ-ing, astral projection, mental telepathy, premonitions and the like. In fact, *The Sixth Sense* is probably the "missing link" show between *One Step Beyond* and *The X-Files*, as it uses the former's core concepts and the lat-ter's devotion to a heroic character seen week in and week out.

Though for a time Harlan Ellison and D.C. Fontana worked on *The Sixth Sense*, they eventually left the series with discontent, and the qual-ity suffered. Today *The Sixth Sense* cannot really be given a fair or objec-tive hearing by critics because shortly after its cancellation in 1972, Universal Studios cut every sixty-minute episode of the series down to thirty minutes so the program could share a syndication package with *Night Gallery*. The removal of a whopping 50 percent of the plots rendered many episodes of *The Sixth Sense* unintelligible and unwatchable.

Before that bit of editorial butchery, however, John Newland came aboard *The Sixth Sense* and directed three episodes for the series' second season. Ironically, Newland was brought aboard not for his incredible expe-rience with the psychic subject matter (96 episodes of *One Step Beyond*!) but because his dear friend Joan Crawford agreed to appear on the series as a guest star only if Newland would direct her. Newland considered this a great compliment and was all too happy to comply with Crawford's request. The duo thus teamed for "Dear Joan: We're Going to Scare You to Death," a story in which guest Scott Hylands (as Jason) attempts to drive the asthmatic Crawford to her death by projecting an image of her dead daughter (*Battlestar Galactica*'s Anne Lockhart), who had drowned a year earlier. The episode pulls out all the stops, featuring telepathic links, premonitions of death, and even psychic communication with the deaf (shades of "Tidal Wave" on *One Step Beyond*!). Though only half of *The Sixth Sense* remains extant, "Dear Joan: We're Going to Scare You to Death" seems a more coherent segment than some other episodes of the series. Interestingly, star Gary Collins did not appear in this episode, allowing Joan Crawford to take center stage.

Gary Collins did not appear in John Newland's second episode of *The Sixth Sense* either, and "Through a Flame Darkly" was another story that could have been lifted right out of the *One Step Beyond* roster with almost no translation or rewriting. In this segment (penned by Dick Nelson) Alice Martin (guest star Sandra Dee) receives the psychic impression that her childhood friend, Beth, is in some kind of terrible danger. Following up on these visions of jeopardy, Alice finds that her friend has been captured by a villainous psychotic (*Dark Shadows*' John Karlen!) who is also the mortician in a small town called Pine Ridge.

"Through a Flame Darkly" came replete with the dismissive, doubting doctor (Peggy Feury) and the helpful law enforcement official (John Anderson) who was willing at least to entertain the idea of psychic powers. "Through a Flame Darkly" also features time-lapse photography in its psychic visions, and culminates in a knock-down, drag-out chase between Sandra Dee and Karlen that manages to get one's blood pumping. Like all episodes of *The Sixth Sense*, it is impossible to assess the quality of "Through a Flame Darkly" with any sense of even-handedness (or even accuracy), since only fifty percent of it remains intact.

Newland's final contribution to *The Sixth Sense* was "And Scream by the Light of the Moon" (also known as "Candle, Candle, Burning Bright"). Unlike the other two episodes, this installment did feature series star Collins, and also an early appearance by Scott Glenn (*The Right Stuff* [1981], *Silence of the Lambs* [1991]). Judging from what survived Universal's chopping block, this appears to be the weakest of Newland's three, featuring a woman under siege by psychic fire. Of his *The Sixth Sense* episodes and the series as a whole, John Newland remembers thinking that "it was a much emptier show than *One Step Beyond*," and that Gary Collins, though a nice guy and a good sport, "was not terribly effective as the lead." Indeed, if one studies *The Sixth Sense* today it does seem a more lurid version of *One Step Beyond*. Most of the characters border on hysteria, the psychic visions are sometimes effective but sometimes overwrought, and there is little of the restraint or attention to detail that still separates *One Step Beyond* from the paranormal pack.

After *The Sixth Sense*, science and fiction on television was out of style for a long spell (though Newland would certainly have been a terrific choice to helm a *Kolchak: The Night Stalker* [1975] episode, with his propensity for almost journalistic objectivity and the documentary approach to the inexplicable). Instead, Newland kept busy directing his friend Angie

Dickinson on *Police Woman* (1974–78) and helming episodes of *The Family Holvak* (1975–77).

TV Movies

Thanks to high quality telefilms such as Steven Spielberg's *Duel* (1971) and Dan Curtis' *The Night Stalker* (1971) and *The Night Strangler* (1972), the 1970s saw a boom in Made-for-Television movies of the horror persuasion. Who can forget *Gargoyles* (1972), with Cornel Wilde; *Satan's School for Girls* (1973), with Kate Jackson and Roy Thinnes; or *Trilogy of Terror* (1974), starring Karen Black? Many of these telefilms are representative not only of great '70s kitsch, but (in a few cases) are motion pictures of some value and quality. Not surprisingly, many of these titles have even prospered and ascended to the vaulted position of classic (well, at least near-classic).

Never one to be left on the sidelines, John Newland was also hard at work in telefilms in the 1970s, and he directed a TV picture that many viewers recall as being one of the most frightening television movies of the epoch: *Don't Be Afraid of the Dark* (1973). A Lorimar Production, *Don't Be Afraid of the Dark* aired near Halloween of 1973 (October 10, actually) on ABC television, and its eerie, atmospheric feel cemented Newland's position as a horrormeister of the tube.

With a teleplay by Nigel McKean, and music by Billy Goldenberg (who had also composed the scores for *Duel* and *The Sixth Sense*), *Don't Be Afraid of the Dark* explored the frightening tale of Sally Farnham (Kim Darby), a woman who comes to live in a country house inhabited by shriveled, monstrous gnomes (led by Felix Silla and Patty Mahoney, of *Buck Rogers in the 25th Century* [1979–81]). Sally's doubting husband (where have we seen that character before?!) refuses to believe that his wife is really being tormented by these black-eyed, ghoulish monstrosities. In the terrifying climax, the nasty critters get their little paws on Sally, who has been drugged, and pull her, body and soul, into a dark basement where she is transformed into one of the brood. A skin-crawling horror novella with an ending that gave impressionable young viewers everlasting nightmares, *Don't Be Afraid of the Dark* may not be recalled by its title. However, those who saw it at the time (and who remember those gruesome trolls) will immediately be struck by how its powerful images remain with them.

The seventies also saw John Newland work on a variety of other Made-for-TV movies, though few were as memorable as *Don't Be Afraid of the Dark*. *The Deadly Hunt*, based on a novel by Pat Stadley, was produced and directed by John Newland. It aired on October 10, 1971, and starred Peter Lawford and Tony Franciosa. *Crawlspace*, based on the novel by Herbert Lieberman, aired on February 11, 1972, with John Newland replacing the original director, Buzz Kulik, on the project.

After *Don't Be Afraid of the Dark* Newland worked on projects such as *A Sensitive Passionate Man* (June 6, 1977) and *Overboard* (1978), both of which starred Angie Dickinson. In some sources *Overboard* has been listed as *Overboard: A Further Step Beyond*, but Newland confirmed with this author that the telefilm had no connection to either *One Step Beyond* or its syndicated sequel, *The Next Step Beyond*.

Part IV

The Next Step Beyond

History

One Step Beyond's incredible success in reruns during the early seventies was a testament to the hard work and love its creative team had lavished on the series during its original run on network TV. That a new generation of viewers would come to love and admire the anthology series through the venue of syndication was a development the program's creators had never expected or anticipated, but it was certainly a delightful surprise. Even better, various overseas markets were also registering high ratings by re-running *One Step Beyond*, making the canceled program a hit across the Atlantic as well as in the United States.

Though John Newland had not slowed down one iota since directing and hosting the original *One Step Beyond*, he and his new film partner, Alan Jay Factor, were not entirely satisfied with how things were going in the business. "It was a particularly infertile time in our careers," Newland remembered. "Alan was a like-minded individual and a friend, and one day we decided to form our own company, put together an office, and make a new show." Clearly, this genesis was a promising decision both creatively and financially because *One Step Beyond* had officially reached the status of "beloved" show, right up there with *Star Trek*, *The Twilight Zone*, *The Outer Limits* and the newer syndicated science-fiction fare of the mid–70s, such as *Space: 1999* (1975–77).

In particular, the British-produced *Space: 1999* was a new genre product that had become a ratings dynamo by airing original episodes through the alternate route of syndicated markets across the country (rather than going the traditional path of network sponsorship). This was an idea that was highly appealing to the team behind the sequel to *One Step Beyond*. Though *One Step Beyond* had lasted for 96 episodes and three years on ABC, thanks to the sponsorship of Alcoa, its real success had come in its second life as a syndicated rerun. Worldvision, who owned the syndicated rights to *One Step Beyond*, was receptive to Factor and Newland's idea of a revival, a new half-hour syndicated series to be called *The Next Step Beyond*. Soon Collier Young was back aboard the project as executive producer, and Merwin Gerard, the creator of *One Step Beyond*, even returned as "special story consultant."

Now listed as "Your Host," Newland was back in front of the camera for a series that was billed as "an exciting encore to the network hit." Behind the scenes on *The Next Step Beyond*, Newland would sometimes share his directing duties with producer Factor. Mark Snow, the remarkable music talent who later devised the sounds of *The X-Files* and *Millennium*, stepped into Harry Lubin's shoes to write the creepy new theme music for the sequel series.

From that auspicious creation, however, things did not pan out quite as Newland and Factor had imagined. Because it was to be a syndicated series produced totally independently, *The Next Step Beyond* was allotted only $92,000 per 30-minute episode, a paltry budget considering the inflation of the time. Because there was so little money involved, the *Next Step Beyond* crew was forced to make many difficult decisions that would affect quality. One of the great joys of the original *One Step Beyond* was that it traveled regularly to a variety of time periods in its accounting of paranormal and psychic experiences. "The Death Waltz," "The Day the World Wept: The Lincoln Story" and "The Executioner" occurred at the time of the American Civil War. "Signal Received," "The Dream" and "Brainwave" were set during World War II. The locale of "Ordeal on Locust Street" and "The Lovers" was the 1880s. There were also *One Step Beyond* stories set during the Revolutionary War ("Night of Decision") and even in the Korean War ("The Return"). Effective costuming allowed *One Step Beyond* to visit not only other times, but other regions of the world as well. "House of the Dead" told its story in Hong Kong, and "The Riddle" played out entirely in India.

Because of its low, low budget, there were to be no significant period pieces or foreign adventures on *The Next Step Beyond*, a fact that immediately reduced the storytelling options of the series considerably. Though the story of Barney and Betty Hill (1961), Roswell (1947), or even the Kennedy assassination (1963) would have been great fodder for an update of *One Step Beyond*, those stories—because of production concerns—were out of its purview.

An even more devastating decision concerned the very look of *The Next Step Beyond*. Again citing monetary concerns, the new series would be lensed entirely on videotape, a visual medium not yet perfected by any standard. Though the benefits of tape versus film were many (including no processing fees, fewer lighting difficulties, higher mobility, and a smaller crew than the 70 or so necessary to run a film enterprise), there was also a regrettable downside, as the creators of *The Next Step Beyond* soon realized. "It was *very* inferior quality," Newland remembers. "We thought videotape was the medium of the future, but the results were not what we had in mind. We switched to 16mm halfway through the series to try to improve its look, but by then it was too late." When questioned whether the decision to shoot in color was another possible reason for *The Next Step Beyond*'s lack of atmosphere, Newland dismissed that notion. "It shouldn't have been an issue."

Because *The Next Step Beyond* lived on so limited a budget, it was not able to select the cream of the Hollywood crop in its character castings. Though several prominent performers and familiar faces to the science fiction and horror crowd appeared, they were often supported by less-than-familiar faces from the world of daytime soap operas. Among the most notable guests of *The Next Step Beyond* were Ana Alicia in "Portrait of the Mind," Lana Wood (*Diamonds Are Forever* [1970]) in "Ghost of Cellblock Two," Grace Lee Whitney and Majel Barrett (of *Star Trek*) in "The Confession" and "Drums at Midnight" respectively, and Mark Goddard of *Lost in Space*. Good actors all, no doubt, but it is significant that none of *Next Step Beyond*'s guest stars went on to more prominent fame, as Warren Beatty, William Shatner, Louise Fletcher and Charles Bronson had all done after their TV appearances on *One Step Beyond*.

The Next Step Beyond's premiere episode, called "Tsunami," aired a full ten months or so before the new series began its regular syndicated run on stations across the country. The pilot (a remake of the third season opener of *One Step Beyond*, "Tidal Wave") bowed on Channel 7, WABC TV, in New York City at 7:30 P.M. on January 5, 1978. It was sandwiched between the national news (with Harry Reasoner and Barbara Walters) and an episode of *Welcome Back Kotter* (1975–79). Despite the awkward placement, the premiere of *The Next Step Beyond* was trumpeted in *The New York Times* with a dramatic advertisement stating that it was a "true story of psychic phenomena" and that the events were real "and unexplainable." As with *Alcoa Presents: One Step Beyond*, John Newland's name was front and center in all the publicity.

Dauntingly, the same issue of *The New York Times* spotlighted a scathing, hostile review of *The Next Step Beyond* by TV critic John J. O'Connor. He concluded that "Tsunami" was so bad that it "could leave demanding critics slipping into weepy gratitude for the existence of game shows, the normal fare of the 7:30 P.M. slot."[1]

From that critical blast, matters got only worse. When the series finally began its syndicated run, it soon became obvious to any fans of the original series that *The Next Step Beyond* was not heading into bold new paranormal territory, but offering remakes of some of *One Step Beyond*'s best episodes. "The Return of Mitchell Campion" was reincarnated as "The Return of Cary De Witt." "The Bride Possessed" reappeared as "Possessed," "Dead Man's Tale" returned as "Greed," and so it went, with very little alteration, let alone innovation. Old stories, coupled with a weak visual component (due to video) crippled *The Next Step Beyond* with a cheap and uninventive texture, despite Newland's still-engaging presence as on-screen narrator. Though his hair had gone white and he now sported a thick pair of black glasses, Newland seemed as sincere and interested in the paranormal material as he had been twenty years earlier.

Today John Newland openly acknowledges that a mistake was made with regards to the types of stories dramatized on *The Next Step Beyond*. "The remakes were a bad idea," he admits. "We thought we could fool the public, and we soon learned that we couldn't."

After just two dozen episodes, *The Next Step Beyond* was canceled, a victim, perhaps, of its own low production values and the misguided stories that failed to break new ground. Though the series eventually had a good run for Worldvision, going for four or five rerun cycles in many regions of the United States, it was not the international success that its predecessor had become.

From a historical standpoint, *The Next Step Beyond* has disappeared into obscurity, and few fans are even aware that there was ever a sequel series to *One Step Beyond* at all. It has never been rerun on The Sci Fi Channel nor been released on videotape by Worldvision. Yet, despite all of its problems, *The Next Step Beyond* was well ahead of its time. Just seven years after it disappeared, anthologies were the flavor of the month again on network TV, and *Alfred Hitchcock Presents* and *The Twilight Zone* were also selected for revival — and met with as little success as the best-forgotten sequel to *Alcoa Presents*.

Ever a man of humility and decency, John Newland candidly shoulders the blame for *The Next Step Beyond*'s failure to measure up to the original series. "It was *my* fault," he emphasizes. "None of us were up to our best speed, including me, and I blame myself for whatever failings there were. I think the major mistake was that we all had the wrong focus. We were trying to crank out the shows as fast as possible; we used the wrong actors; we were too concerned about money; and we were too worried about finding locations."

John Newland's final words on *The Next Step Beyond* express his feelings on the sequel. "I knew early on that we were on the wrong track." He also states that if *One Step Beyond* qualified as the most satisfying experience of his career, *The Next Step Beyond* was certainly the most "disappointing" one.

Critical Reception

"*Next Step*" is stupefying in its sincere exploitation of junk. The dumber the content, it seems, the better the sales and ratings.... — John J. O'Connor. *The New York Times*: "TV: Psychics of *Step Beyond*," Thursday, January 5, 1978.

Unlike the original series, which was in black-and-white, the syndicated version was shot in color. This may have actually hurt its chances, because it lacked the moody texture of the original. At any rate it was in production only during 1978 and never attracted much of an audience.— Tim Brooks, Earle Marsh, *The Complete Directory to Prime Time Network TV Shows, 1946–Present*, 1985, pages 25–26.

...largely a failure. Most episodes are quite poor... — Tony Bell, *Epilog Special #5*, December 1992, page 49.

Cast and Credits

CAST: John Newland (Your Host)
CREW: *Executive Producer:* Collier Young. *Producer:* Alan Jay Factor. *Created by:* Merwin Gerard. *Co-Producer:* Mitchell Gamson. *Director of Photography:* Mike Sweeten. *Art Director:* Elayne Barbara Ceder. *Theme:* Mark Snow. *Music:* Mark Snow, Ron Ramin. *Assistant Directors:* Shelley Jensen, Gary M. Lapoten, David Nicksay. *Stage Managers:* Mitchell L. Factor, Gary Gamson. *Casting:* Marvin Paige. *Assistant Casting:* Skitch Hendricks. *Editors:* Bernard Gribble, Phil Tucker. *Post-Production Supervisor:* Phil Tucker. *Mixer:* Bill Edmondson. *Property Masters:* Alan and Cliff Bernay. *Key Grip:* Doug Campbell. *Gaffer:* Ted Holt. *Make-up:* Penelope Staley. *Hairdresser:* Trilby Taylor. *Costumer:* Cheryl Beasley. *Script Supervisor:* Andrea Walzer. *Location Manager:* Ron Windred. *Transportation Captain:* Tom Blomquist. *Assistant to Producer:* Rivian Bell. *Production Auditor:* Norman Marcus. *Production Assistant:* Mimi Rothman. *Production Secretary:* Deborah. *Videotape Facilities Furnished by:* Compact Video Systems, Inc. *Animation Title by:* Image West Ltd. The Factor-Newland Production Corporation. Distributed by Worldvision Enterprises Inc.

Opening Narration

The dramatization you are about to see is based on an actual investigated and documented case history of psychic phenomenon — it is the Next Step Beyond.[2]— John Newland's weekly introduction to the sequel to *One Step Beyond*.

NOTE: Because *The Next Step Beyond* episodes aired on different days in different markets around the United States, no airdate is included in the episode guide below. Unlike *One Step Beyond* episodes, the actual titles of

The Next Step Beyond episodes appear on-screen during the opening moments of each show.

The Episodes (1978–1979)

1. "Tsunami"
(Written by Merwin Gerard; Directed by John Newland)

SYNOPSIS: In Crescent City in northern California, a wheelchair-bound woman named Mrs. Terence is unaware that an earthquake in Alaska has caused a massive tidal wave, or tsunami, to head in the direction of her home. Her husband is out for the day, and Mrs. Terence is effectively trapped in her beach house ... until a little autistic boy receives a powerful message that she is in danger. But can he get the police to listen to his story in time?

GUEST CAST: Laraine Stephens (Cathy Terence), Craig Littler (Mr. Terence); Angus Duncan, Bryan Scott, Dee Carroll, Martin Rudy, William Wintersole.

COMMENTARY: *The Next Step Beyond* crashes to the shores of syndication with "Tsunami," a dramatic washout that echoes "Tidal Wave," the third season premiere of *One Step Beyond* from the autumn of 1960, in spirit and intent. In fairness, "Tsunami" does alter most of the critical details: the disaster now occurs in California instead of Hawaii; The disaster is called a "tsunami" instead of a "tidal wave"; Mrs. Terence is wheelchair-bound only temporarily instead of a polio victim; and the deaf military man who hears the pleas for help has been supplanted by a little boy who is autistic.

Despite the surface changes, the outline of "Tsunami" is identical to that of "Tidal Wave": A disaster looms, a woman is not evacuated from her home, and an unlikely savior is alerted to her plight through psychic channels. Unfortunately, the alteration of critical plot points in "Tsunami" only serves to forge a disturbing realization: The story is no longer accurate to the facts of the case history.

"Tidal Wave" bolstered some real dramatic resonance on the earlier series because it was based on *real* events that occurred in May of 1960, and it even had the audacity to bring the two people involved in the case on the air for verification of the details. Now that all the details have been changed on "Tsunami," the story is no longer an accurate representation of what actually occurred in 1960. And, since no major tsunamis occurred in California in the seventies, what is one to make of the claim that this is an "authentic" dramatization? Had "Tsunami" been a 1960 period piece, a straight remake of "Tidal Wave," it might actually have been better than "Tsunami," because then at least it would have been accurate. Alternately, "Tsunami" might have concerned the tsunami in the Philippines that struck on August 17, 1976, and killed approximately 8,000 people, instead of this wholly fabricated story.

Alas, the wholesale plundering of *One Step Beyond* stories would become a permanent fixture of *The Next Step Beyond*, and future stories would revamp "The Bride Possessed," "Who Are You?" "The Return of Mitchell Campion," "Echo," "Father Image" and "I Saw You Tomorrow." Now told in color and on videotape, every one of these remakes came off as inferior to the original segments.

Fans of seventies television may recognize guest star Craig Littler in "Tsunami." In the late seventies he had the title role of *Jason of Star Command* (1978–81), a popular Saturday morning space adventure. He is also familiar from a series of commercials in the early 1980s that asked the famous question: "Pardon me, do you have any Grey Poupon?"

2. "The Return of Cary De Witt"
(Written by Merwin Gerard; Directed by John Newland)

SYNOPSIS: During routine surgery Cary De Witt flatlines for a moment and then slips into a coma for ten days. When he awakens, Cary vacations in Tahiti to recuperate, but everybody there, from taxi drivers and bartenders to the hotel clerk, recognizes him from a previous visit he has no knowledge of. DeWitt insists he has never been to Tahiti, but the hotel register and the local police prove him wrong. Worse, Cary is not welcome in Tahiti because of a scandalous affair with a Tahitian girl that ended in tragedy … an affair that occurred simultaneously with his coma in Milwaukee!

GUEST CAST: Lewis Van Bergen (Cary De Witt), Alan Frost (Sergeant Renaud), Wendy Cutler (Hotel Clerk), Anakorita (Madame Auber), Micheal Rougas (George Mason), Lainie Miller (The Nurse), Milton Perlow (The Anesthesiologist), Paul Hampton (The Surgeon).

COMMENTARY: Peering into the operating theater where Cary De Witt lays quiescent in a coma, *The Next Step Beyond* host John Newland faces the camera and declares deadpan that the "real surprises are ahead," an observation that simply does not jibe with the fact that this episode is a flat-out remake of the *One Step Beyond* story "The Return of Mitchell Campion."

In fact, all the revelations in "Cary De Witt" follow the outline of the earlier *One Step Beyond* story in lock-step fashion: a hospital stay; a vacation to recuperate; a case of believed mistaken identity as hotel clerks and natives claim to recognize the protagonist; the intimation of a dangerous romance; and finally the revelation that the protagonist was really in two places at the same time through psychic auspices.

Unfortunately, the elements that worked so well in "Mitchell Campion" fail to work the same magic a second time in "Cary De Witt." The remake is inferior in terms of acting, music, sound quality and even visual appearance. Though *The Next Step Beyond* film crew flew to Tahiti to shoot segments of the story, a fact corroborated by the credits (which thank UTA French Airlines for their cooperation in the "portions" filmed on location in Tahiti), the truth remains that on primitive, grainy video, even beautifully composed shots of the shoreline and roaring ocean appear cheap and grainy, like someone's home movie of a beach vacation. Worse, the sound quality is inferior to that on *One Step Beyond*, with a recurrent rasp infiltrating the background of many shots.

Some minor differences do surface between "Mitchell Campion" and "Cary De Witt." Lewis Van Bergen (De Witt) makes for a more mellow protagonist than the always-on-the-verge-of-exploding O'Neal, and the later variation spends an excessive amount of time lingering on the romance between Cary and Tiera. There is an interlude in which Cary and Tiera make love on the beach to the strains of romantic synthesizer music. The heightened romance angle also makes some of this episode play like "Delia," that *One Step Beyond* story of tragic love.

Otherwise, this remake raises a serious question. Why remake a successful production with inferior actors, inferior sound, inferior picture, and overall inferior production values? At least if *The Next Step Beyond* had consistently dramatized original stories, it would not have faced these invidious comparisons to its worthy predecessor.

"The Return of Cary De Witt" also makes a very minor mistake in terminology. After it is stated (rather vaguely) that the story appeared in "major newspapers around the world," the episode concludes that Cary De Witt was in two places via *teleportation*. Yet teleportation involves the movement of a person from one location to another, not the simultaneous appearance of a person at two locales. Bilocation, astral projection or the "out-of-body experience" would have been more accurate terms to apply to Cary De Witt's ordeal.

3. "Possessed"

(Written by Merwin Gerard; Directed by John Newland)

SYNOPSIS: During a vacation intended to save their failing marriage, Paul and Carolyn Adams face a disturbing "psychic detour" when Carolyn experiences strange feelings of *déjà vu* about a region of the country she has never visited before. Carolyn starts to exhibit even more bizarre behavior, suddenly speaking Spanish and acquiring the knowledge of how to drive, and soon Mr. Adams seeks help from the local police. Now Carolyn claims to be Maria Robles, an Hispanic woman who died three months ago and is believed to have been murdered by her husband, Homero. Has Carolyn been possessed by the spirit of a dead woman, and if so, what is the secret that her spirit so desperately desires to share?

GUEST CAST: Toni Bull Bua (Caroline Adams), Gene Bua (Paul Adams), Sam Chew (Dr. Green), Biff Elliot (The Sergeant), Bobb Hopkins (Officer Gates), Warren W. Smith (The Guard), Marco Lopez (Homero Robles).

COMMENTARY: "Possessed" is a thinly-veiled remake of "The Bride Possessed," the *One Step Beyond* pilot that sold the series to television back in 1959. Unlike "The Return of Cary De Witt," "Possessed" manages to inject a few twists and turns into a familiar premise.

For instance, "The Bride Possessed" concerned a newlywed married couple (the Conroys), while "Possessed" featured a couple on the verge of divorce (the Adams), a sign perhaps of the more "hip" and socially conscious seventies. Likewise, a switcheroo has been pulled regarding the showcased psychic turbulence. The possession in "The Bride Possessed" happened so that a dead woman could establish that she was murdered by her husband. "Possessed" reverses that premise when a dead woman returns from the grave to prove that her death was an accident and that her husband, locked away in jail, is an innocent man. Finally, a Southern belle lost her southern drawl when possessed in "The Bride Possessed," but in *The Next Step Beyond* remake the same character adopts an Hispanic accent upon her possession. These trappings allow "Possessed" to stand on its own better than "The Return of Cary De Witt" did, but its derivative nature nonetheless remains obvious.

As with the earlier shows, "Possessed" suffers from weak technical credits. There is good location shooting at a dam, but again, even that impressive sight looks rotten in the pixelized, grainy video on which the episode was shot. On a similar topic, all of Toni Bull Bua's lines as Maria Robles (with the Hispanic accent) are dubbed by a different actress, and Bull Bua's lips are not well-synchronized to the words racing from her mouth.

Despite the flaws, it is to "Possessed's" credit that it attempts to dramatize the struggle of a very individual couple. Cary De Witt was Mitchell Campion all over again, but the Adams family as seen in "Possessed" are facing a different set of struggles than the newlyweds in "The Bride Possessed." Specifically, Paul is a workaholic who seeks balance in his life. "I only appreciate something when I'm about to lose it," Paul states at one point. The episode promptly puts him in the situation of contemplating life without Caroline, his wife, so he can see just how valuable the marital relationship is. It is still a far cry from *One Step Beyond* in the level of writing quality and acting, but there is evidence in these characters that the creators were not merely picking the bones of a TV classic.

For those who are interested in other antecedents, "Possessed" does echo a facet of the 1972 film *The Possession of Joel Delaney*, starring Shirley MacLaine. In that film (directed by Waris Hussein) a young man also becomes possessed by the spirit of a dead Hispanic. In that case, however, the "possessor" was a crazed serial killer, not an innocent attempting to clear someone of murder.

4. "The Love Connection"
(Written by Christopher Lofton; Story by Merwin Gerard;
Directed by John Newland)

SYNOPSIS: An athletic little girl named Jill faints while at gymnastics practice. When she awakens, Jill is a very different child who does not recognize her own parents. Instead, she insists she is Karen, the daughter of Harriet and Frank Jessup, a couple living across town and in mourning over the death of their daughter, Karen. Jill understands all the details of Karen's life and helps Harriet overcome the grief of her daughter's demise by conveying the message that death ends nothing, least of all love.

GUEST CAST: Luana Anders (Harriet Jesup [sic]), Jean Gillespie (Aunt Alice), Michael Bell (Jeff August), Miles Shearer (Frank Jessup), Lola Fisher (Helen August), Paul Kent (Dr. Morgan), Kelly Gallagher (Jill August), Ray Duke (John Berson), Shawn Michaels (Officer Davis); Lisa Moore (The Nurse), Diane Butler (Sandra).

COMMENTARY: The *One Step Beyond* second season episode "Who Are You?" is dusted off and revamped for *The Next Step Beyond* segment called "The Love Connection" (no relation to the famous "dating game"–style series hosted by Chuck Woolery).

The familiar tale of a woman devastated by the loss of a child but then miraculously buoyed by hope when another girl briefly assumes the characteristics and personality of her dead child, "Love Connection" alters little from the outline of "Who Are You?" The sick girl who becomes the vessel for the dead child suffers not from scarlet fever this time around but from a gymnastics accident at school. The message from the dead child is more explicit this time, however. Little Karen (in Jill's body) may have drowned but she still exists ... somewhere, the episode concludes. And she tells her mother that death ends nothing, least of all love. This is a comforting message to Harriet Jessup (Luana Anders, all grown up in the 20 years since her performance in "The Burning Girl"!), and one that allows her to heal.

As in "Who Are You?" "The Love Connection" concludes with the once-despondent mother learning that she is pregnant, and the consequent continuation of the human life cycle. In contrast to "Who Are You?" "The Love Connection" punctuates its climax with a more explicitly psychic note than its predecessor. Newland establishes that Harriet Jessup's new baby just may be the reincarnation of Karen, suggesting a family reunited at last.

"The Love Connection" is an emotional story, a tearjerker. It is effective in a schmaltzy kind of way, yet is so sincere and heartfelt. Perhaps sincerity should not be mocked in an age of cynical entertainments; and like many episodes of *One Step Beyond*, this episode of *The Next Step Beyond* clearly points the way towards "wholesome" and inspirational drama such as *Touched by an Angel*. Though the dialogue deliveries of young Kelly Gallagher feel pretty stilted at times (her voice modulates mostly by volume rather than tone), her very energy and sincerity in the role of Jill make her an effective and unusual messenger from "the other side."

On the accuracy front, *The Next Step Beyond* makes a basic mistake in nomenclature. At the end of the episode, Newland's narration establishes that Karen's soul was reincarnated briefly in Karen. That is wrong. Reincarnation is believed to occur only when a body dies and the old spirit moves into a new, fresh life — starting over as a baby, as it were.

The events of "The Love Connection" represent a textbook case of possession. The spirit of Karen assumes control of Jill's body (much as Maria Robles assumed control of Caroline Adams' body in the previous "Possession"). Fitting in with possession "lore," Karen returns for a specific purpose (to heal her mother's trauma and allow her to move on) and then vacates the possessed body when the mission is accomplished. It may be that *The Next Step Beyond* writers did not care to name "possession" as the phenomenon of "The Love Connection" because it has a negative, fearsome connotation (thanks to *The Exorcist* [1973], and because the previous episode ("Possession") had dealt explicitly with the topic.

Interestingly, "The Love Connection" fosters the same psychological fallacy that was inherent in its source material, "Who Are You?" In both cases, the arrival of a new baby ends a period of mourning, as if a dead child can ever be replaced by another pregnancy.

5. "Ondine's Curse"
(Written by Merwin Gerard; Directed by John Newland)

SYNOPSIS: Poor Tom Westerly is afflicted with Ondine's Curse, a disease that mimics exactly the appearance of death. Tom wishes he had not hidden this fact from his worried wife when, one night while out driving, he is attacked by a psychotic hitchhiker and left for dead on the side of the road. The authorities assume Tom is dead (though he is not) and set about embalming procedures ... but Tom's wife Sara is driven to search for him by telepathic impressions that he is in danger.

GUEST CAST: Meredith MacRae (Sara Westerly); Nick Holt (Tom Westerly); Robert Cleaves (Anderson); Chrisopher Ellis (The Hitchhiker); Joe Medalis, Steve Mitchell, Sandy Champion, Ed Ness, Don Monte, Tamar Cooper.

COMMENTARY: The fear of being buried alive is one of those so-called "mortal dreads" that fills all human beings with a sense of swelling, escalating fear. The thought of being interred alive is actually an illogical one in this day and age, since "dead" bodies are embalmed before burial, and medical science has a better understanding of the barrier between life and death than ever before. Despite these facts, there is still something discomforting about the notion of such a grim fate. To awaken and find oneself in a box, unable to move or see, with walls all around and six feet of dirt over your head, is perhaps the ultimate nightmare of helplessness. You can scream for help, but soon the air will run out in your little pocket of space, and besides, there is nobody around to hear you....

Accordingly, film and television have often taken advantage of this seemingly universal human fear. *The Premature Burial* (1962), directed by Roger Corman and starring Ray Milland, is one such movie. Another is *The Vanishing* (1993). In 1987 horrormeister Wes Craven employed what *Cinefantastique* referred to as "directorial sadism" to show the audience the exact, harrowing experience of being buried alive in the voodoo-horror picture *The Serpent and the Rainbow*. Significantly, that movie's advertising line was "Don't Bury Me! I'm Not Dead!"

On television, one of the most memorable episodes of *Alfred Hitchcock Presents* was "Breakdown," an installment written by Francis Cockrell and Louis Pollack and directed by Hitchcock himself. In this episode Joseph Cotten (*The Abominable Dr. Phibes* [1972]) played a not-so-nice businessman who was paralyzed after a car accident and thus unable to inform the authorities that he was still alive. His paralysis mimicked death perfectly. Thinking the man had expired, medical and legal authorities prepared the body for funerary rights. The suspenseful climax saw Cotten survive only because one tear drop was seen rolling down his cheek! "Breakdown" was remade in the colorized NBC version of *Alfred Hitchcock Presents* (1985), this time with Andy Garcia and John Heard starring.

On *The Next Step Beyond*, "Ondine's Curse" is a reiteration of the "Breakdown" ethos, with a "road" scenario leading to a crisis in which a man is presumed dead, though he is still alive. In a way, "Ondine's Curse" also reflects the structure of the early *One Step Beyond* episode "Twelve Hours to Live" in that it forges a telepathic link between a worried wife and the husband who is in terrible danger. Though "Ondine's Curse" is not strictly a remake (as are "Tsunami," "The Return of Cary De Witt," "Possessed," and "The Love Connection"), its film and television antecedents are numerous.

Stalwart *Battlestar Galactica* fans may recognize Nick Holt, Tom Westerly of "Ondine's Curse," as the villainous Charka from the sixteenth episode of that series, "Take the Celestra."

6. "Dream of Disaster"
(Written by Merwin Gerard; Directed by John Newland)

SYNOPSIS: Expectant wife Helen Chambers has a recurring nightmare in which a Cessna 172 plummets out of control and crashes, precipitating a disaster. When her doctor witnesses the violent nature of her night terrors, he moves Helen to a motel much closer to her husband's job at the flight tower of a nearby airport. When the "phantom" plane is detected for real in the region, just as Helen predicted it would be, Harry Chambers races to the motel to save his wife and unborn child from a fiery death.

GUEST CAST: Meredith Baer (Helen Chambers), Peter Skinner (Harry Chambers), Leonard Stone (Dr. Whitewood), Eric Howell (Steve Colton).

COMMENTARY: "Tonight at 12:17," a popular and effective premonition story from *One Step Beyond*, gets the remake treatment in "Dream of Disaster." Unfortunately, like many *Next Step Beyond* episodes, "Dream of Disaster" does not improve on its source material and, because of budgetary limitations, actually emerges as a far inferior product. In fact, one shot alone indicates the breadth of *Next Step Beyond*'s problems. In "Dream of Disaster," the camera pans from a shot of the airport landing strip (seen through a window) into the control tower. The lighting is natural (a supposed "benefit" of video) but the interior aspect of the shot is too dark compared with the exterior, and one extra sitting on a stool actually swivels with the camera, looking directly at the lens as it moves in his direction. The shot cuts away to something else just as the extra's non-professionalism becomes plain, but by then it is too late. In this brief moment of screen time, one can detect the rush to get the episode made, the acceptance of inferior lighting, and the casting of locals who do not understand how to behave before the camera. Though low-budget filmmaking is frequently more challenging and powerful than the typical Hollywood product, *The Next Step Beyond* does not use the low budget, "home-made" look to its advantage (as *The Blair Witch Project* does with such finesse). Instead, it relies on old stories, existing locales, and overused 1970s techniques such as zooms. This is a terrible shame because Newland is a talented director when given the time and resources to be creative.

Even in "Dream of Disaster" there are flashes of the old brilliance. There is some solid footage of a plane out of control. Filmed from the cockpit interior, the camera registers the landscape rushing by in a dizzying whirl just outside the plane's front window. And the guest actors employed here do effectively capture the hysteria of the situation. Despite weakness in production values, "Dream of Disaster" produces that all-important surge of adrenaline as Mr. Chambers experiences his moment of realization and races to the motel to save his wife.

The purse strings also show in "Dream of Disaster" during the denouement. The explosion of the motel is actually stock footage from some filmed production, not material original to *The Next Step Beyond*. Though stock footage was often used on *One Step Beyond* (particularly in episodes involving World War II and combat, such as "Brainwave" or "Signal Received"), its use in those instances did not feel inappropriate, and the black-and-white photography hid the jarring transitions. In color, "Dream of Disaster's" shift from video storytelling to filmed stock footage is obvious.

The problems of "Dream of Disaster" are the same as those of virtually every "remake" episode of *The Next Step Beyond*. Since the audience knows the punchline, and since the execution is hampered so much by the low budget, there is little left to really enjoy or appreciate.

7. "Ghost Town"

(Written by Arthur C. Pierce; Directed by John Newland)

SYNOPSIS: A crime of passion from the past resurfaces in the present when a beautiful model goes on a fashion shoot in a strange old ghost town. There Leslie witnesses events of 25 years past: an illicit love triangle and a murder. Leslie is even more disturbed when the murderer, still alive, shows up in the present.

GUEST CAST: Kathleen King (Leslie), Paul Peterson (Mitch), Michael Stroka (Donk/Logan), Barbara George, Michael Potter, Dee Cooper.

COMMENTARY: A murder from the past and a psychic discovery of the crime inform "Ghost Town," a *Next Step Beyond* story that recalls a *One Step Beyond* convention: the echo of a crime committed in the past. In particular, this scenario is reminiscent of "Echo" and "Father Image" (two stories that would be remade as *Next Step Beyond* episodes). Interestingly, "Ghost Town" also occurs in the world of fashion photography, an arena visited by such films as *The Sentinel* (1977), with Cristina Raines, and *The Eyes of Laura Mars* (1978), with Faye Dunaway. That the story of ghosts from the past should occur in a "ghost" town is a funny visual joke, and also in keeping with a long line of "horrors," including *The Devil's Rain* (1975) and even an episode of the *Brady Bunch* (1969–74).

8. "Drums at Midnight"

(Written by Harry Spalding; Directed by John Newland)

SYNOPSIS: An angry woman, Neva, resorts to witchcraft and voodoo when she learns that her dead father has betrayed her. Since he left all of his estate and wealth to his new wife, Neva feels justified in her attempts to destroy her new stepmother. The witchcraft backfires on the perpetrator, however, thanks to a surprise betrayal.

GUEST CAST: Majel Barrett (Neva), Yvonne Regaldo (Montine Gillespie), Crane Jackson (The Doctor), Seheldon Allman (John), Josephine Premice (Mambo).

COMMENTARY: One of the many interesting facets that distinguishes *The Next Step Beyond* from its predecessor is its viewpoint on horror. When the sequel series chose to dramatize new adventures rather than remakes, it often did so well outside of the realm of so-called believable (or provable) paranormal stock. Instead, it dwelt directly in the realm of traditional horror, much like *Rod Serling's Night Gallery* or *Tales from the Crypt* might. Both "The Haunted Inn" and "Drums at Midnight" are indicative of a different approach than that assumed by the restrained *One Step Beyond*. These episodes deal with the horrific aspects of long-cherished genre subject matter, such as ghosts or voodoo curses. These episodes are clearly not dramatized accounts of "personal records" (though on-screen narrations attempt to connect them to such), but rather phantasmagoric stories designed to scare, with only a passing nod toward the literature and study of parapsychology.

When *One Step Beyond* was horrific, it was through paranormal auspices. "The Haunted U-Boat" was a terrifying episode, but it accurately depicted a phenomenon known as "rapping." Likewise with "The Villa," which understood how a premonition could prove scary.

"Drums at Midnight" trades on voodoo (or voudon, as it is called in Haiti), the religion of choice for Hollywood filmmakers who want to establish a supernatural menace with a minimum of fuss. *White Zombie* (1932), *Scream Blacula Scream* (1973) and *The Believers* (1987) are just a few of the many motion pictures that have utilized Western society's misunderstanding of voodoo tenets to evoke an instant sense of menace. On TV, *Tales from the Crypt* used the same material in "Til Death," but the object of voodoo power in that episode was to create love in someone not inclined to experience that emotion. In "Drums of Midnight" voodoo is the tool of a standard "comeuppance" plot in which the perpetrator of a crime actually becomes the victim.

Actress Majel Barrett is beautifully suited to her role in this segment because she had recently portrayed a witch in *Spectre* (1977), a great Gene Roddenberry pilot that should have gone to series but did not. It is nice to see Barrett get an opportunity to really act in "Drums at Midnight," as one feels she often got a bum deal from Paramount (being all but locked out of the *Star Trek* feature films) because she was the boss' wife. Perhaps living well is the best revenge, and Paramount's own "comeuppance" can be seen in Barrett's ascension to role of creator and producer on such series as *Earth: Final Conflict* and *Gene Roddenberry's Andromeda*.

9. "Portrait of the Mind"
(Written by Jerry Sohl; Directed by Alan Jay Factor)

SYNOPSIS: A police sketch artist has the unusual ability to see into the minds of others and then draw what they are thinking. This is a talent that proves useful when a liquor store is robbed and the wrong man is arrested. Can the real criminal be ferreted out through psychic means before an innocent man is convicted?

GUEST CAST: William Campbell (Chad), Eloy Casados (Mendoza), Ana Alicia (Angela Mendoza), Edmund Stoiber (Sam), Tony Canne.

COMMENTARY: On *One Step Beyond* the audience saw *automatic writing* in "Message from Clara" and, bizarrely, automatic typing in "Dead Man's Tale." In *The Next Step Beyond* episode "Portrait of the Mind," a similar concept is used to drive the drama: *automatic art*. In this situation physical action (such as drawing or painting) is driven by a psychic knowledge usually beyond the automatist's control or understanding. Known sometimes as *motor automatism*, this term could also be applied accurately to the *One Step Beyond* third-season episode "Nightmare," in which a painter "unconsciously" drew memories from a previous life. "The Storm" was also a variation on this topic.

As in many episodes of *One Step Beyond*, "Portrait of the Mind" demonstrates how a psychic insight or "power" can be used in a purely practical, legal sense. Here the sketch of the real criminal frees a man from the possibility of imprisonment in jail. Without paranormal assistance, justice would never be done!

"Portrait of the Mind" features two notable and recognizable guest stars, an anomaly for the low-budget *Next Step Beyond*: William Campbell, of *Star Trek* ("The Squire of Gothos," "The Trouble with Tribbles"), and Ana Alicia (*Battlestar Galactica*: "Take the Celestra," *Buck Rogers in the 25th Century*: "Vegas in Space," and *Galactica 1980*: "The Space Croppers").

10. "Other Voices"
(Written by Arthur C. Pierce; Story by Merwin Gerard;
Directed by Alan Jay Factor)

SYNOPSIS: A man returns home to the palatial estate in which he grew up and unexpectedly watches as a drunken man strangles his wife. Though Walter does not realize it, this peek at a violent encounter is one that will soon be repeated in the flesh by his fellow guests at the mansion.

GUEST CAST: Robert Walker (Walter Hastings), Susan Keller (Carrie Jarris), H.M. Wynant (Frank Jarris), Audrey Christie (Elsie), Peter Forster (Jason).

COMMENTARY: In "I Saw You Tomorrow," the fiftieth episode of *One Step Beyond*, an American equipped with an unusual "mental radio" picked up a signal from the future: a vision of murder. That theme is recycled in "Other Voices," *Next Step Beyond*'s remake of the original. The character names are different and the setting is slightly altered, but the rhythm of the 18-year-old Merwin Gerard story is quite the same.

The Cassandra Complex (a seer knows something important via psychic seeing and is disbelieved and ignored) and the time-hiccup (an element seen in "The Visitor," "The Open Window" and "I Saw You Tomorrow") are still in evidence in "Other Voices," but thematically this episode offers nothing new or exciting.

11. "A Matter of Pride"
(Written by Peter Germano; Directed by John Newland)

SYNOPSIS: A worried boxer seeks the help of a hypnotist to make him a force to be reckoned with in the ring again. Unfortunately, the hypnotist passes away after giving the boxer a post-hypnotic suggestion. This suggestion, a personal one involving a diabetic child, becomes the boxer's psychic obsession.

GUEST CAST: Enrique Novi (Manny Guzman), Eileen Dietz (Melissa Guzman), Robert Contreras (Carlos), Martin Rudy (Dr. Hartfield).

COMMENTARY: Hypnotism is always a fun subject to contemplate in genre TV series. That a person could be hypnotized to commit murder (*The Manchurian Candidate* [1962]), act like a chicken, relive a past life (*The X-Files:* "The Field Where I Died") or even (inaccurately) act totally against his or her nature has proven to be a beloved trope of horror. A man was hypnotized into his own death in the early *Night Gallery* episode "The Dead Man," starring Jeff Corey, and a Nazi sympathizer discovered the true nature of evil during past-life hypnosis in the *Beyond Reality* segment "Echoes of Evil."

On *One Step Beyond*, hypnosis was a tool in episodes such as "Emergency Only," "Ordeal on Locust Street," "Moment of Hate" and "The Room Upstairs," to name just a few. On *The Next Step Beyond*, "A Matter of Pride" involves a post-hypnotic suggestion that cannot be ignored if an innocent life is to be saved. Written by Peter Germano, this is an original story, not a remake, even though it momentarily returns to the boxing world dramatized for different purposes in "The Last Round." The crux of the issue here is the boxer's confidence: He seeks outward help for it (hypnosis) and ends up in a web of confusion he has little control over. In the end, however, the boxer is buttressed by his experience, evidence of *The Next Step Beyond*'s belief that psychic experiences, if understood, can also be therapeutic.

12. "Ghost of Cellblock Two"
(Written by Shelly Hartman and Clifford Campion; Directed by John Newland)

SYNOPSIS: A woman wrongly accused of a crime is sent to jail, where she promptly attempts suicide. A friendly sergeant is surprised by the act and learns that half-a-dozen other inmates have all committed suicide in the same cell as well. The curious police officer decides to stay in the cell, and finds herself face to face with a murderous ghost still reliving a crime — and a death — some half-a-century old.

GUEST CAST: Lana Wood (Sgt. Enright), Kathleen Brown (Mary), Lee Warrick (Mrs. Jordan), Pat Renalla (Officer Doug Taylor).

COMMENTARY: Shelly Hartman and Clifford Campion contribute a new story to *The Next Step Beyond*, one that is well in keeping with the history and tenets of *One Step Beyond*. In episodes such as "The Dead Part of the House" and "The Room Upstairs" it was established that a particularly traumatic human event (death, usually) could leave behind a psychic residue or image in a house. "Ghost of Cellblock Two" conforms to that belief, but sets the events of its story in a prison instead of a residence. As inmates are lead to kill themselves, this story also resembles "The Captain's Guests," a *One Step Beyond* episode in which a man was forced by an angry spirit to relive the unhappy events of another life.

Part possession and part ghost story, " Ghost of Cellblock Two" certainly pointed to a setting the world of horror would later exploit. *Prison* (1987), directed by Renny Harlin (*A Nightmare on Elm Street IV: Dream Warriors* [1988], *Die Hard 2: Die Harder* [1990], *Deep Blue Sea* [1999]), saw a dead inmate, formerly imprisoned within the Wyoming State Penitentiary, return to life of a sort as a vicious life-force. On television, the prison has been a setting for psychic phenomena in *The X-Files* ("The List") and *Beyond Reality* ("Justice") as well.

13. "The Legacy"

(Credits unconfirmed)

SYNOPSIS: A young boy's model train set and diorama becomes the central piece in a bizarre psychic puzzle. The spirit of the child's dead grandfather, a former railway worker, manipulates the model to warn authorities about the locations of a series of apparent "accidents" which are, in truth, caused by an extortionist.

GUEST CAST: Stephen A. Clarke (Alan), Delos V. Smith, Jr. (Gus), Tasha Lee Zemrus (Patty), Doug Druse (Lt. Jeff Burns), Whitney Rydbeck (Officer Woodward).

COMMENTARY: Though "The Legacy" was unavailable for review at the time this book was written, it appears to concern physical objects appearing and moving in manners that cannot be explained empirically.

Such objects are referred to as *apports*. In this story, a man's will to see a terrible wrong undone is so strong that he returns from the spirit world to send messages to the living. As in the *One Step Beyond* episode "Goodbye Grandpa," this appears to be a tale that features a grandpa-grandson dynamic.

14. "Cry Baby"
(Written by Ed Burnham; Directed by John Newland)

SYNOPSIS: Larry Elston goes away on a soothing nature retreat for the weekend, leaving his beautiful wife, Susan, at home in their isolated mountain house. A crazed intruder with a knife breaks into the Elston home and threatens to rape Susan while, miles away, Larry inexplicably hears the repetitive cries of an infant. Susan breaks free of her captor and flees the house, but she and the attacker end up plunging down a hill together. Driven to desperation by the cries of a baby, actually the unborn child in Susan's womb, Larry returns home to save his wife.

GUEST CAST: Simone Griffeth (Susan Elston), Joe Bratcher (Larry Elston), Michael Heit (The Man), Julie Parrish (Dr. Elizabeth Turner), George Skaff (The Doctor), Marcia Mohr (The Woman Patient).

COMMENTARY: A tense and frightening setup grants "Cry Baby" a sense of breakneck urgency. In this original story, Susan Elston is left alone for the weekend at her isolated mountain house while her husband attends a seminar about getting "back in touch with nature." On her own, Susan is threatened when an intruder breaks into her house silently, brandishing a knife. From there the chase is on, as the episode becomes a suspenseful game of cat-and-mouse between victim and attacker. Periodically, the episode crosscuts to Mr. Elston as he hears the inexplicable cries of a baby, but the real thrust of the episode is the chase. And what a chase it is! Poor Mrs. Elston (the beautiful Simone Griffeth) faces just about every type of distress imaginable. She is nearly raped. She then falls down the side of a cliff, breaks her ankle, faces a group of rampaging rats, encounters a snake, and is finally pelted by a ferocious rain storm. Talk about your bad day! And, all through all this distress, Mrs. Elston is unknowingly carrying a child in her womb!

While his wife endures every physical trial imaginable, Mr. Elston listens to "the music of planet Earth" but hears a strange tune he did not expect. Somehow he makes contact with the inner voice of his unborn child and, through *clairaudio*, hears the baby's cries for help. Though clairaudio was a concept explored by *One Step Beyond* in "Call from

Tomorrow," and pregnant women had psychic experiences in episodes such as "The Storm," "The Room Upstairs," "Tonight at 12:17" and its *Next Step Beyond* remake "Dream of Disaster," "Cry Baby" still emerges as an original-seeming adventure because this is the first time the twin *Beyonds* have explored the psychic link between fetus and parent.

Delightfully, "Cry Baby" also reverses the trend of stories such as "Twelve Hours to Live," "Dream of Disaster," "Possessed" and "Ondine's Curse" by permitting a man rather than a woman to be an unheeded psychic. Despite being an equal opportunity story, "Cry Baby" complies with *One Step Beyond* tradition by highlighting a spousal relationship threatened and eventually strengthened by a traumatic, psychic experience. All in all, "Cry Baby" is a show that could have appeared on *One Step Beyond*. It fits with accepted psychic research, it is not a remake, and it is shot with an eye towards suspense and pace. Poor Mrs. Elston's traumas may be laid on a bit thick, and one may shake one's head with amazement that she did not miscarry during a series of physical trials that would have made Hercules shudder, but overall this story by Ed Burnham is one of the better episodes of the sequel series.

15. "Greed"
(Written by Merwin Gerard; Directed by John Newland)

SYNOPSIS: Jan and Phil Barlow have lost their farm, are essentially bankrupt, and find themselves living in a hotel room. Phil contemplates returning to his previous career as a newspaper reporter; and later, in the hotel, the couple finds a goldminer's handbook belonging to one Mr. Whitaker. After reading the book, Phil is possessed to type out a strange tale of two brothers obsessed with gold and twisted by greed. When the story is printed, the Barlows find the weird story is true and that the last chapter has not yet been written.

GUEST CAST: Ben Andrews (Philip Barlow), Elaine Princi (Jan Barlow), Virginia Leith (Mrs. Whitaker), Larry Watson (Robert Whitaker), Gil Lamb (Store Proprietor), Larry Barton (Hotel Manager), Max West (Lawrence Whitaker);

COMMENTARY: Though "Greed" is shot on 16mm rather than videotape, this episode of *Next Step Beyond* still appears cheap — not much better than a B-movie of the period. And, continuing a disturbing trend, the Merwin Gerard story slavishly re-uses the teleplay of a *One Step Beyond* episode, this time the third season entry "Dead Man's Tale."

As in the original, the story concerns a couple who have become bankrupt. Like its predecessor, a moral issue is raised (should a story be sold to a newspaper even though it has no corroboration?) and then answered — ultimately by desperation. There is the same sequence of automatic typing, the same discussion of greed destroying a family (two brothers), and the same revelation at the ending. The only real difference comes in the realm of technique. Mired in '70s filmmaking, "Greed" is dependent on the excessive use of the zoom, a technique which distorts the picture and composition of the frame.

One fresh contextual note comes at the end of "Greed." The poison of greed is noted to have blossomed over false riches. The Whitaker gold is nothing but iron pyrite ... fool's gold. In this case, the content alteration is too little too late.

Perhaps the greatest pleasure of "Greed" is the opportunity to see the lovely Virginia Leith in action again. Though it had been some 19 years since "The Bride Possessed" and her wonderful performance as Sally Conroy, Leith is still beautiful in "Greed" and still capable of giving a touching performance. Here she plays Mrs. Whitaker, the wife who lost a husband and brother-in-law to avarice.

16. "Out of Body"

(Written by Bernard Gerard; Directed by John Newland)

SYNOPSIS: Randall Prieste is charged with the murder of Susan Lambert — even though he was away in the mountains, deep in a trance, at the moment of the crime. The real murderer is Susan's married lover, David Peters, but a jury finds Prieste guilty of the crime nonetheless. Once in prison, a vengeful Randall Prieste torments the guilty Peters by astrally projecting himself into the murderer's house.

GUEST CAST: Lawrence Casey (David Peters), James Houghton (Randall Prieste), Sandra McCally (Dorothy Peters), Henry Brandon (The Prosecuting Attorney), Lee Anthony (William Goldman), Marland Proctor (Vincent Tanner), Jay Zuckerman (The Jury Foreman), Deborah Alexakos (Susan Lambert).

COMMENTARY: "Out of Body" is another *Next Step Beyond* original, a "comeuppance" story that accurately depicts the concept of the OBE or Out of Body Experience. Though OBEs had been seen frequently on *One Step Beyond* (in episodes such as "The Return of Mitchell Campion" and "The Explorer"), this is the first time the concept is used in a "just desserts" fashion. Here innocent Randall Prieste is sent to jail for a crime he did not commit, and he uses his powers of concentration and meditation to astrally project himself to the home of his accuser, David Peters.

Peters is driven to distraction and ultimately to death by Prieste, who continues to confront him in this psychic fashion. Of course, Prieste cannot be tried for this murder, since history records he was safely locked away in his cell at the same moment Peters claims to have seen him.

Astral projection or bilocation as a deliberate tool for vengeance is a frightening idea. Interestingly, *The Next Step Beyond* does not adopt a viewpoint on the issue. Is it right of Prieste to kill Peters? Could his OBE merely have forced a confession rather than death? For a peaceful man who has faith in the power of the mind, Prieste certainly subscribes to the theory of an-eye-for-an-eye justice.

"Out of Body" also conforms to other *One Step Beyond* traditions. It concerns a criminal act of passion (a murder committed out of "love"), as in "Echo," "Father Image," "The Haunting," "The Clown," "Justice" and "The Sorcerer." In "Out of Body," Peters' romantic relationship with Susan Lambert is established through the technique of the flashback. In a clever scene of contrasts, David Peters is seen to describe the murder of Susan as he commits perjury on the witness stand under oath. These untruths are intercut with a flashback to the reality of the murder, with Peters becoming angry and killing Susan. In the tradition of all comeuppance stories, Peters is thus visually established as the antagonist, the man who will receive justice via some paranormal mechanism.

Though "Out of Body" may not be in the class of most *One Step Beyond* episodes, together with "Cry Baby" and other non-remakes (such as "The Haunted Inn"), it demonstrates a simple fact. Viewers will give a TV series the benefit of the doubt, even with cheap production values, if the stories are at least moderately original. Accordingly, the non-remakes on *The Next Step Beyond* seem to be the most interesting of all the installments. At the very least, they are variations on a theme rather than carbon copies of beloved, familiar stories.

17. "Key to Yesterday"
(Written by Merwin Gerard; Directed by Alan Jay Factor)

SYNOPSIS: A young man named Dan is surprised to learn that the inheritance from his dead father includes an old burlesque theater. Reopening the old place, Dan has a psychic vision that reveals his father's affair with a showgirl. More disturbing than that, the same vision reveals that the affair ended with Dan's father committing murder!

GUEST CAST: David Gilliam (Daniel Gardner), Henry Brandon (Timothy), Carol Connors (Valerie), Clint Young (The Policeman), Nathan Adler (The Stage Doorman), Sally Swift (Jessie).

COMMENTARY: Though directed by Alan Jay Factor rather than John Newland, "Key to Yesterday" is so obvious a remake of Merwin Gerard's "Father Image" that no one has even bothered to change the character names! David Gilliam thus plays a man named Dan Gardner, just as Jack Lord played him in the original years earlier. Even the awful "The Return of Cary De Witt" at least bothered to alter the names of its protagonists. Newland has gone on record to describe the rushed production schedule that went on behind the scenes of *The Next Step Beyond*, so there is no need to further belabor the point that effort was clearly not going to the right places at this point. The series needed new scripts and new ideas to take it to a "next step" beyond *One Step Beyond*. Instead, it kept recycling Merwin Gerard's old material.

The burlesque theater, the murder from the past, the relationship with a deceased father and the advent of psychic happenstance all re-occur in "Key to Yesterday," an episode of *The Next Step Beyond* that cannot hold a candle to the original "Father Image.

18. "Woman in the Mirror"
(Written by Merwin Gerard; Directed by John Newland)

SYNOPSIS: A guilty man is legally exonerated for the murder of his wife, and he flees town to escape the violent past. While staying at a quaint hotel, Paul experiences a vision of his dead wife firing a revolver at him … but is the assassin (seen only in the mirror) real or imagined? And why has his dead wife's sister chosen this moment in time to show up? Is she out to kill him too?

GUEST CAST: Craig Littler (Paul), Martine Beswicke (Helen Wiley), Noah Keen (Harold), Louie Quinn (Ferris), Olive Dunbar (Mrs. Wyckoff), John Lawrence (The Bartender).

COMMENTARY: Craig Littler (*Jason of Star Command* and "Tsunami") returns to *The Next Step Beyond* with Bond actress Martine Beswicke (*From Russia with Love* [1963], *Thunderball* [1965]) for yet another tiresome remake from the *One Step Beyond* episode catalog. This time the Merwin Gerard story "Echo" is resurrected, with Craig Littler in the Ross Martin role. Like "Key to Yesterday" before it, there is not even a rudimentary attempt to change the story. The lead character has the same name as before (Paul Marlin), and the sole detail switch involves the sex of the visitor in Paul's hotel room. In "Echo" it was a man. In "Woman in the Mirror" it is a woman.

19. "The Haunted Inn"

(Written by Harry Spalding; Directed by Alan Jay Factor)

SYNOPSIS: Having missed his exit by some 60 miles, painter Chris Stabler arrives at an out-of-the-way inn after being directed to it by a beautiful girl in a white dress. Once at the mysterious inn, Chris encounters the beautiful girl, Lucianne, again, and starts to romance her even as the other guest, Miss Argus, warns him that the inn is filled with ghosts. By night, sounds of a boisterous party ring out, but there are no other guests at the inn and the nearest house is half-a-mile away. Soon Chris is confronted with the horrifying truth that his new lover is a ghost and that the inn actually burned to cinders some years earlier!

GUEST CAST: James Keach (Chris Stabler), Patricia Anne Joyce (Lucianne Court), Lorna Thayer (Miss Argus), Buck Young (The Sheriff), Robert V. Barron (Peter Combs).

COMMENTARY: "The Haunted Inn" is like a breath of fresh air on *The Next Step Beyond*. It may not be the best-written or most accurate depiction of a psychic phenomenon ever seen on TV, but the story is fresh and new (*not* a remake), and Alan Jay Factor's fine, suspense-building direction demonstrates a genuine attempt to shake loose a restrictive, conservative format and really scare the heck out of viewers. A story of gothic proportions, "The Haunted Inn" tells the unforgettable "ghost story" of Chris Stabler's brief stay at a little inn off the road that simply does not exist ... a haunted house that supposedly burned down years earlier. Though the episode builds slowly, it becomes a full-blown excursion into terror when the house turns on Chris Stabler, trying to kill him.

Near the end of "The Haunted Inn," Chris is seen in his rented bedroom. He is disturbed by the strange laughing he has heard emanating seemingly from nowhere over the last few days at the bed and breakfast. He has resolved to leave the inn the following morning with his new romantic interest, the lovely Lucianne. Then Lucianne arrives in his bedroom for a midnight visit. In a glowing white gown and grasping a candle, Lucianne approaches the sleeping Chris. When she awakens him and they embrace, Lucianne's eyes suddenly turn a dead white. Horrified, Chris watches as she becomes a laughing embodiment of death, cackling maniacally at him. Chris flees his lover, now revealed to be a ghost, and then finds the white-eyed concierge of the Inn (a ghoulish-looking Peter Combs) strangling the only other guest of the inn, Mrs. Argus. The servant stops this grisly pursuit to face Chris, and his gaunt face (in close-up) is another glimpse into terror. Combs really looks like the malevolent dead, with his slicked back hair, pale skin and oversized mouth (filled with pearly choppers). For pure creepiness, this climax is unmatched in *The Next Step Beyond*. It is miles away from *One Step Beyond* in subject matter, but it is probably the only episode of the sequel series to capture the feeling of slowly-dawning dread and anxiety.

All the elements of "The Haunted Inn" fit together nicely. James Keach makes an appealing lead character, and Lorna Thayer has a rich part as Miss Argus, a woman who desires to see a ghost with her own eyes but does not live long enough to regret that choice. And the end, which reveals the torturous history of Lucianne and her inn, leaves one with shudders. In fact, "The Haunted Inn" is even more disturbing in retrospect, considering that Stabler was in the presence of malevolent entities for some two days before escaping.

Though "The Haunted Inn" is not a perfect episode (like "Dream of Disaster," it also relies on stock footage of a fire for its climax), it still works as unadulterated horror. It sets out to scare, and it accomplishes that goal in an effective, even artful manner.

20. "The Pact"
(Credits unconfirmed)

SYNOPSIS: Three children are tormented by a fortune teller who says they will have a tragic future. One of the children is haunted by this revelation and is driven to obsessive behavior by it. Twenty years later the children reunite as adults, and the prophecy of tragedy comes true.

GUEST CAST: Frank Ashmore (Peter), Tom Gerard (Teddy), Lynn Benesch (Valerie), Diane Hale (The Gypsy), Scott Edward Allen (Young Peter), Jennifer Germaine (Young Valerie), Jeffrey Pinto (Young Teddy), Miles Masters (The Sheriff).

COMMENTARY: Frank Ashmore, of *V* (1984–85) and *Parts: The Clonus Horror* (1978), guest stars in "The Pact," an original *Next Step Beyond* program that focuses on a vision of the future that haunts three children into their adulthood. A prophecy of death similarly haunted three British sailors in "Signal Received," a third season *One Step Beyond* episode. And the idea of a self-fulfilling prophecy of doom also informed the segment called "Doomsday." Before its utilization in "The Pact," gypsy lore appeared also in the *One Step Beyond* episode "Gypsy," though to somewhat different purposes.

21. "Sin of Omission"
(Written by Merwin Gerard; Directed by Alan Jay Factor)

SYNOPSIS: Having recently moved into a new home with her husband, Diane Hollis has a vision of a child in pain in the new sewing room ... a room that was once a bedroom. Diane fears for her sanity because there is a history of mental illness in her family, and the visions of a child in distress persist. Soon Diane's husband Larry sees the ghosts too, particularly an event in time replayed, as a saddened couple lets a terminally ill child pass away by "forgetting" her medicine. When the Hollises confront the former owners about this "sin of omission," the revelation of a little girl's sad death bring an end to years of psychic torture.

GUEST CAST: Mark Goddard (Larry Hollis), Zina Bethune (Diane Hollis), John Harding (Dr. Carl Ferris), Bill Zuckert (Bart Hudson), Ray Stricklyn (Mr. Morrison), Rhonda Hopkins (Mrs. Morrison), Shannon White (The Child).

COMMENTARY: A child's voice comes bellowing from a converted sewing room upstairs, "Mommy, Mommy, please! It hurts!" A terrified woman believes that both she and her unborn child could be plagued by insanity because mental problems run in her family. A terrible secret, a projection of guilt, and a "sin of omission" echo in a newly-leased house, and yet another set of parents reveal they once let their sick daughter expire in "that room upstairs."

If these plot elements sound hauntingly familiar, they should. They are the building blocks not only of *The Next Step Beyond*'s "Sin of Omission," but of the classic "The Room Upstairs," a third season *One Step Beyond* episode that starred Lois Maxwell. In both circumstances, a couple named Hollis confronts the ghost of a now-dead girl and the facts of her terrible, lingering death. It is a good story, certainly — that psychic evidence of sin could remain behind in a house — but it is also old hat.

As in "Key to Yesterday," not even the names of characters have been changed to give "Sin of Omission" a rudimentary sense of originality. The only real difference between original and remake in this case is that "The Room Upstairs" was one of the *One Step Beyond* episodes filmed in England during the last season, and "Sin of Omission" looks like it was filmed in a producer's living room here in the United States. Mark Goddard (Colonel West of *Lost in Space*) has replaced David Knight, and Zina Bethune steps in for Lois Maxwell. Even the twist of having Mr. Hollis see the ghost and therefore freeing his wife of her fear of insanity has been carried over. All these familiar elements bring up a nostalgia for the classy production values and sharp black-and-white photography of *One Step Beyond*.

It would have been no sin to omit this remake from production on *Next Step Beyond*, and as it stands, "Sin of Omission" is guilty of the sin of *re*-mission more than anything else.

22. "Thunderbolt"

(Written by Merwin Gerard; Directed by John Newland)

SYNOPSIS: As a storm gathers high above the city, forked lightning spurs a double premonition in disparate individuals. One woman, Carolyn Peters, dreams of her husband's death at the bank where he works, and at the same time a factory worker realizes his own death will occur on that very day.

GUEST CAST: Debbie Lytton (Carolyn Peters), Thomas Bellin (Alex Peters), Ryan MacDonald (George Chambers), Anne Helm (Ellen Chambers), Gary Vinson (The Factory Foreman), M.G. Kelly (The Paramedic), Sonny Carber (The Bank Guard), Paul E. Richards (The Insurance Broker).

COMMENTARY: Once more into the valley of remakes! This time the tale of psychic lightning called "Forked Lightning" is reincarnated as the similarly named "Thunderbolt." Merwin Gerard is again the so-called "author" of the new material, and, sadly, no one has even bothered to change character names! A woman has a frightening premonition that her husband will die that day. Her husband ends up ignoring her pleas to stay home (making her a Cassandra) because of some illicit activity at the bank. Meanwhile, at the same time, another man also has a vision of his death at the bank that very day and sets about a chain of events that will assure that the "double dream" comes true. No dream at all, "Thunderbolt," so fresh a concept in 1960, seems hackneyed and tired in 1978.

23. "The Confession"

(Credits unconfirmed)

SYNOPSIS: A man is accused of the murder of his wife, and must use psychic means to clear his name. Complicating the case is the fact that the man believes he is guilty of the crime, and he keeps having a psychic vision of the death. Is he really responsible for this death or is the psychic confession originating somewhere else?

GUEST CAST: Grace Lee Whitney (Dr. Dorothy Alsworth), Paulette Breen (Maggie Graham), Michael Christian (Carl Graham), George Ball (Ben Morrison), Peter Griffin (The Guard).

COMMENTARY: *Star Trek's* Grace Lee Whitney (Yeoman Janice Rand) stars in "The Confession," a *Next Step Beyond* episode that utilizes several core concepts of *One Step Beyond*, including the murder scenario (a dead wife), the advent of the psychic (a vision, but from whom?) and the doctor who attempts to investigate and help resolve the situation after much initial skepticism. In "Confession" the interest arises in a question of identity. Who is the *sender* and who is the *receiver* of the telepathic message? Is it naturally occurring or implanted, so as to imply guilt?

Though there was a *One Step Beyond* episode entitled "The Confession," this episode is not a remake of that story.

24. "Trance of Death"
(Written by Arthur C. Pierce; Story by Merwin Gerard; Directed by John Newland)

SYNOPSIS: A woman has a bad accident during her karate class, and she awakens to discover that the fall has seemingly granted her psychic powers. In particular, she has developed the ability to intuit insights from touching objects and people, a skill she will be able to use in a desperate situation that hits close to home.

GUEST CAST: Alexandra Morgan (Sharon Weaver), James Camino (Hank), Nancy Stephens (Chrisiana), Santy Josel (Tadashi), Colby Chester (Mark), Sandra Clark (Debbie).

COMMENTARY: In a few critical ways, "Trance of Death," by Merwin Gerard, echoes the life story of Peter Hurkos, the famous Dutch psychic who was profiled in the *One Step Beyond* two-parter "The Peter Hurkos Story." Where Hurkos fell off a ladder, the protagonist in "Trance of Death" has an accident in karate class. Where Peter Hurkos awoke from a coma to have the power of psychometry (garnering insights from touching an object), Sharon Weaver does likewise. Where Hurkos would often involve himself in solving crimes and helping his fellow man, so does Sharon Weaver follow suit in "Trance of Death."

Psychometry is one of the most interesting sub-categories of psychic "communication," and one that has not been wholly dismissed nor satisfactorily proven. Peter Hurkos was hit-or-miss in his psychic insights, yet strangely accurate for a good percentage of the time. "Trance of Death" believes wholeheartedly in the concept of psychometry, that an object can hold the psychic signature or residue of a person who held or owned it. But, like most of *The Next Step Beyond* canon, "Trance of Death" is remarkable mostly for the fact that its cast consists of unknowns and that it rehashes (if not remakes) the ideas so intelligently explored in its predecessor series.

25. "To Fight a Ghost"
(Written by Harry C. Spalding; Story by Merwin Gerard; Directed by John Newland)

SYNOPSIS: Cathy's husband George has been missing and presumed dead in Venezuela for three years. Unsure whether George is actually alive or dead, Cathy has been unable to move forward in her life and has been stalling Bill, the man who now wants to marry her. Then, one night, Cathy is attacked in the park by a former student named Elton. He attempts to rape her, but is warded off by the spirit of Cathy's husband. This encounter not only saves Cathy's life, it proves to her once and for all that George is dead and she can start living a full life again.

GUEST CAST: Brioni Farrell (Cathy LeMasters), Phillip Clark (Bill Maxwell), Lisa Pera (Mrs. Riva), Radames Pera (Elton Connors), Kathleen Bracken (Joan Watson), Russ Marin (Detective Gans), Dinah Anne Rogers (Eleanor Snyder), John Dresden (Second Man), Paul LeClair (Terry Canfield), Chuck Howerton (George LeMasters).

COMMENTARY: "To Fight a Ghost" could very well have been the subtitle of *The Next Step Beyond* as a TV series. For this is one sequel that never escaped the orbit of *One Step Beyond*, a classic TV program beloved by the world over and a megahit in the universe of syndication. By concentrating so wholeheartedly on remakes of *One Step Beyond*, *The Next Step Beyond* only made its creative "ghosts" all the easier for viewers to detect. A sequel series that legitimately carried on the concepts of *One Step Beyond* while also telling bold new stories may not have resulted in so many invidious comparisons to a glorious past, but all the bloody remakes of *One Step Beyond* classics only reveal the paucity of creativity that went into *The Next Step Beyond*. John Newland and Alan Jay Factor are both good directors, and the sequel series had some episodes that were better than others ("Cry Baby," "Out of Body" and "The Haunted Inn" come to mind immediately). Still, the creative team of Newland, Factor and Gerard were obviously so occupied with keeping the show on budget, on schedule, and finding acceptable locations that the joy and artistry so evident in *One Step Beyond* leaked out somewhere, leaving behind an empty, derivative vessel. In many ways it is a blessing that *The Next Step Beyond* has never been granted much airtime. John Newland, director of "Pigeons from Hell," "Errand of Mercy," "There Aren't Any More MacBanes" and 96 episodes of a genuine TV classic deserves better than to be remembered for this problem-riddled sequel series.

Now to the matter at hand: "To Fight a Ghost" is a remake of "Rendezvous." There are some new wrinkles in the second go-round. Cathy LeMasters is depicted as slightly more desperate and gullible than Kate Maxwell was in the original, even going so far as to hire a medium to communicate with the spirit of her husband so as to determine if he is dead or alive. The medium turns out to be a phony, an amusing conceit for a series that regularly espoused its steadfast belief in psychic phenomena and the validity of concepts such as communication with the dead. Rather than being a marine who died in the war in the Pacific (World War II), the missing husband is described in "To Fight a Ghost" as an archaeologist who disappeared in the jungles of Venezuela. The same idea that a woman cannot move on with her life so long as she "doesn't know" the disposition of her husband is repeated hook, line and sinker, but the charming scene in "Rendezvous" in which a suitor uses a personalized phonograph to propose to Maxwell has been replaced in "To Fight a Ghost" with more standard TV-style exposition.

There is a rapist here too, but this time he is a former student who declares in perfect '70s lingo that Mrs. LeMasters is "the foxiest teacher" he ever had. Playing a full-fledged psycho, Radames Pera gives a slick, disturbing performance as the villainous Elton Connors.

Alas, even the ending of "To Fight a Ghost" is a rehash of the "Rendezvous" climax. The creep in the park is struck down by invisible blows (an unintentionally funny sequence here) dealt by the ghost of the widow's husband come home to protect her from evil.

Though it adheres rigorously to the story of "Rendezvous," "To Fight a Ghost" somehow seems less objectionable a remake than "The Return of Cary De Witt", "Tsunami" or "Dream of Disaster." Perhaps the main reason is Brioni Farrell's performance. She makes for a fetching lead, and the denouement in the park is exciting, if predictable and a little silly.

Beyond the Beyond

Although *The Next Step Beyond* was a grueling and unsatisfying experience from a creative standpoint, it did not stop John Newland from being a force in the world of television. Years after *One Step Beyond* and *The Next*

Step Beyond, and after more than four decades in the industry, Newland continued to contribute to the industry in a new venue: education. Passing on his expertise in the fields of acting and direction to a new generation, Newland recently taught a drama class called "Acting for the Industry" at the University of New Mexico, Taos.

In 1998 John Newland undertook another bold step beyond. He was invited to modernize the RCTI TV network in Jakarta, Indonesia. With a bundle of hand-picked, hand-trained actors, Newland set out to teach the locals about TV acting, camera technique, and western production requirements. In 1999 Newland returned to the United States, mission accomplished.

Newland's production company has not been idle since *The Next Step Beyond* either, producing TV films such as *Timestalkers* (1986), with William Devane, Klaus Kinksi and Lauren Hutton, and the NBC TV movie *Too Good to Be True*, with Loni Anderson and Patrick Duffy. And, as the millennium came to a close, John Newland was still doing what he has always done best: directing. His last project was a production of Julia Cameron's musical *Avalon* at the Taos Community Auditorium, Taos.

Part V

A "Legacy of Love"?
One Step Beyond as Genre TV's Paranormal Bedrock

The game of "which came first?" is a controversial but often illuminating one in the hallowed halls of modern criticism. Historical context remains a vital component in a true comprehension of any art form, whether it be television, photography or painting. Yet if one probes deeply enough into the past, there will inevitably be something to quarrel about; an earlier exploration of the very material that one critic is so loudly trumpeting as being fresh, original, or as the inspiration for later work. In truth, the origins for so many of man's greatest stories arrive from the distant past: our collective mythologies and religions. Considering that reality, to highlight a TV series or a film as a pioneer or originator of any concept may seem foolhardy and unwarranted, if not downright inaccurate.

There is no escaping the reality that every viewer or reader (and yes, every critic) some day encounters a "new" story for "the first time" on a purely personal level. For instance, the film *Alien* (1979) may appear a great, artistic and important original when first experienced ... if a viewer has never seen or heard of *It! The Terror from Beyond Space* (1958). Thus, the responsible critic and historian has an obligation to learn about other productions and works so he may draw an accurate overall picture for the reader. Indeed, one of the many joys of authoring reference books of this type is the amount of learning that goes on behind the scenes, sometimes even at the editorial stage. The editing process forces an author to contend with a voice that brings a different background, different experience, and different preferences and beliefs about what really and truly merits the coveted stamp of "originality." The author who grew up in the 1970s will be prone to trumpet *Star Wars* (1977) as a cornerstone of the space adventure film, but an editor who was a child in the forties will no doubt recall *Flash Gordon* (1939) instead.

Still, it is both possible and worthwhile to write a compelling and cogent study of antecedents and descendants when referencing television. As an art form, TV is a relatively recent development, an invention of the early information age. Thus its history is well documented. That so much of television is still "extant," still available for analysis, permits contemporary critics an opportunity to delve into the past and look at the beginnings, adolescence and maturity of an art form that devours material at so prodigious a rate.

All of this intellectual gamesmanship comes about as a preface to a debate about the historical importance of the paranormal anthology program *Alcoa Presents: One Step Beyond* (1959–61). It is of a distinct time and place (America of the late fifties and very early sixties), and thus it categorically pre-dates the modern glut of paranormal TV programs such as *The Sixth Sense* (1972), *Beyond Reality* (1991–93), *The X-Files* (1993–), *Millennium* (1996–1999), and *The Others* (2000). Because it also arrived on TV a half-season before *The Twilight Zone* (and production realities would dictate it was conceived a year or so before Rod Serling's classic), it might also be called "ahead" of that famous series in at least a chronological sense.

Of course, if the intrepid critic were to back out from the study of television for a moment and delve into the arts of film, theater or even into man's earliest history, *One Step Beyond* might not seem at all like a watershed or momentous production. Indeed, one of the most commonly utilized characters in *One Step Beyond* is a mythological archetype, Cassandra.

In Greek Myth, Cassandra was a Trojan princess and one of Apollo's many lovers. As a gift to Cassandra for her willingness to copulate with him, Apollo bestowed the power of sight (or prophecy) upon her. Cassandra changed her mind about the affair, however. Angry, Apollo spat into her mouth, and Cassandra's gift of insight was mutated. She became doomed to see the future only to never be heeded about it.

In *One Step Beyond* the psychic seers are likewise cursed never to be heeded. They make a fuss, cry, scream and shout about what they have witnessed in premonitions, visions and the like, but nobody believes them ... at least not in time to prevent tragedy. Grace Montgomery Farley envisions the sinking of *Titanic* in "Night of April 14," Ellen Larabee foresees a train crash in "Emergency Only," Carol psychically intuits that her husband has had a car accident in "Twelve Hours to Live," Debbie has a vision that a chandelier will fall from the ceiling in "Premonition," and so forth. These prophecies are met with skepticism, ridicule and a dismissive attitude. Each of these prominent *dramatis personae* owes her situation and dilemma to Cassandra and Greek myth. Though these wretched souls did nothing (one assumes) to evoke a God's wrath or enmity, they share the terrible curse: foreknowledge unheeded.

Perhaps even more to the point, *One Step Beyond* prides itself on dramatizing "true" or "authenticated" stories of the paranormal. Its literate teleplays, though engineered especially for the series, are based on ensconced, even substantiated psychic concepts (possession, OBEs, reincarnation, the collective unconscious, alien abduction, Bigfoot). These notions have been explored outside the artificial realm of drama and art, but are nonetheless a "matter of human record." *One Step Beyond* tales evolve from anecdotes, published accounts, eyewitness reports, archival documentation and current research in the field of parapsychology. Therefore, *One Step Beyond*'s ongoing inspiration is known and very public: so-called true accounts. *One Step Beyond* did not "invent" conceits such as precognition, clairvoyance or automatic writing. Instead, those concepts came from human experience, and *One Step Beyond* dramatizes them in a unique and high-quality fashion.

So, in the limited world of television history, *One Step Beyond* merits the title of pioneer. Though its anthology format obviously derives from any number of TV series, both inside and out of the genre (and including *Alfred Hitchcock Presents* [1955–65]), its choice of content was relatively new for the medium of video. Naturally, there will be those who quarrel with that perception. Rightly, historians may recall *Tales from Tomorrow*, *Inner Sanctum* or *Lights Out*, all of which occasionally took trips to the same paranormal well that TV series such as *One Step Beyond* and later *The Twilight Zone* drank from on a more regular basis. However, the distinction of importance in this argument is that *One Step Beyond* was the first dramatic series to devote itself *exclusively* to the paranormal and inexplicable, rather than directly to horror or science fiction. This distinction means that for 96 weeks (plus reruns), *One Step Beyond* was undoubtedly a primer for an audience unfamiliar with such things. In many cases, these half-hour episodes represented a viewer's very first experience with the quirky, compelling material.

It has often been argued that *Star Trek* (1966–69) was so ubiquitous in reruns in the 1970s that it familiarized America with "technology" such as photon torpedoes, cloaking devices and tractor beams just in time to make *Star Wars* user friendly and comprehensible on a blockbuster level. After a slew of *Star Trek* repeats, the average American viewer was ready to accept the majesty and wonder of *Star Wars*' Zen-like Jedi philosophy because the same viewers had already absorbed the outer space lexicon of *Star Trek*. Again, a similar argument can be applied to *One Step Beyond*.

It educated viewers about parapsychological concepts, and later TV productions were able to take advantage of this familiarity to tell bolder stories. Post–*One Step Beyond* programs such as *The Sixth Sense* or *The X-Files* could take the core concepts of the paranormal as a given and, because of familiarity and audience understanding, tell wider-ranging, more mature tales.

How can *One Step Beyond*'s influence be accurately gauged? A brief glimpse of its history is illuminating in that regard. In 1959 there were only three networks, and *One Step Beyond* was carried on one of the "Big Three" in prime time. This positioning suggests that on any given week from '59 to '61, some 25 to 30 percent of the television viewing audience in America was watching Merwin Gerard's creation. In contrast to those numbers, one might consider that today's genre programming, from *Star Trek: Voyager* (1995–2001) to *Buffy the Vampire Slayer* (1997–) rope in no more than five or six percent of the American viewing audience weekly (and are still judged hits!). During its rerun cycle in the 1970s, *One Step Beyond* often aired with *The Twilight Zone* and *Star Trek* as part of a genre block, making it a perennial favorite and a multi-generational phenomenon. The children who may have watched the series from 1959 to 1961 were parents themselves in the 1970s, exposing a new generation of children to the Newland series. In the 1980s *One Step Beyond* officially became a cult "midnight" hit. Though it was often relegated to late night broadcasts, a new generation of coffee-addicted high schoolers discovered its creepy charms. That it aired so late only made it feel more like a bizarre nightmare to many impressed kids. Then, in the early 1990s, *One Step Beyond* was back on prime time at last: on the cable Sci-Fi Channel. Essentially then, the series has been available to every generation of viewer from 1959 to 1992 (a second life that, sadly, *Tales from Tomorrow*, *Lights Out* and *Inner Sanctum* were denied).

This multi-generational broadcast record clearly puts *One Step Beyond* on the same plateau as series such as *Star Trek* and *The Twilight Zone*. A new genre series airing today (such as *Now and Again* [1999–2000]) would not find the same long-lasting popularity over the years simply because there is now an over abundance of choice on the tube. USA, TNT, TBS, FX, TLC, the Sci-Fi Channel, Animal Planet and other cable stations compete with the "Big Three" networks for valuable viewers, and the end result is the end of an era. The days of "common heritage" TV are probably over.

What this broadcast history establishes is that *One Step Beyond* was there when TV was young, well before any other paranormal TV shows, and it lasted long enough to cover the same topics sometimes three or four times. Then it had a second prominent platform: a long and healthy rerun life. Importantly, the very children who watched the series in the '70s and '80s are now producing their own paranormal programs, and *One Step Beyond* is part of their mental landscape. It is a cornerstone of the genre, acknowledged publicly by the likes of producer Steven Spielberg when he created his own anthology series, *Amazing Stories* (1985–87).

Rod Serling's *The Twilight Zone* was the first genre anthology to follow *One Step Beyond* into prime time (though *Thriller* followed soon after as well). *One Step Beyond* premiered on ABC in the winter of 1959 (January 20, 1959), giving it a 22 episode lead on CBS's *The Twilight Zone*, which was first broadcast on October 2, 1959. On Serling's show, the seemingly miraculous occurred when man intersected with a dimension of irony and cosmic justice. However, *The Twilight Zone* did occasionally stray into the paranormal terrain first blazed by *One Step Beyond*. "Nightmare as a Child" (aired April 29, 1960), by Rod Serling, depicted the story of Helen Foley, a teacher who was warned of impending doom by a projection of her childhood self. This mental projection of young Helen was able to spur Helen's long-repressed memory of her mother's murderer and even prevent Helen from suffering the same violent death. This example of *autoscopy*, of seeing one's doppelganger through the auspices of the mind, was one that would have been right at home on *One Step Beyond*. Accordingly, "phantom" projections of people bearing warnings or saving lives were seen in "Epilogue" (airdate: February 24, 1959), "The Navigator" (airdate: April 14, 1959), "The Aerialist" (airdate: April 28, 1959), and "The Explorer" (airdate: March 15, 1960). It should be noted that all those airdates pre-date "Nightmare as a Child's" initial television broadcast.

On *One Step Beyond* there were various explanations for these projections, from apparitions to out-of-body experiences, whereas on *Twilight Zone* it was merely part of the "zone's" *modus operandi*. Though treated with a different tenor (explanation versus non-explanation), the concept was similar. Again, this is not to declare that *One Step Beyond* originated the concept (it most certainly *did not*), only that if one is choosing to name a certain TV program as "the father" of a genre, *One Step Beyond* has a superior claim to *The Twilight Zone*, since it aired these particular ideas first.

Another popular *Twilight Zone* story was "the disappearance." In stories such as "The Arrival" (airdate: September 22, 1961) and "Little Girl Lost" (airdate: March 16, 1962), people and objects (such as airplanes) disappeared off the face of the Earth. Again, *One Step Beyond* had investigated the idea of bizarre, seemingly inexplicable disappearances in "The Secret" (airdate: April 21, 1959) and "Vanishing Point" (airdate: February 23, 1960). Again, the airdates testify to the fact that *One Step Beyond* explored the concept at an earlier time than did *The Twilight Zone*.

With its OHenry-style twist endings, *The Twilight Zone* also favored the comeuppance/just desserts/cosmic justice stories to a very high degree. This material was explored prominently in "The Fever" (airdate: January 29, 1960), "The Whole Truth" (airdate: January 20, 1961), "The Rip Van Winkle Caper" (airdate: April 21, 1961), "The Mind and the Matter" (airdate: May 12, 1961) and "Death's-Head Revisited" (airdate: November 10, 1961), among others. Again, *One Step Beyond* had explored the same kind of comeuppance story in "The Haunted U-Boat" (airdate: May 12, 1959), "Image of Death" (airdate: May 19, 1959), "Echo" (airdate: June 2, 1959) and "Front Runner" (airdate: June 9, 1959), to name but a few. Again, it would be completely inaccurate, not to mention irresponsible, to suggest that *One Step Beyond* in any way invented the "comeuppance" story. This kind of story was the bread and butter of E.C. Comics long before television explored it (in anthologies such as *Alfred Hitchcock Presents* and *Lights Out*). The point is merely that as a matter of historical record, *One Step Beyond* handled the material before *The Twilight Zone* did, thus punching holes in the theory that *The Twilight Zone* should be preferred as "father of the genre."

These kinds of comparisons could go on forever. *One Step Beyond* aired a haunted submarine story ("The Haunted U-Boat") years before *The Twilight Zone* dramatized a similar story ("The Thirty Fathom Grave"). *One Step Beyond* examined the Lincoln assassination ("The Day the World Wept: The Lincoln Story" [airdate: February 9, 1960]) well before *The Twilight Zone* mined the same history ("Back There" [airdate: January 13, 1961]). The differences in these two exemplary shows were not so much in content or setting, but in intent. *One Step Beyond* really endeavored to be accurate about the details, concepts and "real" cases it dramatized, whereas Rod Serling's series admittedly had no interest in genuflecting to reality. It was a didactic series in every way, offering sterling morality plays.

Lest one forget, television is an art form that thrives on similarities, not differences. One TV series looks very much like another TV series, and networks approve new programs based not necessarily on originality, but by what is already on the air and prospering in the ratings. So, should the world thank *One Step Beyond* for the fact that CBS greenlighted *The Twilight Zone* in the first place? *One Step Beyond*'s ratings were always solid, and it did air for nearly ten months before *The Twilight Zone*, so that bit of speculation is, at least, an arguable one. The success of the Gerard-Newland series *may* have played a part in the decision to proceed with *The Twilight Zone*.

After *The Twilight Zone* followed *One Step Beyond*, the next paranormal-oriented series out of the gate was 1972's *The Sixth Sense*. Like

One Step Beyond before it, this program attempted to dramatize psychic phenomena as a "real" and believable extension of man's mental abilities. Since anthologies were no longer in vogue, a new format was adopted. Dr. Michael Rhodes (Gary Collins) was a psychic researcher (and university professor in parapsychology) who aided those with psychic-oriented problems and visions. *The Sixth Sense* went "one step beyond" *One Step Beyond* by giving its Cassandras (i.e. percipients) a steadfast, heroic advocate. This is something that the protagonists of *One Step Beyond* never had: They were on their own in attempting to understand the world of the inexplicable. Also, *The Sixth Sense* hyped-up and glamorized the paranormal experience to a great extent. Where *One Step Beyond*'s ongoing focus had been the common individual's unexpected encounter with a "larger" world, *The Sixth Sense* made a special effort to have Rhodes assist the most beautiful women imaginable. Carol Lynley, Anne Archer, Lucie Arnaz, Mariette Hartley, Mary Ann Mobley, Stefanie Powers, Cloris Leachman (of "The Dark Room"!), Sharon Gless, Patty Duke, Susan Strasberg, Sandra Dee, Pamela Franklin and Meg Foster were among the lovelies who so gratefully accepted Rhodes' help. On *One Step Beyond* the woman was often the percipient because she was an underdog (and easier to dismiss in a male-dominated world), but on *The Sixth Sense* there was a distinct impression of exploitation and titillation.

The *Sixth Sense* did not hedge its bets in another important realm either: It did not offer a balanced, even-handed view of psychic phenomena. Psychic powers were universally responsible for strange events, whereas *One Step Beyond* at least attempted to remain objective in the face of the unknown. ("Explain it? We cannot.")

Despite these differences, *The Sixth Sense* might be termed *One Step Beyond* with a face-lift: *One Step Beyond* lite. Automatic writing proved that an MIA American soldier was still alive in Vietnam in "I Do Not Belong to the Human World." A spirit haunted William Shatner ("The Promise") in "Can a Dead Man Strike from the Grave?" forcing him to relive a fatal love triangle from another life (a concept on view in "The Captain's Guests," an early episode of *One Step Beyond*). Dr. Rhodes experienced a premonition of murder in "Eye of the Haunted," another familiar idea. "Flying Sepulcher of Death" involved a psychic girl's premonition that a plane would soon crash ("Tonight at 12:17"). Telepathy and a crisis apparition were featured in "Through a Flame Darkly" (directed by John Newland). Indeed, all the core concepts that *One Step Beyond* had dramatized on prime time TV with a great measure of restraint resurfaced on *The Sixth Sense* in a glossy new package replete with white-knight hero, damsels in distress and a concentration on the exploitative elements of psychic phenomena.

Where *One Step Beyond* introduced a concept (such as the OBE or premonition) and devoted 30 minutes to accurately (usually, anyway) exploring it, *The Sixth Sense* offered a swashbuckling adventure (replete with fisticuffs) in each installment. Many stories were simply murder mysteries with "psychic" resolutions. Rather than a legitimate examination of the paranormal or the core concepts of parapsychology, fascinating happenstances were deployed merely as stock solutions in melodrama.

Suspension of disbelief was also harder to come by on *The Sixth Sense* than it had been on *One Step Beyond* because of its very format. It was difficult to believe that a single man (in a year or so of his life) would run into psychic happenstance every week. On *One Step Beyond* the anthology format allowed the psychic to be experienced by different characters each week, and often in vastly differing time periods. *One Step Beyond* visited the time of Washington, the time of Lincoln, World War II, The Korean War and the 1960s, whereas *The Sixth Sense* was limited to the '70s. Despite all these noteworthy differences, *The Sixth Sense* could not have hoped to use psychic phenomena as the solution to its crimes each week had *One Step Beyond* not blazed a trail that familiarized viewing audiences with concepts such as reincarnation and the like.

The 1991–1993 USA series *Beyond Reality* was an interesting synthesis of both *One Step Beyond* and *The Sixth Sense*. Like the former, *Beyond Reality* featured half-hour stories and made the claim that its episodes were based on documented cases of psychic phenomena. Like the latter, *Beyond Reality* was not an anthology, but a "hero" show with performers Shari Belafonte and Carl Marotte playing professors of parapsychology at a major university (cohorts of Dr. Rhodes, no doubt!). And, quite unlike *One Step Beyond*, no documentation or evidence was ever offered that *Beyond Reality* stories were actually true, despite the presence of the opening disclaimer. Still, *Beyond Reality* was clearly an advancement over *The Sixth Sense*. Psychic phenomena were depicted in a mildly more accurate fashion, with less pulchritudinous eye candy and less an obsession with murder mysteries. To wit: Doppelgangers appeared in "The Doppelganger," alien abduction was the subject of "Return Visit" and "Final Flight," reincarnation was the concept informing "Echoes of Evil." "Face off," "The Dying of the Light" and "Asylum" all concerned possession, and "Inner Ear's" focus was telepathy. There was also a heavy concentration on special effects wizardry (a factor missing from *One Step Beyond*).

Interestingly, the producers of *Beyond Reality* soon learned that Merwin Gerard's Law of Parapsychology TV (there are only fifteen original stories) was absolutely true. There were only so many variations on these phenomena that could be explored before the show became repetitive.

Thus it did not take long before *Beyond Reality* lived up to its name and simply went beyond the pale. In no time, its heroes were zapped into alternate dimensions in "Matter of Darkness," "Nightfall," "Let's Play House" and "Facing the Wall." They were catapulted through time in "Dancing with the Man" and "Reunion." They fought demons ("The Box"), vampires ("The Passion"), shape-shifting creatures ("Where There's Smoke"), telepathically created monsters ("Dead Air") and even a succubus ("Siren Song"). Many of these stories were vastly entertaining, and *Beyond Reality* was a good, low-budget series; but it clearly abandoned its pretense of accuracy early on in favor of the fantastic and horrific. By the third season, *Beyond Reality* had dropped its disclaimer of "accuracy" altogether and gone whole hog into terror. After forty-four episodes and two-and-a-half seasons, it was cancelled.

And that brings this discussion to a wonderful series entitled *The X-Files* (1993–). Importantly, this Chris Carter masterpiece is the first paranormal series to last as long (and longer) than *One Step Beyond* did. *The Sixth Sense* lasted for 25 episodes; *The Next Step Beyond* for 25; *Beyond Reality* for 44; and *The X-Files* is still going strong at over 150 hours logged! It is long-lived for very good reason. Written and conceived by Chris Carter with a welcome maturity and an understanding of science not available to *One Step Beyond* in the 1950s, *The X-Files* sought to do something new and exciting. Carter examined the world of the paranormal through the filter of two extremely divergent world views: belief (epitomized by David Duchovny's Mulder) and skepticism (advocated by Gillian Anderson's Scully). This was a brilliant conceit that provided stories of psychic phenomena and the inexplicable a new edge for the first time since *One Step Beyond* aired. Concepts such as the OBE were now merely a take-off point for fascinating dissertations (and heated debates) on biology, genetics, psychology, mental aberration, theology, wish-fulfillment, et al. A sort of paranormal *Equal Time* with Mulder and Scully (instead of Ollie North and Paul Begala), *The X-Files* passionately weighs the arguments on both sides of psychic matters while always permitting the viewer make the ultimate decision. In one sense, this "have it your way" *X-Files* argument was a reflection of *One Step Beyond*'s "prove-it-we-cannot, disprove-it-we-cannot" debate, only with the adrenaline ratcheted up by several degrees.

On the subject of reincarnation, *The X-Files* had a most interesting debate. In "The Field Where I Died," by Glen Morgan and James Wong, a woman (played by Kirsten Cloke) reported a past-life experience. To Mulder this regression was proof positive of reincarnation, but to Scully and science it may all have been a case of multiple personality disorder. At the end of the episode it was certainly arguable which "truth" was real, though Mulder fell for the reincarnation side hook, line and sinker. Many *X-Files* episodes walked this tightrope with great success and artistry.

"Beyond the Sea" witnessed the reality-grounded Scully experiencing visual hallucinations of her dead father. Was she merely in mourning, was her mind playing tricks on her, or was she actually communicating with a spirit? Again, *The X-Files* asked all the right questions, presented all the appropriate documentation on each side, and then moved off the stage, leaving the audience with the chills.

Another *X-Files* episode, called "Pusher," involved an extension of the idea that had been the focal point of the *One Step Beyond* episode called "Moment of Hate": that one person can plant the suggestion to die in another person's mind. In this case, there was a medical excuse. A brain tumor was enhancing the mental potential of Modell (Robert Wisden), the psychic assassin and "ronin" of "Pusher." Interestingly, this murderous character, a mercenary for hire, was just a few "steps beyond" Joanne Linville's character in "Moment of Hate." Karen was coming to terms with a horrible power (the ability to kill with a thought) in "Moment of Hate," whereas Modell, her spiritual descendant, had accepted the power willingly and was actually utilizing it for personal and financial gain.

The X-Files is still not finished, but it has opened up an expansive debate about every paranormal concept imaginable: psychic links ("Oubliette"), precognition ("Clyde Bruckman's Final Repose"), near-death experiences ("The Blessing Way" and "One Breath"), genetic throwbacks ("Home," "The Jersey Devil"), pyrokinesis ("Fire"), possession ("Lazarus"), alien abduction ("Duane Barry"), spirits ("Excelsius Dei," "How the Ghosts Stole Christmas"), the collective unconscious ("Aubrey"), ethnic curses ("Fresh Bones," "Teso Dos Bichos"), OBEs ("The Walk"), anomalous phenomena ("Rain King") and even soul transference ("Dreamland"). In the seventh season *The X-Files* also featured a two-part episode about "Walk-Ins," spirits who are "invited" to enter the bodies of others in what is believed to be a benign variation on possession.

In all these situations the concepts that *One Step Beyond* once examined with such restraint and sincerity is re-examined through the filter of two very dynamic, very radical world views. That new veneer makes *The X-Files* the legitimate "next step" after *One Step Beyond* in paranormal television programs. It is a worthy heir to *One Step Beyond*, and that is, no doubt, a reason behind its remarkable success. It speaks in the "psychic" language popularized by *One Step Beyond*, yet injects a healthy dose of modern science, great visuals, remarkable acting, confrontational perspectives and good stories to carry those concepts to a new level of maturity and originality.

There is no doubt that *The Twilight Zone* deserves much credit for the face of the genre on TV today. It is a highly influential TV series, and its overwhelmingly didactic tone is heavily mirrored in the original *Star Trek* as well as in *The Outer Limits*. However, *The X-Files* is a different animal. Its playground, like that of *One Step Beyond*, is one of belief. In all human beings there is a duality that *The X-Files* recognizes by the very nature of its two dynamo protagonists: the desire to believe something on faith (such as the existence of UFOs or even God), and the lure of the practical, of science, to quantify the world in Euclidian terms. *The X-Files* espouses both world views by giving science and parapsychology a mouthpiece in its incredible adventures.

One Step Beyond manages the same feat by depicting in accurate fashion the documented cases of the paranormal, real-life "X-Files" if you will. It drew no real conclusions, but offered viewers the possibility of the psychic (OBEs et al.) on one hand and the practical (hallucinations, mirages, coincidences) on the other. These two TV programs may be separated in genesis by more than a thirty-year gulf, but they are two sides of the same coin, and *The X-Files* has much more in common both conceptually and thematically with *One Step Beyond* than it does with *The Twilight Zone*.

One Step Beyond's influence does go further as well. Two of its episodes, "The Burning Girl" and "The Peter Hurkos Story," might legitimately be called inspiration for two highly popular Stephen King books, *Carrie* and *The Dead Zone*. And "reality" TV has currently taken up *One Step Beyond*'s mantle of depicting "actual" cases, with such series as the syndicated hit *In Search of* (1976–82) and the more recent *Sightings* (1994–1997).

In viewing these children, it is interesting to see how *One Step Beyond* melded two approaches — drama and journalism — into a successful hybrid. Its children have accordingly been separated into two categories. *The Sixth Sense*, *Beyond Reality*, and *The X-Files* are children of its concepts and dramatic approach, and *In Search of* and its ilk represent a different branch, descended directly from the journalistic or so-called "accurate" approach. One would be hard put to name another TV series that managed to create so many offspring in such vastly different formats.

Conclusion

One Step Beyond made TV history by effectively marrying film technique and craft with a serious (and well-researched) study of its subject matter, the paranormal. Though one need not renounce any long-held skepticism or beliefs about the validity of premonitions, out-of-body experiences, possession and reincarnation over the so-called "evidence" presented on a four-decades-old television anthology program, there are moments in *One Step Beyond* that certainly give one reason to pause (unless one happens to be the Amazing Randi). Perhaps it is John Newland's straight-faced narration and crisp direction that fosters so pleasant a suspension of disbelief, but there is also much to be credited to staff writers Merwin Gerard and Larry Marcus. They artfully constructed their "dramatizations" on substantive, real-life reports (and eyewitness accounts) of the unusual and inexplicable rather than relying merely on the phantasmagoria of their imaginations. In the face of a book like *Futility*, which accurately predicted nearly to the letter the date, nature, context and specifications of the *Titanic* disaster, it is a little difficult to be completely dismissive of life's mysteries. *One Step Beyond*'s steadfast dedication to accuracy stands as a remarkable contrast to the special effects showcases of other paranormal-based TV programs such as *Poltergeist the Legacy*, *The Sixth Sense*, *The Others* and *Psi Factor*.

And that, perhaps, is *One Step Beyond*'s greatest gift to television audiences the world over. It is a sincere program that treats its subject matter with more respect than is common in the world of "lowest common denominator" TV entertainment. Although on occasion a psychic concept is misrepresented by a simple error in terminology ("The Love Connection" and "The Return of Cary DeWitt" are two examples from *The Next Step Beyond*), the vast majority of *One Step Beyond* installments adhere to accepted parapsychological research and dramatize accurate depictions of the concepts (if not the people) involved in such cases. What other TV series can make the same claim?

Perhaps the most interesting element of *One Step Beyond*'s legacy is that it seems to have borne two very distinct types of children. On the one hand are the pure dramas like *The X-Files* and *The Sixth Sense*, which concern themselves mostly with telling good, entertaining stories, not in reflecting truthful accounts of the mysterious. On the other hand are the ventures like *Sightings*, which obsess on "real" case studies to the total exclusion of the dramatic or the artistic. *One Step Beyond* is perhaps the only genre program in history that manages to mesh the stringent requirements of drama with the difficult commitment to accurately reflect research. The series thus balances art and accuracy in a manner most rare, and most welcome.

Every TV series has its adherents, those faithful writers and experts who go out and champion one production to the exclusion of others. In the case of *One Step Beyond*, it has long stood in the shadow of *The*

Twilight Zone, admittedly one of the best TV series ever produced; but in many important categories *One Step Beyond* is equally deserving of respect and admiration. Not only did it come first, but (arguably) it had a much more difficult mission to accomplish. It had to make people believe (or at least *not* disbelieve) at the same time that it kept audiences entertained, off guard and frightened. That *One Step Beyond* succeeded more often than not on the twin fronts of entertainment and accuracy is a testament to its inherent quality.

Many of the talents who imbued *One Step Beyond* with so much integrity and spirit are no longer with us. In that sense, this book was written several years too late. Collier Young and Merwin Gerard passed away some years ago, as did many of the performers who made the series such a memorable experience. Though these artists and creators may have taken that "one step beyond" that John Newland so frequently talked about, they leave behind a television legacy of remarkable interest. For *One Step Beyond* is that rarest of TV birds: a horror show that "gets it." It understands that the best scares originate from the head, not the gut. With its bows to reality and research, *One Step Beyond* always set out to forge a terror of the most cerebral variety. Though the creepy punctuation of most *One Step Beyond* episodes — the realization that inexplicable things really do sometimes occur in life — may not immediately match the visceral gut-punching effect of *Twilight Zone*'s best and most ironic twist endings, regular viewers may find that the *One Step Beyond* climax has a longer lasting impact.

Somehow, sleep is harder to come by in the dark chill of the night knowing that 19 people really had visions of *Titanic*'s sinking before the event, or that Abraham Lincoln dreamed repetitiously of his own death just prior to his assassination, or that Dutch psychometrist Peter Hurkos did have a remarkable (if not consistent) ability to intuit "truth" about people he had never before met merely by touching their belongings. As has long been established, truth is indeed stranger than fiction, and *One Step Beyond* recalls that proverb and tweaks it. Reality, or the appearance of reality, can be scarier than fiction too.

Appendix A:
The Most Common Conventions and Themes in *One Step Beyond*

One Step Beyond was a remarkably consistent series in the types of stories it dramatized and the characteristics of its protagonists and antagonists. Below is a list of some of the most common plots, characters and themes that appeared on this paranormal anthology.

1. *The Cassandra Complex*

Those unfortunate souls who have psychic visions but are disbelieved, often to the detriment of others. Following each episode title is the name of the Cassandra in question and the prediction ignored.

1. "Night of April 14" (Grace Montgomery; sinking of *Titanic*)
2. "Emergency Only" (Ellen Larrabee; train crash)
3. "Twelve Hours to Live" (Carol Jansen; car crash)
4. "Premonition" (Debbie Garrick; falling chandelier)
5. "Delusion" (Harold Stern; death of blood recipient)
6. "The Open Window" (Tony March; death of woman in hotel)
7. "Forked Lightning" (Ellen Chambers; death of husband)
8. "Earthquake" (Gerald Perkins; San Francisco earthquake)
9. "The Day the World Wept" (Mary Lincoln; death of Lincoln)
10. "I Saw You Tomorrow" (Don Stewart; murder in hotel room)
11. "Moment of Hate" (Karen Wadsworth; death of those hated)
12. "To Know the End" (Emily; death of husband in combat)
13. "Tonight at 12:17" (Laura Perkins; plane crash)
14. "The Villa" (Mary Lowe; death of someone in a lift)

2. *You've Come a Long Way (Beyond) Baby*

Wherein women are the real protagonists of *One Step Beyond*, depicted as being psychic, experiencing the paranormal, or having the enhanced potential for psychic experiences. (Notice that there are over 30 such characters in *One Step Beyond*, representing one third of all the episodes produced!)

1. "The Bride Possessed" (Sally Conroy)
2. "Night of April 14" (Grace Montgomery)
3. "Emergency Only" (Ellen Larrabee)
4. "The Dark Room" (Rita Morrison)
5. "Twelve Hours to Live" (Carol Jansen)
6. "The Dream" (Ethel Blakeley)
7. "Premonition" (Debbie Garrick)
8. "The Dead Part of the House" (Ann Burton)
9. "The Secret" (Sylvia Ackroyd)
10. "The Burning Girl" (Alice Denning)
11. "Image of Death" (Charlotte)
12. "Message from Clara" (Miss Morrison)
13. "Forked Lightning" (Ellen Chambers)
14. "Dead Ringer" (Esther Quentin)
15. "Make Me Not a Witch" (Amy Horvath)
16. "Call from Tomorrow" (Helena Stacey)
17. "Who Are You?" (Laurie)
18. "The Day the World Wept" (Mary Lincoln)
19. "Vanishing Point" (Ruth Graham)
20. "The Visitor" (Ellen Grayson)
21. "Tidal Wave" (Margaret North)
22. "Anniversary of a Murder" (Frances Hillier)
23. "The Death Waltz" (Lilly Clark)
24. "If You See Sally" (Sally Willis)
25. "Moment of Hate" (Karen Wadsworth)
26. "To Know the End" (Emily)
27. "Tonight at 12:17" (Laura Perkins)
28. "Legacy of Love" (Mary Ann)
29. "Rendezvous" (Kate Maxwell)
30. "The Gift" (Lola)
31. "The Room Upstairs" (Esther Hollis)
32. "The Prisoner" (Ruth Goldman)
33. "The Villa" (Mary Lowe)
34. "The Tiger" (Miss Plum; Pamela)

3. Dismissive Doctors

Wherein medical authorities dismiss the psychic or paranormal by championing equally farfetched medical and psychological gobbledygook.

1. "Epilogue"
2. "The Open Window"
3. "Moment of Hate"
4. "Dead Ringer"
5. "Tonight at 12:17"

4. *Married Couples Caught in Psychic Circumstances*

Wherein the spousal union is either destroyed or strengthened by the intervention of the paranormal or psychic. Following the episode name is the name of the couple and the end effect of their odd experience.

1. "The Bride Possessed" (The Conroys; strengthened)
2. "Night of April 14" (The Farleys; destroyed)
3. "Twelve Hours to Live" (The Jansens; strengthened)
4. "Epilogue" (The Archers; strengthened — though she dies)
5. "The Dream" (The Blakeleys; strengthened)
6. "The Secret" (The Ackroyds; destroyed)
7. "Image of Death" (The Marquis and Charlotte; destroyed)
8. "The Captain's Guests" (The Courtneys; indeterminate)
9. "The Riddle" (The Barretts; destroyed)
10. "Doomsday" (The Donamoors; destroyed)
11. "Forked Lightning" (The Chambers; destroyed)
12. "Reunion" (Helga and Peter; destroyed)
13. "Dead Ringer" (The Quentins; strengthened)
14. "Forests of the Night" (The Dolivers; destroyed)
15. "Call from Tomorrow" (The Staceys; strengthened)
16. "Who Are You?" (The Warrens; strengthened)
17. "The Day the World Wept" (The Lincolns; destroyed)
18. "Vanishing Point" (The Grahams; destroyed)
19. "The Haunting" (The Chandlers; destroyed)
20. "The Clown" (The Reagans; destroyed)
21. "I Saw You Tomorrow" (The Seymours; destroyed)
22. "Encounter" (The Rands; destroyed)
23. "The Visitor" (The Graysons; strengthened)
24. "The Storm" (The Bernheims; strengthened)
25. "Tidal Wave" (The Norths; indeterminate)
26. "To Know the End" (Emily and Harry; destroyed)
27. "The Trap" (The Donovios; strengthened)
28. "The Promise" (The Bremmers; destroyed...but with hope)
29. "Tonight at 12:17" (The Perkins; strengthened)
30. "Rendezvous" (The Maxwells; indeterminate)
31. "Dead Man's Tale" (The Werrises; strengthened)
32. "The Room Upstairs" (The Hollises; strengthened)
33. "The Villa" (The Lowes; destroyed)
34. "Nightmare" (The Rolands; strengthened)

5. *The Scales of Justice Righted* (a.k.a. *The Comeuppance*)

Wherein bad, guilty people pay for their crimes or general badness by facing judgment at the hand of mysterious psychic phenomena. The following list includes the episode title and the crime to be "righted."

1. "The Devils' Laughter" (arrogance and murder)
2. "The Secret" (marital infidelity and neglect)
3. "The Haunted U-Boat" (Nazism; war crimes)

4. "Image of Death" (infidelity and murder)
5. "Echo" (murder)
6. "Front Runner" (cheating)
7. "Reunion" (murder)
8. "The Stone Cutter" (murder)
9. "The Hand" (murder)
10. "The Justice Tree" (murder)
11. "The Clown" (murder)
12. "Anniversary of a Murder" (infidelity; murder)
13. "The Death Waltz" (conspiracy to commit murder)
14. "The Executioner" (wrongful imprisonment; attempted murder)
15. "The Confession" (withholding evidence; murder)
16. "The Avengers" (Nazism)
17. "The Villa" (infidelity)
18. "The Tiger" (cruelty to a child)

6. Psychic Experiences Misinterpreted

Wherein psychic visions are experienced, but the reading of said visions are wrong, misguided or just a tad off.

1. "Emergency Only"
2. "Premonition"
3. "I Saw You Tomorrow"
4. "The Face"
5. "Nightmare"

7. Pink Elephants (or Alcoholics Make the Best Psychics...)

Wherein people with a history of alcoholism (or even a bout with alcoholism) have persuasive psychic experiences but are dismissed because of their former and or current love of booze.

1. "Epilogue"
2. "Brainwave"
3. "Earthquake"
4. "The Peter Hurkos Story" (admittedly, a brief bout with drink)
5. "Delia" (featuring "Senōr Whiskey" himself!)
6. "The Visitor"
7. "The Executioner"

8. White Men Don't Know Any Better...

Wherein "foreign" (i.e. non–Caucasian) and non–Western ideas offer a deeper insight into the paranormal and supernatural than any Western-born white man or his Christian religion ever could.

1. "The Dead Part of the House" (Asian)
2. "The Riddle" (Indian)
3. "Forests of the Night" (Chinese mysticism)
4. "The Mask" (Egyptology)

5. "Gypsy" (Gypsy magic)
6. "House of the Dead" (Chinese mysticism)
7. "Night of Decision" (Native American legend)

9. Chock Full o' Nuts

Wherein people with a history of nervous breakdowns have persuasive psychic experiences but are dismissed because of their fragile mental states.

1. "Call from Tomorrow"
2. "The Haunting"
3. "The Room Upstairs"

10. The Thin Psychic Line

Wherein psychic or paranormal experiences are had in the heightened, hysterical atmosphere of war.

1. "The Dream" (World War II)
2. "The Vision" (World War I)
3. "The Haunted U-Boat" (World War II)
4. "Brainwave" (World War II)
5. "Reunion" (World War II)
6. "The Mask" (World War II)
7. "The Peter Hurkos Story" (World War II)
8. "The Death Waltz" (post–Civil War)
9. "The Return" (The Korean War)
10. "To Know the End" (World War II)
11. "The Promise" (World War II)
12. "The Executioner" (The Civil War)
13. "The Last Round" (World War II)
14. "Night of Decision" (American Revolutionary War)
15. "Signal Received" (World War II)
16. "The Avengers" (World War II)
17. "The Prisoner" (World War II)
18. "The Sorcerer" (World War II)

11. Bad Seeds?

Wherein children become the unwitting recipients or fulcrum of powerful psychic powers or experiences.

1. "Epilogue" (a little boy is saved by a crisis apparition)
2. "The Dead Part of the House" (a little girl detects ghosts)
3. "The Burning Girl" (a teenage girl starts fires with her mind)
4. "Make Me Not a Witch" (a teenage girl develops telepathy)
5. "The Justice Tree" (a boy is saved by a hangin' tree)
6. "Call from Tomorrow" (a little girl is saved by clairaudio)
7. "Who Are You?" (a child is possessed)
8. "Goodbye Grandpa" (two children receive a psychic message from their dead grandpa)

9. "The Room Upstairs" (a dead child haunts a home)
10. "The Tiger" (an abused child strikes back by mentally projecting a deadly invisible friend)

12. Real Life Disasters

Wherein a terrible real-life calamity is predicted (usually psychically) but dismissed by people, with catastrophic results for many.

1. "Night of April 14" (sinking of *Titanic*, 1912)
2. "Earthquake" (San Francisco earthquake of 1916)
3. "The Day the World Wept: The Lincoln Story" (Lincoln assassination)
4. "Tidal Wave" (Hawaii tidal wave of 1960)
5. "Signal Received" (the sinking of the H.M.S. *Hood*)
6. "Eye Witness" (volcanic eruption at Krakatoa, 1883)

13. Touched by the Paranormal

Wherein the stories of psychic phenomena are ultimately uplifting and inspirational rather than frightening or mysterious. Thankfully, all such stories are *sans* angels.

1. "Who Are You?"
2. "Goodbye Grandpa"
3. "The Promise"
4. "Nightmare"

14. "Say, Mr. Newland, Did I Ever Tell You About the Time that..."

Wherein series host John Newland becomes personally involved with the participants of a psychic-oriented event.

1. "The Inheritance" (Newland "on vacation" in Mexico City)
2. "Vanishing Point" (Newland called in by a cop to investigate)
3. "Delia" (Newland "on vacation" again, this time near San Salvador)
4. "Gypsy" (Newland called in by a warden to investigate)
5. "The Sacred Mushroom" (Newland goes on pilgrimage to Mexico)

15. The (Literal) Blind Leading the (Figurative) Blind (i.e. Non-Believers)

Wherein blind characters have a special insight or relationship with the world of the psychic that ultimately proves superior to the senses of the sighted.

1. "House of the Dead"
2. "The Storm"
3. "The Return"
4. "The Stranger"

16. Pickles and Ice Cream

Wherein pregnant women have experiences with the supernormal or paranormal, but are dismissed out of hand because of their tender physical condition.

1. "The Storm"
2. "Tonight at 12:17"
3. "The Room Upstairs"

17. Murder Most Foul

Wherein psychic experiences revolve around the planned, intentional death of another human being. Closely related to the comeuppance story (which rights the murder).

1. "Image of Death"
2. "Echo"
3. "The Riddle"
4. "Delusion"
5. "Reunion"
6. "The Stone Cutter"
7. "The Hand"
8. "The Haunting"
9. "The Clown"
10. "I Saw You Tomorrow"
11. "Anniversary of a Murder"
12. "Moment of Hate"
13. "The Executioner"
14. "Persons Unknown"
15. "Justice"
16. "The Face"
17. "The Sorcerer"
18. "The Tiger"

18. "It Really Happened!"

Wherein the actual percipient of an "encounter with the world of the unknown" is brought onto *One Step Beyond* to confirm the veracity of the episode at hand.

1. "The Peter Hurkos Story" (Peter Hurkos)
2. "Tidal Wave" (Margaret North)
3. "The Sacred Mushroom" (Dr. Andrija Puharich)
4. "Persons Unknown" (Dr. Atl)
5. "Signal Received" (Robin Hughes)

19. No Trespassing!

Wherein *One Step Beyond* suggests that a certain environment or location can do "strange things" to a man's mind.

1 "The Navigator" (the sea)
2. "The Aerialist" (the circus)
3. "The Clown" (the circus)
4. "The Explorer" (the desert)
5. "House of the Dead" (Hong Kong)
6. "Goodbye Grandpa" (the desert)

Appendix B: A Survey of the Psychic, Paranormal and Inexplicable in Genre Television

Many of the psychic and paranormal concepts that *One Step Beyond* explored on a regular basis from 1959 to 1961 have since become the bread and butter of the rapidly proliferating horror and science fiction genres. Below is a list of concepts (such as reincarnation, possession, astral projection, etc.) that appeared on *One Step Beyond* and again later in other American genre TV series.

1. *Astral Projection (The Out-of-Body Experience)*
   "The Return of Mitchell Campion" (*One Step Beyond*)
   "The Aerialist" (*One Step Beyond*)
   "The Explorer" (*One Step Beyond*)
   "The Sorcerer" (*One Step Beyond*)
   "Justice" (*One Step Beyond*)
   "The Last Laurel" (*Rod Serling's Night Gallery*)
   "Face of Ice" (*The Sixth Sense*)
   "The Return of Cary De Witt" (*The Next Step Beyond*)
   "Out of Body" (*The Next Step Beyond*)
   "Justice" (*Beyond Reality*)
   "Reunion" (*Beyond Reality*)
   "The Walk" (*The X-Files*)

2. *Possession*
   "The Bride Possessed" (*One Step Beyond*)
   "Who Are You?" (*One Step Beyond*)
   "The Return of Andrew Bentley" (*Thriller*)
   "With Affection, Jack the Ripper" (*The Sixth Sense*)
   "Possessed" (*The Next Step Beyond*)

"Asylum" (*Beyond Reality*)
"The Dying of the Light" (*Beyond Reality*)
"Face Off" (*Beyond Reality*)
"Lazarus" (*The X-Files*)
"The Calusari" (*The X-Files*)
"The Inheritance" (*Poltergeist the Legacy*)

3. Reincarnation

"The Riddle" (*One Step Beyond*)
"Nightmare" (*One Step Beyond*)
"Echoes of Evil" (*Beyond Reality*)
"The Burning Judge" (*Beyond Reality*)
"Born Again" (*The X-Files*)
"The Field Where I Died" (*The X-Files*)

4. Telepathy

"Twelve Hours to Live" (*One Step Beyond*)
"Make Me Not a Witch" (*One Step Beyond*)
"The Trap" (*One Step Beyond*)
"Through a Flame Darkly" (*The Sixth Sense*)
"The Confession" (*The Next Step Beyond*)
"The Amazing Falsworth" (*Amazing Stories*)
"Inner Ear" (*Beyond Reality*)
"Beyond the Sea" (*The X-Files*)

5. Alien Abduction

"Encounter" (*One Step Beyond*)
Project U.F.O. (series concept)
"Return Visit" (*Beyond Reality*)
"The X-Files" (pilot) (*The X-Files*)
"Duane Berry"/"Ascension" (*The X-Files*)
"Fearful Symmetry" (*The X-Files*)
Dark Skies (series concept)

6. Bigfoot

"Night of the Kill" (*One Step Beyond*)
"The Secret of Big Foot" (*The Six Million Dollar Man*)
"The Return of Big Foot" (*The Bionic Woman*)
"Big Foot V" (*The Six Million Dollar Man*)

7. Automatic Writing

"Message from Clara" (*One Step Beyond*)
"I Do Not Belong to the Human World" (*The Sixth Sense*)

8. *The Ghostly Hitchhiker*

"If You See Sally" (*One Step Beyond*)
"The Hitchhiker" (*The Twilight Zone*)
"Ghost in the Road" (*Poltergeist the Legacy*)

9. *The Doppelganger*

"The Lonely Room" (*One Step Beyond*)
"Shatterday" (*The Twilight Zone* [remake])
"Doppelganger" (*Beyond Reality*)
"Doppleganger"[sic] (*Poltergeist the Legacy*)

10. *Hauntings and Poltergeists*

"The Dead Part of the House" (*One Step Beyond*)
"The Captain's Guests" (*One Step Beyond*)
"The Lovers" (*One Step Beyond*)
"The Haunting" (*One Step Beyond*)
"The Haunted Inn" (*The Next Step Beyond*)
"How the Ghosts Stole Christmas" (*The X-Files*)

11. *Vanishings*

"The Secret" (*One Step Beyond*)
"Vanishing Point" (*One Step Beyond*)
"Little Girl Lost" (*The Twilight Zone*)

12. *Curses*

"Image of Death" (*One Step Beyond*)
"Doomsday" (*One Step Beyond*)
"The Mask" (*One Step Beyond*)
"The Closed Cabinet" (*Thriller*)
"There Aren't Any More MacBanes" (*Rod Serling's Night Gallery*)
"Drums at Midnight" (*The Next Step Beyond*)
"Black Magic" (*Beyond Reality*)
"Fresh Bones" (*The X-Files*)
"Tesos Dos Bichos" (*The X-Files*)

13. *Precognition/Premonitions*

"Night of April 14" (*One Step Beyond*)
"Emergency Only" (*One Step Beyond*)
"Premonition" (*One Step Beyond*)
"The Dream" (*One Step Beyond*)
"Forked Lightning" (*One Step Beyond*)
"The Stone Cutter" (*One Step Beyond*)
"Earthquake" (*One Step Beyond*)
"To Know the End" (*One Step Beyond*)

"Tonight at 12:17" (*One Step Beyond*)
"Signal Received" (*One Step Beyond*)
"The Villa" (*One Step Beyond*)
"Eye Witness" (*One Step Beyond*)
"Ring-a-Ding Girl" (*The Twilight Zone*)
"The Prediction" (*Thriller*)
"What Beckoning Ghost?" (*Thriller*)
"Eye of the Haunted" (*The Sixth Sense*)
"Coffin, Coffin in the Sky" (*The Sixth Sense*)
"Five Widows Weeping" (*The Sixth Sense*)
"Dream of Disaster" (*The Next Step Beyond*)
"Thunderbolt" (*The Next Step Beyond*)
"You Gotta Believe Me" (*Amazing Stories*)
"Clyde Bruckman's Final Repose" (*The X-Files*)

14. Genetic deformity

"Ordeal on Locust Street" (*One Step Beyond*)
"Squeeze" (*The X-Files*)
"Tooms" (*The X-Files*)
"The Host" (*The X-Files*)
"Home" (*The X-Files*)

15. Apparitions

"The Dark Room" (*One Step Beyond*)
"Epilogue" (*One Step Beyond*)
"The Navigator" (*One Step Beyond*)
"Rendezvous" (*One Step Beyond*)
"The Last Round" (*One Step Beyond*)
"The Death Waltz" (*One Step Beyond*)
"The Room Upstairs" (*One Step Beyond*)
"Nightmare as a Child" (*The Twilight Zone*)
"Echo of a Distant Scream" (*The Sixth Sense*)
"Dear Joan: We're Going to Scare You to Death" (*The Sixth Sense*)
"Gallows in the Wind" (*The Sixth Sense*)
"To Fight a Ghost" (*The Next Step Beyond*)
"Sin of Omission" (*The Next Step Beyond*)
"Range of Motion" (*Beyond Reality*)
"The Bridge" (*Beyond Reality*)
"Theater of the Absurd" (*Beyond Reality*)
"Late for Dinner" (*Beyond Reality*)
"How the Ghosts Stole Christmas" (*The X-Files*)

16. Psychometry

"The Peter Hurkos Story (Parts I & II) (*One Step Beyond*)
"Trance of Death" (*The Next Step Beyond*)

Appendix C: The Fifteen Best Episodes of *One Step Beyond*

With 96 episodes to choose from, it is difficult to select only a dozen or so segments of *One Step Beyond* that could be termed "the best." Nonetheless, the following list comprises this author's choices for the best fifteen episodes of the series, based on a combination of dramatic strengths and cogent "depiction" of psychic phenomena (i.e., evidence presented in favor of the episode's case, or adherence to established paranormal research). Following each choice is a notation about the season of production, the psychic concept explored and, where applicable, the specific incident. Though not by any design, this list includes five episodes from each of *One Step Beyond*'s three seasons.

1. "Night of April 14" (1st year); *premonitions*; sinking of *Titanic*.
2. "If You See Sally" (3rd year); *apparition*; hitchhiker.
3. "The Bride Possessed" (1st year); *possession*.
4. "The Visitor" (2nd year); *apparition/astral projection/time hiccup*.
5. "Epilogue" (1st year); *crisis apparition*.
6. "The Sacred Mushroom" (3rd year); documentary; mushrooms and *ESP*.
7. "The Haunted U-Boat" (1st year); *rapping* on submarine.
8. "The Day the World Wept" (2nd year); *premonitions*; death of Lincoln.
9. "The Clown" (2nd year); *psychic revenge*.
10. "The Hand" (2nd year); *guilty conscience*.
11. "Premonition" (1st year); *gyromancy*; *premonitions*; chandelier.
12. "Moment of Hate" (3rd year); *mind over matter*.
13. "The Villa" (3rd year); *premonition*.
14. "Anniversary of a Murder" (3rd year); *revenge from beyond the grave*.
15. "Image of Death" (1st year); *guilty conscience*.

Runners-up: "Emergency Only," "The Face," "House of the Dead."

Appendix D: John Newland's Directing Contributions to Genre TV Series (1961–1978)

John Newland prospered, with a long directing career outside of *One Step Beyond* and *The Next Step Beyond*. The following is a brief list of genre series episodes he helmed between the two *Beyonds*. Series titles, episode titles and airdates have been included. The list is in chronological order.

1. *Thriller*: "Pigeons from Hell" (June 6, 1961)
2. *Thriller*: "The Return of Andrew Bentley" (December 11, 1961)
3. *Alfred Hitchcock Presents*: "Bad Actor" (January 9, 1962)
4. *Alfred Hitchcock Presents*: "Burglar Proof" (February 27, 1962)
5. *Thriller*: "Man of Mystery" (April 2, 1962)
6. *Alfred Hitchcock Presents*: "The Twelve Hour Caper" (May 29, 1962)
7. *Star Trek*: "Errand of Mercy" (March 16, 1967)
8. *Rod Serling's Night Gallery*: "There Aren't Any More MacBanes" (February 16, 1972)
9. *The Sixth Sense*: "Dear Joan: We're Going to Scare You to Death" (September 30, 1972)
10. *The Sixth Sense*: "Through a Flame Darkly" (November 4, 1972)
11. *The Sixth Sense*: "Candle, Candle Burning Bright" (November 25, 1972)

Appendix E: Remakes

Included below for easy reference is a list of *One Step Beyond* episodes later remade as episodes of *The Next Step Beyond*. Please note, these remakes are all of episodes written by series creator Merwin Gerard.

OSB Episode   *Remade as NSB Episode*

1. "Tidal Wave"   "Tsunami"
2. "The Return of Mitchell Campion"   "The Return of Cary De Witt"
3. "The Bride Possessed"   "Possessed"
4. "Who Are You?"   "The Love Connection"
5. "Tonight at 12:17"   "Dream of Disaster"
6. "I Saw You Tomorrow"   "Other Voices"
7. "Dead Man's Tale"   "Greed"
8. "Father Image"   "Key to Yesterday"
9. "Echo"   "Woman in the Mirror"
10. "The Room Upstairs"   "Sin of Omission"
11. "Forked Lightning"   "Thunderbolt"
12. "Rendezvous"   "To Fight a Ghost"

Notes

Part I: History

1. Ruth Reichl. *The Measure of Her Powers: An M.F.K. Fisher Reader*. Counterpoint, 1999, introduction.
2. Paul Gray. *Time Magazine*: "Those good Old Games." January 17, 2000, p. 84.
3. Richard Goodwin. *Time Magazine*: "Watching Drama Become Farce." January 17, 2000, p. 85.
4. William Boddy. *Fifties Television: The Industry and Its Critics*. University of Illinois Press, 1990, p. 163.
5. Jeff Kisselhoff. *The Box: An Oral History of Television, 1920–1961*. Viking, 1995, p. 234.
6. Patrick Luciano and Gary Colville. *American Science Fiction Television Series of the 1950s*. McFarland, 1998, p. 209.
7. James Robert Parish and Vincent Terrace. *The Complete Actors' Television Credits, 1948–1988*, Second Edition. Scarecrow, 1989, p. 360.
8. Marc Scott Zicree. *Treasures of the Twilight Zone: Inside The Twilight Zone*. CBS Video/Panasonic DVD, 1998.
9. Rick Marshcall. *The History of Television*. Gallery Books, 1986, p. 117.
10. Roger Fulton and John Betancourt. *The Sci-Fi Channel Encyclopedia of TV Science Fiction*. Warner Books, 1997, New York, pp. 309–310.
11. John Javna. *The Best of Science Fiction Television*. Harmony Books, 1987, p. 128.
12. Gary Gerani & Paul Schulman. *Fantastic Television*. Harmony Books, 1977, p. 25.
13. John McCarty. *Starlog #124*: "Taking a Trip *One Step Beyond*." November 1987, p. 91.
14. *Ibid*.
15. Newland-Raynor Productions, Inc., 1999 Promotional Materials, "John Newland." Sunset Boulevard, Los Angeles, California.
16. Myrna Oliver. *The Los Angeles Times*, January 17, 2000.

Part II: The Series

1. Carroll B. Nash, Ph.D. *Parapsychology: The Science of Psiology*. Charles C. Thomas, 1986, p. 166.

2. Milan Ryzl. *Parapsychology — A Scientific Approach.* Hawthorne Books, New York, 1970, p. 171.

3. *Ibid.*, p. 2.

4. John Javna. *The Best of Science Fiction Television.* Harmony Books, 1987, p. 128.

5. D. Scott Rogo. *Parapsychology — A Century of Inquiry.* Taplinger, New York, 1975, pp. 136–137.

6. Carroll C. Calkins (Editor). *Mysteries of the Unexplained.* Reader's Digest Publications, 1982, p. 29.

7. Carroll B. Nash, Ph.D. *Parapsychology: The Science of Psiology.* Charles C. Thomas, 1986, pp. 133–134.

8. Shiresh C. Thakur, M.A., Ph.D. *Philosophy and Psychical Research.* Muirhead Library of Philosophy, George Allen Ltd., New York Humanities Press Inc., 1976, p. 17.

9. Joel Martin and Patricia Romanowski. *Love Beyond Life: The Healing Power of After Death Communications.* HarperCollins, New York, 1997, pp. 56–57.

10. Caroll B. Nash, Ph.D. *Parapsychology: The Science of Psiology.* Charles C. Thomas, 1986, p. 165.

11. Daniel Goleman. *Emotional Intelligence.* Bantam Books, 1995, pp. 114–115.

12. Reginald Omez (translated from the French by Renee Haynes). *Psychical Phenomenon.* Hawthorn Books, 1958, pp. 59–60.

13. Carroll C. Calkins (editor). *Mysteries of the Unexplained.* Reader's Digest Publications, 1982, p. 264.

14. Lois Duncan and William Roll. *Psychic Connections: A Journey into the Mysterious World of Psi.* Delacorte Press, 1995, p. 18.

15. D. Scott Rogo. *Parapsychology — A Century of Inquiry.* Taplinger, New York, 1975, pp. 44–45.

16. Reginald Omez (translated from the French by Renee Haynes). *Psychical Phenomenon.* Hawthorn Books, 1958, p. 60.

17. Bernard Gittelson. *Intangible Evidence.* Fireside, 1987, p. 31.

18. *Ibid.*, p. 296.

19. Gary Gerani and Paul Schulman. *Fantastic Television.* Harmony Books, 1977, p. 26.

20. Carroll C. Calkins (editor). *Mysteries of the Unexplained.* Reader's Digest Publications, 1982, p. 154.

21. *Ibid.*, p. 159.

22. Herbert B. Greenhouse. *The Book of Psychic Knowledge.* Taplinger, New York, 1973, p. 86.

23. *Ibid.*, p. 40.

24. Caroll B. Nash, Ph.D. *Parapsychology: The Science of Psiology.* Charles C. Thomas, 1986, p. 181.

25. Matthew Jones. *X-Pose*, Issue #21: "Cursed Earth." Visual Imagination, April 1998, p. 30.

26. Edgar D. Mitchell. *Psychic Exploration: A Challenge for Science.* G.P. Putnam's Sons, New York, 1974, p. 84.

27. Carroll B. Nash, Ph.D. *Parapsychology — The Science of Psiology.* Charles C. Thomas, 1986, p. 155.

28. Bernard Gittelson. *Intangible Evidence.* Fireside, 1987, p. 147.

29. Carroll B. Nash, Ph.D. *Parapsychology: The Science of Psiology.* Charles C. Thomas, 1986, p. 133–134.

30. Patricia Weintraub. *Omni's Catalog of the Bizarre.* An Omni Press Book, Doubleday and Company, 1985, p. 81.

31. Gary Gerani and Paul Schulman. *Fantastic Television.* Harmony Books, 1977, p. 29.

32. Rémy Chauvin. *Parapsychology — When the Irrational Rejoins Science,* translated by Katharine M. Banham, McFarland, 1985, p. 71.

33. *Ibid.,* p. 70.

34. Carroll C. Calkins (editor). *Mysteries of the Unexplained.* Reader's Digest Publications, 1982, p. 32.

35. John Hairr. *The Anomalist* "High Strangeness Report" — "When Flesh and Blood Fell from the Sky." www.anomalist.com/reports/fleshbood.html, pp. 1–4.

36. Carroll C. Calkins (editor). *Mysteries of the Unexplained.* Reader's Digest Publications, 1982, p. 201.

37. *Ibid.,* p. 198.

38. Rémy Chauvin. *Parapsychology — When the Irrational Rejoins Science,* translated by Katharine M. Banham, McFarland, 1985, p. 146.

39. Ernest Hartmann. *The Nightmare: The Psychology and Biology of Terrifying Dreams.* Basic Books, New York, 1984, p. 135.

40. *Ibid.,* p. 39.

41. David Richardson. *TV Zone,* Issue #41: "Mark Eden from Tibet to the Village." Visual Imagination Limited, April 1993, p. 11.

42. Herbert B. Greenhouse. *The Book of Psychic Knowledge.* Taplinger, New York, 1973, p. 41.

43. Marc Scott Zicree. *The Twilight Zone Companion.* Bantam Books, 1982, p. 429.

Part III: Newland Between Steps

1. Christopher Wicking and Tise Vahimigi. *The American Vein: Directors and Directions in Television.* E.P. Dutton, 1979, p. 73.

2. Stephen King. *Danse Macabre.* Berkley, 1983, p. 227.

3. Scott Skelton and Jim Benson. *Rod Serling's Night Gallery — An After Hours Tour.* Syracuse University Press, 1999, p. 282.

Part IV: The Next Step Beyond

1. John J. O'Connor. "TV: Psychics of *Step Beyond.*" *The New York Times,* Thursday, January 5, 1978.

2. Vincent Terrace. *Television 1970–1980.* A.S. Barnes, 1981, p. 145.

Bibliography

On Television and Film

Brooks, Tim, and Earl Marshe. *The Complete Directory to Prime Time Network TV Shows (1946–Present)*. Third Edition, Ballantine, 1985.

Gerani, Gary, and Paul Schulman. *Fantastic Television*. Harmony, 1977.

Javna, John. *The Best of Science Fiction Television*. Harmony, 1987.

Jeavons, Clyde. *A Pictorial History of War Films*. Citadel, 1974.

Kisseloff, Jeff. *The Box — An Oral History of Television, 1920–1961*. Viking, 1995.

Marill, Alvin H. *Movies Made for Television*. Da Capo, 1980.

Marschall, Rick. *The History of Television*. Gallery, 1986.

Morton, Alan. *The Complete Directory to Science Fiction, Fantasy and Horror Television Series: A Comprehensive Guide to the First 50 Years, 1946 to 1996*. Other World, 1997.

Muir, John. *An Analytical Guide to Television's* Battlestar Galactica. McFarland, 1999.

_____. *A Critical History of* Doctor Who *on Television*. McFarland, 1999.

_____. *Exploring* Space: 1999: *An Episode Guide and Complete History of the Mid-1970s Science Fiction Television Series*. McFarland, 1997.

Parish, James Robert, and Vincent Terrace. *A Complete Actors' Television Credits, 1948–1988*. Second Edition, Scarecrow, 1989.

Rovin, Jeff. *The Great Television Series*. A.S. Barnes, 1977.

Skelton, Scott, and Jim Benson. *Rod Serling's Night Gallery — An After-Hours Tour*. Syracuse University Press, 1999.

Stanley, John. *Creature Features Movie Guide Strikes Again*. Fourth Revised Edition, Creatures at Large Press, 1994.

Terrace, Vincent. *Fifty Years of Television: A Guide to Series and Pilots, 1937–1988*. Cornwall, 1991.

_____. *Television 1970–1980*. A.S. Barnes, 1981.

Vahimagi, Tise. *British Television*. Second Edition, Oxford University Press, 1996.

Wicking, Christopher, and Tise Vahimagi. *The American Vein: Directors and Directions in Television*. E.P. Dutton, 1979.

Zicree, Marc Scott. *The Twilight Zone Companion*. Bantam, 1982.

On Myth, Parapsychology, Philosophy and Psychology

Araoz, Daniel L., and Marie A. Carrese. *Solution-Oriented Therapy for Adjustment Disorders.* Brunner/Mazel, 1996.
Calkins, Carroll C. (editor). *Mysteries of the Unexplained.* Reader's Digest, 1982.
Chambers, Paul. *Paranormal People.* Blandford, 1998.
Chauvin, Rémy. *Parapsychology — When the Irrational Rejoins Science,* translated by Katharine M. Banham, McFarland, 1985.
Duncan, Lois, and William Roll. *Psychic Connections: A Journey into the Mysterious World of Psi.* Delacorte, New York, 1995.
Gibson, Walter B., and Litzka Gibson. *The Complete Illustrated Book of the Psychic Scientists.* Doubleday, 1966.
Gittelson, Bernard. *Intangible Evidence.* Fireside, 1987.
Goleman, Daniel. *Emotional Intelligence.* Bantam, 1995.
Greenhouse, Herbert B. *The Book of Psychic Knowledge.* Taplinger, 1973.
Harris, Melvin. *Investigating the Unexplained.* Prometheus, 1986.
Hartman, Ernest. *The Nightmare: The Psychology of Terrifying Dreams.* Basic Books, 1984.
Haynes, Renee. *The Seeing Eye, the Seeing I — Perception, Sensory and Extra Sensory.* St. Martin's, 1997.
Hopcke, Robert H. *There Are No Accidents — Synchronicity and the Stories of Our Lives.* Riverhead, 1997.
Imich, Alexander, Ph.D. (editor). *Incredible Tales of the Paranormal — Documented Accounts of Poltergeists, Levitations, Phantoms, and Other Phenomena.* Bramble, 1995.
Lewis, James R. *Encyclopedia of Afterlife Beliefs and Phenomena.* Visible Ink, 1995.
Martin, Joel, and Patricia Romanowski. *Love Beyond Life: The Healing Power of After Death Communications.* HarperCollins, New York, 1997.
Mitchell, Edgar D. *Psychic Exploration — A Challenge for Science.* G. P. Putnam's Sons, 1974.
Morford, Mark, and Robert J. Lenardon. *Classical Mythology.* Fourth Edition, Longman, 1991.
Nash, Caroll B., Ph.D. *Parapsychology: The Science of Psiology.* Charles C. Thomas, 1986.
Omez, Reginald (translated from the French by Renee Haynes). *Psychical Phenomena.* Hawthorn, 1958.
Parker, Derek, and Julia Parker. *Atlas of the Supernatural.* Prentice Hall, 1990.
Rogo, D. Scott. *Parapsychology — A Century of Inquiry.* Taplinger, 1975.
Ryzal, Milan. *Parapsychology — A Scientific Approach.* Hawthorne, New York, 1970.
Thakur, Shiresh C., M.A., Ph.D. *Philosophy and Psychical Research.* Muirhead Library of Philosophy, George Allen Ltd., New York Humanities, 1976.
Waley, Arthur (translator). *The Analects of Confucius.* Vintage, 1989.
Weintraub, Patricia. *Omni's Catalog of the Bizarre.* An Omni Press Book, Doubleday, 1985.

Periodicals

Anchors, Gloria. *Epilog Special* #5: "One Step Beyond." December 1992, pp. 40–49.

Bell, Tony. *Epilog Special* #5: "The Next Step Beyond." December 1992, pp. 49–51.

Jones, Matthew. *X-Pose* #21: "Cursed Earth." Visual Imagination, Inc., April 1998, pp. 27–33.

McCarty, John. *Starlog* #124: "Taking a Trip One Step Beyond." November 1987, pp. 88–96.

_____. *Starlog* #130: "John Newland's Errand of Mercy." May 1988, p. 77.

Richardson, David. *TV Zone* #41: "Mark Eden from Tibet to the Village." April 1993, pp. 9–11.

Weaver, Tom. *Starlog* #257: "Times Traveler." December 1998, pp. 69–74.

Index